THE CRIMINAL JUSTICE SYSTEM AND MENTAL RETARDATION

This book is printed on recycled paper.

THE CRIMINAL JUSTICE SYSTEM AND MENTAL RETARDATION

DEFENDANTS AND VICTIMS

edited by

RONALD W. CONLEY, PH.D.
Administration on Developmental Disabilities
Administration for Children and Families
U.S. Department of Health and Human Services
Washington, D.C.

RUTH LUCKASSON, J.D.
Department of Special Education
University of New Mexico
Albuquerque

and

GEORGE N. BOUTHILET, PH.D.
President's Committee on Mental Retardation
Administration for Children and Families
U.S. Department of Health and Human Services
Washington, D.C.

·P A U L·H·
BROOKES
PUBLISHING CO

Baltimore · London · Toronto · Sydney

Paul H. Brookes Publishing Co.
P.O. Box 10624
Baltimore, Maryland 21285-0624

Typeset by The Composing Room of Michigan, Inc., Grand Rapids, Michigan.
Manufactured in the United States of America by
The Maple Press Company, York, Pennsylvania.

Permission to reprint the following quotation is gratefully acknowledged:

Page 55: "Caged Bird" by M. Angelou (1983). *Shaker, Why Don't You Sing?* New
York: Random House.

Library of Congress Cataloging-in-Publication Data
The criminal justice system and mental retardation / edited by Ronald
W. Conley, Ruth Luckasson, and George N. Bouthilet.
    p.cm.
    Includes bibliographical references and index.
    ISBN 1-55766-070-0
    1. Insanity—Jurisprudence—United States.   2. Criminal liability—
United States.   3. Mental health laws—United States. I. Conley,
Ronald W.   II. Luckasson, Ruth.   III. Bouthilet, George N.
KF9242.C75   1992
345.73'04—dc20
[347.3054]   91-18175
                                                               CIP

For the individuals with mental retardation who, as victims of the crimes of others or as defendants accused of committing crimes, must struggle to obtain justice in the American criminal justice system

CONTENTS

CONTRIBUTORS

THE EDITORS

Ronald W. Conley, Ph.D., is a special assistant to the Commissioner of the Administration on Developmental Disabilities in the Administration for Children and Families of the U.S. Department of Health and Human Services. Since becoming employed by the federal government, he has also worked at the National Institute of Mental Health, the President's Committee on Mental Retardation, the Rehabilitation Services Administration, the U.S. Department of Labor, and for the Assistant Secretary of Planning and Evaluation in the U.S. Department of Health and Human Services. He received a B.A. degree in economics from the University of Washington (1958) and a Ph.D. degree in Political Economy from The Johns Hopkins University (1964). His primary focus has been on economic and programmatic issues relating to people with disabilities. He is the author of *The Economics of Vocational Rehabilitation* (The Johns Hopkins Press, 1965) and *The Economics of Mental Retardation* (The Johns Hopkins Press, 1973), and co-author of *Workers' Compensation Reform: Challenge for the 80's* (U.S. Department of Labor, 1979) as well as many articles and chapters. He continues to conduct research in supported employment and other policy issues in the area of disability.

Ruth Luckasson, J.D., is a Professor of Special Education and Coordinator of Mental Retardation at the University of New Mexico, Albuquerque. She was formerly the Managing Attorney of the New Mexico Protection and Advocacy System. Currently she serves as Chair of the American Bar Association Commission on Mental and Physical Disability Law, Chair of the ARC-US Legal Advocacy Committee, and Chair of the American Association on Mental Retardation Terminology and Classification Committee. Professor Luckasson was co-author of the disability Amicus Curiae brief in the *Penry* case, the major mental retardation death penalty case before the U.S. Supreme Court. She is co-author of *Introduction to Special Education* (Allyn & Bacon, 1992), co-editor of *Transitions to Adult Life for People with Mental Retardation: Principles and Practices* (Paul H. Brookes Publishing Co., 1988), co-author of *Classification in Mental Retardation* (9th ed., AAMR, in press), and many articles, chapters, and reports. Currently she is conducting research on crime victims with mental retardation.

George N. Bouthilet, Ph.D., is Coordinator of the Subcommittee on Full Citizenship and Justice with the President's Committee on Mental Retardation (PCMR). He initiated the development of the basic plan and recommended to the Subcommittee (December 1987) that PCMR sponsor a conference on the offender with mental retardation. Subsequently, he served as project officer for the Presidential Forum on the

Offender with Mental Retardation and the Criminal Justice System. Previously, he was the project officer for the Second National Conference on Citizens with Mental Retardation and the Law. Currently, he is project officer for a contract to develop a guide on correctional industry programs for offenders with mental retardation, and is revising and updating *An Historical Review of the PCMR: 1966–1991.* He was formerly Director of the Division of Program Operations (State Planning, Administration and Services; and State Protection and Advocacy Systems) with the Administration on Developmental Disabilities (ADD). He started his federal career at the inception of the mental retardation programs in the mid-1960s and, at various times, was Director of Planning and Evaluation, University Affiliated Programs and Special Projects. Prior to coming to the U.S. Department of Health and Human Services, he was State Program Director for the Community Guidance Services (Mental Retardation) at the Oklahoma State Health Department.

THE CHAPTER AUTHORS

Richard J. Bonnie, LL.B., John S. Battle Professor of Law, Director, Institute of Law, Psychiatry, & Public Policy, The School of Law, The University of Virginia, Charlottesville, VA 22901

Richard H. Burr, J.D., Attorney at Law, NAACP Legal Defense & Educational Fund, Suite 1600, 99 Hudson Street, New York, NY 10013

Philip W. Davidson, Ph.D., University Affiliated Program for Developmental Disabilities, University of Rochester Medical Center, 601 Elmwood Avenue, Suite 671, Rochester, NY 14642

Christine DeMoll, M.S.S.W., 1906 S.E. 51st Avenue, Portland, OR 97215

James W. Ellis, J.D., Professor, School of Law, University of New Mexico, Albuquerque, NM 87131

James G. Exum, Jr., LL.B., Chief Justice, North Carolina Supreme Court, P.O. Box 1841, Raleigh, NC 27602

John W. Finn, Ph.D., Director, Forensic Services, New York Office of Mental Retardation and Developmental Disabilities, 44 Holland Avenue, Albany, NY 12229-0001

W. Lawrence Fitch, J.D., Associate Professor and Director of Forensic Evaluation Training and Research, Institute of Law, Psychiatry, & Public Policy, University of Virginia Law School, Charlottesville, VA 22901

Jane Nelson Hall, Ed.D., Mental Retardation Specialist, Georgia State Prison, Georgia Department of Corrections, HCO 1, Reidsville, GA 30453

Frank J. Laski, J.D., Public Interest Law Center of Philadelphia, 125 S. Ninth Street, Suite 700, Philadelphia, PA 19107

Robert Martin, Cpt., Commanding Officer, Detective Headquarters Division, Los Angeles Police Department, 150 N. Los Angeles Street, Los Angeles, CA 90012

John J. McGee, Ph.D., Associate Professor, Department of Psychiatry and Behavioral Science, Creighton-Nebraska University, 2205 S. Tenth Street, Omaha, NE 68108

Frank J. Menolascino, Ph.D., Chairman and Professor, Department of Psychiatry, Creighton-Nebraska University, 2205 S. Tenth Street, Omaha, NE 68108

Ruth J. Messinger, M.S.W., University Affiliated Program for Developmental Disabilities, University of Rochester Medical Center, 601 Elmwood Avenue, Suite 667, Rochester, NY 14642

John H. Noble, Jr., Ph.D., Professor of Social Work and Rehabilitation Medicine, State University of New York at Buffalo, 191 Alumni Arena, Amherst, NY 14260

Russell C. Petrella, Ph.D., Director of Mental Health Services, Commonwealth of Virginia, Department of Mental Health, Mental Retardation, and Substance Abuse Services, P.O. Box 1797, Richmond, VA 23214

H. Rutherford Turnbull III, LL.M., Professor, Department of Special Education, Haworth Hall, The University of Kansas, Lawrence, KS 66044

David L. White, Co-Director, Office of Special Offenders Services, Courthouse, Lancaster, PA 17603-1881

Hubert R. Wood, M.A., Co-Director, Office of Special Offenders Services, Courthouse, Lancaster, PA 17603-1881

ACKNOWLEDGMENTS

T HE PUBLICATION OF this book results directly from the vision and efforts of many individuals who care about the ability of citizens with mental retardation to achieve justice in the American criminal justice system. The issues addressed could only have come to light through the sustained efforts of courageous defendants and victims, their families and friends, and the professionals around them, who continue to fight for justice even against great odds. Their names may not appear, but their contributions have been essential.

The chapter authors all were generous with their experience and talents. Representing many disciplines, they tackled difficult topics, participated in the vigorous give and take of a multidisciplinary meeting, and wrote fine chapters that capture just how compelling the challenges continue to be. We hope that this book clarifies some of the problems and contributes to the development of strategies to improve the treatment of people with mental retardation in the criminal justice system.

Many organizations were involved in bringing this effort to fruition. We particularly wish to acknowledge the assistance of the President's Committee on Mental Retardation, the Administration on Children and Families in the U.S. Department of Health and Human Services, the U.S. Department of Justice, the U.S. Department of Education, and the University of New Mexico Department of Special Education.

Our publisher, Paul H. Brookes, deserves special credit for this book and for his continuing efforts to make available to readers a body of work that explores the complexity of the lives of people with mental retardation and their families. His skill and enthusiasm, and that of Melissa Behm—knowledgeable, generous, and tireless— made this book on criminal justice issues a reality. Roslyn Sassani Udris, with great competence and efficiency, managed its production and crafted the pieces together. And Vincent Ercolano—nominally our acquisitions editor but really much more— contributed sensitively and creatively throughout the book's development and ultimately assured its completion. Thank you.

FOREWORD

T HE PRESIDENT'S COMMITTEE on Mental Retardation (PCMR) has long been an excellent sounding board and source of advice for the Department of Justice and other federal agencies, offering support when needed . . . and leveling criticism when necessary. Generally, this criticism has been related to civil rights issues such as deinstitutionalization, implementation of Section 504 of the Rehabilitation Act of 1973 (PL 93-112), and enforcement of the Civil Rights of Institutionalized Persons Act of 1980 (CRIPA, PL 96-247). Although criticism is often difficult to take, it is precisely because we have heard it and have taken it to heart that the Justice Department's relationship with PCMR has grown stronger in recent years.

The people who participated in the Presidential Forum on Offenders with Mental Retardation and the Criminal Justice System did so because of their concern for individuals with mental retardation and because of their interest in ensuring that those who work with defendants with mental retardation perform their duties and meet their responsibilities competently. These two groups constitute the two sides of the coin the Forum participants examined—those who deserve special attention, and those charged with providing it. Individuals who deserve special attention include, for example:

The person who is found incompetent to stand trial because of mental retardation, and who will be committed to a state institution because there are no openings in community-based residential or vocational programs

The man who has confessed to something he did not do because he did not understand his *Miranda* rights and because he wanted to please those questioning him

The woman who is not even considered for programs offering alternatives to incarceration, such as pretrial diversion or probation, because those making the decision do not think she can benefit from them

The victim of a crime who cannot clearly explain what happened to him

The first-time offenders, guilty mostly of poor control, who have been given no special consideration—despite disabilities that increase their vulnerability to verbal or physical abuse within a jail or prison

On the other side of the coin are individuals who are in positions to provide special attention to defendants with mental retardation, such as public defenders, prosecutors, police officers, and judges, many of whom too often simply do not know how to deal with a person with mental retardation.

No official endorsement by the U.S. Department of Justice of the views presented in this book is intended by, or should be inferred from, Attorney General Thornburgh's remarks as presented in this foreword.

We have a unique opportunity to consider the challenge posed by the interaction of these two groups, and to consider some creative approaches that have been introduced by various programs, and perhaps, as a consequence, to develop some new approaches of our own.

One such program is managed by David L. White and Hubert R. Wood (see Chapter 8), founders and co-directors of the Lancaster County (PA) Office of Special Offenders Services—a program with which I was associated as governor of Pennsylvania, and one with much to offer to those interested in learning about successful efforts at drastically reducing recidivism.

Through astute recognition of the problems of those with mental retardation who run afoul of the law, Special Offenders Services has developed a program whose purpose is to teach students with mental retardation about laws and about the consequences of breaking those laws. But beyond simple teaching, this program works with those students and provides them with the information to help them improve their decision-making and problem-solving abilities so that they can avoid future problems with the law, and, just as important, so that they can avoid being manipulated by others who would tempt them to break the law.

There is much to be learned from the Lancaster County program, just as there is much to be learned from other innovative programs in states across the nation. Ultimately, that is what will be required—that we learn from each other's experiences and work together to create the correct balance between rights and responsibilities, as well as between the need for "special" treatment or protection and the need for equal opportunity. It is vital to consider how we can achieve this balance within the criminal justice system and from a civil rights standpoint within society as a whole.

As the nation's chief law enforcement officer, I have made my position clear concerning those who violate the laws of our states or our nation—they must be held accountable for their actions, whether they are drug kingpins or drug couriers, white collar criminals or shoplifters, or individuals who commit crimes against people or property. But as we strive to preserve order in our society and protect our citizens from crime, we must also seek methods of ensuring accountability that will preserve the right of due process, provide for support services, and promote rehabilitation.

In some situations, long-term incarceration may be the only method not only of punishing a lawbreaker and protecting society, but also of rehabilitating an offender. However, that should in no way preclude our efforts to find means—outside, or in addition to, incarceration—to prevent and control unacceptable behavior, methods such as counseling, community service, and restitution. This suggestion raises perhaps the most difficult dilemma we must confront: although we must make every effort to integrate people with disabilities into the mainstream of society, we cannot always do so by treating them exactly like people without disabilities. As is true in most areas of disability rights law, equality does not necessarily mean equal treatment. In other words, persons with disabilities must at times be treated differently from others to ensure protection of their rights and to ensure an equal opportunity to benefit from services. People with mental retardation cannot be "processed" exactly like others who come into contact with our criminal justice system because, for them, it may be a system they do not understand or a system that does not understand them. Thus, we must take care to ensure that our criminal justice system does not compound the challenges that individuals with disabilities face in other aspects of their lives.

Although the Justice Department's role as enforcer of federal laws leads me to emphasize accountability, rehabilitation, and concern for victims of crime, the Department's responsibility for federal implementation of civil rights law brings me to the second half of our complicated equation: to guarantee that, outside the criminal justice system, our communities do not create conditions that increase the chances that a person with mental retardation will become a criminal defendant. In short, the criminal justice system does not exist in a vacuum and cannot be isolated from the actions of society in general.

The phrase *society in general* naturally brings to mind the principle of normalization. This principle holds that all individuals with mental retardation must have every possible opportunity to participate in the activities of everyday life, including work, play, travel, learning, shopping, and all the other activities we take for granted. It is a principle that has driven this nation's deinstitutionalization efforts. Beyond deinstitutionalization, however, it is undeniable that individuals who are least likely to become defendants regardless of disabilities are those who have had full opportunities to be productive members of society—those who have enjoyed the benefits of a meaningful education, fruitful employment, strong bonds with family and friends, and spiritual, recreational, and social activities. That, I know, is only a minor variation on the theme of normalization. But it sums up the strongly held convictions behind the Administration's efforts to achieve the goal of maximum opportunity for Americans with disabilities. As an example of this commitment, the Americans with Disabilities Act of 1990 (PL 101-336) holds promise of being the vehicle that brings all citizens with disabilities into the mainstream of American life, enabling us finally to realize the goal of full rights for this long-neglected segment of society. It is my hope that through our collective efforts, with laws such as the Americans with Disabilities Act as a mandate, we can eliminate or compensate for many of those factors in the areas of education, employment, housing, and public accommodations, among others, that may contribute to the criminal involvement of people with mental retardation.

The Department of Justice has had significant responsibilities under the Americans with Disabilities Act with respect to rule-making, technical assistance, compliance efforts, and enforcement. We have pursued our mandate promptly and vigorously, and we will also continue our efforts to ensure compliance by the federal government and by recipients of federal aid with Section 504 of the Rehabilitation Act, and to pursue violations of CRIPA and the Fair Housing Amendments Act of 1988 (PL 100-430).

Since the Fair Housing Amendments Act took effect, the Justice Department has used that legislation to challenge denials of special use permits for group homes and evictions we believe were based on disability. We are continuing to pursue legal action under CRIPA against those who would violate the rights of persons with disabilities in institutions.

In conclusion, thousands of persons have been released from large state institutions in the last several years, many of whom 20 years ago would have been in "out-of-sight-out-of-mind" institutions. Now, most of these persons are with their families, living independently, or in group homes—and that is a blessing. But with that blessing have come the inevitable predictions by those who say that as people with mental retardation face the temptations that exist outside structured institutions, their involvement in criminal activity is destined to increase. We must prove such predictions wrong. We cannot free a significant number of persons with mental retardation from one institution only to see them sent into another—this nation's prison system.

Our final task, then, is to use the criminal justice and social service systems to reach out and respond fully and fairly to the challenge of normalization, rather than leave people with mental retardation to cope alone with a bewildering world. If we can do that, those dire predictions will never come true, and eventually the fears and misunderstandings upon which they are based will evaporate in the warmth of a nation that has used fairness, decency, love, and human kindness to bring its citizens with disabilities and mental retardation into the mainstream of our great and good society.

Dick Thornburgh
Attorney General of the United States
Washington, D.C.
July 1991

INTRODUCTION

THE GREAT MAJORITY of people with mental retardation reside in the community. Like other Americans, they live in apartments or houses, they work, they have social relationships, they travel, and, increasingly, they marry and have children. In large part, people with mental retardation are free to choose which activities they engage in, as well as when, where, and with whom. Even those who require some degree of assistance or supervision usually have considerable leeway to select their activities and friends.

The percentage of people with mental retardation who live in the community, and the extent to which they exercise control over their lives, have increased substantially over the last 30 years. This is true even of people with severe mental retardation. This is because great advances have been made in our understanding of what people with mental retardation can accomplish and in the development of programs designed to assist them to integrate into society.

People with mental retardation are usually law-abiding and productive citizens. But, as with any other group of citizens, there is a small percentage who violate federal, state, or local laws. And inevitably, some individuals with mental retardation themselves become victims of crime. Those individuals who commit offenses should, like any citizen, be held accountable for their acts. And those who are victims must have access to redress through the criminal justice system. But because of their intellectual limitations, important and complicated issues arise that must be considered if our system of justice is to attain genuine integrity. Did the suspect actually commit the act of which he or she is accused? Was there a voluntary and reliable confession? Did the individual who committed the crime understand the nature and consequences of his or her act? Is the defendant competent to stand trial? Are defendants and victims with mental retardation able to provide a meaningful explanation of the circumstances surrounding the alleged offense to law enforcement authorities and to their lawyers? Can they testify competently in court? How should (re)habilitation programs be organized to facilitate their return to society if they are imprisoned?

The issues arising from the interaction between people with mental retardation and the justice system are particularly complex since variations exist among people with mental retardation in their ability to understand and control their actions, to communicate, and to participate in (re)habilitation programs. To date, little attention has been given to the special issues that may arise when people with mental retardation commit crimes or become crime's victims. In the fall of 1989, the President's Committee on Mental Retardation sponsored a presidential forum on these issues. Subsequently, the participants at this forum prepared the papers contained in this volume. These papers represent a rich and comprehensive survey of the issues and problems that arise when persons with mental retardation are accused of committing crimes or become victims of the criminal activities of others.

While it is impossible in just a few pages to summarize all the conclusions and insights found within this volume, there are several critical observations that provide a reasonably concise and telling overview of the issues and problems that require resolution.

EPIDEMIOLOGY

A relatively small but significant number of Americans with mental retardation have committed illegal acts. Roughly, about 14,000 individuals with mental retardation (about 2% of all inmates) are in state and federal prisons and another 12,500 are in residential facilities for people with mental retardation because they have been convicted of, or are suspected of, committing unlawful acts (see Chapter 1, this volume). Additional but unknown numbers of people with mental retardation are in local jails, diversion programs, or residential facilities for people with mental illness, or are on probation. Sometimes, people with mental retardation are placed in residential facilities as a means of preventing them from engaging in illegal, usually aggressive, behavior outside the facility.

Most prisoners with mental retardation in state and federal prisons are male and have mild mental retardation. Offenders with more severe mental retardation usually are placed in specialized residential facilities, although reports persist of prisoners with IQs in the 40–55 range. The percentage of nonwhite persons among inmates with mental retardation is unusually high. Although it is frequently claimed that offenders with mental retardation tend to engage in serious crimes, this assertion is wrong and appears to be due to the fact that most of the statistical evidence is derived from state and federal prisons that are likely to receive inmates who commit serious crimes (see Chapter 1, this volume).

Reported rates of mental retardation range from 0.5% to almost 20% in state and federal prisons. A major reason for this wide variance is the differences in the way mental retardation is identified. Prisons that report data based solely on group tests shortly after admission tend to report rates of mental retardation three times higher than those that employ individual tests at a later point (see Chapter 1, this volume). Little information exists on offenders with mental retardation outside of state and federal prisons.

REASONS FOR CRIMES

People do *not* commit crimes because they have mental retardation. People with mental retardation commit crimes for the same complex reasons other Americans do—childhoods in which appropriate values were not instilled, poverty, unemployment, poor choices of friends, and so forth.

UNDERSTANDING MENTAL RETARDATION

Judges, public defenders, police officers, and defense lawyers often do not understand mental retardation sufficiently to represent defendants with mental retardation appropriately. Cases may be tried without even an awareness that the defendant has mental retardation, or of the effect of the disability on the ability of the defendant to assist counsel, to respond accurately and knowingly to questions, or to understand the consequences of a guilty verdict. Mental retardation often is confused with mental illness. Few states have training programs for judges, lawyers, and correctional officers on the problems posed by the situation of defendants with mental retardation.

EARLY PREVENTION

Programs to prevent people with mental retardation from committing crimes should be instituted during the school years. These students need to be taught the laws and the reasons for them, the responsibilities of citizens to obey the law, and the consequences of law-breaking. They also need to receive information on arrest procedures, rights, detention centers, and placement facilities.

MIRANDA RIGHTS

A fundamental right in the American system of justice is that at the point at which a person is arrested, he or she must be notified of his or her *Miranda* rights (i.e., the right not to answer questions and the right to counsel). Unfortunately, a conventional rapid recitation of the *Miranda* warning, which contains a number of complicated provisions, may be dimly comprehended by the suspect, or may not be understood at all. This is particularly important in view of the eagerness of many people with mental retardation to please people they are involved with (including the police), and their susceptibility to suggestions (e.g., "Why not confess?"). In consequence, suspects with mental retardation may make unwise, misleading, or mistaken statements to the police without the opportunity to talk to a lawyer.

LEGAL REPRESENTATION

The legal representation provided to defendants with mental retardation is frequently inadequate. The quality of legal representation depends largely on the ability and inclination of the defense attorney to recognize and understand the client's limitations. Unfortunately, defense attorneys sometimes do not know how to solicit information from their client or how to present the case. Moreover, public defenders and court-appointed counsel working for a set fee are under pressure to cut corners in criminal defense, which means that inadequate time frequently is spent on the case.

COMPETENCE TO STAND TRIAL

Despite the well-established legal principle that accused persons should not be brought to trial if unable to understand the proceedings, assist their lawyers, or otherwise assist in their own defense, many defendants with mental retardation are tried without an adequate assessment of their competence to stand trial. Many are not even identified as mentally retarded until after they are imprisoned, if at all. The ends of the American criminal justice system cannot be adequately served by trying defendants unable to testify coherently, explain their actions to their attorney, or even understand the significance of a guilty plea.

The question of whether competence to stand trial exists in an individual defendant is complex. There are crucial judgment issues involving how accurately and effectively the accused person must be able to assist in the defense. In addition, defendants may be competent in some ways and not in others. The forensic services necessary to evaluate competence to stand trial are frequently inadequate because of limited resources and a lack of familiarity with mental retardation.

CRIMINAL RESPONSIBILITY

Tests to determine if a defendant with mental retardation is criminally responsible for his or her acts are generally the same ones used for mental illness. This reflects continuing confusion about the two disabilities, and is based on an "either/or approach"—either the individual is fully responsible or has no responsibility at all. An either/or approach is inappropriate since, while many people with mental retardation are aware of the difference between legal and illegal acts and that they may be punished for the latter, their appreciation of these matters may not be as clear as is the case with most people. In some cases, the ability of people with mental retardation to conform their behavior may be even more impaired. The possibility of diminished criminal responsibility due to mental retardation has been proposed, but is not explicit under the laws of any state.

HABILITATION

The most effective (re)habilitation programs for most offenders with mental retardation are those provided in the community. Community programs can take many forms (e.g., they can require that the defendant with mental retardation stay in a supervised residential facility, they can place the defendant on probation on condition that he or she participate in a special program). Ideally, these programs include training, counseling, and other services designated in an individualized plan designed to meet the needs of each offender. Unfortunately, few community programs are available.

(Re)habilitation programs in prisons are limited and those that are available are often inappropriate. It is estimated that fewer than 10% of inmates with mental retardation receive (re)habilitation services (see Chapter 9, this volume). These limited (re)habilitation programs are partly a consequence of limited resources, partly a consequence of a failure to understand the needs of inmates with mental retardation, and partly due to the multiple and conflicting missions faced by prisons, which have primary responsibility for the secure containment of inmates and the maintenance of order.

SERVICE SYSTEM

Many programs and services have an impact on offenders and victims with mental retardation, including all the services that are available specifically to people with mental retardation (residential care, [re]habilitation and employment programs, counseling, etc.), all the activities associated with the criminal justice system (prisons, police, judges, defense attorneys, prosecuting attorneys, etc.), and many other generic services such as the education system, income support (e.g., Supplemental Security Income), health care financing (e.g., Medicaid) and others. It is the combined effect of all these programs that must be taken into account when one considers ways of preventing people with mental retardation from committing offenses and of (re)habilitating them if offenses are committed. There are many deficiencies in this service system for defendants and victims with mental retardation. For example, the issues involving defendants and victims with mental retardation can be dealt with only by the cooperative and combined efforts of individuals in the field of mental retardation and individuals in the criminal justice system. Unfortunately, such cooperation is the exception rather than the rule.

Those who provide criminal justice programs often expect mental retardation programs to provide the services or intervention needed by offenders with mental retardation. However, mental retardation program service providers often are unaware of, or are overwhelmed by, the special needs of offenders with mental retardation. Another frequent problem is the mutual misunderstanding between the criminal justice system and the mental retardation community.

SENTENCING

Sentencing is an attempt to balance the conflicting goals of punishment, rehabilitation, protection of the public, confinement of offenders considered dangerous, and public acceptance of sentencing decisions. Often, the existence of mental retardation is not taken into account when a sentence is set. The criminal justice system tends to emphasize punishment rather than rehabilitation. However, this policy may be self-defeating if offenders are not prepared to make a living and cope with the stresses of outside life when released back to the community.

VICTIMS OF CRIME

The nature of their disability may make some people with mental retardation particularly vulnerable to victimization. In these cases, problems arise similar to those that exist when people with mental retardation are defendants. How can it be determined if a crime was committed, particularly if the victim is unable to provide a coherent description of what happened? How can victims with mental retardation be assisted to press charges? How can it be assured that their testimony will be presented effectively in court and taken seriously, even if they cannot withstand the pressure of cross-examination as well as other people? How can we ensure that people with mental retardation are not devalued and that crimes against them are not considered less important than if they had been committed against other people?

FUTURE STEPS

Many of the problems involved in ensuring that defendants and victims with mental retardation are accorded their full Constitutional rights have yet to be resolved, and, in some cases, will require extensive investigation and debate before solutions are reached. We believe, however, that a clear need exists for the following immediate changes in public policies and activities.

1. There needs to be a sharper focus on the interaction between people with mental retardation and the justice system at all levels of government, as

well as among the components of the justice system and mental retardation programs. Too often, the problems surrounding defendants and victims with mental retardation are overlooked or ignored. It needs to be specifically emphasized that people with mental retardation have the right to fairness in the criminal justice system.

2. The amount and quality of information on people with mental retardation who are accused of committing crimes or who become victims of crimes must be greatly improved. Data must be collected on how often crimes are committed by people with mental retardation, when the disability was first identified by the criminal justice system, defendants' understanding of the effects of their crimes, defendants' characteristics, the types of crimes they are alleged to have committed, the punishments imposed, the (re)habilitation services provided, and the effectiveness of these services.

3. There are many areas in which research should be funded. Examples include projects to identify the risk factors that cause people with mental retardation to commit crimes, to determine the frequency and causes of false accusations and false or coerced confessions among people with mental retardation, to determine the availability and the effectiveness of community support programs, and to identify the extent of crimes against people with mental retardation.

4. Mental retardation should always be taken into account, including when assessments are made concerning criminal responsibility, severity and type of punishment, competence to stand trial, the establishment of (re)habilitation programs, and decisions about parole and probation.

5. The disposition of any case involving a person with mental retardation should be based on an individualized plan that takes account of the recommendations of both mental retardation professionals and correctional experts and in which (re)habilitation is a major goal.

6. Capital punishment should be prohibited for persons with mental retardation.

7. Federal sentencing guidelines should be modified to give greater flexibility to judges in sentencing people with mental retardation who have been convicted of committing a crime.

8. Verdicts of "guilty but mentally retarded" that provide a basis for indefinite imprisonment should not be used.

9. Offenders with mental retardation should not be sentenced to any facility that does not have a (re)habilitation program suitable to such defendants' needs.

10. Truly comprehensive training of individuals in the criminal justice system on issues involving people with mental retardation must be instituted. The police department needs to be trained to recognize when a person might be mentally retarded and how to communicate with him or

her. Lawyers, judges, and probation and parole officers need to appreciate the factors that may cause a person with mental retardation to be accused of a crime, or to confess to a crime he or she did not commit, and how the appropriateness of the sentence may vary because of the disability of a convicted person.

11. All inmates in federal, state, and local prisons with mental retardation should receive habilitation services that are appropriate and in accordance with an individualized program.

12. Public and private programs that provide support and assistance to people with mental retardation and that are part of the correctional services system must work in a more cohesive and coordinated way to achieve the goals of individualized plans for offenders with mental retardation.

13. The quality of forensic services must be improved by training forensic examiners and making increased use of experts in mental retardation.

14. Judicial procedures must ensure that victims with mental retardation are accorded the same redress in court received by other Americans, and that the perpetrators of crimes against them are charged, convicted, and punished.

Support for these and many other actions to ensure that defendants and victims with mental retardation are accorded fair and appropriate treatment in the criminal justice system is articulated throughout this book. Such actions are, of course, but a few more steps in the long journey toward full citizenship for people with mental retardation. They are already long overdue.

THE CRIMINAL JUSTICE SYSTEM AND MENTAL RETARDATION

Chapter 1

POINTS OF VIEW
Perspectives on the Judicial,
Mental Retardation Services,
Law Enforcement, and Corrections Systems

JAMES G. EXUM, JR.,
H. RUTHERFORD TURNBULL III,
ROBERT MARTIN, AND JOHN W. FINN

I F A CITIZEN with mental retardation breaks the law or is suspected of doing so, his or her future usually will be determined by the subsequent and interactive effects of law enforcement agencies, the judiciary, corrections programs, and programs that have been established to serve people with mental retardation. Other programs, such as those providing health care or mental health services, may also be involved.

To set the tone for the Presidential Forum from which many of the chapters in this volume derive their inspiration, representatives from the four primary systems (law enforcement, the judiciary, corrections, and mental retardation services) were asked to present an overview of the issues from the perspectives of these four systems. These remarks subsequently have been expanded and are presented in this chapter—*The Editors.*

THE JUDICIARY

James G. Exum, Jr. Chief Justice,
North Carolina Supreme Court

I suppose I am a pretty good representative of the judiciary because the truth is that judges, by and large, don't know much about mental retardation.

I think this is also true of lawyers. Even criminal defense lawyers don't know a great deal about mental retardation. This is what I see as the great need, so far as the courts and the legal profession are concerned—a need to know. This point can be illustrated by two cases decided in recent years by the North Carolina Supreme Court. One case is *State v. Massey*, which was decided in 1986 (316 N.C. 558, 342 S.E.2d 811). The second is *State v. Moore*, decided in 1988 (321 N.C. 327, 364 S.E.2d 648). Both cases involved defendants with mental retardation. In both cases the prosecution relied heavily on the defendants' confessions to the crimes charged in order to get a conviction. Both crimes were serious felonies. Both carried mandatory life imprisonment under the sentencing scheme in North Carolina.

In both cases the defendants were indigent. Both had court-appointed counsel. Both defendants moved under North Carolina statutes and the federal and state constitutions for a psychiatrist to assist them in their defense. (Although the motions were for the assistance of a psychiatrist, the principles involved would apply as well to psychologists or to any mental health professional qualifiable as an expert in mental retardation.) In *State v. Massey*, that motion was denied by the trial court, and the state supreme court, on appeal, affirmed that denial. In *State v. Moore*, decided two years later, the motion was also denied by the trial court. But our court reversed that denial and held that the defendant Massey was entitled to appointment of a state-paid psychiatrist to assist him in his defense.

What caused the different response in the second case? The difference lay in the level of information and knowledge that the North Carolina Supreme Court had and that each counsel representing each defendant had in *Massey* versus *Moore*.

Something had happened between 1986 when *Massey* was decided and 1988 when *Moore* was decided. To begin with, I, as a member of the state supreme court, had attended an excellent forum at an American Bar Association meeting in New Orleans, at which several speakers delineated the difficulties of people with mental retardation in the criminal justice system. My eyes were opened to these difficulties in a way they had not been in 1986. I recall one speaker eloquently describing how it is almost impossible to accord people with mental retardation due process in our courts, although that is a constitutional guarantee for all of us.

The second thing that happened was that between 1986 and 1988 I became Chief Justice of the North Carolina Supreme Court. That position of leadership helped me persuade my brethren on the court of the difficulties, as I then understood them, that people with mental retardation were having in our judicial system.

The most important distinction between the two cases was the level of information provided the state supreme court by the evidence offered at the trial level—evidence that was adduced by counsel for the defendants. Officially, and often in actuality as well, courts know only what the lawyers tell them. When any case is begun, so far as the court is concerned, it is like a blank slate. The lawyers basically write on that slate, and, often depending upon what they write and how they write it, the decision is made.

In *Moore,* the case in which the defendant with mental retardation won his appeal on the issue of his right to have a court-appointed psychiatrist assist him in his defense, evidence was offered at the trial's hearing that suggested the following: The defendant had an IQ of 51, a mental-age equivalent to that of an 8- or 9-year-old. The defendant's vocabulary was equivalent to that of a fourth- or fifth-grade elementary student. According to expert testimony, the defendant could not understand complicated instructions. According to family members, the defendant could not understand his *Miranda* warnings, read to him by investigators without further explanation. According to expert testimony, the defendant was easily led and intimidated by others. According to a friend of the defendant, the defendant could be "run over" by anybody. The defendant's low intelligence level may have rendered him unable to understand the nature of any statement he may have made. The defendant's mental retardation may have rendered him unable to waive his rights knowingly. The state's case against the defendant was predicated in significant measure on the defendant's confession, because the victim in the case could not identify her assailant.

We outlined the foregoing in our opinion. We also noted in our opinion that when the defendant was being questioned by investigators and was being given his *Miranda* warnings, his only responses to the questions were: "Yes. Yes. Yes, sir. Yes. Yes, sir. Yes. Yes." That kind of response would not have made much of an impression on me in 1986. It did make an impression when I saw it in 1988.

The state supreme court distinguished *State v. Moore* (1988) from *State v. Massey* (1986) because in *Massey* the defendant had failed to make a sufficiently specific demonstration of his need for the assistance of a psychiatrist to present his case. In *Massey,* the defendant did not specify the precise degree of his retardation. Neither did he offer any evidence indicating the effect his particular mental condition might have had on his ability to understand either his rights or the implications of his pretrial statement. To support his motion for funds to hire a psychiatrist to assist him, Massey relied solely on a single psychological evaluation, which indicated that he had mild mental retardation. Because Massey only baldly asserted that because of his mild mental retardation he needed the assistance of a psychiatrist, we held that he did not manifest the requisite threshold level of specific need.

So the difference in the outcome in the two cases rested in part on a difference in the level of the general knowledge on the part of the court about mental retardation. But, more important, it rested on the specific factual and detailed information that counsel in *Moore* was able to gather and present at the trial level.

As is illustrated by these two cases, the judiciary has a need for more information, more knowledge, and more understanding. We need lawyers who understand the difficulties and can present rich, meaningful, and detailed evidence like that in *Moore* for the edification of both the trial court initially and the appellate court ultimately.

THE MENTAL RETARDATION SERVICES SYSTEM

H. Rutherford Turnbull III,
Professor of Special Education, The University of Kansas

Many people with mental retardation are not recognized as having a disability. Yet, mental retardation is indeed a disability, and social justice cannot be achieved without recognition of the limitations inherent in mental retardation.

Mental retardation occurs when significantly subaverage intelligence results or is associated with impairments in a person's ability to adapt to the "normal" world, that is, to those conditions of life to which almost everyone else accommodates easily. It is manifested during the developmental periods.

Inherent in this definition are some important considerations. One of these, as Luckasson and Ellis argue, is that the legal issues involving people with mental retardation often are clouded by issues involving people with mental illness. We must keep in mind that people with mental retardation should not be mistaken for those with mental illness. Although it is true that some people with mental retardation have mental illness, not all of them do, and they should not be treated in the same way by community law enforcement and corrections systems.

A second important consideration inherent in the definition is that the degree or extent of mental retardation varies. Some people with mental retardation have mild mental retardation and often are not easily distinguishable from people who are not mentally retarded. These people with mild mental retardation are regarded as consisting of about 85% of the entire population of people classified as having mental retardation. Others have moderate, severe, or profound mental retardation. Because of the extent of their disability, they are often more easily distinguished from people who do not have mental retardation or who have it only in mild degree. People with mental retardation therefore differ from those who do not have mental retardation and from each other as well.

This brings me to the third important consideration. It is one that is hard, yet necessary, to broach. It is that there are indeed people with mental retardation who break the law. None of us should say that people with mental retardation do not commit crimes. Accordingly, none of us should say that apprehension, trial, sentence, rehabilitation, correction, and punishment are always inappropriate for people with mental retardation. For people with mental retardation who commit crimes, as for people without mental retardation who break the law, certain consequences are warranted.

It is equally true that people with mental retardation are victims of crime and of general lawlessness in our communities. Whatever crimes are committed against people without mental retardation are committed as well against people with mental retardation. Like other members of society, they have a vital stake in being protected from crime by effective and wise law enforcement and corrections systems, and in being fairly judged by courts.

The facts—that people with mental retardation commit and are victimized by crime—are pregnant with meaning. It is our task to address those meanings with a mixture of reality, compassion, and political sagacity.

To be realistic is to say that individualized determinations, which not only are commanded by the constitutional precepts of due process but also undergird the approaches of special education, rehabilitation, and other systems serving people with mental retardation, are mandatory. Just as we would not argue for a generalized application of the law to all people, without regard to various factors that cause or explain behavior and that justify or mitigate punishment, so we should take into account not what is generally true (if anything is) about people with mental retardation but what is particularly and specifically true about a certain person. Still, there is a certain ceiling on their capacities, and this means that certain punishments should never be applied, especially capital punishment.

To be compassionate is to say the special characteristics of mental retardation—significantly subaverage intelligence and coexisting problems in adaption—generally call us to err more on the side of mercy and forgiveness than not. None of us—including those of us like myself who are parents and who have entrusted our students, clients, or children to life in the community—fear any condition of life more than that people with mental retardation will be victims of real criminals or of the deficits of our own police and corrections systems. Even if my son Jay were to die, his death would hurt less than his being victimized by the evil that individuals or systems can do. What we must do, then, is be compassionate.

Finally, to be politically wise is to recognize that we must be leaders who can confront the hard facts about crime, people, and systems, and who can admit that we have huge problems to solve. This mandate applies not just to those of us who are advocates for people with retardation and who are experienced leaders in the field of disability but also to those of us who must police society, correct its criminals, protect its innocents, and pass judgment in courts. We all have something to gain by creating a partnership and avoiding confrontation. If we try to find ways to address together the problems of mental retardation, criminal behavior, and victimization, we can offer a mutually beneficial deal to each other.

To be blunt, we are engaged in risky business. The many rights that have been won in recent decades by people with mental retardation and their families remain imperiled. It took years, efforts by thousands of parents and professionals, billions of tax dollars, and a revolution in the law to dismantle the restrictions that prejudice and social mores placed on people with mental retardation and that the law institutionalized. The task continues today to teach and habilitate. Special emphasis must be placed on teaching people with mental retardation to be effective citizens. As those of us who are advocates for people with mental retardation know well, those rights are too easily jeopardized and can too quickly be jettisoned. Our task—one that requires us to be realistic and compassionate and wise—is to see if together we can find a way to identify those who have mental retardation, correct and prevent their criminal behavior, protect their victimization by individuals and systems, and do all that without weakening a single link of the chain of rights that has been so hard to create.

LAW ENFORCEMENT

Robert Martin, Commanding Officer, Detective Headquarters Division, Los Angeles Police Department

In 1985, I could have summed up everything that law enforcement, particularly the Los Angeles Police Department, was doing with people with mental illness or mental retardation in one sentence. Basically, we had a policy that said: "A person's mental status is not of concern to law enforcement." It was up to the courts to decide what happened to them. If they committed a crime, they went to jail. Let me give you some good news. We are changing that.

Let me tell you a story. We had an incident in Los Angeles in which a person with mental illness and mental retardation entered the 49th Street grade school and shot several children. People in the neighborhood were up in arms. Part of their frustration was that we [law enforcement officials] had had warnings that something might occur, but we didn't do anything about it. As a result of that crime, the chief of police put together a board of inquiry and said, "We need to take a look at what is going on out there." One finding of that inquiry is that tactically we did everything right. But that was not enough. So a group was formed that is now known as the Psychiatric Emergency Coordinating Committee, which consists of all the people who deal with persons with mental illness in Los Angeles. (I use the term mental illness here, because the Los Angeles Police Department doesn't distinguish between people with mental illness and people with mental retardation.) One of the challenges to this group is that we don't keep statistics on whether persons who commit crimes have mental retardation, or are substance abusers, or whatever. But there are many people with mental disabilities who are on probation and parole, and who are defendants in court cases.

In Los Angeles there are seven Regional Centers for the Developmentally Disabled that provide assistance in working with people with mental retardation who commit crimes. However, the extent and quality of this assistance could be greatly improved. For instance, one problem in working with these autonomous centers is the issue of confidentiality. If in our area we come across somebody whom we suspect has mental retardation and we call the regional center to ask if somebody has left, or wandered away, they respond by saying that for reasons of confidentiality, they can't tell us. Consequently, we have no way of returning these individuals to the facilities they came from, even if we believe we know where they belong. I think policies such as these need to be reevaluated.

As a result of the board of inquiry, the Los Angeles Police Department formed a Mental Evaluation Unit, staffed by 10 expertly trained people in the areas of mental retardation, mental health, mental illness, and drug abuse. The Mental Evaluation Unit is headed by a lieutenant who also oversees our Missing Persons Unit. The Mental Evaluation Unit has established ties with the Alzheimer's Foundation, Medic Alert, and Links-to-Life programs.

When a police officer in Los Angeles encounters someone whom we believe has some type of mental problem, whether it be mental retardation, mental illness, or some other condition, that officer calls the Mental Evaluation Unit. The individual in question is then given a preliminary screening to determine where he or she should go. The Mental Evaluation Unit does an excellent job of referring individuals to appropriate programs and resources. We all know the problems we encounter in trying to work together. In Los Angeles, we had difficulty talking to each other. There were programs that, because of procedural problems, refused to take people whom we found to have mental illness. Our new procedures have greatly reduced this problem.

Another large concern that we must address is the issue of statistics. The unit that works for me, the Mental Evaluation Unit, has very detailed statistics, but we don't break these data down by type of mental problem, whether it be mental retardation or some other condition. As a result, and as I indicated earlier, I have no way of knowing how many people with mental retardation are in the criminal justice population in Los Angeles. And without such information, there is no way to develop a comprehensive program.

Finally, I think our major challenge is to improve law enforcement procedures for dealing with offenders with mental retardation. Law enforcement is the critical link between the criminal justice and service systems for persons with mental disabilities. Training of law enforcement personnel in the area of mental disabilities is crucial. For instance, legislation has been enacted in California that mandates training for law enforcement personnel in this area. It will be an excellent program.

We need to understand that there is a difference between believing in something and acting on this belief. I suspect that there is widespread intellectual commitment to improving law enforcement procedures and punishment mechanisms for offenders with mental retardation. But this commitment will have to be coupled with hard work if beliefs are to result in action. We need to do more than just bandy ideas about. We need to start promoting change.

THE CORRECTIONS SYSTEM

John W. Finn, Director, Forensic Services, New York Office of Mental Retardation and Developmental Disabilities

On a cold steel bench in a maximum security state prison sits Richard, a 28-year-old man with mild mental retardation. Richard has just had 6 months of good time taken away for fighting. This is the fourth infraction in the last 6 months, and the prison disciplinary review board is becoming increasingly more punitive toward Richard. The guards assigned to Richard's cell block know that something is not quite right with Richard, but they don't know how to keep him out of trouble. Richard isn't sure either, but he feels he can't stop fighting, or else the other inmates will harass him even more and he will never be safe. The judge who sentenced Richard to 3½–7 years in prison for second-degree criminal mischief did so because he didn't know what else to do with Richard. After five arrests in three years, he felt he had no choice but to incarcerate Richard. Staff from the community residence where Richard was living told the judge that they had tried everything they could to help Richard, but that he was resistive to services and they did not know what else to offer. The police officer who arrested Richard was willing to work out an informal disposition, but nobody seemed to have any suggestions about what to do with Richard. So Richard sits, and the best minds in both criminal justice and human services are at a loss about what to do with him.

One thing is clear. For the next 3½–7 years, Richard will be the responsibility of a correctional institution. The prospects of how that time will be spent are far from encouraging. Richard has become part of an enigma. Society says, "We should be kind to persons with disabilities and give them assistance to meet their needs." Society also says, "Criminals should be severely punished." To unravel the enigma, we must be able to discriminate between the person with mental retardation who is having trouble with the law and the criminal who may also have mental retardation.

It is generally accepted that persons with mental retardation and developmental disabilities present unique problems and challenges to the human services and criminal justice systems. The problems associated with providing services to incarcerated persons with mental retardation involve legal, ethical, political, and financial considerations. To some extent, these issues are reflective of larger issues facing the entire criminal justice and human services systems. Perhaps the most central of these involves defining the role of criminal justice systems on the one hand and human services programs on the other, in meeting societal expectations for maintaining public safety and providing humanistic services in the context of shrinking public resources. It is essential to the success of any initiatives in this area that these overlapping, sometimes conflicting, and critical questions of public policy be fully explored and integrated within the larger missions of both systems.

In New York State we have been reasonably successful at developing a working consensus that allows both the human services and criminal justice systems to address the problems of offenders with mental retardation from each system's perspective. Some of the programs that have been initiated are jointly administered by both systems and some are separate, but all share a commitment to focus services on the specific needs of individual clients whenever possible.

My comments here concentrate on issues, problems, and recommendations regarding persons with mental retardation and developmental disabilities who are incarcerated in local lockups and county jails, as well as state prisons and penitentiaries. Regardless of the location or size of the prison, the most important element in formulating a sound response to the needs of incarcerated offenders with mental retardation is the preincarceration system of screening, evaluation and, where appropriate, diversion. For any response to the problems of incarcerated clients to be effective, it must be part of a comprehensive response to the problems of offenders with mental retardation throughout the criminal justice process. In New York this response includes extensive training of criminal justice and human services staff in the nature and needs of offenders with mental retardation; provision of technical assistance and expert clinical evaluations to attorneys and courts concerning defendants with mental retardation; consultations with criminal justice and human services staff concerning clients' criminal justice problems; assistance to courts in depositional planning for offenders with mental retardation and developmental disabilities; and provision of training, program design assistance, and case-specific consultative services to the staff of correctional facilities.

The problems associated with serving persons with mental retardation and developmental disabilities in prisons and jails are seen by some as so overwhelming as to essentially preclude the possibility of meaningful habilitation within incarceration settings. Although this perception may be an overstatement, several fundamental problems must be recognized if programs are to succeed. Perhaps the most basic of these problems concerns the underlying theoretical differences in the way most prison systems operate, compared to the approaches of most human services programs. Human services programs are usually based upon values such as personal growth, individual opportunity, and cooperative helping relationships. In contrast, in most correctional situations, security, maintenance of order, adherence to rules, and respect for authority are most valued. "Cooperative helping" may not only be foreign to the average correctional officer's perspective, but it might well endanger the officer's safety if he or she were to practice it on the cell block. Programs for inmates with mental retardation and developmental disabilities are thus often at odds with the primary security mission of the prison. The staff of habilitative programs may feel that their clinical perspectives are not valued within the prison. This, in turn, can make program staff feel isolated and unsupported in their efforts. When program staff do not feel supported, have no peer group of colleagues to relate to, and are working with such difficult clients, burnout becomes almost inevitable. To help avoid burnout, it is important that program and correctional staff be brought together for regular training and case conferences and that they work jointly to resolve issues concerning inmate behavior and treatment. Program staff must also be supported by regular contact with colleagues from outside the prison system. Administrators must remain aware of the warning signs of staff burnout and be prepared to address it when it occurs.

Another major problem concerns the lack of an advocacy group for prisoners with mental retardation and developmental disabilities. It has been said that when we combine prisons with human services programs we get the best of neither world and the worst of both. This may be particularly true for advocacy. The traditional role of an advocate within the human services system involves a combination of friendship to the client, critical evaluation of the system, and exertion of sometimes unpleasant pressure on the system when the advocate perceives it is failing to meet the client's needs or to protect the client's rights. Traditional human services advocates do not usually include inmates with mental retardation within the scope of their responsibilities; nor are these advocates generally welcomed in correctional settings.

Within the prison system there often exists a form of advocacy somewhat different from that usually found in human services programs. Often prisoner advocacy is more self-initiated and less formal. To protect one's own rights, one must first be aware of and understand what rights one is entitled to. One must then have the skills and abilities to pressure the system on one's own behalf. Yet, even those inmates with mental retardation who are aware of their rights tend to have greater difficulty asserting them in the face of the overwhelming authority of the prison system.

A second form of self-advocacy is inherent to all incarceration settings. Within correctional institutions there exists a commodity variously referred to as "juice," "heat," or "drag." Essentially, these terms refer to the ability of an inmate to bring about that which he wishes to happen. When an inmate is able to obtain a choice work assignment, he or she is said to have "used some juice." The reality of prison life is that persons with mental retardation and developmental disabilities are usually not able to master the informal systems of accumulating and then using "juice" to improve their situations. Even typical prisoner's rights groups are generally not suited to the situations of persons with mental retardation who may be reluctant to reveal their disability for fear of abuse from other inmates or guards.

To appreciate fully the problems encountered by incarcerated persons with mental retardation, one must first understand something about the characteristics of offenders with mental retardation and developmental disabilities. In general, inmates with mental retardation are relatively high functioning. In New York State nearly 95% of the clients referred to the Office of Mental Retardation and Developmental Disabilities Bureau of Forensic Services are persons with mild mental retardation (see Table 1). Most offenders with mental retardation are male, and most are young. In New York over 53% are under age 30, and over 82% are under age 40 (see Table 1). Most clients commit their crimes in concert with others, and a wide range of criminal behaviors is alleged (see Table 1). Most significantly, offenders with mental retardation tend to be aware of their disabilities and, whether motivated by mistrust of large systems or by fear of abuse, they generally work very hard to

Table 1. Forensic data and referral system: Characteristics of persons referred

Characteristics	Percentage
Age of person:	
Over 50 years	2.6
40–49 years	15.0
30–39 years	29.3
20–29 years	32.7
Under 20 years	20.4
Total	100.0
Level of mental retardation:	
Mild	94.6
Moderate	3.4
Severe	1.3
Profound	0.7
Total	100.0
Type of crime charged:	
Against person	35.9
Sexually related	22.2
Against property	20.3
Arson	11.1
Other	10.5
Total	100.0

convince others that they do not have mental retardation. The results can be catastrophic. Not only do clients fail to take advantage of the rights they have and probably do not understand, but the very services that they could benefit from (i.e., adult functional education, vocational training, and literacy training) are the ones they will most likely avoid for fear that their disabilities will become apparent if they participate.

We also know that the responses of inmates with mental retardation to situations where they feel threatened are more likely to be physical rather than verbal or intellectual. They are, therefore, more prone to getting into fights and becoming a correctional management problem both because of their outbursts and their high potential for victimization by others. From the human services perspective, these types of clients are usually seen as resistive to programming, uncooperative and, therefore, unworthy of special program effort. We know, therefore, that when inmates with mental retardation are considered for release to parole, they will likely have a poor prison record with little program participation, many infractions and violations, and a very weak postdischarge plan. Also, inmates with mental retardation generally do not do well in interviews with the parole board, since those types of intense verbal interactions are particularly difficult for them. Once released from prison, the likelihood is that people with mental retardation will be no more successful at navigating the parole supervision situation than they were at being a successful inmate within the correctional institution. It should not be surprising, therefore, that compared to people who do not have mental retardation, the inmate with mental retardation does more time, does harder time, gets less out of his time, and is more likely to be returned once released from prison.

Given this admittedly generalized profile of the inmate with mental retardation, the problems in identification and classification can be put into perspective. Not the least of these problems is whether it is reasonable to screen out persons with mental retardation and developmental disabilities if there are no appropriate services to offer them. In addition, it is likely that the prison staff who conduct the screenings will not be skilled or experienced in the fine points of assessing persons with mental retardation and developmental disabilities. This, in turn, can lead to an overrepresentation of the numbers of clients, since the tendency of inexperienced evaluators is to underestimate intellectual capabilities, particularly when the person being tested is not being cooperative. Certainly, the widely used group screenings of intellectual function such as the Revised Beta should not be used to determine if an inmate has mental retardation.

Classification problems are compounded by a lack of programs at the various levels of security for inmates with mental retardation. Most programs for inmates with mental retardation are operated at the maximum security level, since this allows prison administrators the flexibility of placing moderate and minimum security inmates as well as maximum security inmates into a single program. The result is that inmates who are diagnosed as having mental retardation may be placed at more restrictive security levels than they would have if their disabilities had not been detected. Programs for inmates with mental retardation also face funding problems; problems associated with controlling access to and exit criteria from the programs; problems associated with inmates who have multiple disabilities; problems in obtaining training, and retaining good correctional staff to work in these types of programs; problems in gaining access to institutional resources such as gym equipment, inmate work programs, and vocational training shops. Given the myriad of problems, one might reasonably ask, "What should we do with the inmate who has mental retardation?"

The answer, at least in New York State, begins long before the client is sentenced and placed in a correctional facility. The accompanying diagram (see Figure 1) illustrates the conceptual framework within which individual cases are handled. The paradigm has two dimensions. Along the vertical dimension are issues of public safety. At the lowest level are public safety issues of relatively low impact such as victimless crimes, petty larceny, and minor violations. At the upper level are severe attacks on the public safety such as murder, rape, and arson.

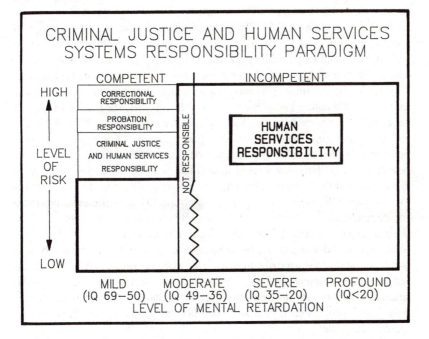

Figure 1. Criminal justice and human services systems responsibility paradigm.

Along the horizontal dimension of this paradigm is the individual's level of mental retardation or developmental disability. This dimension ranges from only slightly disabled on the left axis to profoundly disabled on the far right axis. When one attempts to determine the appropriate system response to any individual case, it is the relative relationship of these two dimensions (public safety and level of disability) that will determine the roles that the human services and criminal justice systems should play in any individual case. Within this matrix of possibilities, there are some established parameters of system responsibility. For example, if one begins at the far left axis of mild disability and proceeds to the right, one encounters a point where the level of disability is so severe as to render the client incompetent to stand trial. In these cases, the human services system will have responsibility for the care and treatment of the client, regardless of the degree of danger to public safety or the threat associated with the client's criminal behavior. If one begins again at the far left axis of mild disability and proceeds to the right, but not so far that the client is deemed incompetent to stand trial, one encounters the point of diminished criminal responsibility. This client, although capable of standing trial, is disabled to the extent that at the time of committing the crime, the client was not criminally responsible for his or her actions.

These clients are also the responsibility of the human services system, regardless of the degree to which public safety is threatened. One will notice that the area of lack of criminal responsibility is relatively narrow for persons with mental retardation. This is because of the nature of the condition of mental retardation and the order in which the issues of competency to stand trial and criminal responsibility are decided before the court. Because mental retardation is a relatively stable condition, it is likely that if an individual were so disabled at the time he committed a criminal act that he was unable to understand the nature and consequences of his actions, the probability is that he would still have substantial disabilities when competency to participate in the trial is assessed. Because the issue of competency to stand trial is resolved prior to considerations of criminal responsibility, most persons with mental retardation who have substantial disabilities will be found incompetent to stand trial and the issue of criminal responsibility will never be raised. However, because the criteria for criminal responsibility are different from those for competency to stand trial, the possibility exists that a client could be deemed capable of understanding the legal proceeding and of participating in his or her own defense (e.g., be competent to stand trial), but be disabled to the degree that at the time of committing the alleged criminal act he or she was not criminally responsible for his or her behavior. In New York State approximately 50 clients are deemed incompetent to stand trial annually, whereas only 2 or 3 persons each year are found not criminally responsible owing to mental retardation.

For those clients whose disabilities are not severe enough for them to be deemed incompetent or not criminally responsible, the degree to which public safety is threatened is important in determining the appropriate systematic and individual response. At the extremes of this area, there is usually little disagreement as to responsibility. In the instance of the marginally competent client who commits a low-level offense, most people would see the human services system as the focal point of services. Likewise, in the case of the extremely dangerous person with only slight disabilities, most people would see the criminal justice system as having primary responsibility. The two extremes having been eliminated, the remaining category can best be seen as an area of joint criminal justice system and human services involvement. The specific roles each system should play can best be determined on a case-by-case basis. This matrix of systems responsibility enables one to gain a better understanding of the characteristics of those persons with mental retardation and developmental disabilities who are most likely to be incarcerated. Corrections-based programs can then be designed to address the needs that these clients will present. Such an approach requires confidence that persons conducting pretrial and trial-based assessment and evaluation services have sufficient knowledge and sensitivity to the issues involved in competency and culpability assessments of persons with mental retardation and developmental disabilities. The human services system should assist the criminal justice system in this regard by making available clinical expertise in forensic evaluations of persons with mental retardation and by offering specific expert evaluations when requested by a court or attorney.

When the pretrial system of evaluation and assessment is working effectively, the clients with the most severe disabilities will be diverted from the criminal justice process prior to incarceration. It must be acknowledged, however, that some persons with mental retardation and developmental disabilities will continue to be sentenced to correctional institutions. If we can trust our systems of pretrial and trial-based competency and culpability assessments, then the clients for whom we should be designing correctional programs are persons who have mild disabilities and are quite dangerous. The responsibility of correctional institutions for these clients is probably quite similar to their responsibilities for the general inmate populations. They should certainly ensure that inmates with mental retardation are kept safe and free from harm or abuse. They should offer them opportunities for services that will help them grow in areas where they have needs. They should protect and advocate on behalf of those clients who are not capable of self-advocacy. They should ensure that their policies and operations do not impose a more severe burden upon inmates with mental retardation than upon nondisabled inmates. Overall, they should help inmates with mental retardation do their time with as little trouble as possible, while also helping them to make their incarceration as productive as possible.

Both the criminal justice and human services systems must accept their responsibilities for people with mental retardation and developmental disabilities who become involved in the criminal justice system. Neither system should be seen as having total responsibility, and both should be held accountable for incorporating the needs of these very challenging people within their total mandate to serve.

Before concluding, let me return to Richard, who has remained incarcerated, confused, and underserved. He continues to be both a victim and a victimizer. Given the current circumstances, the prospects for his future are only marginally better than hopeless. To a certain extent, Richard's failure is our failure; but his success could be our success. If we are truly concerned about people like Richard, we must be willing to extend the limits of our systems and accept responsibility for shedding light upon the enigma that they represent. If we are not, then the lost potential of Richard's life will become our own dubious legacy.

Chapter 2

Toward an Epidemiology of Relevant Attributes

John H. Noble, Jr.
and Ronald W. Conley

M OST PEOPLE WITH mental retardation are able to live in the community, either independently or with social supports. The majority can work in integrated employment and participate in community activities, such as going to theaters, shopping, using public transportation, maintaining friendships, and so forth. Unfortunately, like other groups in society, a small percentage of people with mental retardation disobey the law. In these cases difficult issues of apprehension, adjudication, punishment, and rehabilitation arise.

This chapter examines some of the existing epidemiological data on offenders with mental retardation as a foundation for assessing the impact of recommended changes in policy and practice and for identifying areas where additional research is needed. Such information is particularly helpful in assessing how many people with mental retardation will be affected by, and what may be the likely costs of, the different options for improving the criminal justice system. Unfortunately, as will become apparent, there has been little systematic collection of data about offenders with mental retardation.

THE CRIMINAL JUSTICE SYSTEM

In general, the data presented in this chapter describe the flow of cases through the criminal justice system, from the point at which the alleged crime is committed to the offender's final release from confinement or his or her completion of some other kind of punishment or rehabilitation. This case flow can be divided into five segments for purposes of defining the types of data required. The first is the commission of a crime. The second involves the

17

identification and apprehension by law enforcement officials of the individual who allegedly committed the crime. The third involves the adjudication and disposition of the case, which usually consists of arraignment and trial but may follow a different route if the person is identified as having a disability. The fourth segment involves the incarceration or other punishment of the offender and his or her rehabilitation. The fifth segment refers to the release of the offender from the criminal justice system, usually to probation or by transfer to a treatment facility. (Of course, many variations and complications are typically introduced into this flow of events, reflecting the great diversity of courts, programs, procedures, and the possible dispositions of a case.)

The Crime

One can never know with certainty how many crimes are committed by people with mental retardation, since, with rare and unimportant exceptions, the guilty person must be apprehended to determine whether mental retardation is implicated. Many crimes go unsolved.

Apprehension

Once an individual is identified as having committed a crime or is suspected of committing a crime, there is at least the possibility of determining whether or not the individual has mental retardation. However, between the time of apprehension and the trial (if there is one) there are numerous reasons why the identification of suspects as having mental retardation is likely to be erratic.

At the time of arrest, the police usually have no easily available means by which to ascertain whether or not the person has mental retardation. There are exceptions to this generalization, of course, as when prior investigation has disclosed that the suspect has mental retardation or when obvious visual clues exist. But even in the latter case, the clues suggesting mental retardation may be confounded by the existence of other factors such as the influence of alcohol or drugs, language problems, uncontrolled behavior, and so on. At best, the police will have simple guidelines by which to attempt to identify persons who may have mental retardation.

Even after arrest, it is unlikely that many police stations have the capacity to accurately diagnose mental retardation, or that much interest exists in doing so. Moreover, the accused person or the person's guardian may be unwilling to consent to a test.

Disposition

After apprehension, the flow of offenders with mental retardation through the criminal justice system becomes more complex. A case can be handled in at least four ways. First, the defendant can be sent to trial to determine guilt or innocence and to reach a decision about punishment or other disposition. Second, the defendant can be judged mentally incompetent to stand trial and the court can direct that he or she be institutionalized to attempt to restore competency to stand trial or to await the possible spontaneous return of competency. Third, the defendant can be placed directly in a community treatment or diversion program, again without a formal determination of guilt or innocence. Finally, the defendant can be released—possibly to enter or return to a habilitation program.

If tried in court, there are several possible scenarios. If found guilty, the offender may be sentenced to a prison term or probation, or given a fine or warning, depending upon the nature of the crime. The offender may also, in consideration of recognized mental retardation, be committed to an institution for care and treatment, or be placed in a community program. Another possibility is for the court to find the individual not guilty by reason of mental disability.

Clearly, some dispositions require knowledge of the offender's mental retardation, since a person cannot reasonably be institutionalized or placed in a special program without such prior knowledge. In other cases, however, trial and sentencing may take place without any effort to identify possible mental retardation.

Punishment and Rehabilitation

Upon determination of guilt, the court imposes punishment (e.g., imprisonment, fine) and/or a program of rehabilitation. This is the segment of the criminal justice process in which more testing is likely to occur in an effort to ascertain whether or not the adjudicated offender has mental retardation. If the offender is imprisoned or institutionalized, such testing may be routinely administered. It is not surprising, therefore, to find that most existing data on offenders with mental retardation are based on prison records. Nevertheless, the data on incarcerated persons are incomplete. Not all correctional facilities—especially local jails and lockups—assess the intellectual status of inmates. In fact, almost no information is available on the incidence of mental retardation among prisoners in local jails. The data are further limited by the fact that many prison assessments are themselves suspect in nature.

Release

The final segment in the criminal justice cycle is release to the community, which occurs when the offender has completed the prison sentence or, if institutionalized or placed in a supervised community program, when a determination has been made that the offender is no longer a danger to the community. Release may also be conditional (e.g., parole).

EPIDEMIOLOGICAL ISSUES

Many methodological difficulties are encountered in evaluating existing information on offenders with mental retardation. This section examines several definitional problems and their implications for data collection.

Definition of Mental
Retardation and Identification

The most widely accepted definition of mental retardation is "significantly subaverage general intellectual functioning existing concurrently with deficits in adaptive behavior and manifested during the developmental period" (American Association on Mental Deficiency, 1983, p. 1). "[S]ignificantly subaverage . . . intellectual functioning" is usually defined as an IQ below 70, although clinicians may occasionally regard individuals with even higher IQs as having mental retardation. "[D]evelopmental period" is defined as the period of time before age 18. And "deficits in adaptive behavior" are defined as "significant limitations in an individual's effectiveness in meeting the standards of maturation, learning, personal independence, and/or social responsibility that are expected for his or her age level and cultural group . . ." (American Association on Mental Deficiency, 1983).

Each of these components of the definition of mental retardation presents significant problems when used to identify people with mental retardation. To begin with, the phrase "deficits in adaptive behavior" is conceptually vague and ill-defined. Despite the existence of many scales that claim to measure adaptive behavior, there is no clear indication as to how severe the maladaptive behavior must be before a person is identified as having mental retardation. Although at some level the lack of adaptive behavior is easy to identify, there are no empirical standards for determining the cutoff point between behavior considered "normal" versus "abnormal." Second, the *presumption* of a close relationship between deficits in adaptive behavior and limited intellectual functioning is false. Many factors in addition to impaired cognitive ability may affect adaptive behavior among people with mental retardation, including other disabilities, age, lack of motivation, lack of opportunities, disabling environments, abuse and neglect, and so forth—each of which may interact and cause people to fall below normal social expectations. In fact, the service system for people with mental retardation is currently undergoing major changes based on accumulating evidence that individuals with severe mental limitations are capable of far greater social adjustment (e.g., living and participating in the community, working in integrated jobs, and so on) than was previously believed.

The requirement that the mental retardation originate before age 18 raises additional concerns. Regardless of whether the event (e.g., accident, substance abuse) causing mental limitations happened before or after age 18, criminal justice system officials must confront the same problems of social adaptation and offer the same kinds of services to assist the affected individuals to respond appropriately to the due process requirements of the criminal justice system and, if found guilty and sentenced to prison, to help them adjust to prison life and prepare for subsequent release.

Finally, there are many problems with intelligence tests. The key characteristic in mental retardation is *significant* limitation in intellectual functioning. However, tests of intelligence provide, at best, a rough approximation of the level of intelligence. For one thing, these tests measure some aspects of intelligence, such as memory and reasoning ability, better than other aspects, such as creativity. In addition, IQ tests are frequently criticized for systematically understating the intelligence of persons who are poor, nonwhite, or non–English speaking, or from a different cultural background. Furthermore, IQ tests can give misleading results if used to measure the intelligence of persons with emotional problems or physical handicaps such as blindness, deafness, or cerebral palsy. Finally, the attitudes of the person being tested can be a biasing factor. Despite continuing efforts to improve IQ tests, problems with their use and interpretation remain unresolved and are perhaps unresolvable.

The dichotomous nature of the judgment about mental retardation is another problem. The existence of mental retardation is not an either/or condition, as is measles, polio, and so forth. Intellect is distributed continuously along a curve approximating the shape of the normal probability distribution in which the percentage of persons with IQ scores below a specific value declines rapidly as the specified value falls increasingly farther below the mean value of the distribution of IQ scores. Thus, assuming a mean of 100 and a standard deviation of 16, one would expect to find about 3% of the population with IQs below 70. However, the expected percentage would rise to 4.6% for IQs below 73, and would reach 5.9% for IQs below 75.[1]

These concerns regarding the definition of mental retardation and identification of people with mental retardation have several consequences. First, despite frequent exhortations about the limitations and questionable validity of IQ tests and the importance of applying measures of social competence, most efforts to measure the number of people with mental retardation rely on IQ tests.

Second, there will always be a large number of persons just above any arbitrary IQ cutoff point who differ only in minor ways from persons below the cutoff, and whose need for special consideration will be just as valid. In fact, given the difficulties of measuring intelligence, the differences between people slightly over or under the cutoff point may reflect random variation rather than true differences among people. In terms of many criminal justice issues, the situation of an individual with an IQ of 72 may not differ substantively from an individual with an IQ of 68, and, indeed, the variance may fall within the standard error of measurement of most IQ tests. Reliance on rigid IQ criteria to determine whether an offender is entitled to special consideration may lead not only to inequities among people who differ only slightly in

---

[1]For a number of reasons, IQs will not be distributed exactly according to the normal probability curve at these low levels, but the order of magnitude of the relative distribution of low IQs can be expected to remain roughly the same as described in the text.

mental competency but also to inappropriate sentencing and rehabilitation decisions. This is because the ability to distinguish right from wrong, to be competent to stand trial, to plead guilty, to be a witness, or to participate meaningfully in rehabilitation programs depends on many factors, among which level of intelligence is only one.

Definition of Developmental Disabilities

The term *developmental disabilities* appears frequently in the literature. Federal law (PL 98-527) defines a developmental disability as a severe chronic disability of a person that:

1. Is attributable to a mental or physical impairment or a combination of mental and physical impairments.
2. Is manifested before age 22.
3. Is likely to continue indefinitely.
4. Results in substantial functional limitations in three or more of the following areas of major life activity: self-care, receptive and expressive language, learning, mobility, self-direction, capacity for independent living, and economic self-sufficiency.
5. Reflects the person's need for a combination and sequence of special interdisciplinary or generic care, treatment, or other services that are of lifelong or extended duration and are individually planned and coordinated.

Two basic distinctions separate people with developmental disabilities from those with mental retardation. First, the term *developmental disabilities* encompasses *all* types of severe disabilities originating before age 22. Mental retardation is only one of many such disabilities, although one of the most prevalent. Second, only individuals with very severe disabilities qualify as having developmental disabilities. For instance, some individuals with mild mental retardation do not qualify under the federal definition of a developmental disability.

Nevertheless, the term *developmental disabilities* is often used almost synonymously with *mental retardation*. Moreover, *developmental disabilities* is sometimes used to encompass all persons who are defined as having mental retardation, to the exclusion of most other kinds of severe disabilities originating before age 22. Accordingly, when *developmental disabilities* is used to describe the composition of a database, it is important to ascertain precisely which individuals are included.

It is not the intent of this chapter to detail all the problems involved in constructing a reliable and valid operational definition of developmental disabilities. However, it is important to note that the concept is vague, ambiguous, and encompasses an extremely heterogeneous population and, as such, provides an extremely weak foundation on which to establish empirical parameters for identifying individuals, for conducting epidemiological studies, or for designing rehabilitation and other programs.

Definition of Offender with Mental Retardation

There are also definitional ambiguities in the term *offender with mental retardation*. In principle, the term refers to people with mental retardation who violate the law. However, under American jurisprudence, the guilt or innocence of any individual, whether or not he or she has mental retardation, is a matter that the courts must decide. Consequently, unless the individual confesses to a crime, the alleged offender must first be accused and then must stand as a defendant in a court proceeding and be found guilty. If found not guilty, the accused person is not an offender, even though he or she has been deeply enmeshed in the criminal justice system and requires appropriate assistance. Another definitional problem arises when the individual is found to have mental retardation, but no action is taken against the individual, or he or she is placed in a program for treatment, rehabilitation, or institutional care instead of being charged or categorized as an offender. Still another definitional problem arises when an act committed by a person with mental retardation would lead to criminal charges if committed in the general community but not when committed in an institutional setting or group home.

These definitional problems are not cited here to argue for labeling as "offenders" all individuals with mental retardation who commit unacceptable or antisocial acts. Nonetheless, it is important to recognize that a number of persons with mental retardation who violate the law may never be formally charged.

Incidence and Prevalence

Epidemiologists distinguish between incidence and prevalence. Incidence refers to the number of times a given event occurs in a known population during a particular time period (e.g., the number of persons in the U.S. population incarcerated annually). Prevalence refers to the number of such cases that exist in a known population at a point in time (e.g., the total number of persons incarcerated as of January 1, 1991). Incidence and prevalence are usually expressed as rates per some standard unit of population (e.g., per 10,000 or 100,000 population).

Epidemiologists also distinguish between *true* and *treated* incidence and prevalence (Monahan & Steadman, 1984). The distinction has special relevance when considering reports of crime and imprisonment. For example, the rate at which crime actually occurs would be its true incidence, whereas the rate at which the criminal justice system detects crime and imposes punitive sentence on those involved would be its treated incidence.

SPECIAL POPULATIONS

There are special populations in which it is sometimes hard to distinguish among those who have, or do not have, mental retardation. A number of these conditions or characteristics are outlined in the subsections following.

Traumatic Brain Injury

Medical technology is now able to save many people who only 10 years ago would have died from traumatic brain injury (TBI) sustained in automobile accidents, falls, sports injuries, near-drowning, assaults, and other types of accidents. Sometimes, however, these individuals survive with major deficits in cognitive and behavioral functioning. The de facto loss of intelligence combined with major problems in adaptive behavior (Brooks, 1989) causes many survivors to be labeled as "mentally retarded." Estimates of the incidence of TBI vary considerably as a result of substantial differences in definitions among studies, procedures for identifying cases, the time-frame within which data are collected, and other important differences in methodology (Kraus, 1980). Males are roughly twice as likely as females to sustain traumatic head injuries, with the highest incidence occurring in the 15- to 24-year-old age group (Axelrod, 1986). Race and social class differences tend not to be reported.

In addition to loss of intellectual functioning, among the most noticeable sequelae of TBI are behavior disorders, including overactivity, restlessness, destructiveness, aggression, tantrums, impulsiveness, and socially uninhibited behavior (McGuire & Rothenberg, 1986), which sometimes cause the TBI victim to run afoul of the law. McKinlay, Brooks, Bond, Martinage, and Marshall (1981) reported that 12 months after injury, 19% of persons with serious TBI had behavior disorders and 54% had emotional problems. Extrapolating these percentages to conservative estimates of the number of live hospital discharges in the United States in 1988 with "severe" and "severe/moderate" TBI, as measured by the Glasgow Coma Scale (Teasdale & Jennett, 1974), would place the annual incidence of behavior disorders among persons with TBI at between 7,039 and 19,861, and the annual incidence of emotional problems at between 10,878 and 30,666 (Noble, Laski, Conley, & Noble, 1990).

Little is known about how many persons with TBI actually enter the criminal justice system at various stages. A survey by the New York State Commission on Quality of Care for the Mentally Disabled (Sundram, 1989) provides a basis for estimating the prevalence of adult prisoners with TBI in New York State and local correctional facilities. Among the 140 sample inmates with Beta IQs below 80 (18% of the total adult inmate population), 2 (1.4%) had known histories of serious head trauma. This sketchy information yields an estimated TBI prevalence rate of 0.26% in 1988 among all adult prisoners in New York State and local correctional facilities. This would indicate that 109 of the 42,288 New York State adult prisoner population had *both* a low Beta IQ score and a history of TBI.

Recently, Lewis, Pincus, Feldman, Jackson, and Bard (1986) reported the results of clinical evaluations of 15 death-row inmates, chosen for examination because of the imminence of their executions. All had histories of severe head injuries with evidence of varying neurological problems, including periodic blackouts, leading Lewis and colleagues to conclude that many persons sentenced to death (and, by implication, others sentenced to lesser punishments) "probably suffer unrecognized severe psychiatric, neurological, and cognitive disorders relevant to considerations of mitigation" (p. 838). Although Lewis and colleagues did not explicitly mention mental retardation as one of the identifiable cognitive disorders, it is well known that clinicians sometimes confuse subnormal intellectual functioning when coupled with significant maladaptive behavior with psychiatric symptomatology. In any event, Perlin (1987, p. 85), commenting on these findings about death-row inmates, criticized the U.S. Supreme Court for not giving sufficient consideration to the possible existence of severe mental impairment as a mitigating factor when passing judgment in capital punishment cases, despite an apparent historical aversion to concurring in the execution of demonstrably insane persons.

Identification of TBI is complicated by the tendency of the affected individuals and their families to deny the reality of mental impairment because of the stigma attached to the term. Indeed, as reported by Lewis and colleagues (1986, p. 841), most of the death-row inmates attempted to minimize their disorders, "preferring, it seemed, to appear 'bad,' rather than 'crazy.'"

The growing number of people with TBI naturally means that an increasing number will violate the law. In cases where the intellectual functioning of TBI victims is comparable to that of people with mental retardation, identical problems will arise with respect to the identification, representation, punishment, rehabilitation, and management of the enormously diverse behaviors, emotional problems, levels of comprehension, and programmatic needs of individuals.

Alcohol and Drug Abuse

There is evidence of relatively high use of alcohol and drugs among persons with mental retardation and developmental disabilities who enter the criminal justice system. The earlier-mentioned survey by the New York State Commission on Quality of Care for the Mentally Disabled (Sundram, 1989) indicated that 64% of the sample at risk for developmental disabilities had histories of alcohol abuse; 43% had histories of drug abuse; and 30% had histories of both alcohol and drug abuse. The Monroe County Developmentally Disabled Offender Project (Rockowitz, 1986a) reported histories of drug/alcohol abuse in 66% of its clients. The Buffalo (N.Y.) State College Developmental Disabilities Criminal Justice Project (K.L. Curry, August 1989, personal communication) reported that 35%–40% of all persons screened at the Erie County Holding Center and the Niagara County Jail had histories of alcohol/drug abuse, and that 5.3% of these alcohol/drug abusers were identified as being developmentally disabled. Finally, P.J. Jericho (letter of July 14, 1988, to Steven M. Eidelman, deputy secretary of mental retardation, Commonwealth of Pennsylvania) reported that 51% of the population with mental retardation served by the Erie, Pennsylvania, Court of Common Pleas Special Probation Services also abused drugs and alcohol or had personality disorders, antisocial behavior, or other mental health diagnoses. The combination of low intelligence and substance abuse often exacerbates maladaptive behavior in persons with mental retardation and developmental disabilities.

Functional Illiteracy

Many prisoners with mental retardation and developmental disabilities are functionally illiterate and are school dropouts. The New York State Commission on Quality of Care for the Mentally Disabled survey (Sundram, 1989) reported that only 6% of the prison inmates with low Beta IQs had completed high school or received an equivalency diploma; 47% had dropped out before completing the 9th grade, and 23% had not completed elementary school. Reading achievement tests indicated that 45% were reading at or below the 5th grade level; mathematics achievement tests showed that 51% had mathematics skills at or below the 5th grade level, and 25% had mathematics skills below the 3rd grade level. The earlier-mentioned Developmental Disabilities Criminal Justice Project (Curry, 1987) reported that 98.9% of offenders diagnosed as having developmental disabilities were school dropouts; 21% of these dropped out by the end of the 8th grade, 46% by the end of the 9th grade, and 74% by the end of the 10th grade.

Dual Diagnosis

The term *dual diagnosis* refers to a combination of mental retardation with alcohol or substance abuse, or mental retardation with mental illness. In a sample of 964 adult offenders with IQs below 55 (Brown & Courtless, 1971), only 11 cases (1.1.%) received a psychiatric or medical diagnosis as a result of special testing or examination. In sharp contrast, 12% of the prison inmates in the New York State Commission on Quality of Care for the Mentally Disabled survey (Sundram, 1989) had received inpatient psychiatric care. The Monroe County Developmentally Disabled Offender Program (Rockowitz, 1986a) indicated that 37.3% of its clients with mental retardation, other developmental disabilities, learning disabilities, or communication disorders also had a neurotic or psychotic disorder.

Victims

Persons with mental retardation may become victims as well as offenders. This raises a host of legal and ethical issues as victims with mental retardation seek redress against alleged offenders with or without mental retardation, or as prosecutors seek to convict the alleged offenders (see also Luckasson, chap. 11, this volume). Accordingly, one can anticipate the need to obtain an estimate of the number of people with mental retardation who are victims of crime in order to judge the possible impact on them of future changes in law or procedures relating, inter alia, to competency to give evidence.

OFFENDERS WITH MENTAL RETARDATION IN PRISONS AND INSTITUTIONS

Most data on offenders with mental retardation are collected from prisons and institutions.

Data from Prisons

Most, but not all, inmates of state and federal prisons are given intelligence tests at the time of admission. The results of these tests, however, are not easily accessible in published form. More important, there are many problems of accuracy and consistency among the data that are available.

Lack of accuracy stems from numerous causes. To begin with, testing procedures are usually suspect. Prisons usually rely on group intelligence tests rather than individually administered IQ tests, the latter of which is required by the American Association on Mental Retardation (AAMR) when making a diagnosis of mental retardation. In some cases, however, individualized testing is administered to persons who score low on group tests. In addition, the people administering the tests are not always properly trained in test administration. Further, the tests are often given shortly after arrival at prison—a time in which the inmate is most likely to be disoriented, depressed, upset, suspicious, and hostile, and with little incentive to cooperate in completing the tests. Another problem arises because a large percentage of the prison population comes from low-income and minority groups, raising the possibility of cultural bias (New York State [NYS] Office of Mental Retardation and Developmental Disabilities, 1987, pp. 8–9). Finally, it is often difficult to filter out the effects of intellectual limitation from the effects of other conditions such as substance abuse or mental illness. As a consequence, some persons will test in the IQ range indicating mental retardation, when in fact they are functioning at a much higher level.

In the case of developmental disabilities other than mental retardation, "prisons generally do not have resources to gather developmental and social historical information to determine whether or not the onset of a disability occurred during an individual's developmental period" (NYS Office of Mental Retardation and Developmental Disabilities, 1987, p. 9).

Lack of consistency in prison data arises because of widely varying levels of accuracy across various prisons, the use of different criteria for determining mental retardation, and the use of different tests to measure intelligence. As a result, estimated rates of mental retardation vary widely.

National Studies   Two major national studies have been conducted to estimate the percentage of people with mental retardation in state and federal prisons (see Table 1).

1. *Brown and Courtless (1971) study.* This survey was initiated in December 1963 and remains one of the most frequently cited studies on the prevalence of people with mental retardation in federal and state penal and correctional institutions. All penal and correctional institutions in the United States other than local jails and workhouses were asked to supply IQ and other relevant information for their populations. Completed questionnaires were received from over 80% of the institutions surveyed, with IQ scores reported on slightly more than 90,000 inmates.

A prisoner was defined as having mental retardation if his or her IQ fell below 70. Approximately 9.5% of the reported IQ scores fell below 70. Approximately 1.6% of the surveyed population had IQ scores below 55. A small proportion of prisoners had IQs below 40, and a few cases even fell below an IQ of 25. These data represent national averages of data reported by state and federal prisons that administered various types of intelligence tests under widely varying conditions.

To test the reliability of these data, a small follow-up study of 60 inmates with IQ scores falling below 70 was conducted in five states. On retest with the WAIS, 26% of the sample obtained IQ scores of 70 or above. However, about one-third of these persons were in the borderline range of 70–74.

On the grounds that the more refined procedures utilized in the follow-up testing create more reliable results, it is tempting to conclude that the prevalence of mental retardation in the prison population should be reduced by

Table 1.   National studies on the prevalence of prison inmates with mental retardation (MR)

Study	Year	MR criteria	Type test	Population	Percentage with MR
Brown and Courtless (1971)	1963	70	Various tests	All	9.5
Denkowski and Denkowski (1985)	1985	70[a]	Various tests	All	
Group tests only					6.2
Individual tests					2.0

[a] Sometimes below 71.

roughly one-quarter of the original 9.5% estimate. On the other hand, there is unavoidable variation in the scores individuals obtain on IQ tests. Consequently, an unknown percentage of individuals who were reported as having IQs above 70 would probably score below 70 on a retest, so that the appropriate adjustment would be less than 25%. Unfortunately, we cannot determine by how much less.

2. *Denkowski and Denkowski (1985) study.* In a national survey published in 1985, Denkowski and Denkowski sent a questionnaire to the administrator of each state's adult corrections system. Responses were received from all but two states.

Of the 48 states responding, it was found that 36 routinely assessed incoming inmates for mental retardation. The methods of assessment varied widely. Of the 36 states responding, 20 used individual WAIS-R tests to measure intelligence. Of these 20 states, 16 states administered a group test before using the individual WAIS-R test. The other 4 states apparently only tested cases where mental retardation was suspected. Table 2 presents the estimated prevalence of mental retardation in prisons in states that utilized the individual WAIS-R intelligence test for final determination of mental retardation. Table 3 presents the estimated prevalence of mental retardation in prisons in states that relied on some form of group test only. The great majority of states used an IQ cutoff point of 60 or 70 to determine whether a person had mental retardation. In the case of states that employed group IQ tests only, the estimated prevalence of mental retardation ranged from 1.5% to 19.1%, with an average of 6.2%. In states that employed individual WAIS-R IQ tests, the estimated prevalence of mental retardation was much lower, varying from .05% to 5.3%, with an average of 2%.

The prevalence of mental retardation in prisons in states that gave individual WAIS-R tests was less than one-third the rate of states that typically utilized the Beta 1 or Beta 2 group tests only. The obvious implication is that relying solely on group tests causes the prevalence of mental retardation to be greatly overstated. On the other hand, the bias may not be three times greater. The wide variance in the estimated percentage of prisoners with mental retardation among states would indicate that other factors are involved (e.g., Do states that utilize the WAIS-R test all prisoners that have a high probability of having mental retardation? Are states that give individual WAIS-R tests more likely to place offenders with mental retardation in alternative facilities?). It should be recalled that the earlier-mentioned Brown and Courtless (1971) study estimated that the percentage of false positives was only about one-third, rather than the two-thirds that might be inferred from the Denkowski and Denkowski (1985) data.

Single-State Studies Several reports have been published analyzing the prevalence of mental retardation within the penal institutions of single states (see Table 4).

Table 2. Total inmate population, inmate population with mental retardation (MR), MR prevalence rate, IQ cutoff score, and adaptive behavior assessment process of state prison systems that routinely diagnose mental retardation with the WAIS-R

State	Total inmate population	Number inmates with MR	Prevalence rate (%)	Cutoff score	Adaptive behavior scale used
Alabama	9,112	89	1.0	69	AAMD[a]
Arizona	5,064	50	1.0	60	Vineland[b]
Connecticut	5,000	50	1.0	70	Informal[c]
Florida	27,500	322	1.2	70	None
Kentucky	1,440	58	4.0	69	Informal
Maine	1,391	29	2.1	70	Informal
Massachusetts	5,730	45	0.8	70	Informal
Mississippi	5,445	188	3.5	69	Vineland
Nebraska	1,512	20	1.3	60	AAMD
New York	29,850	746	2.5	70	Informal
North Carolina	17,208	465	2.7	69	Informal
North Dakota	409	3	0.7	70	None
Ohio	17,795	224	1.3	69	None
Oregon	4,139	75	1.8	78	Informal
Pennsylvania	10,582	502	4.7%	70	Informal
Rhode Island	950	5	0.5	69	AAMD
South Carolina	9,520	250	2.6	70	AAMD
South Dakota	804	2	0.2	70	None
Texas	36,950	703	1.9	70	None
Wyoming	732	39	5.3	69	None
Total	191,133	3,865	2.0	NA	NA

From Denkowski, G.C., & Denkowski, K.M. (1985) The mentally retarded offender in the state prison system: Identification, prevalence, adjustment, and rehabilitation. *Criminal Justice and Behavior, 12*(1), Table 1; reprinted by permission of Sage Publications, Inc.

Note: All states except Massachusetts, North Dakota, Oregon, and South Dakota test only inmates who score in the MR range on a group screening scale.

[a] American Association on Mental Deficiency Adaptive Behavior Scale.

[b] Vineland Social Maturity Scale.

[c] Essentially clinical judgment based on available historical data and observation by the evaluator.

1. *Florida* (Spruill & May, 1988). In 1978, about 4% of the population of Florida state prisons were identified as having mental retardation at the time of intake on the basis of the Revised Beta IQ score. To test the reliability of this estimate, a representative sample of 68 subjects who were identified as having mental retardation was drawn and tested on the WAIS-R. The results were startling. Only 18 of the original 68 who tested as having mental retardation had a WAIS-R IQ score below 70. This constituted about 1% of the prison

Table 3. Total inmate population, inmate population with mental retardation (MR), MR prevalence rate, and cutoff score of state prison systems that routinely diagnose mental retardation with a group intelligence test

State	Total inmate population	Number inmates with MR inmates	Prevalence Rate (%)	Cutoff score	Aptitude test used
Arkansas	3,781	276	7.3[a]	60	Beta[b]
California	32,065	720	2.3	69	Beta
Louisiana	9,436	1,801	19.1	70	Beta II
New Mexico	1,750	88	5.0	70	Beta
Oklahoma	5,777	462	8.0	75	Beta II
Tennessee	8,218	509	6.2	69	Beta
Utah	1,367	20	1.5	Varies	Shipley[c]
Virginia	9,369	738	7.9	69	Beta II
Washington	5,914	166	2.8	Varies	Beta
West Virginia	1,456	146	10.0	70	Beta II
Total	78,688	4,926	6.2	NA	NA

From Denkowski, G.C., & Denkowski, K.M. (1985) The mentally retarded offender in the state prison system: Identification, prevalence, adjustment, and rehabilitation. *Criminal Justice and Behavior, 12*(1), Table 1; reprinted by permission of Sage Publications, Inc.

[a] Another 8.0, or 296, were reported to have scored between 60 and 69. A more meaningful accounting of Arkansas's number and prevalence would be to include those inmates, yielding 572 (number of MR inmates) and 15.1% (prevalence rate). Using those adjustments, the total prevalence rate reported in this table would be 6.7%.

[b] Revised Beta I and revised Beta II (Buros, 1976, 1980).

[c] Shipley Intelligence Test (Buros, 1980).

population. Subsequently, 54 of the original sample of 68 subjects who were still in prison were again given the Revised Beta test by the prison psychologist. On the second test, only 15 of the subjects retested had Revised Beta IQ scores below 70. The authors concluded that these dramatically lower rates on retest were primarily due to inherent biases resulting from administering IQ tests to inmates at time of admission.

2. *Georgia* (Irion, 1988). During 1986 and 1987, a sample of 318 inmates was drawn from all prisoners entering Georgia prisons. One out of three prisoners was selected who scored below an IQ of 85 on the Culture Free Intelligence Test (CFIQ)—a total of 253 inmates plus 65 prisoners who could not be tested at admission because of physical or emotional handicaps or other problems. Eighty-five of the 253 inmates tested on the CFIQ scored 70 IQ points or below, representing about 3.9% of the population admitted.

The WAIS-R was given to 317 inmates in the sample (1 inmate refused to be tested). Of these, 115 scored 70 IQ points or below on the WAIS-R, representing about 5.4% of the admitted population. Thirty-seven of the 65 inmates who were not tested under the CFIQ had a WAIS-R IQ below 70. If

Table 4. State studies on the prevalence of prison inmates with mental retardation (MR)

Study	Year	MR criteria (IQ cutoff)	Type test	Population	Percentage with MR
Florida (1)	Variable	70	Beta[a]	All	4.0
Florida (2)	1978	70	Beta-Revised	All	1.0
Florida (2)	1978	70	WAIS-R[b]	All	1.1
Georgia	1986–1987	71	WAIS-R	Admissions	5.4
Georgia	1986–1987	71	CFIQ[c]	Admissions	3.9
Texas (1)	1974	70	Unknown	Admissions	6.9
Texas (2)	1970–1971	70	WAIS-R	Admissions	7.0
Texas (2)	1970–1971	70	Slosson[d]	Admissions	13.2
Texas (2)	1970–1971	70	PPVT[e]	Admissions	23.4
Texas (2)	1970–1971	70	Various tests	Admissions	12.6
New York	1989	70	Beta	All	8.0

Note: Two separate studies were conducted in Florida and Texas, identified here as studies 1 and 2 for each state. Several differing estimates were made on the basis of alternative measures of intelligence in Florida, Georgia, and Texas.

Sources: Florida—Spruill and May (1988); Georgia—Irion (1988); Texas—Texas Department of Mental Health and Mental Retardation (1973:4); New York—Sundram (1989).

[a] Beta I.Q. test (Buros, 1976, 1980).

[b] WAIS-R = Wechsler Adult Intelligence Scale–Revised (Buros, 1980).

[c] CFIQ = Culture Free Intelligence Test (Buros, 1980).

[d] Slosson = Slosson Intelligence Test (Buros, 1980).

[e] PPVT = Peabody Picture Vocabulary Test (Buros, 1980).

these individuals are added to the number who scored below 70 on the CFIQ, the resultant total of 122 is slightly greater than that derived by the use of the WAIS-R only. However, the existence of physical and emotional handicaps is a major reason for not being able to complete the CFIQ, and these additional handicaps may have contributed to low IQ scores.

The great similarity of these estimates based on different IQ tests is noteworthy, since the CFIQ is group administered and given at admission, whereas the WAIS-R was individually administered and given at some later time after admission.

3. *Texas* (Texas Department of Mental Health and Mental Retardation, 1973: 4). During December 1970 and January 1971, the Texas Department of Mental Health and Mental Retardation administered IQ tests to all male admissions to Texas prisons. The total sample consisted of 500 prisoners. On the basis of the usual testing employed by Texas institutions at admission, 12.6% of the sample had IQs below 70. Various IQ tests were employed. Each person in the sample was tested using the WAIS-R, Slosson, and Peabody Picture Vocabulary tests of IQ. On the basis of the WAIS-R, 1% of the prison population had IQs between 50 and 59, 6% had IQs between 60 and 69, and 11% had IQs between 70 and 79. Thus, a more rigorous measure of intelligence reduced the estimated number of persons with IQs below 70 by about half.

On the basis of the Slosson IQ test, however, the percentage of admissions scoring below 70 rose to 13.2%. Five people who scored below 70 on the WAIS-R scored above 70 on the Slosson. Finally, 23.4% of admissions scored below 70 on the Peabody Picture Vocabulary Test. These results are indicative of the widely varying results that may be obtained from different IQ tests on the same population.

4. *New York* (Sundram, 1989). The state of New York is conducting an extensive examination of adults in correctional facilities to determine how many meet the criteria of developmental disabilities. As discussed earlier, developmental disabilities includes, but is not limited to, mental retardation.

One of two preliminary reports of this study (Sundram, personal communication, Feb. 28, 1991, citing November 1990 report) permits several important observations. Based on an examination of the records, 8% of the population in adult correctional facilities had Beta IQs below 70. A small sample of 294 individuals was drawn, of whom about one-fourth had a Beta IQ below 70, another one-fourth scored between 70 and 80, and slightly more than one-half had Beta IQs above 80. After extensive examination, only 7 persons were considered to have developmental disabilities, and the prevalence of people with developmental disabilities was estimated at between 1.8% and 2.2%. Surprisingly, only 3 of these individuals had Beta IQs below 70, indicating an overall prevalence rate of mental retardation of 1% or less among the New York prison population. This undoubtedly understates the actual prevalence of mental retardation, because of the application of more stringent criteria for developmental disabilities than for mental retardation. These results are consistent with those of other studies that have disclosed the tendency of IQ scores based on group tests at admission to significantly understate the intellectual capacities of many prison inmates. In this case, the results are confirmed by use of an adaptive behavior test instead of by a more rigorous IQ test, as was the case in other studies.

5. *Other studies*. Several other studies of prison inmates with mental retardation should be briefly mentioned:

- The Atlanta Association for Retarded Citizens estimated that 27% of inmates in Georgia had mental retardation (in Santamour & West, 1982).
- Lampert (1987) reported that 6.9% of a sample of 520 inmates admitted to the Texas Department of Corrections during December 1974 had IQs below 70, a percentage that is probably low, since IQ scores were not available on about 10% of the sample.
- Prescott and Van Houten (1982) reported that about 21% of juveniles in correctional facilities in New Jersey had IQs below 80, and that about 6% had IQs below 70.
- Santamour and West (1982) reported that the South Carolina Department of Corrections estimated that 8% of inmates in South Carolina had mental retardation.
- Steelman (1987) estimated that approximately 3% of the New York prison population had mental retardation.
- Wood (1976) estimated that 10% of prisoners in Missouri had mental retardation.

Data from Juvenile Correctional Facilities

Morgan (1979) conducted a national survey of juvenile correctional facilities. Replies were received from 204 facilities in 45 states, the District of Columbia, and 3 territories. Almost 27,000 juveniles resided in these facilities.

The survey questionnaire requested that the respondents base their estimates of the number of persons with mental retardation on definitions contained in PL 94-142, the Education for All Handicapped Children Act, which requires states to identify children with handicaps who are institutionalized. The way in which diagnoses were made was not explicitly stated, but it can be safely assumed that a variety of individualized and group IQ tests were employed.

The survey reported that 7.69% of the persons in juvenile correctional facilities were classified as "educable mentally retarded" and that 1.84% were "trainable mentally retarded," a combined rate of 9.53%.

A project in Texas tested all juveniles under age 21 admitted to the Texas Youth Council program between September 1, 1969, and August 31, 1970 (Texas Department of Mental Health and Mental Retardation, 1973: 5). Out of a sample size of 1,495 males and 175 females, 12.9% of males and 16.6% of females were found to have mental retardation.

Carefully noting the specific criteria used, Murphy (1986) summarized studies reporting the prevalence of mental retardation among juvenile delinquents and students in the general population. The estimates of mental retardation ranged from 1.3% to 2.3% among all school-age children. Estimates among juvenile delinquents ranged from 6% among 11- to 21-year-old children in New Jersey correctional facilities to 30% of 40 juvenile delinquents from a detention home in New Mexico.

As in the case of adult prisoners, the widely varying reported rates of mental retardation result from many causes: the criteria of mental retardation applied, the types of test used, the rigor with which tests are conducted, the characteristics of the sampled population, and so on. Even the term *juvenile* has different meanings across states. Offenders less than 18 years old are classified as "juvenile" in most states, whereas those 18 to 22 years old are classified as "youthful" offenders. Other states, including California, classify offenders up to 24 years old as "juvenile" (Murphy, 1986).

Data from Residential Facilities for Persons with Mental Retardation

One placement option for people with mental retardation who commit offenses is a residential facility for persons with mental retardation. As we expected, there is little readily available information on the frequency of such placements. Farzaneh-kia, Hill, and Lakin (1983) drew a nationally representative sample of 91 newly admitted persons from state institutions for persons with mental retardation and 81 newly admitted persons from licensed community residential facilities for persons with mental retardation during 1978 and 1979. They reported that 3.3% of the admissions to state institutions and 1.2% of the admissions to community residential facilities had engaged in criminal activities, although there was no indication as to whether these activities precipitated the placement decision. These authors suspect that Farzaneh-kia and colleagues' estimate substantially understates the number who could be regarded as offenders. For example, Farzaneh-kia et al. (1983) also reported that 18.5% of new admissions to community residences and 35.2% of new admissions to state institutions engaged in actions that injured other people, and that 7.4% and 9.9%, respectively, broke or damaged property. It is not surprising that 11.1% and 31.9%, respectively, of new admissions to these facilities were admitted because of problems in managing behavior.

Lakin, Hill, Hauber, and Bruininks (1982) randomly selected a sample of 220 new admissions and 210 readmissions from 75 public residential facilities (institutions). Forty-two percent of new admissions and 38.5% of readmissions engaged in actions that injured others, and 19.2% of new admissions and 23.4% of readmissions engaged in actions that damaged property. However, only 3.1% of new admissions and 7.4% of readmissions were reported as having engaged in criminal activities within the previous year. Given these data, it is not surprising that unmanageable or intolerable behavior was given as the reason for approximately 21% of all admissions and readmissions.

A more recent survey of persons living in residential facilities for persons with mental retardation (Lakin, Hill, Chen, & Stevens, 1989) reported that 28.5% of residents sometimes attempted to hurt others physically, and that about 15.7% of the residents sometimes stole from other persons. Based on these data an estimated 46,000 institutionalized persons with mental retardation in the United States sometimes attempt to hurt others, and an estimated 25,000 sometimes steal. These rates roughly apply, regardless of whether the facility is large (16 or more residents) or small (under 16 residents) and regardless of whether it is certified as an intermediate care facility for persons with mental retardation (ICF/MR).

These data provide evidence that a significant number of people in residential facilities for persons with mental retardation have committed acts that may be unlawful.

Data from Residential Facilities
for Persons with Mental Illness

Some offenders with mental retardation are placed in institutions for persons with mental illness. This is particularly likely to be true for people with mental retardation who are in the mild or borderline range of mental retardation and/or who are dually diagnosed.

In 1980, 7.3% of all admissions to state and county mental hospitals were *involuntary criminal admissions*. About 0.1% of admissions to private psychiatric hospitals and about 0.7% of admissions to separate inpatient psychiatric services of nonfederal general hospitals were for this reason (Rosenstein, Steadman, MacAskill, & Manderscheid, 1986). In all, about 32,000 offenders and alleged offenders were admitted to residential facilities for people with mental illness in 1980 (Steadman, Rosenstein, MacAskill, & Manderscheid, 1988). Almost half (45%) were admitted because they were incompetent to stand trial, and 25% were transferred from prisons. Unfortunately, these statistics do not disclose how many of these admissions involved mental retardation.

Data from Community Programs

Little published information exists on the number of people with mental retardation who are in community programs because they have committed unlawful acts. Wood (1976) estimated that 6% to 7% of persons on probation and parole in Missouri had mental retardation.

Summary and Observations

Two important observations can be drawn from the preceding data. First, a significant number of persons with mental retardation are: 1) incarcerated in prisons and jails because of criminal activities or 2) placed in restrictive residential care facilities either because of criminal activities or because it is believed there is a possibility they will engage in unlawful or unacceptable activities if not restrained. Although prevention usually refers to changing behavior so that individuals will not commit crimes, another way to prevent crimes is to place high-risk persons in restrictive residential facilities where their activities can be carefully monitored and controlled or hidden from the community. The data point to considerable use of detention for this purpose.

Second, existing estimates of the percentage of people in prisons who have mental retardation vary widely within the approximate range of 2% to 10%. Most estimates are based on data from individual prison or state surveys. The reasons for this wide variance are well known, and many have already been addressed here. Although reconciliation of the various estimates is extremely difficult we believe that many published estimates of the prevalence of mental retardation among persons in state and federal prisons overstate true prevalence.

One possible reason for the variance is that some prisons undoubtedly have a greater percentage of persons with mental retardation than others. This may occur because some states make more of an attempt to identify offenders with mental retardation and divert them to other programs. Or the finding may result from the types of prisons surveyed. Prisons that primarily contain perpetrators of white collar crime are unlikely to contain many people with mental retardation.

But the way that mental retardation is diagnosed is undoubtedly the most important explanation for the variance in reported statistics. This is not because the criteria for defining mental retardation vary significantly. In almost all cases the diagnosis of mental retardation is based on a measure of IQ. Adaptive behavior is rarely considered, except for the study being conducted in New York State (Sundram, 1989, 1990).

The procedure for measuring IQ appears to make a difference in results. Average IQ scores tend to be lower: 1) among persons tested shortly after being admitted to prison, 2) among persons who undergo a group test in contrast to individualized testing, and 3) among persons tested on an IQ test other than the WAIS-R. All three factors are interrelated, making it impossible to determine the unconfounded influence of each. For example, if IQ testing occurs shortly after entering prison, a group test is usually administered— most frequently the Beta IQ test. The studies that utilized the WAIS-R consistently reported the lowest rates of mental retardation (Denkowski & Denkowski, 1985; Irion, 1988; Texas Department of Mental Health and Mental

Retardation, 1973). The WAIS-R is always individually administered by a trained individual. The one exception was the Florida study (Spruill & May, 1988), which used both the WAIS-R and the Beta IQ tests on a *retest* of inmates and reported similar rates of mental retardation.

Based on the authors' belief that the most reliable estimates are those based on the individualized WAIS-R test, these writers believe that the best estimate of the prevalence of mental retardation in prisons is 2%. This estimate is derived largely from information provided by Denkowski and Denkowski (1985) on states that employed individualized WAIS-R tests for prison inmates, and is reasonably consistent with data from New York (Sundram, 1989) reporting, on the basis of adaptive behavior, that almost two-thirds of prison inmates who had an IQ score below 70 did not have developmental disabilities, giving rise to a prevalence rate of about 3%. The estimate of 2% prevalence is about one-fifth of the widely publicized rate reported by Brown and Courtless (1971).

The growth rate in the U.S. prison population has been remarkable during the past 8 years. The number of inmates in state and federal prisons (as of December 31st of each year) grew from 330,000 in 1980 to 627,000 in 1988. Assuming that the prevalence of people with mental retardation among the U.S. prison population is 2%, the number of persons with mental retardation in state and federal prisons in 1988 would be approximately 12,500. If one assumes a 3% prevalence rate, the number would be about 18,800. The growth of the prison population shows no signs of abatement. Recently released statistics from the Bureau of Justice Statistics, U.S. Department of Justice (in *Buffalo News*, September 11, 1989) indicated that a record 6-month increase occurred in the U.S. prison population. If the number of prisoners with mental retardation increased proportionately, then our estimates must be revised upward to indicate that there are between 14,000 and 20,000 persons with mental retardation in state and federal prisons.

It appears that over one-third of admissions to institutions for persons with mental retardation (ICFs/MR) results from behavior that may violate existing laws. Moreover, it can be reasonably assumed that residents who are admitted because of violence or the tendency to steal are less likely to be released than other persons, so that the resident population of these facilities probably contains an even greater percentage of people who are admitted for these reasons.

As of June 30, 1987, there were slightly over 250,000 persons in residential facilities for persons with mental retardation. The authors do not wish to give the impression that this is a population with a propensity to criminal behavior. The great majority—over three-fourths—have moderate, severe, or profound mental retardation, and the very concept of willful criminal behavior is probably inappropriate in these cases. Further, it is probable that many of the problems that existed at admission were minor to begin with and responded to treatment soon after admission.

Based on existing information on the proportion of admissions to residential facilities for people with mental retardation and other developmental disabilities (ICFs/MR) resulting from law violations during the previous year, one can conservatively estimate that at least 5% of the population of these facilities, or about 12,500 persons, has previously been involved in serious criminal activities.

Combining the estimate of the number of offenders with mental retardation in federal and state prisons with the estimate of the number in institutions for persons with mental retardation, yields an estimated total of 26,500 to 32,500 offenders with mental retardation who are currently imprisoned or institutionalized because of violations of the law. This estimate is probably low. It does not include offenders with mental retardation who are in institutions for persons with mental illness, in local jails, or in diversion or other local treatment programs. Nor does it include noninstitutionalized people with mental retardation who committed criminal acts but were not apprehended, or if apprehended, were not charged, or if charged, were not confined, or if confined, have been released.

Relative to the estimated population of more than 6 million persons with mental retardation in the United States, the number of offenders among them is a small fraction of the total. Nevertheless, the existing number presents a significant challenge to both the criminal justice system and the existing service system for people with mental retardation.

TYPES OF CRIMES

It is surprisingly difficult to generalize about the types of crimes committed by offenders with mental retardation. Based on a small sample, Brown and Courtless (1971) reported that first-degree murder was the most frequent offense committed by incarcerated persons with mental retardation—about 21% of the sample. Other criminal homicides accounted for about another 18%. About 18% of the sample were incarcerated for breaking and entering (burglary).

These high rates of serious crimes are consistent with more recent reports from New York (Sundram, 1989), where 38% of inmates in state prisons with Beta IQs below 70 have committed or attempted to commit murder, manslaughter, assault, robbery, kidnapping, and sexual offenses. In addition, Santamour (1989, p. 6) reported: "Research on prison populations suggests that retarded offenders as a whole are more frequently convicted of crimes of burglary and breaking and entering (38 percent); 13 percent committed homicide and 5 percent committed rape and sexual crimes."

Although frequently cited, these data on the frequency of serious crimes committed by persons with mental retardation are misleading. To begin with, as noted by Brown and Courtless (1971), the prisons from which these data are derived house individuals who commit the more serious types of crimes. Offenders with mental retardation who are in local jails or are placed into community diversion programs would generally be expected to have committed much less serious crimes. In addition, one would expect the percentage of severe crimes reported among all prison inmates to be greater than among new admissions, since inmates who commit the more severe crimes will usually receive longer prison sentences and over time will represent an increasing proportion of inmates who remain in prison.

Consistent with this observation is a report by the Illinois Mentally Retarded and Mentally Ill Offender Task Force (1988), which concluded: "Despite common misconceptions that this population commits the majority of violent felony crimes, in reality the overwhelming majority of offenses committed by persons who are mentally retarded and/or mentally ill are misdemeanors, less serious felonies, and public disturbances." Similarly, White and Wood (1985, 1986), reporting on a special community program for offenders with mental retardation, noted that over half of the program participants had committed only misdemeanors.

PERSONAL CHARACTERISTICS

Sex

As one would anticipate (based on the general profile of state prison inmates [Bureau of Justice Statistics, 1988]), offenders with mental retardation are usually male. As examples, 88% of the prison admissions in Georgia with IQs of 70 and below were male (Irion, 1988), and 99% of prison inmates in New York with mental retardation were male. Similarly, White and Wood (1986) reported that 83% of the clients of a community program for offenders with mental retardation were male. Rockowitz (1986a) reported that 92% of the clients in a community program in Monroe County, New York, were male.

Race

A large percentage of offenders with mental retardation are nonwhite. For example, Irion (1988) reported that black inmates in Georgia prisons comprised 81% of admissions with a WAIS-R IQ of 70 and below; in contrast, 58% of total admissions during the time period tested were black. Even more astonishing, Sundram (1989) reported that only 5% of the inmates in New York prisons with IQ scores below 70 were white. Black and Hispanic inmates comprised 51% and 44%, respectively, of the population of offenders with IQs below 70. In the general prison population, 50% of inmates were black and 31% Hispanic. Other studies have reported similar findings. In Missouri, Wood (1976) reported that 75% of persons with mental retardation in prison were black, compared to 45% of all inmates and 10% of the general state population. The Texas Department of Mental Health and Mental Retardation (1973) reported that 68.6% of inmates with mental retardation were black, compared to 34.6% of inmates who tested in the normal IQ range. Brown and Courtless (1971) reported that approximately 42% of a sample of 964 adult offenders with IQs below 55 were white and that 58% were non-white. Interestingly, the community program in Lancaster County, Pa. reported that 91% of its clients were Caucasian (White & Wood, 1985, 1986), and the community program in Monroe County, N.Y. reported that 52% were Caucasian (Rockowitz, 1986a).

The high percentage of incarcerated offenders with mental retardation who are nonwhite results from the combination of above-average rates of incarceration for nonwhite Americans and an above-average percentage who test in the range for mental retardation. This is a topic in urgent need of further investigation. Are nonwhite persons more likely to go to jail than white persons who commit the same type of crimes? How reliable are IQ tests when administered to individuals who are poor and nonwhite?

Age

Irion (1988) reported that inmates who scored 70 or lower had an average age of 35, compared to an age of 30 for all admissions. Similarly, the Texas study indicated that the average age of inmates with mental retardation was 26.75, compared to 24.65 for inmates without mental retardation (Texas Department of Mental Health and Mental Retardation, 1973). In New York State, inmates with Beta IQ scores below 70 were about one-half a year older than other inmates. These age differences are too slight to attach much significance to them. However, they may reflect the tendency for offenders with mental retardation in prison to have greater difficulty in obtaining parole compared to other residents.

Level of Disability

It is generally reported that the vast majority of inmates in prison with mental retardation are in the mild and high-moderate ranges of mental retardation. Steelman (1987), for example, noted that most inmates with mental retardation have IQs in the 60–70 range, and that very few have IQs in the 50s. Irion (1988) reported that 97% of the sample of Georgia inmates with WAIS-R scores below 70 had IQs in the 60–69 range. Brown and Courtless (1971) reported that 83% of the inmates identified as having mental retardation had IQ scores above 55.

PUNISHMENT, REHABILITATION, AND OUTCOMES

Lampert (1987) observed that inmates with mental retardation tend to be passed over for parole as poor risks. One can assume that this provides at least a partial explanation for Lampert's observation that, in a sample of Texas prisoners, inmates with mental retardation served 41% of their sentences, in contrast to inmates with normal intelligence who served 36% of their sentences. However, this conclusion is confounded by the fact that the average sentence of Texas inmates with mental retardation was only about half the average sentence of other inmates.

Prisoners with mental retardation who are released from prison also exhibit difficult adjustment problems. The New York State Office of Mental Retardation and Developmental Disabilities (1987) observed that persons with mental retardation are more likely to violate their probation and to be reincarcerated as a result.

These adjustment difficulties while in prison and after release can only be ameliorated by adequate and appropriate training, rehabilitation, and work programs. In the case of inmates with mental retardation, these programs must be shaped to meet their special needs. The National Institute of Justice, U.S. Department of Justice, recognizes the special needs of many inmates and identifies inmates with *severe* mental retardation as one type of inmate requiring special management and protection (in McGee, Warner, & Harlow, 1985).

The widespread need for improved and expanded special programs for many inmates was made apparent in the National Institute of Justice survey of 63 prisons throughout the United States (McGee et al., 1985). Almost 30% of the 22,000 inmates within these prisons were identified as needing special protection, special controls, or special professional treatment. Unfortunately, the survey did not provide a breakdown of the 22,000 inmates needing special management by their defining characteristics (e.g., mental retardation). Thirty-four of these prisons provided additional information. Of these, 50% rated the need for providing protection for inmates with severe mental retardation as "most serious," 32% as "average," and 18% as "least serious." Surprisingly, and obviously incorrectly, none of the 34 prisons reported inmates with severe mental retardation as requiring special professional care. Only psychotics, former mental patients, mentally unstable persons, and medically disabled prisoners were identified as requiring special professional attention.

Coffey, Procopiow, and Miller (1989, p. 23) summarized what is known from state studies about the percentage of persons with mental retardation or learning disabilities in adult and juvenile correctional facilities who require special educational services. The estimates of the population in need of special educational services varied widely, from 16.6% of the adult prisoner population in Wisconsin with mental retardation to 1.4% of the prisoners in adult and juvenile facilities in New Jersey with learning disabilities. Unfortunately, no statistics were given on the percentage of these inmates who were actually receiving special educational services.[2]

Rehabilitation programs for offenders with mental retardation, whether in or out of prison, appear to be the exception rather than the rule. Nevertheless, several outstanding programs exist. Coffey et al. (1989) described five different model programs serving offenders with mental retardation. The capacities of these programs include 800 beds in the Texas Windham consolidated prison school district, 96 beds in the Georgia State Prison, 32 beds (plus 18 day-care slots) in South Carolina's Stevenson Correctional Institution, 169 beds in an intermediate care facility in the Camarillo State Hospital, California, and community-based services for 60 individuals in Lincoln, Neb., where an individual justice plan is used as an alternative to incarceration (see also Hall, chap. 9, this volume). The Nebraska program seeks to provide a community-based alternative to incarceration based on considerations of accountability, competency, due process, least restrictive alternative, normalization, and the possibility of exercising control by some means other than incarceration.

Several other community-based programs have been described. The frequently cited Lancaster, Pennsylvania, Offenders Program for persons with mental retardation (White & Wood, 1985, 1986; see also Wood & White, chap. 8, this volume) served a total of 75 clients with an average WAIS IQ of 66 in 5¼ years (September 1980–December 1985). The Erie, Pennsylvania, Court of Common Pleas Special Probation Services served a total of 42 clients with an average WAIS of 66 between January 1986 and June 1988 (P.J. Jericho, letter of July 14, 1988, to Steven M. Eidelman, deputy secretary of mental retardation, Commonwealth of Pennsylvania). The Monroe County, New York, Developmentally Disabled Offender Project (Rockowitz, 1986a), in the course of 2½ years from October 1983 to April 1986, served 222 clients with an average IQ of 73.9 (range was 40–104). Another program also located in Monroe County, the Monroe Secure Unit for Intensive Treatment (Wolfe, 1988), begun in May 1978, has the capacity to serve 24 seriously assaultive/aggressive adults with mild mental retardation.

The data on the number of persons in these special programs for offenders with mental retardation are too limited to attempt to estimate the number in rehabilitation programs in prison or in the community. The small number of programs, however, leads us to conclude that many, probably most, adults with mental retardation in prisons fail to receive special services appropriate to their habilitation needs. This conclusion is supported by a survey recently

---

[2]Citing Keilitz and Dunivant (1987) that habilitation programming can improve institutional adjustment and the chances of postrelease success, the National Institute of Corrections *Guide for Correction Administrators* (Coffey, Procopiow, & Miller, 1989) provides excellent legal guidelines and model program standards for special educational programming in adult and juvenile correctional facilities.

conducted by the New York State Commission on Quality of Care for the Mentally Disabled (Sundram, 1989). Among the 42,288 adult inmates of New York State and local correctional facilities, only 45% of those with Beta IQs less than 70 and only 31% with Beta IQs between 70 and 79 were enrolled in prison academic programs, despite considerable evidence of poor academic attainment and skills. Only 4% had been placed on specialty units designed for offenders with developmental disabilities.

The availability of special services for incarcerated children and youth with handicaps may be considerably better than for adults. Under the federal Education of the Handicapped Act of 1986 (20 U.S.C. 1402 [1], [6], and 1423 [a]; 34 C.F.R. 300.2 [b] [4]), children housed in state or local institutions, including correctional facilities, are entitled to a free and appropriate public education through age 21.

Rutherford, Nelson, and Wolford (1985) surveyed 85 state departments of corrections (juvenile, adult, and combined juvenile/adult) and 50 state departments of special education and found that, as of August 1984, according to state corrections administrators, 30% of 399,636 adults in state correctional facilities were receiving educational services, in contrast to 92% of the 33,190 juvenile offenders in state correctional facilities. Rutherford and colleagues properly cautioned against accepting these findings in the face of an unacceptably wide variation in the percentage (0%–90%) of inmates with handicaps reported by administrators of state correctional facilities. They hypothesized that federal pressure to comply with PL 94-142 (the Education for All Handicapped Children Act) and the potential for litigation may have induced some states to understate the total number of offenders with handicaps and/or to overstate the number of offenders with handicaps in special education programs.

Eggleston (1984) surveyed correctional educators and administrators from every state, as well as Puerto Rico and the Virgin Islands, to obtain information about the implementation of special education programs pursuant to PL 94-142. Of 94 questionnaires mailed, 48 were returned from 37 states. Sixty percent of the reporting states acknowledged having a special education program for wards and inmates of correctional institutions, the majority locating it in youth programs or programs serving both youth and adults. Eighty percent of these programs serving youth or both youth and adults received PL 94-142 funds. Special education was offered to *all* eligible students in only 50% of the reporting states.

Eggleston's (1984) survey highlights the substantial problems that correctional education programs have in complying with the provisions of PL 94-142, most notably with the requirements of parental or surrogate parental involvement, proper screening and identification procedures, the provision of related services, and meeting procedural time-lines as well as program implementation requirements. As noted by Smith, Ramirez and Rutherford (1983), these problems result from a lack of resources, including an inadequate supply of teachers with certification in all areas of exceptionality. Eggleston (1984, p. 17) concluded:

> Although there are a number of exemplary programs across the country, the level of service provision for the special needs learner in correctional facilities continues to be below the levels mandated by P.L. 94-142. A wide service delivery disparity exists between the states as well as differences in orientation toward the handicapped. Confusion appears to continue among various state programs. The application of P.L. 94-142 mandates does not seem to be clearly understood. . . . Often expressed, however, was a concern that some of the requirements cannot work in corrections. . . . Guidelines should be developed to facilitate coordinated service delivery for special education. . . . Currently, implementation is based on idiosyncratic responses to the federal mandates, and these are biased by personality and/or structural variables.

As pointed out by Warboys and Shauffer (1986), state education and correctional administrators who are out of compliance with the provisions of PL 94-142 run a high risk of litigation. Of particular concern are failure to adequately identify persons in need, failure to adequately evaluate them, failure to develop and implement an individualized education program designed to meet individual needs, failure to provide related services, failure to provide procedural safeguards, and failure to implement protection against improper discipline, suspension, and exclusion.

Obviously, much more information is needed to obtain a valid picture of programs for offenders with mental retardation and their effectiveness. For example, what is the recidivism rate for offenders with mental retardation released from prisons or institutions? How is this rate affected by the availability of special vocational education or industrial programs in prisons?

TOWARD AN EPIDEMIOLOGY OF RELEVANT ATTRIBUTES

The epidemiological literature relating to offenders with mental retardation has improved considerably since the earliest days when such authorities as Goddard claimed in 1914 that between 25% and 100% of the inmates of adult and juvenile correctional facilities were "feebleminded," or even much later when Brown and Courtless contended in 1971 that better administration of intelligence tests would result in higher percentages of offenders being identified as having mental retardation. At least we now understand (Spruill & May, 1988) that *better* administration of intelligence tests is likely to identify a *lower* percentage of people with mental retardation.

There is little point in trying to nail down to the nearest decimal point the percentage of people with mental retardation and other mental disabilities who reside in the nation's prisons. We know that the number is significant and that many inmates with mental retardation are not receiving appropriate services.

Moreover, given record-breaking increases in prison populations ("Prison Rolls," 1989), and overcrowding, it is unlikely that identification and treatment of the offender with a mental disability is a priority matter for most of those who are caught up in the day-to-day administration of justice.

Ultimately, much more is needed than the simple identification of the existence of mental retardation among persons accused or convicted of crimes. Mental retardation is a broad term encompassing a large number of people with widely varying capacities, skills, and attitudes, widely varying capabilities for independent action, and many other attributes, even for people at the same level of mental retardation. In consequence, the level of culpability will also vary widely and influence the appropriateness of various punishments and the most effective methods of rehabilitation.

The behavior of people with mental retardation, including whatever tendency may exist toward violating the law, is a result of the interaction of all of these attributes and not just the intellectual limitation. In fact, whether people with mental retardation become offenders is dependent primarily on these other attributes. In general, whether or not these persons become productively employed, are able to interact meaningfully with other people, and perform many other actions that most of us take for granted will depend less on their intellectual limitation than on the stability of the families in which they were raised, their role models, the values they were taught, the effectiveness of schools, the availability of appropriate jobs, and many other factors. To determine the appropriateness of various punishments, to develop effective rehabilitation programs, or even to prevent the offense in the first place, it is necessary to identify the extent to which these attributes exist among offenders with mental retardation. Without such information, our understanding of this population will necessarily remain superficial.

Accordingly, we need to develop methods not only for improving the count of the number of offenders with mental retardation but also for beginning the more difficult task of estimating the number with other attributes that largely determine their behavior. In addition to such obvious factors as level of education, type of vocational training, and the type of family in which offenders with mental retardation were raised, there is a need to measure the extent to which offenders:

Deny their disability as a possible cause of their criminal behavior
Lack the motivation to follow through on actions given the stimulus of others
Lack the ability to respond accurately to questions asked of them
Are impulsive in their actions
Lack the ability to distinguish between right and wrong behaviors
Have significant language deficits
Have significant memory deficits

In addition, there is a need to measure the extent to which these attributes influenced the offender's behavior in specific situations. As examples, what percentage of offenders with mental retardation:

Were influenced by a need to be accepted by their peers?
Could understand the consequences to other individuals (victims, family) of the crime?
Could understand the punishment that may follow from the crime?
Falsely confessed because of susceptibility to authority and desire for approval?
Could provide accurate information to assist their counsel in preparing a defense?
Could follow the line of testimony at a trial?
Were capable of performing activities required by a program of punishment/rehabilitation?

The preceding short list of personal attributes and behaviors is admittedly not comprehensive, but represents the minimum that should be considered in reaching an understanding of the issues that arise when people with mental retardation commit a criminal offense. These personal attributes and behaviors were derived from a number of sources, the most important being Ellis and Luckasson (1985), who identified *behavioral attributes* of people with mental retardation at various stages of the criminal justice process.[3]

Personal attributes and their behavioral consequences are neither easy nor inexpensive to measure (which partly accounts for the limited information that is available). Nevertheless, methods of measurement can be developed. For example, future studies can be designed to collect information on the aforementioned personal attributes and their behavioral consequences, making use of prosecutors and the defending attorneys as primary sources of data.

RECOMMENDATIONS FOR THE FUTURE

The dearth of epidemiological data relating to people with mental retardation and other severe disabilities who enter the criminal justice system can be remedied only by making a substantial investment in the systematic collection

---

[3]Other sources included: Barry (1986); Barth et al. (1983); Braunling-McMorrow, Lloyd, and Fralish (1986); Corrigan and Hinkeldey (1987); Davidoff, Laibstain, Kessler, and Mark (1988); Ehrlich and Barry (1988); Fisher (1985); Gaspard and Boyce (1985); Imes (1983); Jacobs (1988); Kewman, Yanus, and Kusch (1988); Lam, McMahon, Priddy, and Gehred-Schultz (1988); Lewin, Grossman, Rose, and Teasdale (1979); Lezak (1978); Miller (1979); Postuma and Wild (1988); Price (1986); Prigatano et al. (1984); Rimel, Giordani, Barth, Boll, and Jane (1981); Rosen (1986); Thomsen (1984); Uzzell, Dolinskas, and Langfitt (1988); Van Zomeren and Vandenburg (1985); and Wehman et al. (1989).

of fresh data. To begin with, it will be necessary for the U.S. Departments of Justice, Education, and Health and Human Services to create some permanent interdepartmental mechanism, such as a standing committee or task group, to plan and oversee the design and execution of a variety of studies to address the issues and questions raised by our review of the current state of knowledge.

We furthermore urge that the following recommendations he implemented by federal agencies:

1. The U.S. Department of Justice should routinely obtain data identifying the number of persons with mental retardation (as well as other types of handicapping conditions) among prison inmates when conducting its 5- to 7-year periodic Survey of Inmates of State Correctional Facilities (Bureau of Justice Statistics, 1988). Standardized reporting of statistics on the inmates with mental retardation/developmental disabilities is needed to determine trends in prevalence as well as criminal history, sociodemographic characteristics, prearrest employment and income, prior history of probation, incarceration, parole, and possible enrollment in prison educational or rehabilitation programs.

2. The U.S. Department of Justice should routinely request data on persons with mental retardation (as well as other types of handicapping conditions) when collecting data for publication in *Correctional Populations in the United States* (Bureau of Justice Statistics, 1989) so that the movement (change of status) of persons with mental retardation/developmental disabilities under correctional supervision can be understood and compared to that of the rest of the juvenile and adult corrections populations in the United States.

3. All federal, state, and local correctional facilities should improve the accuracy of intelligence testing by adopting the procedures recommended by Spruill and May (1988) that would: 1) give inmates time to adapt to the prison system before testing, 2) administer a group test for screening purposes to small groups with thorough explanation of the purposes and procedures, and 3) confirm the results of group testing by administering an individual WAIS-R to all those who score below 85 on a group intelligence test.

4. The U.S. Department of Justice should support development of a better adaptive behavior scale than the American Association on Mental Retardation and Vineland Social Maturity Scales, which are not normed for use in the prison setting (Denkowski & Denkowski, 1985). In addition, up-to-date neuropsychological test batteries should be adapted for use in prisons.

5. The U.S. Department of Education, in conjunction with the U.S. Department of Justice, should develop improved information to provide technical assistance to state correctional education programs. Both departments should also consider joint issuance of special guidelines for implementing the Individuals with Disabilities Education Act (PL 101-476) mandate in correctional facilities.

6. The U.S. Congress should consider earmarking funds for training grants and student assistance to increase the available supply of qualified special education and support staff for youth correctional facilities.

7. Special epidemiological studies should be mounted with federal support that go beyond narrowly defined measures of the existence or nonexistence of mental retardation among offenders with mental retardation and focus on the more complicated personal attributes and their behavioral consequences, which are the underlying causes of the criminal activity and are crucial to reaching just decisions about appropriate punishment and rehabilitation. In addition, IQ and adaptive behavior measures of mental retardation should be augmented, when appropriate, with more sensitive neuropsychological test batteries coupled with physical measures of brain functioning. Although this type of investigation is more costly than continued polling of criminal justice officials who are constrained to respond on the basis of arguably inadequate records, the much greater payoff in usable knowledge would seem to justify the extra cost.

REFERENCES

American Association on Mental Deficiency. (1983). *Classification in mental retardation* (H.J. Grossman, Ed.). Washington, DC: Author.

Axelrod, D. (1986). *Head injury in New York State: A report to the governor and the legislature.* Albany: New York State Department of Health.

Barry, P. (1986). A psychological perspective of acute brain injury rehabilitation. *Cognitive Rehabilitation, 4*(4), 18–21.

Barth, J., Macciocchi, S., Giordani, B., Rimel, R., Jane, J., & Boll, T. (1983). Neuropsychological sequelae of minor head injury. *Neurosurgery, 13*(5), 529–533.

Braunling-McMorrow, D., Lloyd, K., & Fralish, K. (1986). Teaching social skills to head-injured adults. *Journal of Rehabilitation, 52*(1), 39–44.

Brooks, N. (1989). Closed head trauma: Assessing the common cognitive problems. In M.D. Lezak (Ed.), *Assessment of the behavioral consequences of head trauma* (pp. 61–85). New York: Alan R. Liss.

Brown, B.S., & Courtless, T. (1971). *The mentally retarded offender.* DHEW Pub. No. (HSM) 72-90-39. Washington, DC: U.S. Government Printing Office.

Bureau of Justice Statistics. (1988, January). *Profile of state prison inmates, 1986.* Washington, DC: U.S. Department of Justice.

Bureau of Justice Statistics. (1989, February). *Correctional populations in the United States, 1986.* Pub. No. NCJ-111611. Washington, DC: U.S. Department of Justice.

Buros, O.K. (Ed.). (1978). *The eighth mental measurements yearbook* (2 vols). Highland Park, NJ: The Gryphon Press.

Carson, D. (1989, February). Prosecuting people with mental handicaps. *Criminal Law Review,* 87–94.

Coffey, O.D., Procopiow, N., & Miller, N. (1989, January). *Programming for mentally retarded and learning disabled inmates: A guide for correctional administrators.* Washington, DC: U.S. Department of Justice, National Institute of Corrections.

Corrigan, J.D., & Hinkeldey, N.S. (1987). Comparison of intelligence and memory in patients with diffuse and focal injury. *Psychological Reports, 60*(3), 899–906.

50 / Noble and Conley

Curry, K.L., (1987, June 30). *Developmental disabilities criminal justice project.* Buffalo, NY: Buffalo State College Developmental Disabilities Criminal Justice Project.

Davidoff, D.A., Laibstain, D.F., Kessler, H.R., & Mark, V.H. (1988). Neurobehavioral sequelae of minor head injury: A consideration of post-concussive syndrome versus post-traumatic stress disorder. *Cognitive Rehabilitation, 6*(2), 8–13.

Denkowski, G.C., & Denkowski, K.M. (1985). The mentally retarded offender in the state prison system: Identification, prevalence, adjustment, and rehabilitation. *Criminal Justice and Behavior, 12*(1), 53–70.

Dikmen, S., Temkin, N., McLean, A., Wyler, A., & Machamer, J. (1987). Memory and head injury severity. *Journal of Neurology, Neurosurgery, and Psychiatry, 50*(12), 1613–1618.

Eggleston, C.R. (1984, February). *Results of a national correctional/special education survey.* New Paltz, NY: SUNY College at New Paltz, Educational Studies.

Ehrlich, J., & Barry, P. (1988). Rating communication behaviours in the head-injured adult. *Brain Injury, 3*(2), 193–198.

Ellis, J., & Luckasson, R. (1985). Mentally retarded criminal defendants. *George Washington Law Review, 53*(3–4), 414–493.

Farzaneh-kia, H.F., Hill, B.K., & Lakin, K.C. (1983). *Institutional versus community residential placement of mentally retarded people leaving home.* Minneapolis: University of Minnesota, Department of Psychoeducational Studies.

Finch, J. (1983). *Mental disabilities and criminal responsibility.* (Review.) *Law Quarterly Review, 99*(4), 324–325.

Fingarette, H., & Hasse, A.F. (1979). *Mental disabilities and criminal responsibility.* London: University of California Press.

Fisher, J. (1985). Cognitive and behavioral consequences of closed head injury. *Seminars in Neurology, 5*(3), 197–204.

Gaspard, N., & Boyce, B. (1985). Rehabilitation nursing: Care of the adolescent male with traumatic head injury. *Journal of Rehabilitation, 51*(2), 58–61.

Goddard, H.H. (1914). *Feeblemindedness: Its causes and consequences.* New York: Macmillan.

Illinois Mentally Retarded and Mentally Ill Offender Task Force. (1988, July 19). *Mentally retarded and mentally ill offender task force report.* Springfield: Author.

Imes, C. (1983). Rehabilitation of the head injury patient. *Cognitive Rehabilitation, 1*(6), 11–19.

Irion, J. (1988). *Mentally retarded inmates in Georgia's prison system.* Atlanta: Georgia Department of Corrections.

Jacobs, H.E. (1988). The Los Angeles head injury survey: Procedures and initial findings. *Archives of Physical Medicine and Rehabilitation, 69*, 425–431.

Kalsbeek, W.D., McLaurin, R.L., Harris, B.S., & Miller, J.D. (1980). The national head and spinal cord injury survey: Major findings. *Journal of Neurosurgery, 53*, S19–S31.

Keilitz, I., & Dunivant, N. (1987). The learning disabled offender. In C.M. Nelson, R. Rutherford, & B.I. Wolford (Eds.), *Special education in the criminal justice system.* Columbus: Charles E. Merrill.

Kewman, D.G., Yanus, B., & Kusch, N. (1988). Assessment of distractibility in auditory comprehension after traumatic brain injury. *Brain Injury, 2*(2), 131–137.

Kraus, J.F. (1980). Injury to the head and spinal cord: The epidemiological relevance of the medical literature published from 1960 to 1978. *Journal of Neurosurgery, 53*, S3–S9.

Lakin, K.C., Hill, B.K., Chen, T.H., & Stevens, P.H. (1989). Persons with mental retardation and related conditions in mental retardation facilities: Selected findings from the 1987 National Medical Expenditures Survey. Minneapolis: University of Minnesota, Institute on Community Integration.

Lakin, K.C., Hill, B.K., Hauber, F.A., & Bruininks, R.H. (1982). *New admissions and readmissions to a national sample of public residential facilities*. Minneapolis: University of Minnesota, Department of Psychoeducational Studies.

Lakin, K.C., Jaskulsi, T.M., Hill, B.K., Bruininks, R.H., Menke, J.M., White, C.C., & Wright, E.A. (1989). *Medicaid services for persons with mental retardation and related conditions*. Minneapolis: University of Minnesota, Institute on Community Integration.

Lam, C., McMahon, B., Priddy, D., & Gehred-Schultz, A. (1988). Deficit awareness and treatment performance among traumatic head injury adults. *Brain Injury, 2*(2), 235–242.

Lampert, R.O. (1987). The mentally retarded offender in prison. *Justice Professional, 2*(1), 60–69.

Levin, H., Grossman, R., Rose, J., & Teasdale, G. (1979). Long-term neuropsychological outcome of closed head injury. *Journal of Neurosurgery, 50*, 412–422.

Lewis, D.O., Pincus, J.H., Feldman, M., Jackson L., & Bard, B. (1986). Psychiatric, neurological, and psychoeducational characteristics of 15 death row inmates in the United States. *American Journal of Psychiatry, 143*(7), 838–845.

Lezak, M. (1978). Living with the characterologically altered brain injured patient. *Journal of Clinical Psychiatry, 39*, 592–598.

McGee, R.A., Warner, G., & Harlow, N. (1985, March). *The special management inmate*. Washington, DC: U.S. Department of Justice, National Institute of Justice.

McGuire, T.L., & Rothenberg, M.B. (1986). Behavioral and psychosocial sequelae of pediatric head injury. *Journal of Head Trauma Rehabilitation, 1*(4), 1–6.

McKinlay, W.W., Brooks, D.N., Bond, M.R., Martinage, D.P., & Marshall, M.M. (1981). The short-term outcome of severe blunt head injury as reported by the relatives of the injured person. *Journal of Neurology, Neurosurgery, and Psychiatry, 44*, 527–533.

Mentally Retarded and Mentally Ill Offender Task Force, The Administrative Office of the Illinois Courts. (1989). *Illinois initiatives to address the issues of the offender with mental retardation*. Chicago: Author.

Miller, E. (1979). The long-term consequences of head injury: A discussion of the evidence with special reference to the preparation of legal reports. *British Journal of Social and Clinical Psychology, 18*, 87–98.

Mitchell, J.V. (Ed.). (1985). *The ninth mental measurements yearbook* (2 vols.). Lincoln, NE: Buros Institute of Mental Measurement.

Monahan, J., & Steadman, H.J. (1984, September). Crime and mental disorder. *National Institute of Justice Research in Brief*. Washington, DC: U.S. Department of Justice, National Institute of Justice.

Morgan, D.J. (1979). Prevalence and types of handicapping conditions found in juvenile correctional institutions: A national survey. *Journal of Special Education, 13*(3), 283–295.

Murphy, D.M. (1986). The prevalence of handicapping conditions among juvenile delinquents. *Remedial and Special Education, 7*(3), 7–17.

National Institute of Corrections. (1985, March). *Source book on the mentally disordered prisoner*. Washington, DC: U.S. Department of Justice.

New York State Office of Mental Retardation and Developmental Disabilities. (1987). *Mentally retarded offenders: Considerations for public policy*. Albany: Author.

Noble, J.H., Laski, F., Conley, R. W., & Noble, M.A. (1990). Issues and problems in the treatment of traumatic brain injury. *Journal of Disability and Policy Studies, 1*(2), 19–45.

Papaleo, L.A. (1985). The mentally retarded and the criminal justice system. *Law Institute Journal, 59*(9), 947–951.

Perlin, M.L. (1987). The Supreme Court, the mentally disabled criminal defendant, and symbolic values: Random decisions, hidden rationales, or "doctrinal abyss?" *Arizona Law Review, 29*(1), 1–98.

Postuma, A., & Wild, U. (1988). The use of neuropsychological testing in mild traumatic head injuries. *Cognitive Rehabilitation, 6*(2), 22–24.

Prescott, M., & Van Houten, E. (1982). The retarded juvenile offender in New Jersey: A report on research in correctional facilities and mental retardation facilities. In M.B. Santamour & P.S. Watson (Eds.), *The retarded offender* (pp. 166–175). New York: Praeger.

Price, P. (1986). Facilitating client-directed vocational planning in head-injured adults. *Vocational Evaluation and Work Adjustment Bulletin, 19*(3), 117–119.

Prigatano, G., Fordyce, D., Zenner, H., Roueche, J., Pepping, M., & Wood, B. (1984). Neurological rehabilitation after closed head injury in young adults. *Journal of Neurology, Neurosurgery, and Psychiatry, 47*, 505–513.

Prison rolls post record increase. (1989). *The Buffalo News*, September 11, p. A1.

Rimel, R., Giordani, B., Barth, J., Boll, T., & Jane, J. (1981). Disabilities caused by minor head injury. *Neurosurgery, 9*(3), 221–228.

Rockowitz, R.J. (1986a, March). *Developmentally Disabled Offender Project—final report*. Grant #90-DD0046. Rochester, NY: Developmentally Disabled Offender Project.

Rockowitz, R.J. (1986b). Developmentally disabled offenders: Issues in developing and maintaining services. *Prison Journal, 66*(1), 19–23.

Rosen, M. (1986). Denial and the head trauma client: A developmental formulation and treatment plan. *Cognitive Rehabilitation, 4*(6), 20–22.

Rosenstein, M.J., Steadman, H.J., MacAskill, R.L., & Manderscheid, R.W. (1986, October). *Mental Health Statistical Note no. 178*. Bethesda, MD: U.S. Department of Health and Human Services, National Institute of Mental Health.

Rutherford, R.B., Nelson, C.M., & Wolford, B.I. (1985). Special education in the most restrictive environment: Correctional special education. *Journal of Special Education, 19*(1), 59–71.

Sachs, P.R. (1984). Grief and the traumatically head-injured adult. *Rehabilitation Nursing, 9*(1), 23–27.

Santamour, M.B. (1989). *The mentally retarded offender and corrections*. Washington, DC: American Correctional Association.

Santamour, M.B., & West, B. (1982). The mentally retarded offender: Presentation of the facts and a discussion of the issues. In M.B. Santamour & P.S. Watson (Eds.), *The retarded offender* (pp. 7–36). New York: Praeger.

Smith, B.J., Ramirez, B.A., & Rutherford, R.B. (1983). Special education in youth correctional facilities. *Journal of Correctional Education, 34*(4), 108–112.

Spruill, J., & May, J. (1988). The mentally retarded offender: Prevalence rates based on individual versus group intelligence tests. *Criminal Justice and Behavior, 15*(4), 484–491.

Steadman, H.J., Rosenstein, M.J., MacAskill, R.L., & Manderscheid, R.W. (1988).

A profile of mentally disordered offenders admitted to inpatient psychiatric services in the United States. *Law and Human Behavior, 12*(1), 91–99.

Steelman, D. (1987). *The mentally impaired in New York's prisons: Problems and solutions.* New York: Correctional Association of New York.

Sundram, C. (1989, August). *Developmentally disabled offenders in New York State prisons: An interim report.* Albany: New York State Commission on Quality of Care for the Mentally Disabled.

Sundram, C. (1990, November). *Inmates with developmental disabilities in New York correctional facilities.* Albany: New York State Commission on Quality of Care for the Mentally Disabled.

Teasdale, G., & Jennett, W.B. (1974). Assessment of coma and impaired consciousness. *Lancet, 2,* 81.

Texas Department of Mental Health and Mental Retardation. (1973). *Project CAMIO* [Correctional Administration and the Mentally Incompetent Offender] (Vols. 4, 5). *The Mentally Retarded in an Adult Correctional Institution.* Austin: Author.

Thomsen, I. (1984). Late outcome of very severe blunt trauma: A 10–15 year second follow-up. *Journal of Neurology, Neurosurgery, and Psychiatry, 47,* 260–268.

Uzzell, B.P., Dolinskas, C.A., & Langfitt, T.W. (1988). Visual field defects in relation to head injury severity. *Archives of Neurology, 45*(4), 420–424.

Van Zomeren, A., & Vandenburg, W. (1985). Residual complaints of patients two years after severe head injury. *Journal of Neurology, Neurosurgery, and Psychiatry, 48,* 21–28.

Warboys, L.M., & Shauffer, C.B. (1986). Legal issues in providing special educational services to handicapped inmates. *Remedial and Special Education, 7*(3), 34–40.

Wehman, P., Kreutzer, J., Wood, W., Stonington, H., Diambia, J., & Morton, M.V. (1989). Helping traumatically brain-injured patients return to work with supported employment: Three case studies. *Archives of Physical Medicine and Rehabilitation, 70,* 109–113.

White, D., & Wood, H. (1985). *Mentally Retarded Offenders Program—program summary.* Lancaster, PA: Mentally Retarded Offenders Program.

White, D., & Wood, H. (1986). The Lancaster County, Pennsylvania, Mentally Retarded Offenders Program. *Prison Journal, 65*(1), 77–84.

Wolfe, G.R. (1987). Clinical neuropsychology and assessment of brain impairment: An overview. *Cognitive Rehabilitation,* (September/October), 20–25.

Wolfe, R. (1988, February 10). *Program overview and admission criteria for Munroe Secure Unit for Intensive Treatment.* Albany: New York State Office of Mental Retardation and Developmental Disabilities.

Wood, H.V. (1976). The retarded person in the criminal justice system. In *Proceedings of the One Hundred and Sixth Annual Congress of the American Correctional Association* (pp. 142–146). College Park, MD: American Correctional Association.

Chapter 3

The Evaluation of Defendants with Mental Retardation in the Criminal Justice System

John J. McGee and Frank J. Menolascino

> . . . But a caged bird stands on the grave of dreams
> his shadow shouts on a nightmare scream
> his wings are clipped and his feet are tied
> so he opens his throat to sing.
>
> The caged bird sings with a fearful trill
> of things unknown but longed for still
> and his tune is heard on the distant hill
> for the caged bird sings of freedom.
> —Maya Angelou, *Caged Bird* (1983)

THE EVALUATION OF a person involved with the criminal justice system must be considered within its psychosocial context, regardless of whether the person has or does not have mental retardation. However, the presence of mental retardation creates substantive differences in causation, culpability, and intervention strategies. As is true of most suspects or criminals in general, a disproportionate percentage of defendants with mental retardation are poor, living at the margin, and powerless. They primarily comprise racial minorities, slum dwellers, and school dropouts, as well as chronically unemployed, homeless, illiterate, and politically disenfranchised individuals. They have

55

little pride in the past or hope for the future. Although significant progress has been made in integrating persons with mental retardation into "normal" family and community life during the past three decades, defendants with mental retardation remain on the fringe of advocacy and community service systems. They are the last to be served, the least likely to be served, and the most subjected to abuse, neglect, and social abandonment. Nearly 30 years ago, the President's Panel on Mental Retardation (1962) pointed out that the possibility of ensuring justice for this population and thus of fulfilling the function of the law, depends on two conditions: correct appreciation of the relevant circumstances and a suitable range of possible dispositions. The panel stated that justice is indeed blind if it does not inquire into the significance of mental retardation as a relevant circumstance, and impotent if it has no dispositional variants suited to the conditions it finds. Haggerty, Kane, and Udall (1976) summarized this challenge to the legal system: "Simply put (in almost all cases) the mentally retarded suspect who has been charged with a crime cannot tell his side of the story, and cannot help his lawyer defend him. If no one realizes he is retarded, this greatly hinders his chances for a fair trial" (p. 59). Thus, the evaluation process needs to consider a galaxy of issues that include not only intellectual level and adaptive behavior but also the sociocultural reality of the individual: poverty, family support, unemployment, range of friendships, on-again/off-again social programs, illiteracy, and racism.

John Steinbeck (1937) described the impact of mental retardation in his fictional account of Lennie, a young man with mild mental retardation, who depended on his friend, George, for his well-being, occasional work, and moral guidance. Lennie found safety and security in his relationship with George, and feelings of affection in his love of mice—caressing them, talking to them, regarding them as companions in an otherwise absurd and meaningless world. Without his mouse or his only friend, Lennie was buffeted by the winds of prejudice and loneliness. When Lennie was invited to touch a young woman's hair, he was innocently happy:

> The woman said, "Feel right aroun' there an' see how soft it is." Lennie's big fingers fell to stroking her hair.

But the woman, afraid that her hair would be messed up, told him enough was enough. She told him to stop. Lennie became nervous. She ordered him to let go, but he continued.

> Lennie was in a panic. His face was contorted. She screamed then, and Lennie's other hand closed over her mouth and nose. "Please don't," he begged. "Oh! Please don't do that. George'll be mad . . . George gonna say I done a bad thing. He ain't gonna let me tend no rabbits. . . ." And she continued to struggle, and her eyes were wild with terror. . . . And her body flopped like a fish. And then she was still, for Lennie had broken her neck. He looked down at her. . . . "I don't want ta hurt you," he said, "but George'll be mad if you yell. . . ." (pp. 99–100)

At the moment of apprehension, Lennie was not able to defend himself, nor was he able fully to understand the nature of the act, its existential meaning, or its consequences. He said, "I wasn't doin nothing bad with it, George. Jus' strokin' it" (p. 137).

An evaluation of anybody's life condition must include both personal and social history so that as comprehensive an assessment as possible might be rendered at the earliest opportunity. In Lennie's case, this would have involved analysis of the impact of: lack of schooling, rigidity of thought, simplicity of emotional life, dependence on his only friend for moral guidance, inability to discriminate between the death of a mouse and that of a human being, paucity of language, poor impulse control, lack of sex education and socialization skills, lack of stability in work and personal relationships, meager understanding of reality, and the narrowness and superficiality of his perception of the deed. An evaluation should not serve as a mere walk through the haunted graveyard of someone's being, while his or her remains are left to rot away; its intent should be to serve as a pathway for fair and appropriate intervention that will enable justice to be done.

EVALUATION OF MENTAL RETARDATION

Understanding Mental Retardation

The evaluation of mental retardation in a person accused of a criminal act, or in an individual already incarcerated, requires an understanding of the disability's systemic nature and impact on the person's total well-being, self-identity, and social valorization. It involves much more than determining an intelligence quotient. It is based on the understanding that persons with mental retardation are complete human beings whose cognitive development, although proceeding in the same order as other individuals, is slower and stops at an earlier stage (Inhelder, 1968). This results in a different developmental pattern, not only in timing but also in degree. It causes qualitative differences in modes of thinking, as opposed to quantitative differences alone, since each stage of human development forms a structured whole. The diagnosis of mental retardation is a descriptive process intended to explain or deepen our understanding regarding this expression of the human condition. The person with mental retardation has many gifts, attributes, and talents that many others do not have, such as a simplicity of life, spontaneous expression of likes and dislikes, loyalty, and tolerance. The evaluation process needs to lay the groundwork for an excusal from mitigation of certain penalties due to the nature of mental retardation, while at the same time recognizing the full humanness and citizenship of the individual.

Empirical evidence demonstrates, however, that psychological evaluations are often not performed on persons with mental retardation prior to trial or sentencing, with the result that their condition is not discovered until incarceration, when it is too late to receive a fair trial (Santamour & West, 1977). Defendants with mental retardation are often simply viewed as slow and uncooperative, especially in cases involving minority defendants. This too-little, too-late approach results in their being left to fend for themselves—frightened, unable to argue their case, and excluded from full due process.

An evaluation needs to take into account mental retardation's global impact on every dimension of the person's being and identity: rigidity in thinking, perseveration, expressive and receptive language, socialization skills, interactions with others, attention, memory, impulse control, immature or incomplete concept of causation, understanding of the social situation and morality, self-concept, suggestibility, biased responding, motivation, problem-solving ability, intelligence quotients, and adaptive behaviors. Identification of these dimensions can be quite difficult, since most individuals in this population appear to be "high functioning"; yet, the appearance of functionality has little to do with understanding the surrounding world and possessing the range of skills and emotions necessary to interact fully within it. Any screening and evaluation process needs to consider this existential reality and interpret the total psycho-socio-cultural essence of the person.

Cognition and Decision Making

Individuals with mental retardation have rigid thought processes that lead to a difficulty or failure to learn from mistakes, resulting in counterproductive behaviors. Possible reasons for this rigidity and persistence center on a limited repertoire of social and communication skills. Physical acts are often the quickest way to express anger, frustration, or stress in the face of diminished cognitive ability and impairments in attention and skill acquisition. Decision making depends upon goal selection, cognitive control, input selection, and short-term memory (Carr, 1979). Performance and awareness of performance require attentional capacity. Mental retardation affects information processing, reactions to events, and planning of alternative actions and interactions (Campione & Brown, 1977). These factors can lead to impairments related to impulse control and difficulty in dealing with stress and frustration. Seemingly insignificant stressors can lead to temper tantrums involving self-injury, aggression, or withdrawal. Sperber and McCauley (1984) found that people with mental retardation encode information in an extremely limited manner, and Ellis and Meador (1985) reported that this population loses information at a much faster rate. Spitz and Borys (1984) pointed out that when tasks require planning, individuals with mental retardation are likely to fail. Their world is very concrete and rooted in the here and now. They have a limited ability to generalize learned skills, so that what they learn in one reality has little bearing on another. An individual with mental retardation might behave quite well in a structured setting but, when placed in a different environment, will often not be able to use what he or she has previously learned. This is especially true in stressful or frustrating moments. Persons with even mild mental retardation generally lack the ability to resolve life's complex problems and will require special support across their life spans to a degree distinct from their nonretarded peers. Yet, persons with mental retardation often live "independently" and lack social support networks. They generally have little trouble with routine functioning skills. However, emotional well-being is often erroneously assumed if "functional" skills are present, and the paradoxical result is that many individuals are pushed into "independent" living, or are simply abandoned to street-life, without any recognition of their basic need for ongoing support and guidance.

Cognition and Social Understanding

An evaluation also needs to encompass the person's understanding of social situations. Social purposiveness in interpersonal relationships involves the ability to understand the roles of others, in addition to possessing repertoires of understanding and interpersonal resources that allow use of varied social tactics in different situations (Weinstein, 1973). These factors mediate social behavior and interactions so that the individual can make inferences about others' covert psychological experiences (Shatz, 1977). The person with mental retardation has extreme difficulty understanding the perspectives, feelings, or thoughts of others. Although persons with mental retardation are whole, sentient beings, often in ways much more honest and authentic than their nonretarded peers, the depth and constancy of such feelings are limited, fixed on one dimension of an object or event to the exclusion of others, and based on rigid, egocentric reasoning (Inhelder, 1966). Simeonsson (1978) found that adults with mental retardation have limited insight into the motivations and characteristics of others. Their perception of others is bound in concrete, simplified perceptions. If one were to ask an adult with mental retardation, "Do you like him?" the response would likely be sincere, but innocent (e.g., a simple yes or no). However, the same question posed to a nonmentally retarded individual would yield a more sophisticated description, with an increase in the use of qualifiers such as *because, when,* or *but.* Such sophistication does not generally exist in a person with mental retardation. Along with impairments related to insight, the disability also presents major communication barriers. Communication is not only a function of vocabulary or IQ but of taking into account the listener's needs. Social cognition involves knowledge of oneself, of other persons, and the relation between self and others (Brooks-Gunn & Lewis, 1978). Although an individual might appear "street-wise" or have the ability to "pass," it is likely that, outside familiar situations, he or she would lack the social understanding necessary for acceptable human interaction.

Cognition and Moral Reasoning

The evaluation process needs to consider the central question of the nature and degree of the individual's moral reasoning and social responsibility—an ability that develops in stages across time and involves quantitative as well as qualitative transformations. Just as distinct patterns can be seen in childhood development, distinctions can similarly be made between individuals with and without mental retardation. The ability to make moral judgments flows from the ability to transcend the self and to see the impact of behaviors and interactions as they relate to "the other." Full moral judgment involves a substantive transition from preoperational and concrete, consequence-based judgments to those that take into account both intent and consequence, combined with the depth of understanding involved in each (Piaget, 1965; Piaget & Inhelder, 1947). A morally autonomous individual is independent of adult authority, is able to make moral judgments, and is able to formulate moral principles based on mutual respect rather than conformity to moral authority (Kohlberg, 1969, 1981). However, persons with mental retardation have extreme difficulty in these complex operations. Research has shown that their moral judgment is comparable to that of mentally age-matched persons without mental retardation and follows a delayed developmental sequence (Foye & Simeonsson, 1979; Gargiulo & Sulick, 1978; Perry & Krebs, 1980). They function through simple rules much like preadolescents—unable to think abstractly and logically in systems of axioms (i.e., "if, then") and do not go beyond the concrete world of reasoning governed by outside authority (Grossman, 1983). It is a morality of constraint rather than cooperation, and a world of "is" rather than "ought" (Kohlberg, 1981). If there is no external authority available, the individual is often left floundering in a hostile and confusing world. Thus, an evaluation of the individual's moral reasoning is the critical dimension required to analyze how and to what extent the person perceives reality, as well as the nature and degree of external support and guidance that the individual has received and needs to receive.

Mental Retardation and Socio-Economic-Cultural Factors

Mental retardation represents more than intellectual handicap and deficits in adaptive behavior. It does not exist in isolation. Indeed, it is influenced by factors such as racism, poverty, unemployment, underemployment, lack of social support, illiteracy, segregation, social isolation, deinstitutionalization, repeated institutionalization, and poor educational-vocational orientation. Most studies have indicated that a disproportionate percentage of incarcerated offenders with mental retardation are Afro-Americans or Latinos (Brown & Courtless, 1971; Haskins & Friel, 1973) who come from economically impoverished families and are poor and unemployed themselves (Denkowski, Denkowski, & Mabli, 1984; Hochstedler, 1987). Haskins and Friel (1973) evaluated 1,666 juvenile inmates in Texas and found that 12.9% of the males and 16.6% of the females had mental retardation. Most were from minority groups, had not graduated from primary school, and were from economically impoverished families. Haskins and Friel also evaluated 500 male inmates in Texas prisons and found that inmates with mental retardation tended to be older, were members of minority groups, and were less likely to be granted probation. These sociocultural factors and their impact need to be taken into account in the evaluation process.

Mental Retardation and Allied Mental Illness

An additional question that needs to be examined is the coexistence of mental illness—including the entire range of psychiatric disorders (Menolascino, 1983)—with mental retardation (Balthazar & Stevens, 1975; Eaton & Menolascino, 1982; Lewis & MacLean, 1982). The presence of mental illness multiplies the impact of mental retardation on a person's behaviors, social perception, and moral reasoning. Among incarcerated offenders with mental retardation, Steiner (1984) found that 30% had a dual diagnosis, and White and Wood (1988) found that 47% had a dual diagnosis. These offenders were described as immature, impulsive, and passive-dependent (i.e., easily led by others and subjected to the pressure and influence of peers). Thus, it is critical to consider the possibility of any of a host of allied psychiatric disorders, such as schizophrenia, bipolar affective disorders, and personality disorders, based on thorough clinical histories, in-depth interviews with the person and significant others, observations of and interactions with the person, as well as specific tests of personality and affective states.

Mental Retardation and Criminal Activity

The evaluation of mental retardation also needs to consider the type of crime involved from the perspective of the individual's history, level of mental retardation and allied disorders, and the degree of community support mobilized around the person. Many persons with mental retardation have little exposure to normal peer relationships, socialization experiences, and human sexuality. Shapiro (1986) found that 33% of these individuals were convicted of sexual offenses, most often sexual assault on young girls and indecent exposure. He also found that 83% had been previously involved in stealing at some point in their lives. White and Wood (1988) reported that most offenses were related to theft and burglary. Steiner (1984) found crimes against property, 63%; crimes against persons, 23%; and sexual offenses, 15%. Denkowski et al. (1983) observed that adolescents most often engaged in physical and verbal aggression, property destruction, stealing, and running away. The evaluation needs to indicate the range of sociocultural factors that might have led to these particular acts and the impact of mental retardation on them, as well as reach a judgment relative to the probability of future recurrence if given adequate and appropriate supports.

Extent of the Problem

The evaluation process is burdened by old problems that die hard. Fernald's (1922) characterization of the situation almost 70 years ago often holds true today:

Mental hospitals claim such an offender is not mentally ill. The traditional institutions for the retarded complain that they do not have appropriate facilities for the offender . . . . correctional institutions would like to remove such persons from their populations on the grounds that programs available in the correctional setting are totally inadequate and in many cases inappropriate. . . . (p. 19)

Current prevalence data show a relatively high percentage of persons with mental retardation in the nation's prison system, although the data are tainted by unreliable measurement methods and racial prejudice. Brown and Courtless (1971) reported a prevalence rate of 9.5%, and other studies have yielded rates ranging from 3.9% (Levy, 1954) to 10.0% (Haskins & Friel, 1973), with marked geographic variations found (e.g., 2.6% in the mountain states compared to a 24.3% rate in the east south central region, strongly indicating bias from one area of the nation to the next). Shilit (1979) investigated reasons for the overrepresentation of persons with mental retardation in the criminal justice system and found that law enforcement officials have little understanding or training in mental retardation and are confused and uncertain about how to deal with this population. Since most communities have no systematic approach for dealing with individuals with these needs, the suspects enter the criminal justice system without external support and advocacy.

Beyond these issues, police officers are not trained to detect mental retardation, nor do they have readily available options even if it is apparent. The courts are ill-prepared to deal with the issue. Prisons make little provision for their rehabilitation. Within state and local mental retardation systems, offenders with mental retardation are often the last, and the least likely, to be served. Few communities offer options for their well-being. Deinstitutionalization, without community alternatives, has left many persons to fend for themselves. Maloney (1983) descried the marginalized situation in which persons with mental retardation find themselves: "a mildly retarded defendant from a poor family, with little education, is punished much more harshly than an honor student from a good family. The honor student is seen as a potential asset to society, the other defendant as more likely to be a lifelong disability" (p. 10). Those who need the most help are left out in the cold—nowhere to live with any degree of stability, few social supports, unemployed or underemployed, segregated in psychiatric ghettoes, and extremely vulnerable to exploitation and criminal engagement.

IDENTIFICATION, EVALUATION, AND SCREENING

Identification

The identification of individuals with mental retardation in the earliest stages of the criminal justice system, though desirable, is highly unlikely in many communities across the nation. It does not depend on screening and testing instruments so much as on community involvement, commitment to integrate, and professional and advocate vigilance. Unfortunately, even in communities where comprehensive service systems exist, this population tends to be shunted aside and virtually abandoned. Menninger's (1969) description of how it must feel to be arrested is representative of accused individuals with mental retardation: "a confused, unlettered, frightened, friendless man in handcuffs, standing in a police station" (p. 33). Indeed, an individual with mental retardation is further enmeshed in a world defined by the very nature of the disability, and most often lacking any outside support. Unless there is an advocacy program in the jail house designed to protect the rights of the accused person at the earliest moments, the individual will be left to flounder. Lack of early identification also means that it is unlikely that the criteria for personal recognizance or bail can be met, since the individual is probably unemployed and friendless. Empirical evidence has indicated that mental retardation is not likely to be identified until the time of arraignment or after incarceration. McAfee and Gural (1988) found that 52.3% of those accused were identified as having mental retardation at arraignment or pretrial; 27.3% were so identified at the time of arrest; 9.1% at trial; and 9.1% during imprisonment. Those identifying them were: lawyers, 56.8%; arresting officers, 29.5%; judges, 18.2%; corrections officers, 9.1%; and corrections psychologists, 4.5%. Moreover, many persons with mental retardation are never identified, because they are perceived as quiet, cooperative, and "normal" in appearance. No state has established a formal identification procedure for persons with mental retardation accused of crimes, and current practices in prisons are haphazard at best.

Some locales report partial systems for early identification. White and Wood (1988) cited a countywide program that utilizes outside case advocates to consult with police prior to charges being filed. Behar (1988) described a statewide program for the protection of the rights and habilitation of children and adolescents with mental retardation considered to be at risk or actually involved in the juvenile offender service system. The first step involved the identification of these people by agencies based on at-risk criteria. Without early identification and subsequent confirmation through evaluation, the person with mental retardation can be denied due process and is likely to confess or plead guilty, without full comprehension of the process (Moschella, 1982). Brown and Courtless (1971) found that: 7.7% of defendants with mental retardation were not represented by an attorney, 59% pleaded guilty, 40% of those pleading guilty waived rights to a jury trial, 66% made confessions or incriminating statements, 78% received no pretrial psychological evaluation, in 92% of the cases competency to stand trial was not raised as an issue, and no appeals were made in 88% of the cases. Garcia and Steele (1988) concluded that testing and referral are often controlled by personnel who are untrained in the identification of mental retardation. Since the person is unlikely to be aware of his or her right to refuse legal counsel or to refuse to answer incriminating questioning, it behooves society to initiate extraordinary precautions and safeguards, even though Parry (1987), in commenting upon the United States Supreme Court's decision in *Colorado v. Connelly,* observed that the Court turned back the clock of constitutional law by divorcing the issue of voluntariness of a confession from that of the confessor's mental capacity. Bazeleton, Boggs, Hilleboe, and Tudor (1963) noted that this population is particularly vulnerable to threats and coercion, as well as friendliness, and that it is unlikely that individuals with mental retardation can see the implications.or consequences of their statements in the same way as other persons.

Screening

A fundamental issue centers on how to screen for mental retardation at the earliest possible moment as a prelude to a comprehensive evaluation so that justice can be served. Screening depends on trained, experienced, and sensitive professionals working in conjunction with police officers and other law enforcement personnel. Krause (1973), elaborating on issues of appropriate and timely screening and testing, concluded that, without knowledge of the presence of mental retardation, an adequate defense may never be prepared, since the individuals are generally more susceptible to coercion.

However, since the reliability and validity of tests to screen for mental retardation are highly questionable, they should only be administered individually by competent professionals, and should be regarded as an early warning system signaling the possible need of a thorough evaluation. Doss, Head, Blackburn, and Robertson (1986) described the use of the Kent Series of Emergency Scales (E-G-Y) and the Quick Test, and reported positive correlations with the more thorough Wechsler Adult Intelligence Scale–Revised (discussed in the next sections under "Evaluation"). However, the E-G-Y, designed for children and adolescents (ages 5–14), serves only as a simple and informal mental test and does not sufficiently discriminate levels of mental functioning, nor can it be used in place of longer tests (Mensh, 1953). The even briefer Quick Test is a picture vocabulary test of intelligence that provides an index of overall cognitive functioning in the form of IQ, mental age, and percentiles (Ammons & Ammons, 1962; 1979). However, like the E-G-Y, it is not a valid or reliable measure of intelligence and, at best, serves as a screening tool where precise estimates of particular abilities are not needed (Swartz, 1984). Among the more acceptable screening tests is the Peabody Picture Vocabulary Test–R (PPVT–R), which measures the receptive vocabulary ability of children and adults. It is the most commonly used measure of language for persons with mental retardation and allows for scores as low as 40 (Pickkett & Flynn, 1983). Although many correctional institutions utilize group screening tests to measure mental ability, often without any follow-up confirmation through individualized evaluations (Denkowski & Denkowski, 1985), currently accepted practice strongly recommends against such procedures, since they are notoriously unreliable (Grossman, 1983).

The basic technology exists for large-scale screening for the presence of mental retardation. White and Wood (1988) described a successful case advocacy system in which professionals outside the criminal justice system work directly with police prior to filing charges against suspects, and with the court, once filed. Communities that have fragmented service delivery systems will not be able to identify or screen mentally retarded offenders. A critical dynamic rests in the political consciousness and mobilization of parent advocacy associations that struggle for justice and decency for all. It is only within such a culture that specific screening tools can assume a useful role. The most effective and fair approach for early identification and screening is for mental retardation and mental health professionals, as well as advocates, to become involved in the early stages of the criminal justice system at the local level, rather than turning away from the problem or only intervening once the person has been incarcerated.

Evaluation

Ellis and Luckasson (1985) urged that evaluation of mental retardation be performed by mental retardation professionals, and pointed out that its diagnosis can be made with less ambiguity than courts typically encounter with issues related to mental illness. Integrating the range of issues affecting a person with mental retardation is a complex process involving questions of competence and mitigating circumstances, such as the level of mental retardation; the extent and impact of adaptive and maladaptive behaviors; the past and present mental state of the individual; the ability of the person to understand and express himself or herself; and the sociocultural factors surrounding the individual's history. Luckasson (1988) cited the following competence areas that need to be analyzed: waiving the *Miranda* right to remain silent, confessing to a crime, standing trial, plea bargaining, pleading guilty, and testifying. These issues require a through evaluation, including personal interviews, interactions, and an understanding of the individual's clinical history.

The most widely accepted test for the evaluation of intelligence in adults is the Wechsler Adult Intelligence Scale–Revised (WAIS–R). It contains 11 subtests divided into two domains and yields a verbal and performance IQ as well as a full-scale IQ. It takes approximately 75 minutes to administer. It is regarded as highly valid and reliable for the general population; however, little standardization has been completed relative to people with mental retardation, especially those with more severe mental retardation (Spruill, 1984). It was designed to assess IQs above 50, which makes it impossible to delineate any meaningful intelligence quotient for persons with less than moderate mental retardation. Questions have also been raised regarding its reliability among persons with mild mental retardation. Some evidence suggests that the WAIS–R overestimates ability at the mild to "borderline" levels of intelligence by an average of 13 points when compared to the prerevision Wechsler Intelligence Scale for Children (Zimmerman, Covin, Woo-Sam, Lotz, & Bley, 1984; Zimmerman & Woo-Sam, 1972). However, others hold that the discrepancy is negligible (Flynn, 1985; Spitz, 1986). Goldman (1987) reported that the overall effect of the WAIS–R is that it expands the "borderline" category by "demoting" persons previously considered "normal" and inflates the mildly retarded category by "promoting" persons previously considered moderately retarded. The WAIS–R should be administered and interpreted with special sophistication for persons with less than mild mental retardation. The Stanford-Binet Form L-M is another traditional test designed to measure intelligence (Thorndike, 1973). Some evidence suggests that this test emphasizes verbal abilities too much at the upper levels. It is standardized on a small number of adults; however, it serves as a valuable tool for measuring the intelligence of persons with severe mental retardation (Lindemann & Matarazzo, 1984). A common alternative to the WAIS-R and Binet is the Bender Gestalt test (Brown & McGuire, 1976), which is easier to administer and relatively independent of language, but centers on the evidencing of neurological impairment. It is regarded as a useful tool in conjunction with a more comprehensive psychological test battery (Sattler, 1982).

The most broadly accepted definition of mental retardation includes the consideration of adaptive proficiencies in addition to a measure of intelligence (Grossman, 1983). Although a number of adaptive behavior measurement tools exist (Walls & Werner, 1977), the two most formalized and standardized measures of adaptive behavior are the Vineland Adaptive Behavior Scales (Sparrow, Balla, & Cicchetti, 1984) and the American Association on Mental Deficiency (AAMD) Adaptive Behavior Scales (Nihira, Foster, Shellhaas, & Leland, 1974). Louttit (1947) described the original Vineland Scales as a means of evaluating social competency by providing a systematic description of actual behavior observed daily in a variety of situations. The current Vineland assesses personal and social adaptability from birth to age 18 as well as that of lower-functioning adults. It involves a scoreable, structured interview procedure and is to be conducted by trained personnel. It examines several domains: communication, daily living, socialization, and motor skills. It yields a composite score for adaptive behavior and another for maladaptive behavior with good reliability and validity (Holden, 1984). The AAMD scales are quite similar and result in a profile comprising 10 scores for different aspects of adaptation and 14 scores for aspects of maladaptation such as aggression, violent and destructive behavior, withdrawal, and hyperactivity.

Denkowski and Denkowski (1985) found that 36 state prison systems routinely assessed incoming inmates for mental retardation. However, such practices are based on a too little, too late approach. Twenty states used individual WAIS–R testing to establish the disability. Of these, 16 performed group tests to screen for that condition and then confirmed scores below preestablished cutofis with the administration of the WAIS-R. Fourteen states incorporated adaptive behavior tests such as the AAMD Adaptive Behavior Scales or the Vineland Adaptive Behavior Scales. Massachusetts, North Dakota, Oregon, and South Dakota did not screen, but used the WAIS–R when staff suspected the possibility of mental retardation. Thirty states relied on group IQ testing in the diagnostic process, using the Revised Beta I or II, a prototype of nonlanguage group tests developed by the United States Army during World War I for screening foreign speaking and illiterate recruits (Anastasi, 1988). Arizona and Rhode Island screened all inmates with the Culture Fair Test—an instrument designed to provide a culturally unbiased measure of intelligence. However, occasionally its results are no better than traditional tests (Anastasi, 1988). Most states set their cutoff scores at 69 or 70, with the exception of Nebraska and Arizona (60) and Oregon (78). Most states reported group testing, ranging from 5 to 50 inmates at one time. These tests were often administered by bachelor's level psychologists (12 states). In 11 other states these tests were administered by teachers, counselors, social workers, and classification analysts. In the nation's two largest prison systems, California and Texas, and one of its smallest, Utah, group IQ tests were conducted by clerks. States reporting the use of the WAIS–R indicated that it was administered by psychologists with master's degrees. States that rely exclusively on group testing to diagnose mental retardation had notably higher prevalence rates. Whereas the prevalence rates in states using the WAIS–R was extrapolated at 2.0%, the 10 states using group tests were considerably higher. However, only Louisiana approached the prevalence rate found by Brown and Courtless (1971). The average prevalence rate for these 10 systems was found to be 6.2%. Spruill and May (1988), using individual tests, agreed with this lower prevalence rate.

Due to the possible coexistence of mental illness with mental retardation, the evaluation process also might involve the use of personality-projective tests and inventories, as well as attitude tests designed or adapted for use among persons with mental retardation. Although incorporating the range of issues involved in mental retardation, the issue of mental illness presents an exceptional challenge since most traditional tests require communication skills. Traditional personality tests, such as the Minnesota Multiphasic Personality Inventory (MMPI), require an understanding of verbal items and a modicum of educational skills, and their use among persons with mental retardation is extremely limited (Blanchard, 1981). A number of authors have suggested the use of projective techniques, such as the Rorschach inkblot test, for differentiating capacity and efficiency in cognitive functioning, as well as for suggesting the presence of an active psychosis (Hurley & Sovner, 1982). Rating scales, such as the Psychopathological Instrument for Mentally Retarded Adults (Matson, Kazdin, & Senatore, 1984), are recommended as a means for overcoming communication barriers. The Beck Depression Inventory has been used successfully among adolescents and adults with mental retardation to measure affective state (Beck, Carlson, Russell, & Brownfield, 1987; Kazdin, Matson, & Senatore, 1983). Because of poor verbal skills among persons with mental retardation, in-depth interviews with the individual and with his or her significant others, along with observations and interactions with the person, provide deeper insights and help overcome communication deficits.

Several conclusions can be made regarding current practices in testing for mental retardation in the criminal justice system. There is little systematic assessment at the time of apprehension or pretrial for suspected mental retardation. Some assessment occurs after imprisonment, although reliability is a serious problem, owing to group testing and unqualified test administrators, as well as the use of often invalid and unreliable tests. Only 20 out of 50 states predicate final diagnosis on individually administered WAIS–R tests. About three-fourths of those states further incorporate some type of adaptive behavior assessment. Most states have adopted the AAMR cutoff criteria (i.e., an IQ of 70 or below on standardized intelligence measures), along with significant deficits in adaptive behavior. Nevertheless, without any standardized assessment and evaluation procedures, it is unlikely that most individuals are fairly identified—some are misdiagnosed and others undiagnosed. Much concern exists regarding the cultural dimensions of any testing because of the large numbers of non–English-speaking defendants and other minorities.

The evaluation process needs to consider a host of technical testing questions as well as sociocultural issues. The choice of test instruments is the easier part of the process, provided one has competent, trained, and sensitive professionals involved. The more complex dimension relates to offering insight into mental retardation's total impact on an individual, plus an analysis of the impact of sociocultural factors and individual traits.

The Role of Families, Guardians, and Advocates

The nuclear and extended family is at the heart of society and represents the very nature of human interdependence. It is within the confluence of family and community life that children develop a sense of identity, learn right from wrong and the underlying values of the culture, and acquire the skills for interacting with the surrounding world. The impact of socioeconomic factors on family life and their relationship to the development of the personality are critical. Many defendants come from families so disorganized or dysfunctional because of the ravages of poverty that the defendants have little chance of avoiding criminal activity and are virtually "born in captivity" (Laing, 1971). They are shunted out of mainstream schools and into separate ones among other children and adolescents with similar vulnerabilities. They are also often subjected to the power of punishment such as programs and classrooms operating on token systems, time-out rooms, seclusion, restraint, and denial of privileges. They tend to be educated in a culture of violence, often drop out of school, and receive their education on the street. They live in a world that is blind to human suffering, shrugs off unemployment, tolerates illiteracy, places more value on material possessions than human existence, and marginalizes those who are black, brown, or poor. Society has yet to establish a system that is desirous or capable of embracing its weakest citizens and bringing its most marginalized members into the community. Families are unlikely to receive help from outside the family unit and are equally unlikely to have the financial resources to defend their son or daughter.

Evaluations are essentially meaningless if government does not offer support to vulnerable individuals and their families. Although these issues have been on the national agenda for nearly 30 years (President's Panel on Mental Retardation, 1962), most offenders with mental retardation and their families still await support and the fulfillment of their rights.

Role of Mental Retardation Professionals

Local community-based services need to reach out to the families of these vulnerable individuals with services such as income support, respite care, improved education, tutoring, local residential options, and vocational training and placement. Evaluations hold no real value unless they lead to intervention strategies for the individual, the family, and the community. Yet local programs often reject or expel persons with these needs due to ideological, legal, political, and financial reasons. In addition, even when supportive programs are available (Scheerenberger, 1983), law enforcement personnel and the courts generally fail to call upon mental retardation professionals. Menolascino (1974) stated that few specialized or effective programs have been forthcoming despite the continuing complaints. French (1983) cited the victimization of persons with mental retardation who are unceremoniously dumped into society with minimal or no follow-up care. Most persons with mental retardation need lifelong support and, if dumped, they are vulnerable to antisocial activities—not because they have mental retardation per se, but because they lack the necessary personal-social supports. Cunningham (1982) described them as "a constant challenge to society as they cause us to question our values, they test our compassion, and remind us that ability is not all" (p. 174).

A number of diversion models have evolved in recent years to meet the developmental, psychological, and legal needs of defendants with mental retardation. Prisons are the most undesirable settings for these individuals because other inmates take advantage of them, subjecting them to physical brutality, rape, and extortion. Correctional personnel often lack the knowledge and skills to deal with them, and habilitation programs are rare (DeSilva,

1980). Morrow (1976) has cited several diversion models: 1) central referral systems that interface with the courts, 2) community councils that assume responsibility for training police and other criminal justice system personnel, and 3) community advocacy programs that work with local legal systems.

Menolascino (1974) described a comprehensive system that takes into consideration prevention, advocacy, and treatment. Prevention involves family and personal support of potential offenders through the enhancement of the home environment, counseling, school testing programs, and specialized educational and vocational programs. It also involves public and professional education for teachers, mental health and mental retardation professionals, and law enforcement personnel. Advocacy encompasses several dimensions including personal, legal, and legislative intervention as well as public education. Finally, no diversionary system would be complete without a range of residential, educational, and vocational alternatives: early intervention; thorough evaluations and prescriptive treatment plans; individual and group counseling; follow-up supportive services to the individual and family; supported and ongoing educational, vocational, and socialization experiences; and community residential options, ranging from case-managed independent placements to structured group homes. Morton (1983) cited the partial implementation institutions; out of a national capacity of 737 placements, the typical capacity of individual programs was 50 individuals, with a high of 120–150 individuals in California. On a more promising note, 5 states reported opportunities to avoid the need for incarceration. Denkowski et al., and Mabli (1983) reported several emerging practices in 14 states. Twelve states had developed special programs on the grounds of corrections or mental retardation institutions; out of a national capacity of 737 placements, the typical capacity of individual programs was 50 individuals, with a high of 120 – 150 individuals in California. On a more promising note, 5 states reported community-based residential programs—group homes for offenders with mental retardation located in the community and providing 24-hour care and habilitative services. Unfortunately, these group homes tended to be small, housing 10 15 residents, with a range of 8 – 20 and a nationwide capacity of 185 individuals. Denkowski and colleagues also concluded that community-based habilitation appears to be geared to clients with minor and low-frequency aggressive behavior. These diversion programs were usually administered by either Departments of Mental Retardation or Mental Health–Mental Retardation. Such agencies administered about 68% of the available placements, whereas Departments of Corrections operated the balance. Denkowski et al. (1983) surveyed state alternatives to incarceration and reported: 1) entry into programs for offenders with mental retardation was typically initiated through court order; 2) institution-based options received funding through Medicaid, but community-based programs received no such federal financing; 3) staffing ratios were less than 1:7; and 4) most programs used behavior modification as the primary treatment strategy. Behar (1988) summarized the basic programmatic needs in serving this population as: a complete system of services with linkages among the various components within the system (i.e., mental health, mental retardation, criminal justice, and child/adult protection agencies); flexibility in funding and in decision making; backup services; individualized treatment; and a "zero-reject" policy. Without guaranteed service options, evaluation is an empty act.

RECOMMENDATIONS

The identification, screening, and evaluation of persons with mental retardation accused of crimes is a complex social, economic, political, and psychological problem that does not lend itself to facile conclusions or superficial recommendations. Evaluation is pointless if it does not yield deeper insights into the human condition and if it is not used as an instrument for personal and social transformation. Based on the current reality, it appears that the following research and programmatic support systems need to be initiated and established within the social fabric of the United States if justice is to be granted to persons with mental retardation:

1. Empirical research into the nature and vulnerability of some persons with mental retardation to become engaged in antisocial conduct, including identifying at-risk factors related to such behavior (not only in terms of the persons themselves but their families, friends, and communities).

2. Applied research into the interactional dimensions of mental retardation, especially as it relates to the integration of persons with retardation into family and community life, as well as ways to enhance social understanding and moral development with a focus on human reciprocity, mutuality, and interdependence rather than functional skills and independence.

3. Demonstration and study of screening procedures early in life that identify severe behavioral problems, and pedagogical procedures that teach prosocial behaviors and interactions.

4. Integration of community-based mental retardation service delivery systems into the criminal justice system at the local level to effectuate identification and screening by mental retardation professionals at the time of apprehension.

5. Descriptive research related to victimization in the legal continuum: false accusations, false or coerced confessions, scapegoating, physical abuse in prison systems, subjection to excessive restraint and punishment in the name of treatment, and the lack of community support upon release.

6. Demonstration of diversion programs that focus on community-based and violence-free alternatives, and the investigation of the long-term effect of such programs, as compared to the effects of incarceration or institution-based diversion programs.

7. Establishment of jailhouse watches and advocacy programs by community-based volunteer organizations to effectuate justice at the earliest possible moment.

8. Systematic integration of issues related to defendants with mental retardation into university-affiliated curricula to better prepare educators, special educators, psychologists, social workers, lawyers, and practitioners in other related disciplines to serve this population.

9. Development of national standards for relevant agencies regarding the rights of people with mental retardation in the justice system as well as a revision of current federal and state mental health and mental retardation standards as they relate to defendants with mental retardation.

10. Establishment of separate diversion programs for children, adolescents, and adults, to protect more vulnerable younger children and adolescents.

11. Increased monitoring of community-based and institution-based diversion programs to ensure habilitation and freedom from cruel and unusual punishment.

12. Recruitment of racial and cultural minority group members into leadership positions in special education, psychology, social work, law, and other related disciplines to create a more sensitive and responsive approach to the issue of mental retardation and justice in general, and to its existence among the disenfranchised in particular.

13. Establishment of local inpatient emergency services that are able and willing to serve people with mental retardation who are "a danger to self and others," for purposes for interdisciplinary diagnosis and short-term treatment.

14. Establishment of comprehensive community-based mental retardation services systems that are capable of serving all people with mental retardation, including defendants, in a spirit that is nonviolent, habilitative, integrative, and conducive to stability.

15. Abolition of the death penalty as a politically symbolic act congruent with basic human rights and the highest expression of a culture of life.

POSTSCRIPT

Recently, I evaluated a young man who was sentenced to die in 2 weeks' time. At first, I was disgusted with the murders that he had committed—life is sacred, no matter what the justification or mitigating circumstance. Yet, as despicable as the crimes were, a culture of life should apply equally to

*everyone—rich and poor, black and white, the powerful and the powerless.
Like Lennie in Steinbeck's* Of Mice and Men, *this young man was humble,
simple, timid, and filled with fear. I watched him enter the interview room and
thought:*

A small, bowed man enters,
Legs and hands manacled,
Feet shuffling in a deathlike march,
Hands clasped as if in prayer,
But to a deaf God.
And I wondered,
"What do I say to a man
With fourteen days to live?"
But words fell from his black, quivering lips,
"I want to go home . . . go home . . . home . . ."
And each sound was like a tear rolling down his face.
The minutes passed by.
As I left,
He stood,
Head bowed,
Eyes wet,
Feet bound,
The shadow of the death-chamber casting itself
Onto both of us.
But I,
I went home.

*He did not want to talk with me or anybody. He refused a handshake, not
out of hatred, but out of despair. He was almost totally withdrawn and had no
understanding of what was transpiring. He was able to communicate, but on
a simple, concrete level; able to acknowledge his deeds, but unable to express
any intentionality; aware that he was to die, but without any understanding of
death's meaning; conscious of the gravity of his situation, but floating in a
cloudy world of unreality. Steinbeck's George eloquently sums up the reality
of our nation's Lennies: "Guys like us got no family. . . . They ain't got
nobody in the worl' that gives a hoot in hell about 'em" (p. 114).*

*Persons with mental retardation have a right to receive justice. The
ultimate challenge of the evaluation process is not to count heads or discover
what the individual and the community are lacking, but, rather, to serve as the
first step toward positive intervention and change.—John J. McGee*

REFERENCES

Ammons, R.B., & Ammons, C.H. (1962). The Quick Test (QT): Provisional manual.
Psychological Reports, 11 (Monograph Supplement I–VII), 111–161.

Ammons, R.B., & Ammons, C.H. (1979). Use and evaluation of the Quick Test (QT):
Partial summary through October 1979: I. Publishing papers. *Psychological Reports, 45,* 943–946.

Anastasi, A. (1988). *Psychological testing* (5th ed.). New York: Macmillan.

Angelou, M. (1983). "Caged Bird." In *Shaker, why don't you sing?* New York: Random House.

Balthazar, E., & Stevens, H. (1975). *The emotionally disturbed, mentally retarded: A historical and contemporary perspective.* Englewood Cliffs, NJ: Prentice-Hall.

Bazeleton, D.L., Boggs, E.M., Hilleboe, H.E., & Tudor, W.W. (1963). *Report of the task force on law: The President's Panel on Mental Retardation.* Washington, DC: U.S. Government Printing Office.

Beck, D., Carlson, G., Russell, A., & Brownfield, F. (1987). Use of depression rating instruments in developmentally and educationally delayed adolescents. *Journal of the American Academy of Child Psychiatry, 26,* 97–100.

Behar, L. (1988). North Carolina's Willie M. Program. In J. Stark, F.J. Menolascino, M.H. Albarelli, & V.C. Gray (Eds.), *Mental retardation/mental health: Classification, diagnosis, treatment, services.* New York: Springer-Verlag.

Blanchard, J.S. (1981). Readability of the MMPI. *Perceptual and Motor Skills, 52,* 985–986.

Brooks-Gunn, Jr., & Lewis, M. (1978). Early social knowledge: The development of knowledge about others. In H. McGurk (Ed.), *Issues in childhood social development.* London: Methuen.

Brown, B.S., & Courtless, T.F. (1971). *Mentally retarded offender.* Washington, DC: National Institute of Mental Health, Center for Studies of Crime and Delinquency.

Brown, W.E., & McGuire, J.M. (1976). Current psychological assessment practices. *Professional Psychology, 7,* 475–485.

Campione, J.C., & Brown, A.L. (1977). Memory and metamemory development in educable retarded children. In R.V. Kail & J.W. Hagen (Eds.), *Perspectives on the development of memory and cognition.* Hillsdale, NJ: Lawrence Erlbaum Associates.

Carr, T.H. (1979). Consciousness in models of human information processing: Primary memory, executive control, and input regulation. In G. Underwood & R. Stevens (Eds.), *Aspects of consciousness.* London: Academic Press.

Cunningham, C. (1982). *Down's syndrome: An introduction for parents.* London: Souvenir Press.

Denkowski, G.C., & Denkowski, K.M. (1985). The mentally retarded offender in the state prison system: Identification, prevalence, adjustment, and rehabilitation. *Criminal Justice and Behavior, 12,* 55–70.

Denkowski, G.C., Denkowski, K.M., & Mabli, J. (1983). A 50-state survey on the current status of residential treatment programs for mentally retarded offenders. *Mental Retardation, 21,* 197–203.

Denkowski, G.C., Denkowski, K.M., & Mabli, J. (1984). A residential treatment model for MR adolescent offenders. *Hospital and Community Psychiatry, 35,* 279.

DeSilva, B. (1980). The retarded offender: A problem without a program. *Corrections Magazine, 6,* 24–31.

Doss, G., Head, D., Blackburn, V., & Robertson, J.M. (1986). Quick measure of mental deficiency among adult offenders. *Federal Probation 50* (4, Dec.), 57–59.

Eaton, L.F., & Menolascino, F.J. (1982). Psychiatric disorders in mentally retarded: Types, problems and challenges. *American Journal of Psychiatry, 139,* 1297–1303.

Edgerton, R. (1981). Crime, deviance, and normalization: Reconsidered. In R. Bruininks, C. Meyers, B. Sigford, & K. Lakin (Eds.), *Deinstitutionalization and community adjustment of mentally retarded people.*

Ellis, J., & Luckasson, R. (1985). Mentally retarded criminal defendants. *George Washington Law Review, 53,* 414–421.

Ellis, N.R., & Meador, I.M. (1985). Forgetting in retarded and nonretarded persons under conditions of minimal strategy use. *Intelligence, 9,* 87–96.

Fernald, W.E. (1922). Annual report of the Massachusetts State School for the Feebleminded. Springfield: Massachusetts State School for the Feebleminded.

Flynn, J.R. (1985). Wechsler intelligence tests: Do we really have a criterion of mental retardation? *American Journal of Mental Deficiency, 90,* 236–244.

Foye, H., & Simeonsson, R.J. (1979). Quantitative and qualitative analyses of moral reasoning in children, adolescents, and adults of similar mental age. *Journal of Pediatric Psychology, 4,* 197–209.

French, S. (1983). The mentally retarded and pseudoretarded offender: A clinical/legal dilemma. *Federal Probation, 47,* 55.

Garcia, S.H., & Steele, H.V. (1988). Mentally retarded offenders in the criminal justice and mental retardation service system in Florida: Philosophical placement and treatment issues. *Arkansas Law Review, 41,* 809–822.

Gargiulo, R.M., & Sulick, J.A. (1978). Moral judgment in retarded and nonretarded school age children. *Journal of Psychology, 99,* 23–26.

Goldman, J.J. (1987). Differential WAIS/WAIS–R IQ discrepancies among institutionalized mentally retarded persons. *Mental Retardation, 91*(6), 633–635.

Grossman, H.J. (Ed.). (1983). *Classification in mental retardation.* Washington, DC: American Association on Mental Deficiency.

Haggerty, D., Kane, L., & Udall, D. (1976). An essay on the legal rights of the mentally retarded. *Family Law Quarterly, 6,* 59–71.

Haskins, J., & Friel, C. (1973). The mentally retarded in an adult correctional facility. In J. Haskins & C. Friel (Eds.), *Project Camio* (Vol. 4). Huntsville, TX: Sam Houston State University.

Hochstedler, E. (1987). Twice-cursed: The mentally disordered defendant. *Criminal Justice & Behavior, 14*(3), 251–267.

Holden, R.H. (1984). Vineland Adaptive Behavior Scales. In D.J. Keyser & R.C. Sweetland (Eds.), *Test critiques.* Kansas City: Test Corporation of America.

Howard, D.V. (1983). *Cognitive psychology.* New York: Macmillan.

Hurley, A.D., & Sovner, R. (1982). Use of the Rorschach technique with mentally retarded patients. *Psychiatric Aspects of Mental Retardation Newsletter, 1,* 4–7.

Inhelder, B. (1966). Cognitive-developmental contributions in the diagnosis of some phenomena of mental deficiency. *Merrill-Palmer Quarterly, 12,* 299–319.

Inhelder, B. ([1943] 1968). *The diagnosis of reasoning in the mentally retarded.* New York: Day.

Kazdin, A., Matson, J., & Senatore, V. (1983). Assessment of depression in mentally retarded adults. *American Journal of Psychiatry, 140,* 1040–1043.

Kohlberg, L. (1969). State and sequence: The cognitive-developmental approach to socialization. In D.A. Goslin (Ed.), *Handbook of socialization theory and research.* New York: Rand McNally.

Kohlberg, L. (1981). *The philosophy of moral development* (Vol. 1). San Francisco: Harper & Row.

Krause, F. (1973). *Police, courts, and the M.R. offender.* Washington, DC: Superintendent of Documents.

Laing, R.D. (1971). *The role of politics in the family and other essays.* New York: Pantheon Books.

Levy, S. (1954). The role of mental deficiency in the causation of criminal behavior. *American Journal of Mental Deficiency, 58,* 455–464.

Lewis, M., & MacLean, W. (1982). Issues in treating emotional disorders. In J. Matson & R. Barrett (Eds.), *Psychopathology in the mentally retarded*. New York: Grune & Stratton.

Lindemann, J.E., & Matarazzo, J.D. (1984). Intellectual assessment of adults. In G. Goldstein & M. Hersen (Eds.), *Handbook of psychological assessment*. New York: Pergamon.

Louttit, C.M. (1947). The Vineland Social Maturity Scale. In I. K. Buros (Ed.), *The third mental measurements yearbook*. Highland Park, NJ: Gryphon Press.

Luckasson, R. (1988). The dually diagnosed client in the criminal justice system. In J. Stark, F.J. Menolascino, M.H. Albarelli, & V.C. Gray (Eds.), *Mental retardation/mental health: Classification, diagnosis, treatment, services*. New York: Springer-Verlag.

Maloney, J. (1983). The J. B. factor. *Saturday Review,* November/December, 10–13.

Matson, J.L., Kazdin, A.E., & Senatore, V. (1984). Psychometric properties of the Psychopathological Instruments for Mentally Retarded Adults. *Applied Research in Mental Retardation, 5,* 81–89.

McAfee, J., & Gural, M. (1988). Individuals with mental retardation and the criminal justice system: The view from the state attorneys general. *Mental Retardation, 6,* 5–12.

Menninger, K. (1969). *The crime of punishment*. New York: Viking Press.

Menolascino, F.J. (1974). The mentally retarded offender. *Mental Retardation, 12,* 7–11.

Menolascino, F. J. (1983). Overview. In F.J. Menolascino & B.M. McCann (Eds.), *Mental health and mental retardation: Bridging the gap*. Baltimore : University Park Press.

Mensh, N. (1953). Kent Series of Emergency Scales. In I.K. Buros (Ed.), *The third mental measurements yearbook*. Highland Park, NJ: Gryphon Press.

Morrow, C. (1976). An attorney's experiences in a legal center for retarded persons. In P. Browning (Ed.), *Rehabilitation of the mentally retarded offender*. Springfield, IL: Charles C Thomas.

Morton, J. (1983). *The Special Offender Project training manual*. Lincoln, NE: Crime and Community.

Moschella, S. (1982). The mentally retarded offender: Law enforcement and court proceedings. In M.B. Santamour & P.S. Watson (Eds.), *The retarded offender*. New York: Praeger.

Nihira, K., Foster, R., Shellhaas, M., & Leland, H. (1974). *AAMD Adaptive Behavior Scale*. Washington, DC: American Association on Mental Deficiency.

Parry, J. (1987). Involuntary confessions based on mental impairment. *Mental and Physical Disabilities Law Review, 18*(1), 2–6.

Perry, J.E., & Krebs, D. (1980). Role-taking, moral development, and mental retardation. *Journal of Genetic Psychology, 136,* 95–108.

Piaget, J. ([1932] 1965). *The moral judgement of the child*. New York: Free Press.

Piaget, J., & Inhelder, B. (1947). Diagnosis of mental operations and theory of intelligence. *American Journal of Mental Deficiency, 51,* 401–406.

Pickett, J.M., & Flynn, P.T. (1983). Language assessment tools for mentally retarded adults: Survey and recommendations. *Mental Retardation, 21,* 244–247.

President's Panel on Mental Retardation. (1962). *A proposed program for national action to combat mental retardation*. Washington, DC: Superintendent of Documents.

Santamour, M., & West, B. (1977). *The mentally retarded offender and corrections*. Washington, DC: U.S. Department of Justice.

Sattler, J.M. (1982). *Assessment of children's intelligence and special abilities.* Boston: Allyn & Bacon.

Scheerenberger, R. (1983). *A history of mental retardation.* Baltimore: Paul H. Brookes Publishing Co.

Shapiro, S. (1986). Delinquent and disturbed behavior within the field of mental deficiency. In A. V. S. deReuck & R. Porter (Eds.), *The mentally abnormal offender.* New York: Grune & Stratton.

Shatz, M. (1977). The relationship between cognitive processes and the development of communication skills. In B. Keasey (Ed.), *Nebraska Symposium on Motivation, 1,* 42.

Shilit, J. (1979). The mentally retarded offender and criminal justice personnel. *Exceptional Children, 46,* 16–22.

Simeonsson, R.J. (1978). Social competence. In J. Wortis (Ed.), *Mental retardation and developmental disabilities: An annual review* (Vol. 10). New York: Brunner/Mazel.

Sparrow, S.S., Balla, D.A., & Cicchetti, D.V. (1984). *Vineland Adaptive Behavior Scales.* Circle Pines, MN: American Guidance Services.

Sperber, R., & McCauley, C. (1984). Semantic processing efficiency in mentally retarded. In P.N. Brooks, R. Sperber, & C. McCauley (Eds.), *Learning and cognition in the mentally retarded.* Hillsdale, NJ: Lawrence Erlbaum Associates.

Spitz, H.H. (1986). Disparities in mentally retarded persons' IQs derived from difference intelligence tests. *American Journal of Mental Deficiency, 5,* 588–591.

Spitz, H.H., & Borys, S.V. (1984). Depth of search: How far can the retarded search through an internally represented problem space? In P.N. Brooks, R. Sperber, & C. McCauley (Eds.), *Learning and cognition in the mentally retarded.* Hillsdale, NJ: Lawrence Erlbaum Associates.

Spruill, J. (1984). Wechsler Adult Intelligence Scale–Revised. In D.J. Keyser & R.C. Sweetland (Eds.), *Test critiques.* Kansas City: Test Corporation of America.

Spruill, J., & May, J. (1988). The mentally retarded offender: Prevalence rates based on individual versus group intelligence tests. *Criminal Justice Behavior, 15*(4), 484–491.

Steinbeck, J. (1937). *Of mice and men.* New York: Viking Press.

Steiner, J. (1984). Group counseling with retarded offenders. *Social Work, 29,* 181–182.

Swartz, J.D. (1984). Quick test. In D.J. Keyser & R.C. Sweetland (Eds.), *Test critiques* (Vol. 1). Kansas City: Test Corporation of America.

Thorndike, R.L. (1973). *Stanford-Binet Intelligence Scale, Form L-M, 1972 norms tables.* Boston: Houghton Mifflin.

Walls, R.T., & Werner, T.L. (1977). Vocational behavior checklists. *Mental Retardation, 15,* 30–35.

Weinstein, E.A. (1973). The development of interpersonal competence. In D.A. Goslin (Ed.), *Handbook of socialization theory and research.* Chicago: Rand McNally College Publishing Co.

White, D.L., & Wood, H. (1988). Lancaster County MRO Program. In J.A. Stark, F.J. Menolascino, M.H. Albarelli, & V.C. Gray (Eds.), *Mental retardation/mental health: Classification, diagnosis, treatment, services.* New York: Springer-Verlag.

Zimmerman, I.L., Covin, J., Woo-Sam, J.M., Lotz, H., & Bley, N. (1984). *A longitudinal comparison of the WISC-R and WAIS-R.* Paper presented at the American Psychological Association Convention, Toronto.

Zimmerman, I.L., & Woo-Sam, J.M. (1972). *Clinical interpretation of the WAIS.* New York: Grune & Stratton.

Chapter 4

DEFENDANTS WITH MENTAL RETARDATION IN THE FORENSIC SERVICES SYSTEM

RUSSELL C. PETRELLA

M ENTAL HEALTH AND mental retardation professionals provide a broad range of services to the legal system. Increasingly, expert witnesses are being relied upon to assist the courts in resolving legal questions. Definitions of the appropriate role of the professional have been proposed ranging from that of a dispassionate evaluator to a zealous advocate. Clinicians who conduct evaluations for the courts balance their professional identity as "helping professionals" with the demands of the legal system, which, at times, requires offering opinions contrary to the best interests of the client. For example, not uncommonly, a clinical evaluation will result in findings that increase the likelihood of a defendant's being incarcerated. Few situations are more vexing to forensic clinicians than those associated with individuals with mental retardation in the criminal justice system. There is an intuitive sense that the laws, rules, and procedures of the criminal justice system are not developed with these individuals in mind, reducing the likelihood that justice will prevail.

It also seems apparent that in cases where defendants with mental retardation are involved, out of necessity and sometimes convenience, the usual rules are not strictly adhered to, and all of the participants act upon their own version of what is in the client's best interest. This tendency was revealed to me in a startling fashion several years ago after I conducted a competency-to-stand-trial evaluation of a man with mild mental retardation. The individual,

The author would like to thank Tamson L. Six for her contributions to this chapter.

who was accused of killing his stepfather, appeared frightened and naive during a clinical evaluation and exhibited very concrete thinking. He exhibited a rather unsophisticated view of the legal system, believing that the jury consisted of friends of the judge and of police officers, all of whom were motivated to put him in jail. He also reported that he did not trust his attorney, since he was obviously friendly with all of these other individuals. He refused to discuss the case with his attorney and in fact, planned to do nothing in his own defense because he believed it would not help.

An opinion was offered to the court that the defendant was currently incompetent to stand trial but probably could be restored to competency after a period of treatment. Somewhat to my surprise, I was subjected to extremely rigorous cross-examination by his defense attorney. Typically, defense attorneys favor a finding of incompetence to stand trial and offer little resistance to this suggestion. This attorney, however, argued that he was perfectly content with the mental state of his client, that he preferred for the client to defer decisions to him, and that he did not need his client's assistance in preparing a defense. He noted that in his opinion the defendant was quite competent. He undertook a lengthy line of questioning regarding my lack of experience as a trial attorney and questioned how I would know what was necessary for a client to assist his attorney in the preparation of a defense. His basic argument was that if he was content with his client's competency, I should be as well. When I suggested that it would be in his client's best interest to be able to make rational decisions about the legal options available, he made it clear that the best interests of the client were something he would take care of.

I later learned that the recommendation of incompetence was threatening a somewhat fragile plea bargaining agreement that might not hold together during the "time out" required by a finding of incompetence.

This case highlights one of the major paradoxes underlying this subject area. Advocates and professionals alike have stressed the critical importance of identifying defendants with mental retardation. However, identification is a double-edged sword. The "special treatment" it affords may sometimes hinder as much as help. This was noted succinctly in 1974 by the President's Committee on Mental Retardation:

> The mentally retarded person is in a uniquely damned position before the courts. If his disability remains undetected, his chances of receiving proper court handling is reduced. But if his impairment is recognized, he may receive a long term institutional commitment without a trial for the alleged offense. (President's Committee on Mental Retardation [1974] as cited in Santamour and Watson [1982], p. 14)

Although numerous aspects of the structure of forensic systems and the nature of forensic evaluations might contribute to the underidentification of defendants with mental retardation, it must be observed that many defendants with mental retardation are *identified* and then *unidentified* because it better serves their legal interests. The common assumption that, if only individuals with mental retardation were identified, they would be appropriately served, may not be valid. Perhaps, in some cases, this label creates more difficulties and limits the available options more significantly than any lack of identification.

This chapter describes how forensic services are provided, it reviews the available data regarding persons with mental retardation in the forensic services system, and it draws some preliminary conclusions from the data.

OVERVIEW OF FORENSIC SERVICES SYSTEMS

A working definition of forensics is the application of a body of scientific knowledge and principles to issues in the legal system. There are forensic experts in many professions. For example, a ballistics expert is able to assist a trier of fact in determining that a specific handgun was fired at the scene of a crime. It is also expected that the mental health/mental retardation professional has specialized expertise to assist the trier of fact in arriving at a legal conclusion. Although forensic professionals are involved at every point in the legal process, from arrest to incarceration and eventual release, this chapter focuses on the issues of competency to stand trial and criminal responsibility, the two key legal issues that forensic professionals are usually asked to address. There has been considerable controversy regarding the appropriateness of mental health professionals' involvement in the courts, but this author accepts this as a given. For example, the standards by which mental health testimony is admitted and by which it is judged relevant have been vigorously debated (Melton, Weithorn, & Slobogin, 1985), as have the relevance, reliability, and validity of expert opinions in criminal cases (Bonnie & Slobogin 1980; Morse, 1978). Despite some concern about the way expert testimony is prepared and utilized, mental health professionals are likely to remain a permanent fixture in the criminal justice process.

Forensic evaluations are typically ordered by the court at the request of the defense, the prosecutor, or the court itself. In the past, most forensic evaluations took place on an in-patient basis at a secure hospital operated by a state department of mental health. In recent years, however, a number of states (Virginia, Tennessee, Ohio, Florida) have begun to provide forensic services on a regional or community basis. It is important to note that historically and continuing to the present, forensic services have been offered by departments of *mental health*. Secure hospital facilities, where forensic patients are treated for restoration to competency or as not guilty by reason of insanity, are operated by departments of mental health and, in a few cases, departments of correction. For many years, it has been recognized that persons with mental retardation are not well served in a mental health facility. A

National Institute of Mental Health survey (Kerr & Roth, 1987) revealed that 16.7% of patients in state-operated mental health forensic facilities had mental retardation. This is clearly not the placement of choice, but few states have a forensic program focusing specifically on the needs of individuals with mental retardation.

The American Bar Association's (ABA's) *Criminal Justice Mental Health Standards* (1989) describe useful guidelines by which forensic evaluations should be ordered and conducted. Standard 7-3.11 establishes the qualifications for mental health and mental retardation professionals to serve as expert witnesses and testify on mental conditions. Three criteria must be met:

> (i) has sufficient professional education and sufficient clinical training and experience to establish the clinical knowledge required to formulate an expert opinion; and
> (ii) has either:
>   (A) acquired sufficient knowledge through forensic training or an acceptable substitute therefor, relevant to conducting the specific type(s) of mental evaluation actually conducted in the case . . . ; or
>   (B) has had a professional therapeutic or habilitative relationship with the person whose mental condition is in question; and
> (iii) has performed an adequate evaluation. . . . (American Bar Association, 1989, p. 132)

It appears that on issues related to mental retardation, standard practice falls far short on each of these dimensions.

A consideration of these criteria, starting with (i) "sufficient professional education and sufficient clinical training . . ." reveals a number of problems. Most states define, by statute or case law, who is permitted to conduct evaluations and provide testimony regarding issues of competency and criminal responsibility. Psychiatrists and, in many states, psychologists are the primary evaluators for these issues. This is logical if the issue relates to mental illness. However, when there are questions about the defendant's intellectual functioning or possible mental retardation, most psychiatrists and many psychologists are not qualified to conduct a proper examination. Psychiatrists receive virtually no training in issues related to mental retardation. Most psychologists' training is limited to the administration of intelligence tests and, possibly, tests of adaptive functioning. A typical graduate program in clinical psychology provides neither extensive classroom coverage nor practical experience with individuals with mental retardation. Thus, the law in most states has defined a category of individuals "qualified" to conduct evaluations who may, in fact, be unqualified to evaluate a disability such as mental retardation.

The second ABA criteria stipulates that the professional must have specialized knowledge regarding the legal matters on which the expert will testify or a professional relationship with the individual. Once again, most forensic evaluators' expertise is on mental health forensic issues. They will certainly be familiar with the legal standards for competency and criminal responsibility and offer opinions regarding these matters. However, a careful examination of what is required in conducting an evaluation reveals a lack of more specialized knowledge. When offering an opinion that an individual is incompetent to stand trial, the *Jackson v. Indiana* (1972) doctrine requires the professional to offer an opinion regarding the probability that a defendant may be restored to competency. There should be serious doubts about the ability of most forensic professionals to offer an accurate assessment of whether or not an individual with mental retardation can be restored to competency. One might speculate on whether the bias would lean toward "restorable" or "unrestorable." Anecdotal information suggests the presence of bimodal errors. Some professionals may believe that people with mental retardation have limited capacity to change, whereas others may believe that such defendants could function better if they were truly motivated. In addition, mental retardation professionals who have a relationship with the individual would rarely have adequate training or experience regarding legal forensic issues. Frequently their academic credentials would not permit offering an opinion owing to the limitations of state law.

Finally, the third criterion requires the performance of an "adequate evaluation." Given the concerns already noted, an adequate evaluation regarding issues of mental retardation would be a chancy affair at best. Many of the "qualified examiners" are not qualified to administer intelligence tests or scales of adaptive functioning. They may have minimal experience observing and interviewing defendants with mental retardation and limited exposure to the unique clinical presentation. Consultation with, or referral, to other professionals for more in-depth evaluations (e.g., psychological testing) frequently does not occur, because of time constraints or fiscal limits. Most mental retardation professionals who have the expertise to conduct a clinical evaluation of current functioning and make reasonable recommendations regarding future prognosis have minimal experience and knowledge about forensic issues.

Thus, it appears that one of the first formal screens for identifying people with mental retardation and diverting them from the criminal justice system is not as fine as assumed. The courts and attorneys may have misplaced confidence in this screening system.

EMPIRICAL DATA

Despite universal agreement that individuals with mental retardation are not appropriately dealt with in the criminal justice system, there are little empirical data to back up the frequent anecdotal accounts. The available data, including that in this chapter, must be viewed with caution. The integrity of the data, including that in this chapter, is compromised by a lack of uniform definitions and measurement techniques. The term *mental retardation* appears to have different meanings depending on the situation in which it is applied.

Information collected for the National Institute of Corrections (NIC) underscores these problems, notwithstanding that the institute's report is an invaluable source of information and an admirable attempt to come to grips with these complex issues. Figure 1, from the NIC data (1985), provides an overview of the reported percentage of the inmate population classified as having mental retardation by 44 state departments of correction. A review of this figure reveals a number of curious findings. Nine state departments of correction reported no inmates with mental retardation, and another 17 reported that less than 1% of their inmate population have mental retardation. Thus, 60% (26 of 44) of the reporting departments classified less than 1% of their total inmate population as having mental retardation. This contrasts with the fact that three departments account for over 50% of the inmates with mental retardation reported nationwide. The conclusion that prisoners with mental retardation are unequally concentrated around the country seems unlikely. However, these findings point to serious problems with the data and classification systems themselves. A closer examination of how each state

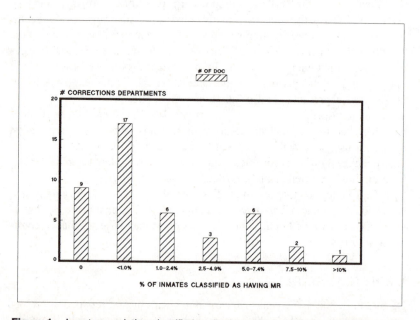

Figure 1. Inmate population classified as having mental retardation (MR) in 44 U.S. departments of corrections (DOC, Department of Corrections). (From National Institute of Corrections. Washington, D.C., 1985.) (Data in this figure were obtained from the *Sourcebook on the Mentally Disordered Prisoner* compiled by the New York State Department of Correctional Services under grant number EW-1 from the National Institute of Corrections and may be copied.)

arrived at the estimate of inmates with mental retardation provides insight into these wide variations. Most states use a combination of intelligence tests and screening interviews to assess mental retardation. However, the wide discrepancies in the training levels of the professional staff employed, as well as the broad range of psychological tests (17 identified) utilized, introduce a set of uncontrolled variables leading to obvious spurious results.

In general, although flawed, a review of the available data can provide temperature readings at different points in the criminal justice system, hinting at the weather but, certainly, not permitting firm conclusions about the climate. By combining information from a number of sources, this author attempts here to compensate partially for the scarcity of data and provide an overview of defendants with mental retardation at critical points in the forensic process.

Identification of Defendants with Mental Retardation after Arrest

Soon after an arrest, decisions are made by defense attorneys, prosecutors, and judges that may determine whether charges are dropped, whether civil sanctions are considered, or whether a defendant is referred for a forensic evaluation. An analysis of the disposition of persons with mental retardation at the time of arrest would provide valuable information regarding rates of identification and diversion. This author uncovered no recent data providing information about the prevalence of mental retardation in an arrestee population. Thus, it was not possible to determine what percentage of individuals with mental retardation is diverted or referred for forensic evaluation.

Defendants Referred for Forensic Evaluation

Individuals are referred for a forensic pretrial examination at the request of the defense attorney, prosecutor, or the judge, typically, for an evaluation of competency or criminal responsibility. This is the first formal occasion where a defendant with mental retardation might be identified. Forensic evaluations are rather rare occurrences in the criminal justice system. For example, in Virginia, in 1987, out of approximately 350,000 arrests, there were approximately 1,500 forensic evaluations. Thus, only .43% of the arrested population received a pretrial forensic evaluation. These evaluations regarding competency to stand trial or criminal responsibility address both mental illness and mental retardation issues. It may be fair to conclude that at least 2.2 percent, or 7,700 (estimated prevalence in general population), of the arrested population in Virginia had mental retardation. Thus, it seems likely that a large number of defendants with mental retardation proceed to trial without a pretrial evaluation.

How well represented are these defendants with mental retardation in referrals for evaluations? Data from six different states, summarized in Table 1, provide information on the prevalence of mental retardation in this referred population. A total of 4,364 defendants were evaluated and 261 (6%) were

Table 1. Diagnosis of mental retardation in forensic evaluation conducted in six states

Study	# Evaluations	% MR
Connecticut Reich and Wells (1985)	390	5.9% (23)
Michigan Sauget, Wightman, and Everett (1988) Thompson and Boersma (1988)	784	6.0% (47)
Missouri Petrila, Selle, Rouse, Evans, and Moore (1981)	480	7.3% (35)
Ohio Mahoney (1989)	662	2.7% (18)
Pennsylvania Heller, Traylor, Ehrlich, and Lester (1981)	196	2.5% (5)
Virginia Institute of Law, Psychiatry and Public Policy	1,852	7.2% (133)
Total	4,364	6.0% (261)

MR, mental retardation.

found to have mental retardation (Figure 2). These data permit some speculation. Assume, as stated earlier, that in a given year in Virginia, 1,500 forensic evaluations were conducted. An average of 7.2% of those referred (108) are identified as having mental retardation. During this same time period, the Virginia Department of Corrections received approximately 7,400 new inmates. Approximately 9.2% (680) inmates were identified as having mental retardation at the time of admission to the Department of Corrections (Virginia Department of Corrections, 1989). At a minimum, then, 572 individuals identified as having mental retardation entered the Department of Corrections with no forensic evaluation conducted. Perhaps not all of these individuals should have had such an evaluation, but the likelihood of a significant portion of this group being incompetent to stand trial is very high.

A series of studies in Michigan (Sauget, Wightman, & Everett, 1988; Thompson & Boersma, 1988) provides more detailed information. The study researchers carefully classified defendants either as having mental retardation, borderline mental retardation, or as "normal" and reported the results of 784 consecutive forensic evaluations. This review yielded rates of 6.1% with mental retardation, 8.3% borderline, and 85.6% without mental retardation (Figure 3). The percentage without mental retardation is almost identical to what one would predict from the general population. The rate of mental

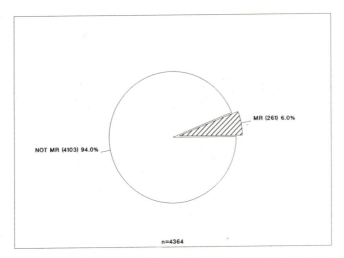

Figure 2. Prevalence of mental retardation (MR) reported in 4,364 forensic evaluations, conducted in six states. (Sources listed in Table 1.)

retardation was higher than expected, and the rate of diagnoses of borderline mental retardation was lower than expected. The Virginia data revealed a similar prevalence of mental retardation (7.2%) in the referred population. Thus, it appears that individuals with mental retardation are properly identified if they are referred for evaluation.

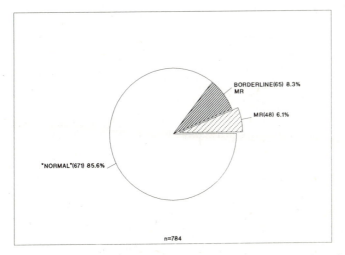

Figure 3. Intellectual classifications reported in 784 consecutive forensic evaluations. (From Center for Forensic Psychiatry, Ann Arbor, Michigan.)

Competency of Defendants
with Mental Retardation

Individuals identified as having mental retardation during a forensic evaluation have been recommended as incompetent to stand trial at widely varying rates, depending upon the data source. Rates of incompetence to stand trial for this population were reported as 17% in Missouri (Petrila, Selle, Rouse, Evans, & Moore, 1981), 12.5% in Connecticut (Reich & Wells, 1985), and 33% in Michigan (Thompson & Boersma, 1988). From a total sample of 1,674 cases in Virginia, 312 defendants (15.7%) were recommended as incompetent to stand trial. Of the 110 defendants identified in Virginia's sample as having mental retardation, 38 (34.5%) were recommended incompetent to stand trial. Thus, in Virginia, defendants with mental retardation are recommended as incompetent to stand trial twice as often as other referred defendants. It appears that in a given group of defendants identified as having mental retardation, approximately one-third may be incompetent to stand trial.

The likelihood of being recommended incompetent to stand trial varies significantly with the severity of the retardation. Twenty-three percent of defendants in Virginia with mild mental retardation were recommended incompetent, whereas 68% of defendants with moderate retardation had an incompetent recommendation (Figure 4). These data support the intuitive conclusion that the likelihood of incompetence increases with the severity of mental retardation.

The Michigan studies (Sauget et al., 1988; Thompson & Boersma, 1988) evaluated the records of 43 defendants with mental retardation referred for competency evaluation. They found that 33% (14) were recommended as incompetent, a finding very similar to the Virginia findings. A comparison of the competent and incompetent defendants with mental retardation on a number of variables produced interesting results. Demographically (age, sex, race, marital status, prior arrests), the two groups were not significantly different. IQ scores for the competent group averaged eight points higher than those for the incompetent group. However, the most significant differences were related to the groups' relative understanding of their legal situation. The competent group demonstrated appropriate concern about the outcome of their legal case, whereas the incompetent group had no appreciation of the consequences of a conviction. The groups also differed significantly in their ability to provide a coherent narrative about the alleged offense. Ninety-seven percent of the competent group could provide this information, yet only 35% of the incompetent group could give a rational account of the offense. The incompetent defendants were less likely to understand the purpose of the evaluation, and approximately half were unable to demonstrate appropriate conduct, including behavioral control and responsiveness to questions. The

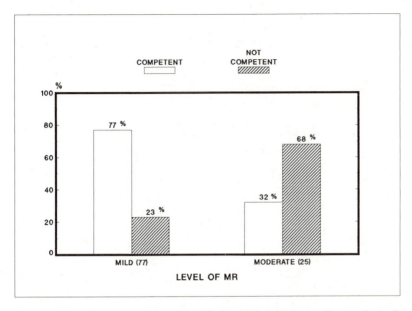

Figure 4. Opinions on competency to stand trial of 102 defendants with mental retardation (MR): Virginia, 1985–1989. (From Institute of Law, Psychiatry, and Public Policy, Charlottesville, Virginia.)

two groups demonstrated significant differences on the functional issues directly related to competency.

Restorability of Incompetent Defendants with Mental Retardation To Stand Trial

The U.S. Supreme Court ruled in *Jackson v. Indiana* (1972) that a defendant who is incompetent to stand trial can only be held involuntarily if there is a substantial likelihood of regaining competency in the foreseeable future. This decision eliminated the lifetime commitments of incompetent defendants with mental retardation and forced the courts and forensic examiners to address the issue of a defendant's "restorability" to competency. This concept is appropriate when considering a defendant with mental illness whose condition will typically remit with a specified course of treatment, "restoring" the defendant to his or her previous competent state. Indeed, most individuals adjudicated incompetent to stand trial due to a mental illness are restored to competency within a short period. However, for defendants with mental retardation, the question of restorability is more difficult. Little data are available on the subject. The opinions on restorability of 38 incompetent defendants with mental retardation in Virginia are presented in Figure 5. Only about 16% were viewed as likely to be restored; in about 66% of the cases, it was believed that

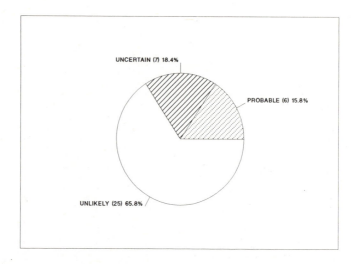

Figure 5. Opinions on "restorability" of 38 incompetent defendants with mental retardation: Virginia, 1985–1989. (From Institute of Law, Psychiatry, and Public Policy, Charlottesville, Virginia.)

restoration was unlikely. Figure 6 highlights the likelihood of restorability for defendants with mild and moderate mental retardation. The severity of the intellectual impairments affects the probability that a defendant will be restored to competency to stand trial.

Evaluation of Criminal Responsibility

Evaluations of criminal responsibility or legal insanity address the culpability of the defendant regarding the specific criminal act. A defense attorney might utilize the results of such an evaluation to pose an insanity defense or as leverage in a plea bargaining agreement. One might expect that an attorney faced with a client with mental retardation would find this a useful tool in preparing a defense. Even in circumstances when a finding of not guilty by reason of insanity (NGRI) might have negative consequences, a referral for evaluation would still yield valuable information.

Several sources are available to examine the prevalence of defendants with mental retardation in populations referred by attorneys for a criminal responsibility examination. In Virginia, for example, diagnostic information is available on 991 defendants during a 4-year period. Seventy-eight of the defendants were found to have mental retardation, or 7.9% of the population. In Ohio, Mahoney (1989) noted that 2.7% of the referred population of 662 defendants were found to have mental retardation. Studies in Colorado (Pasewark, Jeffrey, & Bieber, 1987) and Wyoming studies (Randolph & Pasewark, 1983) yielded rates of 3% and 7.4%, respectively.

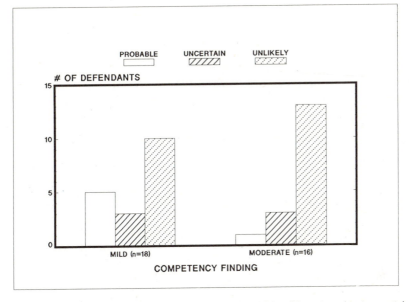

Figure 6. Likelihood of "restorability" of defendants with mild and moderate mental retardation: Virginia, 1985–1989. (From Institute of Law, Psychiatry, and Public Policy, Charlottesville, Virginia.)

Individuals identified as having mental retardation and undergoing evaluations were recommended as not criminally responsible in 11.4% of the reported cases in Virginia. This compares to 9.8% for all examinations conducted during the same period. It appears that a defendant with mental retardation is recommended as not criminally responsible to the court slightly more often than the average rate for the entire referred population. The degree of intellectual impairment appears to have a significant effect on the recommendation of exculpability (Figure 7). Defendants with mild retardation were recommended not responsible in 6.8% of the reviewed cases and defendants with moderate retardation in 33.3% of the cases.

Thompson and Boersma (1988) found that of 43 defendants with mental retardation, 8.6% were recommended as not criminally responsible. This finding approximates the 5-year average of 9.6% not criminally responsible findings for all individuals evaluated at the Michigan Center for Forensic Psychiatry. The overall rate of not criminally responsible findings is almost identical in the Michigan and Virginia studies. The rates for defendants with mental retardation are close to the finding for the population without mental retardation; thus, this diagnosis, in and of itself, does not appear to increase the likelihood of a not criminally responsible recommendation under current procedures. Defendants with mental retardation (if competent to stand trial) are likely to be held responsible for their criminal acts.

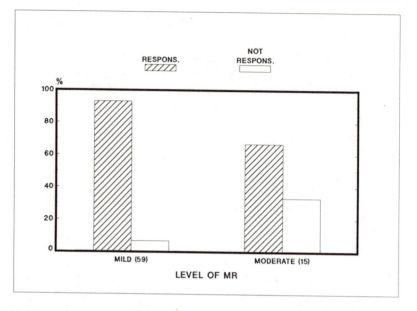

Figure 7. Opinions on criminal responsibility of defendants with mental retardation (MR): Virginia, 1985–1989. (From Institute of Law, Psychiatry, and Public Policy, Charlottesville, Virginia.) (Slash marks = criminally responsible, no slash marks = not criminally responsible.)

Insanity Acquittees

Individuals acquitted by reason of insanity are typically subject to an automatic, short-term period (e.g., 45–60 days) of evaluation in a forensic facility to determine the need for continued treatment. This inpatient evaluation provides an opportunity for a careful diagnostic evaluation. Several studies have examined groups of insanity acquittees admitted to, or currently residing in, forensic facilities. These reports provide an estimate of the prevalence of mental retardation in a population of insanity acquittees. Table 2 provides an overview of these studies.

As with the corrections data described earlier, the wide variation in prevalence rates of mental retardation among insanity acquittees—from 8.5% in the Virginia data to .19% in California—is striking and suggests the need for a cautious interpretation of these findings. The prevalence of mental retardation in a population of insanity acquittees is close to the prevalence of mental retardation in the general population. Although one might expect a higher percentage, a closer analysis provides an explanation. As Figure 8 demonstrates, if an individual with mental retardation is competent to stand trial, he or she is likely also to be found criminally responsible. However, if recommended incompetent to stand trial, a finding of not criminally responsi-

Table 2. Diagnosis of mental retardation in insanity acquittees

Study	# NGRI acquittees	% with MR
Mandella (1986)	1,028	.19% (2)
Menninger (1986)	278	3.2% (9)
Pasewark, Pantle, and Steadman (1979)	225	2.2% (5)
Rogers, Bloom, and Manson (1984a)	373	4.6% (17)
Rogers, Bloom, and Manson (1984b)	316	4.7% (15)
Virginia Department of Mental Health, Mental Retardation and Substance Abuse Services (1989)	200	8.5% (17)
Wettstein and Mulvey (1988)	125	1.6% (2)
Total	2,545	2.6% (67)

NGRI, not guilty by reason of insanity.
MR, mental retardation.

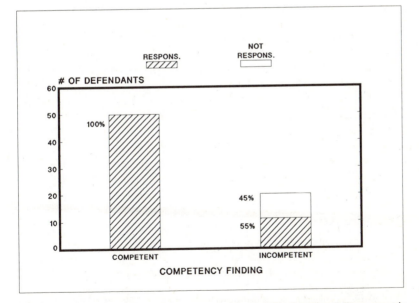

Figure 8. Findings of competency to stand trial and criminal responsibility among defendants with mental retardation: Virginia, 1985–1989. (From Institute of Law, Psychiatry, and Public Policy, Charlottesville, Virginia.) (Slash marks = criminally responsible, no slash marks = not criminally responsible.)

ble is a greater likelihood. It is also striking that 55% of the defendants with mental retardation found incompetent to stand trial are recommended as criminally responsible for their acts. Perhaps the incompetency to stand trial is due to mental illness as opposed to mental retardation factors. In addition, are these defendants "restored" to competency and then held responsible for their acts? This finding warrants further investigation.

CONCLUSIONS AND RECOMMENDATIONS

Forensic services systems play a critical role in the handling of individuals with mental disabilities in the criminal justice system. This chapter has attempted to review some of the flaws in the system, as well as to provide an overview of the current empirical data. The major factors and findings include:

- Identification of defendants with mental retardation may have negative as well as positive consequences.
- Forensic evaluation and treatment systems are focused on individuals with mental illness.
- Individuals qualified to conduct forensic evaluations may not be qualified to assess mental retardation.
- The nature of forensic evaluations in the public sector does not encourage consultation with mental retardation experts.
- Data on individuals with mental retardation in the forensic system are scarce and must be viewed with caution.
- Data are questionable on defendants with mental retardation, owing to varying definitions and assessment techniques.
- Approximately 6% of the individuals referred for forensic evaluation have mental retardation.
- Defendants with mental retardation are found incompetent to stand trial about twice as often as others referred for evaluation.
- The greater the severity of mental retardation, the more likely that one is incompetent to stand trial.
- Restoration to competency is unlikely for approximately two-thirds of incompetent defendants with mental retardation.
- Recommendations regarding criminal responsibility are similar to those for populations without retardation.
- Populations of identified NGRI (not guilty by reason of insanity) patients have varying prevalence rates of mental retardation.

On the basis of these preliminary findings, a number of recommendations are offered here to improve services for individuals with mental retardation in the criminal justice system:

- There is a critical need for improved data regarding individuals with mental retardation in the criminal justice system. The states should be encouraged to collect this type of information at various points in the criminal justice process, for use in future policy decisions.
- A standard model should be proposed for screening individuals with mental retardation who enter correctional facilities. This might include a standard interview and psychological tests to decrease the wide variability currently found.
- States should consider recasting their laws regarding who is qualified to perform forensic evaluations. Flexibility should be incorporated so that individuals with expertise in mental retardation can be included in the process.
- Efforts should be made to train forensic mental health professionals in mental retardation issues and to train mental retardation professionals in forensic issues.
- The states should be encouraged to develop specialized residential forensic programs for individuals with mental retardation.
- Careful review should be made of the disposition of defendants with mental retardation who are incompetent to stand trial.

In conclusion, the critical need for more research and better data must be stressed. Defendants with mental retardation will not be well served in the criminal justice system so long as policy and funding decisions are based on speculation, guesswork, and intuition. Considerable effort will need to be expended so that we may begin to reverse the current situation and find solutions to our long-standing questions.

REFERENCES

American Bar Association. (1989). *ABA Criminal Justice Mental Health Standards, 1989.* Washington, DC: Author.

Bonnie, R.J., & Slobogin, C. (1980). The role of mental health professionals in the criminal process: The case for informed speculation. *Virginia Law Review, 66,* 427–522.

Heller, M., Traylor, W., Ehrlich, S., & Lester, D. (1981). Intelligence, psychosis, and competency to stand trial. *Bulletin of the American Academy of Psychiatry and Law, 9,* 267–274.

Institute of Law, Psychiatry and Public Policy. (1989). Unpublished raw data. Charlottesville: University of Virginia.

Jackson v. Indiana, 406 U.S. 715 (1972).

Kerr, C., & Roth, J. (1987). *Survey of facilities and programs for mentally disordered offenders* (DHHS Pub. No. ADM 86-1493). Washington, DC: U.S. Government Printing Office.

Mahoney, C. (1989, March). Unpublished raw data. Ohio Department of Mental Health, Bureau of Forensic Services, Columbus.

Mandella, R. (1986). Letter of January 1984 to Forensic Services Branch, California Department of Mental Health. In K. Menninger, Thoughts on the idiocy defense. *International Journal of Law and Psychiatry, 8,* 354.

Melton, G., Weithorn, L., & Slobogin, C. (1985). *Community mental health center and the courts.* Lincoln: University of Nebraska Press.

Menninger, K. (1986). Thoughts on the idiocy defense. *International Journal of Law and Psychiatry, 8,* 354.

Morse, S. (1978). Crazy behavior, morals, and science. *Southern California Law Review, 51,* 527–563.

Morse, S. (1982). Foiled explanations and criminal responsibility: Experts and the unconscious. *Virginia Law Review, 61,* 971–1084.

National Institute of Corrections. (1985, March). *Source book on the mentally disordered prisoner.* Washington, DC: U.S. Department of Justice, National Institute of Corrections.

Pasewark, R., Jeffrey, R., & Bieber, S. (1987). Differentially successful and unsuccessful insanity plea defendants in Colorado. *Journal of Psychiatry and Law, 55,* 55–71.

Pasewark, R., Pantle, M., & Steadman, H. (1979). Characteristics and disposition of persons found not guilty by reason of insanity in New York State, 1971–1976. *American Journal of Psychiatry, 136,* 655–660.

Petrila, J., Selle, J., Rouse, P., Evans, C., & Moore, D. (1981). The pretrial examination process in Missouri: A descriptive study. *Bulletin of the American Academy of Psychiatry and Law, 9,* 61–84.

President's Committee on Mental Retardation, Legal Rights Work Group. (1974). The compendium of law suits establishing the legal rights of mentally retarded citizens. (Washington, DC: Department of Health, Education & Welfare). In M. Santamour & P. Watson (Eds.). (1982). *The retarded offender.* New York: Praeger.

Randolph, R., & Pasewark, R. (1983). Characteristics, dispositions, and subsequent arrests of defendants pleading insanity in a rural state. *Journal of Psychiatry and Law, 11,* 345–360.

Reich, J., & Wells, J. (1985). Psychiatric diagnosis and competency to stand trial. *Comprehensive Psychiatry, 26,* 421–431.

Rogers, J., Bloom, J., & Manson, S. (1984a). Insanity defenses: Contested or conceded? *American Journal of Psychiatry, 7,* 885–888.

Rogers, J., Bloom, J., & Manson, S. (1984b). Oregon's new insanity defense system: A review of the first five years, 1978–1982. *Bulletin of the American Academy of Psychiatry and Law, 12,* 383–402.

Sauget, M.F., Wightman, L.H., & Everett, M. (1988). *Comparison of competent and incompetent mentally retarded defendants.* Unpublished manuscript, Center for Forensic Psychiatry, Ann Arbor, MI.

Thompson, J.S., & Boersma, D.C. (1988). *Competency to stand trial and the mentally retarded defendant: An empirical investigation.* Unpublished manuscript, Center for Forensic Psychiatry, Ann Arbor, MI.

Virginia Department of Corrections. (1989). Unpublished raw data.

Virginia Department of Mental Health, Mental Retardation and Substance Abuse Services, Office of Forensic Services. (1989, August). Unpublished raw data.

Wettstein, R., & Mulvey, E. (1988). Disposition of insanity acquittees in Illinois. *Bulletin of the American Academy of Psychiatry and Law, 16,* 11–24.

Chapter 5

THE COMPETENCY OF DEFENDANTS WITH MENTAL RETARDATION TO ASSIST IN THEIR OWN DEFENSE

RICHARD J. BONNIE

O N FIRST REVIEW, the applicable legal rules relating to the competency of defendants with mental retardation to assist in their own defense[1] seem both well settled and well suited to promote fairness in the criminal process. "It has long been accepted that a person whose mental condition is such that he lacks the capacity to understand the nature and object of the proceedings against him, to consult with counsel, and to assist in preparing his defense may not be subjected to trial."[2] Whenever a defense attorney has a good faith doubt regarding the competency of his client, the attorney is obligated to seek an evaluation of the issue and to bring his or her doubts to judicial attention.[3] Further, the trial judge is obligated to hold a hearing, whether or not the defense has requested one, whenever a bona fide doubt arises regarding the defendant's competency.[4] This obligation applies at all stages of the proceedings.

The material in this chapter has previously been published in Volume 82, Number 3, of the *Journal of Criminal Law and Criminology,* pages 419–446. Copyright © 1990 by Northwestern University School of Law. Reprinted here by permission.

A defendant with mental retardation who is found to be incompetent to stand trial may not be convicted.[5] However, the defendant may be committed for the purposes of assessing the probability that competency can be effected in the foreseeable future and for making efforts to do so.[6] Although the long-term character of the disability precludes prosecution in many cases, some competency-enhancing interventions may be efficacious.[7]

Notwithstanding the clarity of these broad legal principles, two problems require attention. First, and most important, there is reason to doubt that, in practice, the interests of defendants with mental retardation are adequately protected. Second, latent ambiguity concerning the concept of incompetency, and the values it is designed to serve, has raised unresolved questions regarding the legal significance of mental retardation in some cases. The problem is most evident in the controversy regarding whether a defendant who is competent to be tried may be found incompetent to plead guilty. This chapter addresses each of these problems.

THE PROBLEM OF UNDERIDENTIFICATION

According to most analysts, legally significant impairments due to mental retardation are largely unrecognized by attorneys and courts.[8] As Ellis and Luckasson have observed, "Efforts that many mentally retarded people typically expend in trying to prevent any discovery of their handicap may render the existence or the magnitude of their disability invisible to criminal justice system personnel."[9] Impairments become visible enough to trigger evaluation, it is thought, mainly when the defendant is also mentally ill or acts in a bizarre or disruptive fashion.

Although the "underidentification" hypothesis is widely accepted, empirical data on the issue are sparse. The hypothesis rests on two suppositions—first, that a substantial proportion of defendants with mental retardation are not referred for competency assessment, and, second, that this low rate of referral is attributable to a general failure to recognize the "existence or magnitude" of the disability.[10] As for the low rate of referral, the main source of empirical support is a 1966 case study of 31 prison inmates with mental retardation that showed that pretrial psychological assessments had occurred in only three cases.[11] Although this is the only study providing direct empirical support for the "underidentification" hypothesis, indirect support can also be found in studies of defendants who *are* referred for pretrial forensic evaluation, in which the prevalence of diagnosed mental retardation ranges between 2% and 7%,[12] compared with about 10% of the correctional population.[13]

In the absence of any contradictory data, it seems reasonable to assume that a substantial proportion (perhaps half) of defendants with mental retardation are not referred for competency evaluation. The more problematic question, however, is the degree to which this low rate of referral is attributable to underrecognition of the disability. It is conceivable that attorneys and courts are aware of the disability in many of these cases but have concluded that the impairment is not of sufficient magnitude to warrant evaluation. To the extent that this alternative hypothesis is accurate, the key question is whether *legally significant disabilities* (i.e., disabilities severe enough to amount to incompetency under the applicable legal "tests") are going unrecognized. This question can be answered empirically only by studying a representative sample of defendants with mental retardation who have *not* been referred for evaluation, and comparing them, in terms of legally relevant incapacities, with defendants referred for evaluation who are, and are not, found to be incompetent. This, of course, has not been done.

In the absence of a definitive empirical investigation, it is reasonable to assume that the low rate of referral of defendants with mental retardation for pretrial evaluation does, in fact, reflect a relatively common failure to recognize the "existence or magnitude of the disability" *and* that underrecognition of the disability compromises the defendants' constitutional interests. Even though available information does not warrant a firm conclusion that significant numbers of "legally incompetent" defendants with mental retardation are being unfairly prosecuted and convicted,[14] it *is* clear that the steps being taken now are inadequate to assure sufficient representation for the much larger number of such defendants who are legally competent to proceed.

In cases involving defendants with mental illness, it is likely that forensic and judicial practice errs in the direction of finding incompetence, at least in the early phases of the pretrial process. This is so for a variety of reasons, including the perceived need for therapeutic restraint and the provisional nature of the finding of "incompetency" in most cases. Where the defendant with *mental retardation* is concerned, however, forensic and judicial practice probably tilts in the other direction, primarily because a finding of incompetency is likely to be a perpetual bar to adjudication. Again, this assertion cannot be "proven" empirically, but most forensic clinicians in the mental retardation field believe it to be true.

If, in practice, the threshold of competency for defendants with mental retardation is set relatively low, the fairness of adjudication in cases involving minimally competent defendants depends largely on the ability and inclination *of the attorney* to recognize and compensate for the client's limitations. In this sense, enhanced competence of attorneys is necessary to ensure adequate representation of marginally competent clients with mental retardation.

The pressures to cut corners in criminal defense, especially for public defenders and court-appointed counsel working for a set fee, are well known. Unfortunately, the risks of inadequate representation are magnified when the client has mental retardation, not only because the client is in no position to monitor the attorney's performance even in a superficial way, but also because attorneys are likely to spend *less* time interviewing clients with mental retardation when *more* time is really needed.

If the attorney fails to employ discerning interviewing techniques to offset the well-documented tendency of persons with mental retardation to attempt to conceal their disability, important facts are likely to be masked or distorted. Clients with mental retardation tend to act as though they understand their attorneys when they do not, and to bias their responses in favor of what they believe their attorneys want them to say or in the direction of concrete, though inaccurate, responses. Only attorneys who have had specialized training or experience in representing clients with mental retardation are likely to be aware of these problems. For others, the risk of unwittingly inadequate representation is serious.

When viewed from this perspective, the failure of the legal system to develop mechanisms to assist lawyers representing marginally competent defendants—a problem that is much graver when the client has mental retardation than when he or she is mentally ill—is more significant, in practical effect, than the underidentification of "incompetent" defendants.

Two corrective arrangements are available. One is to ensure that any defendant with obvious deficiencies in intellectual capacity is evaluated by forensic clinicians who have specialized skills in dealing with persons with mental retardation. Referrals, within the framework of the attorney–client relationship, should be arranged in such cases to assess "legal competency" *and* to ensure that the client is carefully and thoroughly interviewed about the alleged offense. Implementing this proposal would require major changes in current practice, not only because the referral rate is so low but also because most forensic clinicians lack specialized understanding of mental retardation.

A second corrective arrangement is to draw on specialized services for persons with mental retardation. In some cases, interested family members or guardians now play an active role in facilitating communication between defendants with mental retardation and their attorneys and in helping the client to make decisions. However, most defendants with mental retardation lack interested family representatives. In theory, at least, it ought to be possible to provide adjunctive assistance in these cases through judicially designated "representatives" or "consultants," not only to identify dispositional alternatives but also to facilitate informed representation by counsel.

THE MEANING OF INCOMPETENCY

It is often observed that the meaning of incompetency is open-textured and highly contextual in application. As noted in the commentary of the Criminal Justice Mental Health Standards of the American Bar Association (ABA), "competence is functional in nature, context-dependent and pragmatic in orientation."[15] Recognition of the functional dimension of the competency determination has led forensic clinicians to develop checklists and protocols for assessing various functions that a "competent" defendant is expected to perform.[16] Because increasing proportions of forensic evaluations are being conducted by clinicians who have received specialized training, it is likely that this functional approach is now more widely utilized in forensic practice than 10 years ago. The ABA's Mental Health Standards themselves have contributed to improvements in forensic practice. Clinicians are now more likely to recognize that incompetency is a legal concept, that a defendant who has mental retardation (or is psychotic) is not necessarily incompetent for legal purposes, and that the relevant functional capacities relate to various forms of participation in the criminal process, not to mental condition at the time of the offense (i.e., to issues of "responsibility").[17]

The increasing sophistication of forensic practice has helped to expose a latent ambiguity in the construct of incompetency, one that has particular bearing on the assessment of defendants with mental retardation. In its most general formulation, the question is whether competency to participate in one's own defense is a single, open-textured construct or a multiple construct. The most significant subsidiary question, which has befuddled courts and observers, is whether competency to plead guilty is subsumed within a broader construct of trial competency, or whether a defendant who is competent to assist counsel (and proceed to trial) might not be competent to plead guilty.

According to one view, a defendant is not competent to plead guilty if he or she is not capable of understanding the alternatives and making a "reasoned choice" among them.[18] Under this view, a defendant with limited intelligence and limited conceptual ability may not be competent to plead guilty even though he or she is competent to be tried. Although this view has been endorsed by most analysts[19] and by the ABA Standards,[20] it has been rejected by most courts.[21] The prevailing judicial view appears to be that the "test" for competency to plead guilty is the "same" as the test for competency to stand trial.

This author endorses the view that competency to participate in the criminal process is a multiple construct and that competency to plead guilty (or to make other decisions) is conceptually (and clinically) distinct from competency to assist counsel. However, the debate about whether the "test" for competency to plead guilty is more demanding than the test for competency to stand trial has largely obscured the underlying questions raised when defendants with limited intelligence plead guilty—questions concerning the nature and quality of the interaction between these defendants and their attorneys.

Why Incompetency Matters

Although this is not the place for an elaborate analysis of the competency construct, brief treatment of the subject is necessary to establish a frame of reference and a conceptual vocabulary for the discussion following. It is important initially to ask why a defendant's incompetency matters at all. A review of cases and commentary yields three conceptually independent rationales that, for convenience of reference, might be labeled "dignity," "reliability," and "autonomy."

First, a person who lacks a rudimentary understanding of the nature and purpose of the proceedings against him is not a "fit" subject for criminal prosecution and punishment. To proceed against such a person offends the moral *dignity* of the process because it treats the defendant not as an accountable person but, rather, as an object of the state's effort to carry out its promises. The dignitarian rationale is implicated only in cases involving defendants who lack a meaningful moral understanding of wrongdoing and punishment. The procedural bar against prosecution in such cases would seem to be uncontroversial.

Beyond those cases in which prosecution of a defendant with mental retardation would offend the dignitarian rationale, the main purpose of the incompetency construct is to bar definitive adjudication in those cases, and under those circumstances, where the defendant is incapable of providing whatever assistance is necessary to instill confidence in the *reliability* of the outcome. To proceed against a defendant who lacks the capacity to recall relevant information and to communicate this information to his or her attorney would be unfair to the defendant and would undermine society's independent interest in the integrity of its criminal process. This is what the U.S. Supreme Court had in mind when it stated that the bar against trying the incompetent defendant is "fundamental to an adversary system of justice."[22] When viewed from the perspective of reliable adjudication, the concept of incompetency is instrumental in nature and is operationalized within the context of the attorney-client relationship: a defendant is competent if he or she is able to communicate with counsel and to provide whatever assistance counsel requires to explore and present an adequate defense on the defendant's behalf.

A third dimension of the competency construct, which is conceptually independent of the other two dimensions, is derived from legal rules requiring that certain decisions regarding the defense or disposition of cases must be made by defendants themselves. Some construct of "decisional competency" is an inherent, though derivative, feature of any legal structure that prescribes a norm of client *autonomy*. In theory at least, it is possible to imagine a system of criminal adjudication that leaves no room for client self-determination— one that bars self-representation, that does not permit guilty pleas, and in which all decisions regarding the conduct and defense of the case are made by counsel, not the defendant. Under these legal arrangements, a defendant's decisional competency would not be relevant. But this is not our system. In our system, some decisions regarding the defense or disposition of the case are committed, by law, to the defendant and not to the lawyer. According to all authorities, these include decisions regarding the plea and, if the case is to be tried, regarding whether it should be tried before a jury, whether the defendant will be present, and whether the defendant will testify.

Decisional Competency and Autonomy

Notwithstanding that decisional competency rests on a different conceptual foundation from other competencies required of criminal defendants, it is often included as a component of a unitary formula for what is usually called "competency to stand trial" (CST).[23] Forensic "checklists" used for CST assessments typically include items relating to capacity to "make decisions after receiving advice,"[24] "plan . . . legal strategy"[25] or "appreciat[e] the consequences of various legal options."[26] The commentary to the ABA Standards refers to "a capacity . . . to advise and accept advice from counsel, to elect an appropriate plea and to approve the legal strategy of the trial."[27] According to one frequently cited commentary, the *Dusky* standard requires "the capacity to make decisions during the course of the proceedings in response to alternatives explained by the attorney."[28]

For a number of reasons, one might wonder whether decisional competency is properly understood as a component of a unitary competency standard. In the first place, there are a number of discrete contexts in which the law is incompatible with this view. In recent years, courts have recognized that defendants who are "competent to stand trial" may not be competent to make specific decisions, such as whether to raise an insanity defense[29] or whether to decline to introduce mitigating evidence in capital cases.[30] As noted earlier, courts are divided on whether the same should be said of competency to plead guilty.

Second, it seems doubtful that courts are inclined to preclude adjudication altogether in cases involving defendants who understood the charges and are able to assist counsel but who are not competent to make an "informed decision" about issues requiring complex risk-benefit judgments, such as whether to plead guilty or whether to waive a jury trial. In practice, it seems likely that most courts avoid the consequences of a finding of "incompetency to stand trial" in such cases, either by closing their eyes to the defendants' decisional incompetency or by splitting off the decisional competency issue and dealing with it separately.

McCarlo v. State[31] is illustrative. McCarlo, the defendant, was charged with rape and attempted sexual assault. After being found incompetent to stand trial due to mental retardation, he was committed to an institution for 6 months, during which the facility staff "worked with [him] to improve his understanding of the judicial system and the criminal proceedings he faced."[32] He was then found competent to stand trial. However, the trial court repeatedly refused to accept McCarlo's proffered guilty pleas on the grounds that he "did not have sufficient understanding of the rights he would give up by pleading guilty."[33]

At the trial, McCarlo waived jury trial and, after a colloquy with him, the judge accepted the waiver, notwithstanding the fact that "the dialogue . . . indicate[s] substantial confusion on McCarlo's part concerning the specific nature of the proceedings he was involved in, as well as considerable uncertainty about the precise role of a jury."[34] Although the Alaska Court of Appeals affirmed the trial court's decision, it obviously was a bit puzzled about how to explain this result.

On the one hand the court noted that McCarlo's "competency to waive jury trial is implicit in the trial court's determination of his competency to stand trial,"[35] an obviously fictional conclusion since McCarlo was found competent to stand trial before this issue arose, and the trial judge obviously thought it required separate attention. On the other hand, the appellate court also appeared to recognize that McCarlo's decisional competency required an independent determination and went on to set a relatively low standard. McCarlo's waiver was said to be valid, in effect, simply because he was able to express reasons for not wanting a jury—he trusted the trial judge and a jury would make him nervous.[36] Regardless of the court's technical legal explanation for affirming the "finding" of decisional competency, it is clear that the most salient factor was that McCarlo's attorney "acquiesced in the waiver of jury trial and affirmatively indicated his belief that it was appropriate to proceed with a non-jury trial."[37]

As *McCarlo* shows, questions about decisional competency, which implicate the principle of autonomy, must be exposed for independent scrutiny if they are to be sensibly resolved. The reasons (dignity and reliability) for barring adjudication when the defendant is unable to understand the nature and purpose of the criminal process or is unable to assist counsel do not apply when the defendant's deficits relate solely to the capacity to make sufficiently "autonomous" decisions regarding the defense or disposition of the case. Even though our system obligates attorneys to adhere to the wishes of competent clients on certain issues, it does not follow that adjudication should be barred if defendants are not competent to make those decisions; other legal responses (e.g., allocating decisional responsibility to the attorney or directing the attorney to follow a "default" rule) are possible in such cases.

Further, there is no reason, in principle, why the definition or "test" of decisional competency would necessarily be the same in connection with all decisions. For example, a demanding test of competency might be utilized if the defendant insists, over the attorney's advice, on pleading guilty to a capital offense or refusing to introduce mitigating evidence, whereas a less demanding standard might be appropriate if the defendant is acceding to his or her attorney's recommendation that a jury trial be waived, as in *McCarlo*. In short, the criteria for decisional competency are likely to be highly contextual, depending on the value placed on client autonomy and the practical consequences of alternative approaches.

A Conceptual Vocabulary

The remainder of this chapter employs a conceptual vocabulary that differentiates the dignity, reliability, and autonomy dimensions of competency determinations in the criminal process and disaggregates the functionally distinct features of the "open construct" typically called "competency to stand trial." A distinction is drawn between a baseline concept of "competency to proceed" and a highly contextualized concept of "decisional competency." "Competency to proceed" refers to the minimum conditions for participating in one's own defense.[38] Although there is some room for debate about what the law "is" in this context, courts and commentators generally refer to: 1) capacity to understand the charges and the nature and purpose of the adversary process and 2) capacity to communicate with counsel about the facts of the case.[39] (As customarily defined, the criteria serve both the dignitarian and reliability rationales described earlier.)[40]

A defendant who is not competent to assist counsel in the sense just described is (by definition) not competent to make decisions regarding defense or disposition of the case. However, a defendant who is (provisionally) competent to assist counsel may not be competent to make specific decisions that are encountered as the process unfolds. As has been noted, the "relevant decisions" are those that are committed, by law, to the [competent] defendant and not to the lawyer—or, in other words, those that counsel is not permitted to make on his or her own—whether they are made prior to trial, at trial, or in lieu of trial. "Decisional competency" cannot be addressed in the abstract or in the general sense described earlier, but in the context of the specific decision that is encountered as the process unfolds. Decisional competency *requires* a contextualized inquiry.

Although "trial competency" is a purely derivative application of the two concepts already discussed, it requires separate elaboration to clarify terminology and also to demonstrate how these concepts become operationalized in the context of trial proceedings.[41] In the small proportion of cases that are actually tried, the defendant must be competent to participate, to the extent necessary to ensure a fair trial, in his or her own defense. This means the defendant must be "competent to proceed" to trial in the baseline sense described previously—capable of understanding the proceedings and of engaging in rational communication with counsel, as needed, during the proceedings.[42] A few discrete issues regarding "decisional competency" may arise at the trial itself if they have not been anticipated, and resolved, during pretrial interactions with the attorney[43] or, if the defendant's decision must be verified on the record, in a waiver of jury trial.[44] One particularly intriguing issue concerns the competency of a defendant to waive his or her right to be present at trial, a problem that usually arises in connection with disruptive conduct in the courtroom.[45]

The stage is now set to explore the application of those concepts in cases involving defendants with mental retardation. The rest of this subsection illustrates the relatively straightforward notion of "competency to proceed," followed by, in the remainder of the chapter, a discussion of the problem of decisional competency in relation to guilty pleas.

Competency to Proceed: Illustrative Cases

As noted earlier, most observers believe that judicial practice tilts against determinations of incompetency in cases involving defendants with mental retardation, in order to avoid the dispositional dilemmas presented in such cases. It is nonetheless clear, however, that the construct of incompetency does have normative content. Empirical studies of forensic facilities consistently show that about 10% of the defendants found incompetent have mental retardation,[46] and appellate courts reverse trial court findings of competency with sufficient frequency to demonstrate that the ancient ban against adjudication has continuing normative force.

A review of appellate opinions on the subject[47] yields a relatively clear picture of the requirements for baseline competency to proceed. Two recent cases are illustrative. In *State v. Benton*,[48] the Tennessee Court of Criminal Appeals reversed the aggravated rape and aggravated sexual battery convictions of Benton, a 43-year-old man whose full-scale WAIS-R score was 47 and whose performance on the various domains of the Vineland Adaptive Behavior Scales was roughly equivalent to that of an average 5- or 6-year-old child.[49] Benton's incapacities clearly implicated the dignitarian rationale of the incompetency doctrine: he was apparently unable to understand the nature and purpose of the criminal proceedings or the nature of the charges against him. According to a widely shared judicial intuition, prosecution, conviction, and punishment in cases of this nature would mock the moral integrity of the criminal process.

In *State v. Rogers*,[50] a divided Louisiana Supreme Court reversed a trial court finding of competency in a case that illustrates the reliability rationale for the bar against adjudication. Rogers, the defendant, had been charged with aggravated rape. Although all three psychiatrists who evaluated Rogers agreed that he had mental retardation, they disagreed about the severity of his disability. In finding Rogers to be competent, the trial court had relied primarily on the testimony of one psychiatrist whose opinion, though equivocal, tilted in the direction of competency, and had rejected the testimony of two other psychiatrists who estimated Rogers' IQ to be about 50 and who raised substantial doubts about his ability to assist his attorney.

Because the case came to the Supreme Court on an interlocutory appeal, the state's evidence against Rogers was not before the Court. Although nothing was said in the opinion about the evidence introduced at the preliminary hearing, the impression clearly emerges that the Court was worried about the reliability of any conviction that might ensue. According to the preponderance of psychiatric opinion, Rogers had "extreme difficulty in recalling events and circumstances" and had "periods of time up to an hour and a half when he [did] not know what happened."[51] As a result, he "would not be able to assist in his defense by recalling his whereabouts, locating witnesses or testifying without confusion or contradiction."[52] Under these circumstances, the majority of the Court apparently concluded that the risk of an erroneous conviction was unacceptably high.

Taken together, *Benton* and *Rogers* reveal the normative structure of the concept of what this author is calling baseline competency to proceed. The ability to understand the nature and purpose of the criminal proceedings, and the essence of the charge of wrongdoing, is a relatively determinate precondition for competency to proceed; it is not dependent on the evidence against the defendant, and reflects a widely accepted moral intuition regarding the integrity of the criminal process. The ability to recall and describe events—to communicate with and assist counsel—is a less determinate requirement and is, in practice, highly contextual. What is required in each case is a qualitative judgment regarding whether the defendant has *sufficient* ability to recall and describe events (including mental "events") to enable the attorney to explore and present an adequate defense.[53] What is sufficient, in a given case, will depend on the evidence against the defendant and the plausible lines of defense. When the defendant has mental retardation, the disabilities that most warrant attention are those relating to capacity to recall and describe relevant events, including states of mind.

Decisional Competency:
The Guilty Plea Problem

As already noted, decisional competency is conceptually and clinically distinct from competency to understand the criminal process and to assist counsel. Although the relevant psychological capacities may overlap, decision making about defense strategy obviously encompasses conceptual abilities, cognitive skills, and capacities for rational manipulation of information that are not directly pertinent to competency to proceed. The key question is how demanding the test for decisional competency should be.

Although forensic experts have not yet conceptualized the clinical content of alternative tests of decisional competency in the context of criminal defense, the formulations developed by P. Appelbaum and T. Grisso in their continuing research on decisional competency for medical treatment can serve as a starting point.[54] The *ability to understand relevant information* about a particular decision is the criterion most often utilized in many decisional contexts. This "test" involves the basic idea that clients who cannot understand the relevant considerations after they have been conveyed, or do not understand their own prerogatives as decision makers, are not competent to decide whether to accept or reject the attorney's advice. This test, which is purely cognitive, can vary in its stringency according to what considerations are held to be relevant, and therefore must be understood. This point is especially pertinent in connection with defendants with mental retardation who may have the capacity to understand some considerations (e.g., the nature of the alternative courses of action—plea or trial, jury trial or bench trial) but may not be able to understand others (e.g., the risks or consequences of choosing one course or the other).

A defendant who is able to comprehend relevant information may be *unable to appreciate the significance of that information* in his or her own case. Finally, a defendant who can understand information relevant to a decision and can appreciate the "meaning" of the decision in his or her situation may nonetheless lack the capacity to use logical processes to compare the benefits and risks of the decisional options. Again, assuming the person is able to understand relevant information, *inability to engage in rational manipulation of information* (or to engage in a rational decisional process) may be relevant in cases involving defendants with all forms of mental disability.

As this summary of alternative clinical formulations demonstrates, the legal "test" for decisional competency can be made more or less demanding. Moreover, it is clear that the choice of a "test" must turn on a theory of autonomy, in the context of the attorney-client relationship, and on the consequences of a determination of incompetency. Although a comprehensive discussion of these issues far exceeds the ambition of this chapter, an exploratory analysis is offered here of the problem in the context of the controversy over the "test" for competency to plead guilty.

When analyzed within this conceptual framework, guilty pleas by defendants with mental retardation implicate two different concerns that must be isolated for separate consideration. First, the admissions embedded in a guilty plea may not be reliable; to the extent that this is the underlying concern, a finding that the defendant is competent to make the necessary admissions is a necessary condition for a fair adjudication *if* the adjudication is to be accomplished by a guilty plea. Second, even if the reliability of the defendant's admissions are not in doubt, the defendant may be regarded as "incompetent" to plead guilty (and to waive his or her constitutional rights) because he or she lacks the capacity to render a sufficiently "autonomous" decision. Because decisional competency in this sense is not a necessary condition for a fair adjudication, the "test" for competency to plead guilty, when viewed from this perspective, depends entirely on the theory of autonomy that is, or should be, reflected in the law.

Reliability   Substantial reliability concerns are raised whenever a defendant with mental retardation pleads guilty. All of the concerns about reliability of confessions described by Ellis[55] are even more pronounced when the inculpatory (incriminating) admissions are embedded in a plea of guilty. Limited conceptual skills, biased responding, and submissiveness to authority may mask significant doubts about criminal liability, especially in relation to culpability elements. The risk of unreliable pleas is further magnified by all the structural arrangements in criminal justice administration that encourage negotiated pleas. Public defenders or appointed lawyers often spend little time probing the more subtle aspects of criminal liability that may be most pertinent in the defense of persons with mental retardation.

This problem is illustrated by *Gaddy v. Linahan*.[56] Gaddy and his uncle were charged with murder and burglary in a case involving the stabbing of the victim in his home. They were apprehended two days after the offense, following a high-speed automobile chase. Shortly after the indictment, Gaddy's uncle pled guilty to both charges. About a month later, Gaddy, a 30-year-old man who could neither read nor write, pled guilty to "malice murder" pursuant to a plea agreement under which the prosecution agreed not to seek the death penalty and to dismiss the burglary indictment.

After noting, for the record, Gaddy's "limited education and his inability to read," the trial court asked the prosecutor to read the indictment, and then asked Gaddy whether he had talked to his attorney about the charge, whether he understood it, whether he understood that he was waiving various rights by pleading guilty, whether he had made up his own mind to do so, and other aspects of the standard plea colloquy. Gaddy answered, simply, "Yes, sir" to virtually all of these questions. The trial court then accepted the plea and sentenced Gaddy to a life term. Proceedings were subsequently initiated in state court to set aside the plea on a variety of grounds, including the allegation that Gaddy did not understand the elements of the offense of "malice murder." After these efforts were unavailing, habeas proceedings were filed in federal court.

Based on the description of the evidence in the opinion by the Eleventh Circuit Court of Appeals, it seems likely that this is what happened: Gaddy's attorney met with him briefly a couple of times. Although Gaddy said that he was "innocent" because his uncle had stabbed the victim, the attorney quickly concluded that Gaddy was criminally liable as an accomplice to felony murder because he had been present during the alleged burglary and the killing. There is no indication, however, that the attorney interviewed Gaddy carefully about Gaddy's awareness of, or degree of participation in, his uncle's conduct, or that the attorney ever tried to explain to him the "elements" of complicity or felony-murder on which the plea of guilt was predicated. The record also shows that none of this occurred during the plea colloquy.

In the absence of a more complete understanding of the charge, Gaddy's plea was hardly "an intelligent admission of guilt" and might well have been an unreliable one. (Gaddy probably understood that he was pleading guilty to the offense of "murder," which he understood in a lay sense, but he did so because his lawyer led him to believe that he could be sentenced to death if he didn't plead guilty.) As the Eleventh Circuit said:

> The transcripts of the plea hearing and the state habeas hearing fail to indicate whether petitioner had any understanding of the elements of malice murder, whether the facts of his case fit those elements, or whether the state had proof sufficient to obtain a conviction at trial. Neither petitioner nor his attorney represented at either hearing that they had discussed details of the crime. The record does reveal that defense counsel believed that petitioner's conduct fulfilled the elements of the crime of malice murder. But counsel never said that he had explained his conclusion to petitioner. All we learn from counsel's testimony is that he and the petitioner talked with each other about the constitutional rights petitioner would be waiving by pleading guilty and that petitioner would not have the benefit of the prosecutor's recommendation of a sentence of life imprisonment if petitioner opted for a trial.
>
> The only evidence the State can rely on to establish the fact that petitioner knew and understood the elements of malice murder is the one-sentence indictment that the prosecutor read to petitioner during the plea hearing. The terms "murder" and "malice aforethought," as they appear in the indictment, are not readily understandable by a layman, particularly one of minimal intelligence. They are complex legal terms, the discussion of which consumes pages of Georgia case law. Considering the petitioner's lack of intelligence, his expressed confusion, the complexity of the case, and the extraordinary consequences of pleading guilty to malice murder, a more thorough explanation of the nature of the crime and its elements was required to satisfy the tenets of due process.[57]

In cases involving defendants with normal intelligence, attorneys are likely to elicit relevant information regarding the offense and are likely to explain the elements of legal guilt to the defendant. As a result, guilty pleas are more likely to represent reliable admissions of guilt. However, in cases involving defendants with subnormal intelligence, special precautions are required to offset the many factors that propel the system toward efficient outcomes rather than reliable ones.[58] Gaddy may have had the capacity to understand the offense and to make an intelligent admission of guilt, but his interactions with his attorney and the court were insufficient to ensure that he did so in fact.

Insofar as reliability is the underlying concern, the capacities required for competent guilty pleas are substantially congruent with those required for competency to proceed. The defendant must have a sufficient understanding of the charges, in lay terms, and a sufficient understanding of what happened at the time of the offense, to "understand and agree that he performed some acts and that those acts are unlawful."[59] Whether the acts admitted by the defendant provide a sufficient foundation for the plea is a legal judgment that must be made initially by the attorney and then by the court. In *this* respect, then, the "test" for competency to plead guilty is not "higher" than the test for competency to proceed, but this formulation of the issue misses the key point:

The fact that the defendant has been "found" competent to proceed (i.e., to "stand trial") does not establish the reliability of the admissions that may subsequently be embedded in a guilty plea. This matter requires careful attention by counsel and independent scrutiny by the court at the time of the plea. The *"competency" of the defendant with mental retardation to plead guilty must be given heightened consideration, not because the "test" is higher but because careful scrutiny is necessary to ensure that the defendant's admissions, when taken together with other evidence, provide a reliable foundation for the plea.*

Autonomy   The complexion of the "competency-to-plead-guilty" issue changes considerably when viewed in terms of autonomy. Consider the facts of *Allard v. Helgemoe.*[60] Allard was charged with burglary. He apparently admitted that he had broken and entered the building where the crime occurred and had taken property there. He apparently understood that these acts were wrong. It appears, however, that, according to his imperfect recollection of the relevant facts, he may not have had a conscious purpose to steal when he entered the building and may have "succumbed to the temptation" to steal after he was already there. This fact is legally significant because he would not be guilty of the offense of burglary if he lacked the "intent to steal" at the time he broke and entered.

Allard's attorney had done what Gaddy's attorney failed to do. He had carefully interviewed his client and reached a judgment that Allard was guilty of breaking and entering and theft, but that his liability for the more serious burglary offense was at least open to doubt. Notwithstanding this doubt, he concluded that Allard would probably be convicted of burglary if he went to trial and recommended a guilty plea in anticipation of a more lenient sentence.

Allard's attorney tried to explain all this to him. However, due to his limited intelligence, Allard was apparently unable to understand the relevant legal distinction.[61] The judge's colloquy at the time the plea was made and accepted did not expose the problem. In a subsequent challenge to the validity of the guilty plea, Allard's new attorneys argued that he had not been competent to decide to plead guilty because he lacked the capacity to make a "reasoned choice" among the alternative courses of action. The central contention was that "an understanding of the elements of the offense with which one is charged is essential in practical terms to make any kind of informed evaluation of the probability of success at trial."

Resolution of the issue posed in Allard's case requires a theory of autonomy. Allard knew and understood that the decision to plead guilty or go to trial was his to make, that he could get a more severe sentence if he went to trial, and that his attorney had recommended a guilty plea. But Allard was not able to make his "own" evaluation of the alternatives. At best, he was able to decide to follow his attorney's advice. Is this enough? If not, it would seem likely that many defendants with mental retardation are not competent to plead guilty.[62]

The same issue arises in medical treatment decision making. In that context, legal rules requiring informed consent have been designed to create conditions conducive to autonomous patient decision making, even though most patients choose to defer in practice to their physicians' recommendations. If a patient is unable to understand a salient aspect of the disease or the possible effect of a proposed treatment, it might be said that the patient is not "competent" to give informed consent. Although physicians often rely on incompetent "assents" under these circumstances, avenues of surrogate decision making are typically available.

How should the problem of "incompetent assents" be handled in the context of attorney-client decision making in criminal defense? There are three possibilities. One is to adopt legal rules that reflect a "softer" or "weaker" theory of autonomy than that which was implicit in the argument advanced in *Allard*. It can be explicitly recognized, for example, that a "reasoned choice" by the client is an idealized norm, not a legal predicate for a valid decision (here, a valid guilty plea). Although the *lawyer* is expected to make a "reasoned choice" among alternatives, based on his or her specialized knowledge, and the client is *entitled* to exercise an independent prerogative, client deference to the attorney's judgment is the expected norm. Under this view, the law would require only that the client know and understand that the decision is his or hers to make, and that the lawyer make an effort to inform the client of the relevant considerations. However, since a reasoned choice among alternatives is *not* the legally prescribed norm for client decision making, an inability to do so does not constitute decisional incompetency. This was the position taken by the First Circuit Court of Appeals in *Allard:*

> We must accept the obvious fact that different defendants will have different abilities (as will their counsel) in making all legal decisions, including the decision whether or not to plead guilty as opposed to going to trial. Most will have no choice but to rely heavily on the advice of their counsel in evaluating all the factors affecting their chances of success at trial.[63]

A second possibility is to adopt a more demanding theory of autonomy, one that envisions a more active client role in decision making. Under this view, which has been endorsed by many analysts and a minority of courts, a guilty plea is not valid if the defendant lacks the capacity to make a "reasoned choice." As suggested earlier here, this position implicitly rests on a set of expectations regarding client autonomy in the attorney-client relationship that is somewhat heroic when compared with actual practice. Nevertheless, a serious practical objection to this approach—under which "incompetent assents" to negotiated guilty pleas would be invalid—is that it bars only one of the decisional options. The other option, going to trial, remains legally available—assuming, of course, that the defendant is able to understand the proceedings and assist counsel in that context. As a result, those defendants who are competent to be tried, but who are (unrestorably) incompetent to plead guilty, are denied the possible advantages of plea bargaining.[64]

The analogy to medical treatment suggests a possible solution to the problem—reliance on surrogate decision making. The idea of using a surrogate decision maker for "decisionally incompetent" criminal defendants may appear farfetched at first glance. Indeed, in *Commonwealth v. Delverde*,[65] the Supreme Judicial Court of Massachusetts emphatically rejected the defense attorney's effort to utilize a surrogate decision maker to enter a guilty plea on behalf of a defendant with mental retardation. It is important to recognize, however, that Delverde was also incompetent to stand trial, and that *any* conviction in the case, by plea or otherwise, would have violated the constitutional prohibition against convicting defendants who lack "baseline" competency to proceed.[66] In contrast, when the standard for decisional competency is *elevated* in a specific context, and a defendant *is* sufficiently competent to be tried, some form of surrogate decision making might be a plausible response to a difficult problem. In other words, if neither dignitarian nor reliability concerns arise, and the only basis for decisional incompetency is an inability to make sufficiently "autonomous" decisions, surrogate decision making would not contradict the principles of fairness embodied in the due process clause. Nor is surrogate decision making altogether unprecedented in the criminal process. An increasing number of courts have held that a mentally ill defendant who is "competent to stand trial" may not be competent to decide whether or not to invoke the insanity defense.[67] These cases can sensibly be understood as permitting the attorney (or the judge) to serve as surrogate decision maker.[68]

Reliance on surrogate decision making to "solve" problems of decisional incompetency might be regarded as problematic when the defendant is refusing to do what the attorney believes to be in his or her best interests. When the "surrogate" overrides the defendant's objections in such a case—which is equivalent to the imposition of medical treatment over a patient's incompetent refusal—the subject's known preferences are ignored on the basis of the controversial assertion that they are not entitled to respect. However, in cases involving incompetent "assents," surrogate decision making provides a costless solution to the problem of decisional incompetency: it provides a device for vindicating the best interests of the subject when he or she may not be able to do so, and it also provides a mechanism for monitoring the judgment of attorneys and physicians, a task that "normal," self-interested clients or patients are expected to perform for themselves.

As these observations imply, the real issue in cases involving marginal decisional competency is not autonomy, but quality assurance. In cases involving defendants with mental retardation who are otherwise competent to assist counsel, some form of contemporaneous monitoring would be desirable to ensure that the attorney's judgments are in the client's best interests. At present, neither the court nor any formal surrogate decision maker is serving this function. As was suggested earlier, however, designated "representatives" might usefully be utilized in this context. They could serve in a formal surrogate role if the "test" for decisional competency is a demanding one, such as "capacity for reasoned choice," or in an adjunctive role if the "test" for competency is a less demanding one.

Summary   Capacity for "reasoned choice" is too demanding a test for decisional competency. It reflects a conception of autonomy that is at odds with a realistic understanding of the attorney-client relationship in criminal defense. A less demanding test of "understanding," similar to the one formulated in *Allard v. Helgemoe,* is sufficient. However, this is not to say that the test for competency to plead guilty is the "same" as the test for competency to proceed (or to stand trial), or that a finding of competency to proceed obviates the need for assessing competency to plead guilty, as many courts seem to have assumed.

The competency of a defendant with mental retardation to plead guilty requires careful assessment to ensure that the admissions embedded in the plea are reliable *and* that the defendant understands the nature and consequences of the plea. Routine attorney-client interactions and routine plea colloquies will not do the job. Adjunctive involvement by family members or advocacy services can ameliorate the difficulties in communication between attorney and client, and, if plea decisions are to be made, they can provide an independent assessment of the attorney's recommendation.[69]

CONCLUSIONS

This chapter has focused on one central theme, that the critical normative issue raised by current practice is whether defendants with mental retardation are receiving adequate legal representation. As a practical matter, the procedures for assessing and judging the competency of defendants with mental retardation must be designed and administered to enhance the competency of *counsel.*

The low rate of referral for pretrial forensic evaluation suggests that some defendants with mental retardation who "should" be found incompetent are now being convicted. But the more significant problem is that lawyers are probably providing inadequate representation for the much larger number of marginally competent defendants whose disabilities can be counteracted by skillful interviewing and counseling. This problem can be ameliorated by providing thorough forensic assessment and consultative assistance by appropriately trained clinicians—in any case involving a defendant with significantly subaverage intellectual abilities—and by appointing trained representatives to assist persons with mental retardation.

When viewed from this perspective, the controversy regarding the correct "test" for competency to plead guilty comes into clearer focus. To the extent that guilty pleas by defendants with mental retardation raise concerns about the reliability of the admissions embedded in the pleas, these concerns can be ameliorated by ensuring that counsel is able to make an informed judgment about the reliability of the defendant's acknowledgments of guilt and by guaranteeing that courts carefully scrutinize the factual foundation for these pleas. Judicial sparring over the correct "test" for competency to plead guilty tends to obscure the real problem.

Guilty pleas by defendants with mental retardation (or other decisions regarding the defense or disposition of the case) may also be regarded as problematic, owing to doubts about the defendants' capacity for "autonomous" decisions. Put simply, the issue is: How should the law deal with decision making by marginally competent defendants who assent to the advice of their attorneys even though they are unable to understand all of the relevant considerations? The way in which this issue is resolved depends on what steps are thought necessary to ensure that the decisions made are in the defendants' best interests. A "default" rule against guilty pleas (or against waiver of other constitutional rights) would often *not* be in these defendants' best interests; this is why a demanding standard of decisional competency is undesirable, at least in the absence of a procedure for surrogate decision making. However, uncritical acceptance of simple "assent" in these circumstances would also be undesirable in light of the significant danger of ill-considered legal advice. Some form of adjunctive participation by designated representatives for defendants with mental retardation, together with careful judicial monitoring of these decisions, would help to provide necessary incentives for improved legal representation.

NOTES

1. Although criminal defendants are constitutionally entitled to waive their right to counsel and to represent themselves (Faretta v. California, 422 U.S. 806 [1975]), this issue is not of practical significance in cases involving defendants with mental retardation.
2. Drope v. Missouri, 420 U.S. 162, 171 (1975).
3. American Bar Association, (1986), *Criminal Justice Mental Health Standards* (Std. 7-4.2[c] and commentary), G. Bennett, reporter (Washington, DC: Author).
4. Drope v. Missouri, 420 U.S. 162 (1974); Pate v. Robinson, 383 U.S. 375 (1966).
5. Pate v. Robinson, 385 U.S. 375, 378 (1966), noting and apparently endorsing the government's stipulation "that the conviction of an accused person [who] is legally incompetent violates due process. . . ." Incompetency does not bar "innocent only" adjudications. Whether it bars factual determinations that establish the necessary predicate for restrictive civil commitment statutes is a controversial issue. See American Bar Association, *Criminal Justice Mental Health Standards* (Std. 7-4.13 and commentary).
6. Jackson v. Indiana, 406 U.S. 715 (1972).

7. See, generally, I. Keilitz, B.A. Monahan, S.L. Keilitz, & C. Dillon, (1987, April 30), *Criminal defendants with trial disabilities: The theory and practice of competency assistance*, Grant No. G008535166, Unpublished manuscript, Institute on Mental Disability and the Law, National Center for State Courts, Williamsburg, VA.

8. See, for example, J.W. Ellis & R.A. Luckasson (1985), Mentally retarded criminal defendants, *George Washington Law Review 53*(3–4), 414–493; I. Mickenberg (1981), Competency to stand trial and the mentally retarded defendant: The need for a multi-disciplinary solution to a multi-disciplinary problem, *California Western Law Review, 17*, 365–402; J.B. Person, (1972), The accused retardate, *Columbia Human Rights Law Review, 4*, 239–266.

9. Ellis & Luckasson, Mentally retarded criminal defendants, p. 458.

10. As noted elsewhere in the text, forensic clinicians who are not trained to assess mental retardation probably fail to recognize the magnitude of the disability even in cases referred for evaluation.

11. B.S. Brown & T.F. Courtless, (1968), The mentally retarded in penal and correctional institutions, *American Journal of Psychiatry, 124*, 1164–1170; R.C. Allen, (1968), The retarded offender: Unrecognized in court and untreated in prison, *Federal Probation, 32*, 22–27.

12. The most comprehensive data are those compiled by the University of Virginia Institute of Law, Psychiatry and Public Policy, which encompass a substantial proportion of forensic evaluations conducted in Virginia from July 1985 through June 1989. The proportion of defendants diagnosed as retarded was 4.7% (see Petrella, chapter 6, this volume). This proportion was 5.9% in J. Reich & J. Wells, (1985), Psychiatric diagnosis and competency to stand trial, *Comprehensive Psychiatry, 26*, 421–431; the proportion was 7.3% in J. Petrila, J. Selle, P. Rouse, C. Evans, & D. Moore, (1981), The pretrial examination process in Missouri: A descriptive study, *Bulletin of the American Academy of Psychiatry and the Law, 9*, 61–84; and the proportion was 2.5% in M. Heller, W. Traylor, S. Erhich, & D. Lester, Intelligence, psychosis and competency to stand trial, *Bulletin of the American Academy of Psychiatry and the Law, 9*, 267–275.

13. Brown & Courtless, Mentally retarded in penal and correctional institutions.

14. It is instructive in this connection. to note the clinical opinions reached by forensic evaluators in those cases that have been referred for evaluation. In the two most comprehensive studies, about one-third of the defendants with mental retardation were found incompetent. See, for example, Petrila et al., Pretrial examination process in Missouri; and Petrella, chapter 4, this volume. Petrella, R. *Supra* note 12.

15. American Bar Association, *Criminal Justice Mental Health Standards* (commentary to Std. 7-4.1), p. 175.

16. See, for example, P. Lipsett, D. Lelos, & A. McGarry, (1977), Competency for trial: A screening instrument, *American Journal of Psychiatry, 128*, 105–109; A. Robey, (1965), Criteria for competency to stand trial: A checklist for psychiatrists, *American Journal of Psychiatry, 122*, 616–621. See, generally, T. Grisso, (1986), *Evaluating competencies: Forensic assessments and instruments* (New York: Plenum). R.A. Luckasson and C. Everington have developed a specialized instrument for defendants with mental retardation, the "Competence Assessment for Standing Trial for Defendants with Mental Retardation" ("CAST-MR"). See C. Everington (1990), The competence assessment for standing trial for defendants with mental retardation (CST-MR): A validation study, *Criminal Justice and Behavior, 17*, 147–168. This instrument is available from the authors.

17. For earlier critical studies, see, for example, N.G. Polythress, & H.V. Stack, (1980), Competency to stand trial: A historical review and some new data, *Journal of Psychiatry and Law, 8,* 131–146; C.R. Vann, & F. Morganroth, (1964), Psychiatrists and competence to stand trial, *University of Detroit Law Review, 42,* 75–85.

18. See, for example, United States v. Masthers, 539 F.2d 721 (D.C. Cir. 1976); Seiling v. Eyman, 478 F.2d 211 (9th Cir. 1973).

19. See, for example, B.A. Weiner, (1985), Mental disability and the criminal law, in S.J. Brakel, J. Parry, & B.A. Weiner, (Eds.), *The mentally disabled and the law* (3rd ed.), (pp. 693, 696–697) (Chicago: American Bar Foundation); G. Melton, J. Petrila, N. Polythress, & C. Slobogin, (1987), *Psychological evaluations for the courts: A handbook for mental health professionals and lawyers* (New York: Guilford).

20. See American Bar Association, *Criminal Justice Mental Health Standards* (Std. 7-5.1 and commentary at 266). (Std. 7-5.1 "embodies the Association's judgment that a special norm ought to govern plea proceedings.")

21. See, for example, Curry v. Estelle, 531 F.2d 766 (5th Cir. 1976); Suggs v. LaVallee, 570 F.2d 1092 (2d Cir.), *cert. denied,* 439 U.S. 915 (1978).

22. Drope v. Missouri, 420 U.S. 162, 172 (1974).

23. Everyone agrees that "competency to stand trial" is a misnomer because 90% of criminal cases are not actually tried. R. Roesch and S.L. Golding have suggested "competency for adjudication."

24. Group for Advancement of Psychiatry, (1974, February), *Misuse of psychiatry in the criminal courts: Competency to stand trial,* (Vol. 8, Rep. 89) (pp. 896–897), (New York: Author).

25. A.L. McGurry, (Principal Investigator), (1974), *Competency to stand trial and mental illness,* (Proj. No. 7R01-MH-18112-01) (New York: Harvard Medical School, Laboratory of Community Psychiatry).

26. S.L. Golding, R. Roesch, & J. Schreiber, (1984), Assessment and conceptualization of competency to stand trial: Preliminary data on the interdisciplinary fitness interview, *Law and Human Behavior, 8,* 321–34.

27. American Bar Association, *Criminal Justice Mental Health Standards* (Commentary to Std. 7-4.1, p. 174).

28. Mickenberg, Competency to stand trial, p. 385.

29. See, for example, Treece v. State, 313 Md. 665, 547 A.2d 1054 (1988); Frendak v. United States, 408 A.2d 365 (D.C. 1979).

30. See, for example, Fisher v. State, 739 P.2d 523, 525 (Okla. Crim. Appl. 1987); Commonwealth v. Crawley, 514 P.2d 539, 550 n.1, 526 A.2d 334, 340 n.1 (1987).

31. McCarlo v. State, 677 P.2d 1268 (Ct. App. Alaska 1984).

32. Id. at 1270.

33. Id.

34. Id. at 1273.

35. Id. at 1272, n.3.

36. Id. at 1273–74.

37. Id. at 1273, n.1.

38. Because this construct is meant to refer to a baseline of competence, a defendant who is incompetent to proceed is also not competent to make whatever decisions might be required in defense of the case, however low the "standard" of decisional competency is set in any given context.

39. This is, of course, a restatement of the "test" articulated in Dusky v. United States, 362 U.S. 402 (1960). In addition, the concept probably encompasses a "motiva-

tional" component pertaining to capacity to cooperate with one's attorney, thereby enabling the attorney to perform his or her assigned role in the process (cf. State v. Johnson, 133 Wisc. 2d 212, 395 N.W.2d 179 [1986]). The puzzle in these cases is that of differentiating between "can't" and "won't," a problem not apt to arise in cases involving defendants with mental retardation in the absence of a "dual diagnosis" of mental illness.

40. This construct also has a chronological dimension, which helps to explain how it ordinarily becomes operationalized. In most cases involving defendants with mental illness, questions about "competency to proceed" arise at the outset of the process, before significant interactions with counsel have occurred and before strategic decisions regarding defense of the case have been encountered or considered.

41. "Trial proceedings" is meant to include the sentencing phase of the trial in capital cases, and any other proceedings involving an evidentiary hearing.

42. A focus on the trial emphasizes the dynamic and sequential dimensions of competency assessment. A defendant who was regarded as sufficiently competent during earlier stages of the process (or who was restored to competency) may deteriorate under the stresses of a trial. In those cases where the defendant's testimony is necessary for a fair adjudication, capacity to testify on one's own behalf is a component of competency to proceed to trial. A defendant with mental disability who was able to communicate coherently with counsel may be unable to do so in the context of a trial.

43. Cases have arisen, for example, in which defendants convicted of capital crimes have sought to preclude their attorneys from introducing mitigating evidence or arguing for leniency at the sentencing phase of their trials; in states where appellate courts have held that the attorney is obligated to adhere to the defendant's wishes, the courts have also directed trial judges to make contemporaneous assessments of the defendants' competency. This author discussed this problem in 1988 in The dignity of the condemned, *Virginia Law Review, 74,* 1363–1391.

44. See, for example, McCarlo v. State, 677 P.2d 1268 (1984).

45. See, for example, Sweezy v. Garrison, 554 F.Supp. 481 (1982). Some decisions may also be required as part of the sentencing process itself, such as the exercise (or waiver) of the right of allocution. See, for example, Wotjowicz v. United States, 550 F.2d 186 (2d Cir. 1977).

46. Data compiled by the University of Virginia Institute of Law, Psychiatry, and Public Policy (July 1985–June 1989) show that 8.2% (38 of 312) of those found incompetent had mental retardation; R. Roesch & S.L. Golding, (1980), in *Competency to stand trial* (Urbana-Champaign: University of Illinois Press), found that 18% (23 of 130) of those found incompetent had mental retardation (p. 149); and J. Petrila et al., in Pretrial examination process in Missouri, reported that around 10% (6 of 59) of those found incompetent had mental retardation.

47. See, generally, D.B. Dove, (1983), Competency to stand trial of criminal defendant diagnosed as 'mentally retarded'—modern cases, *American Law Reports* (4th ed.), *23,* 493–551.

48. State v. Benton, 759 S.W.2d 427 (Tenn. Cr. App. 1988).

49. According to the appellate court in State v. Benton:

> The record reveals that the defendant intellectualizes as a child five to seven years old does. Efforts to educate him were abandoned after he attended his first (and only) day of school. Consequently, he is unable to read or write and reached age nine or ten before beginning to talk. . . . The defendant . . . has always lived at home with his parents who treat him as a child. Almost everything he

does requires adult supervision. . . . He is never allowed to go anywhere alone because he passes out almost every time he is in a crowd of people. He is unable to run a simple "go get" type of errand; that is he "doesn't understand what you tell him and forgets before he gets to where he's going." (759 S.W.2d at 430–31)

50. State v. Rogers, 419 S.2d 840 (La. 1982).
51. Id. at 843.
52. State v. Rogers, 419 S.W.2d at 842.
53. Cf. Schulte v. State, 512 P.2d 907, 914 (Alaska 1973):

The defendant must have some minimum ability to provide his counsel with information necessary or relevant to his defense. . . . But this does not mean that a defendant must possess any high degree of legal sophistication or intellectual prowess. In determining competency, the standard of judgment must be a relative one. . . .

54. See generally P. Applebaum & T. Grisso, (1988), Assessing patients' capacities to consent to treatment, *New England Journal of Medicine, 319,* 1635–1638.
55. Ellis, J. (1989, September). Competence to confess and be a witness. In *Offenders with Mental Retardation and the Criminal Justice System.* Symposium conducted by the President's Committee on Mental Retardation, Bethesda, MD.
56. Gaddy v. Linahan, 780 F.2d 935 (11th Cir. 1986).
57. Gaddy v. Linahan, 780 F.2d at 945–46.
58. I am putting to one side the concern with undermining the finality of adjudications based on guilty pleas that has led the Supreme Court to state that it "'may be appropriate to presume that in most cases defense counsel routinely explain the nature of the offense in sufficient detail to give the accused notice of what he is being asked to admit'" (Marshall v. Lonberger, 459 U.S. 422, 436 [1983], quoting Henderson v. Morgan, 426 U.S. 637, 647 [1983]). For present purposes, the important point is that attorneys often fail to do so if the defendant's intelligence is limited, as the Supreme Court noted in *Henderson,* 426 U.S. at 647.
59. Allard v. Helgemoe, 572 F.2d 1, 6 (1st Cir. 1978).
60. Allard v. Helgemoe, 572 F.2d 1 (1st Cir. 1978).
61. The district court's finding on this issue was as follows:

The petitioner may have understood the intent requirement of burglary at some time for a brief period, but he did not carry that understanding with him to his plea hearing nor was he ever able to thoroughly comprehend the importance of the element of the crime. . . . It is unlikely that he will ever be able to comprehend the element of intent required, and the other elements of burglary as they distinguish it from the crime of breaking and entering, and retain that comprehension for any length of time. (Allard v. Helgemoe, 572 F.2d 2, n.1)

62. For an example of a case in which the defendant was found competent to stand trial (for rape) but not competent to plead guilty because "he did not have a sufficient understanding of the rights he would give up by entering a guilty plea," see McCarlo v. State, 677 P.2d 1268, 1270 (Ct. App. Alaska 1984). *McCarlo* demonstrates that the gap between competency to proceed and decisional competency (to plead guilty) can arise even in jurisdictions that have rejected the *Sieling* "reasoned choice" formula (see 677 P.2d at 1272, n.2).
63. Allard v. Helgemoe, 572 F.2d at 6.
64. Although it has been suggested that defendants found incompetent to plead should be able to "enforce" any plea agreement previously arranged, or should be entitled

to whatever sentencing leniency would otherwise have been accorded, these solutions are not feasible.

65. Commonwealth v. Delverde, 496 N.E.2d 1357 (Mass. 1986).

66. The opinion does not elaborate on Delverde's capacities, so it is not possible to ascertain the respects in which he was incompetent.

67. See, for example, Treece v. State, 313 Md. 665, 547 A.2d 1054 (1988); Frendak v. United States, 408 A.2d 364 (D.C. 1979).

68. A "pure" version of surrogate decision making would involve appointment of a "guardian" to make the decision on the defendant's behalf. This solution is preferable to allowing the judge or the defendant's attorney to make the decision. A law-trained guardian would be preferable to the judge because the surrogate should stand in the defendant's shoes (whether the perspective is substituted judgment or "best interests"), something the judge is in no position to do. A law-trained guardian would also be preferable to the defense attorney because he or she could monitor the attorney's reasoning in a way similar to that of a "competent" defendant.

69. This same analysis is applicable to all other contexts in which decisions regarding the defense of the case are allocated, by law, to the defendant rather than the attorney. As a practical matter most decisions (other than those regarding the plea) concern issues that arise at trial such as whether to be tried by a jury and whether or not to testify.

Chapter 6

MENTAL RETARDATION AND CRIMINAL RESPONSIBILITY

W. LAWRENCE FITCH

To OBTAIN THE fullest possible understanding of mental retardation and criminal responsibility, one should bring to the topic an understanding of the historical development of "mental abnormality" as a criminal defense.

MENTAL ABNORMALITY AS A CRIMINAL DEFENSE: A HISTORICAL PERSPECTIVE

Early in Anglo-American law it was established that "idiots" and "lunatics" were exempt from criminal liability. W. Blackstone wrote:

> The second case of a deficiency in will, which excuses from the guilt of crimes, arises also from a defective or vitiated understanding, *viz.* in an "idiot" or a "lunatic" . . . . In criminal cases therefore "idiots" and "lunatics" are not chargeable for their own acts, if committed when under these incapacities: no, not even for treason itself.[1]

Persons regarded as "idiots" and "lunatics" in Blackstone's day suffered from the more serious forms of disorders we currently know as mental retardation ("idiocy") and mental illness ("lunacy"). The level of disability contemplated by "idiocy" was particularly great, arguably "corresponding to what is called 'profound' or 'severe' retardation today."[2] Writing in 1524, Fitzherbert described such a person as one:

> who cannot account or number twenty-pence, nor can tell who is his Father, or Mother, nor how old he is, &c, so as it may appear that he hath no understanding of Reason what shall be for his Profit or what for his Loss.[3]

The idea was that no one so disabled could exercise sufficient free will to be regarded as morally accountable.

121

By the early 17th century, many English courts had begun to assess the criminal responsibility of persons with mental disability in terms of their capacity to distinguish right from wrong. "[I]f one that is 'non compos mentis,' or an ideot, kill a man, this is no felony, for they have not knowledge of Good and Evil. . . ."[4] In time, the courts moved away from the view that the accused's mental disability must have been so great as to preclude *any* understanding of right and wrong, and toward a more case-specific view, focusing on the defendant's knowledge of the wrongfulness of the particular offense charged. In 1843, the English House of Lords endorsed this view in its pronouncement of the so-called M'Naghten test of "insanity":

> It must be clearly proved that, at the time of committing the act, the party accused was laboring under such a defect of reason, from disease of the mind, as to not know the nature and quality of the act he was doing, or if he did know it, that he did not know he was doing what was wrong.[5]

For more than 100 years, the "right-wrong" test set forth in M'Naghten has governed determinations of insanity in England. The test has had a significant impact on the development of insanity laws in the United States as well. Some form of the right-wrong test appears in the laws of all but two of the states that currently recognize a defense of nonresponsibility due to mental disability.[6] The right-wrong test, however, is not the only nonresponsibility test the law has recognized. Indeed, even before M'Naghten, the right-wrong test had its critics. Sir Isaac Ray, a noted Connecticut psychiatrist, objected to the test's narrow cognitive focus, arguing that its failure to take into account the accused's ability to control his or her behavior was morally indefensible.[7] In response to this criticism, the "irresistible impulse" test was devised, allowing for the exculpation of persons with mental disability who, although cognitively intact, "had lost the power . . . to avoid doing the act in question."[8] Various irresistible impulse formulations have appeared in the law; most have required extreme volitional (control) dysfunction. Virginia's law is typical, calling for "total deprivation of the mental power to control or restrain the act."[9] In jurisdictions that have adopted the irresistible impulse test, some cognitive test also is available, so that a defendant might win acquittal by reason of insanity on either volitional or cognitive grounds.

Although recognition of a volitional prong to the insanity defense significantly broadened the basis for mental nonresponsibility, the law remained controversial. Many physicians believed that the "mind function[ed] as an integrated whole and that it [was] impossible to isolate the separate functions of cognition and control."[10] In deference to this view, the British Royal Commission on Capital Punishment in 1953 proposed (as one of two alternate reforms of English nonresponsibility law) "to abrogate the [M'Naghten] Rules and to leave the jury to determine whether at the time of the act the accused was suffering from a disease of the mind (or mental deficiency) to such degree that he ought not to be held responsible."[11] Although the recommendations of the Royal Commission fell on deaf ears in England, they were warmly received by David L. Bazelon, judge of the U.S. Court of Appeals for the District of Columbia and a leading figure in the movement to reform mental health law in the United States in the 1950s and 1960s.[12] In *Durham v. U.S.*, Judge David L. Bazelon ruled that "an accused is not criminally responsible if his unlawful act was the product of mental disease or defect."[13]

Judge Bazelon's "product" test of responsibility, although binding only on District of Columbia courts,[14] generated significant excitement among scholars in mental health law throughout the country. In practice, however, his test proved disastrous. Without clear direction as to which mental disorders qualified as mental diseases or defects, psychiatric experts were free to decide for themselves who was so afflicted. In 1957, the psychiatric staff of St. Elizabeth's Hospital (the facility that provided experts for the District of Columbia criminal courts) voted to recognize "sociopathic personality disturbance"[15] as a mental disease or defect for the purposes of the insanity defense.[16] The result was a dramatic increase in the rate of acquittal by reason of insanity in the District.[17] In 1962, the D.C. Court of Appeals reined in the psychiatrists, ruling that only those disorders that "substantially affect[ed] mental or emotional processes and substantially impair[ed] behavior controls" could provide the basis for the defense of insanity.[18] "Definitional problems persisted,"[19] however, and in 1972, the court abandoned the "product" test altogether in favor of a test proposed some years earlier by the American Law Institute (ALI) for inclusion in its Model Penal Code and already adopted in many states.

The American Law Institute (ALI) test was devised in response to charges that the tests prevailing at that time—the M'Naghten test and the irresistible impulse test—were overly rigid and clinically unrealistic, requiring virtually complete cognitive or volitional incapacity. Rather than take the *Durham,* or "product," approach and leave to the trier of fact virtually unfettered discretion as to the conditions of nonresponsibility, the ALI chose to retain the cognitive-volitional inquiry but to express it in terms that recognized as potentially exculpating a broader range of mental impairment:

> A person is not responsible for criminal conduct if at the time of such conduct as a result of mental disease or defect he lacks substantial capacity either to appreciate the criminality (wrongfulness) of his conduct or to conform his conduct to the requirements of the law.[20]

The ALI test, although not without its critics,[21] has enjoyed immense popularity in the United States, and currently is used in more than half the states.[22]

RECENT INSANITY DEFENSE REFORMS: THE ABA/APA POSITIONS AND GUILTY BUT MENTALLY ILL

After the acquittal by reason of insanity of John Hinckley in 1982 (for the shooting of President Ronald Reagan a year earlier), calls for the reform of the insanity defense were heard throughout the country. Within a matter of months, both the American Bar Association (ABA)[23] and the American Psychiatric Association (APA)[24] had issued position statements on the defense. Considering the traditionally disparate views held by these two organizations, their recommendations on this issue are remarkably similar.[25] Both forcefully oppose abolition of the insanity defense, calling instead for modification. Both would eliminate the volitional, or control, prong of the defense but retain a cognitive prong employing the "appreciation of wrongfulness" language of the ALI test. Finally, both would expressly recognize mental retardation as an applicable threshold condition.[26]

The ABA Test

(a) A person is not responsible for criminal conduct if, at the time of such conduct, and as a result of mental disease or defect, that person was unable to appreciate the wrongfulness of such conduct.
(b) When used as a legal term in this standard *mental disease or defect* refers to:
   (i) impairments of mind, whether enduring or transitory; or,
   (ii) mental retardation, either of which substantially affected the mental or emotional processes of the defendant at the time of the alleged offense.

The APA Test

A person charged with a criminal offense should be found not guilty by reason of insanity if it is shown that as a result of mental disease or mental retardation he was unable to appreciate the wrongfulness of his conduct at the time of the offense.

As used in this standard, the terms mental disease or mental retardation include only those severely abnormal mental conditions that grossly and demonstrably impair a person's perception or understanding of reality and that are not attributable primarily to the voluntary ingestion of alcohol or other psychoactive substances.

The most notable feature of the ABA and APA proposals, of course, is their repudiation of the irresistible impulse defense. The ABA's rationale for eliminating this defense is two-fold:

first that the "appreciation of wrongfulness" formula is sufficiently broad to take into account the morally significant effects of severe mental disorder; and second, that any independent volitional inquiry involves a significant risk of "moral mistakes" in the adjudication of criminal responsibility.[27]

Addressing this second concern—that volitional impairment defies reliable assessment—the APA observed: "The line between an irresistible impulse and an impulse not resisted is probably no sharper than that between twilight and dusk."[28]

The organizations' selection of a cognitive test that speaks in terms of "appreciation" rather than "knowledge" of wrongfulness is significant. As commentary to the ABA Standards observes:

> The focus of the inquiry into criminal responsibility should not be limited, as the term "know" [as in *knowledge* of wrongfulness] might suggest, to a defendant's superficial intellectual awareness of the law or prevailing social morality. Instead, the non-responsibility test should take into account all aspects of the defendant's mental and emotional functioning relating to an ability to recognize and understand significance of personal actions. The language of the standard allows a proper latitude for experts to testify fully concerning the defendant's mental and emotional condition and for juries to consider this testimony in deliberating on the issue of mental non-responsibility.[29]

Assuming (and it seems a fair assumption) that volitional impairment in the degree necessary to satisfy the requirements of an irresistible impulse defense is unlikely to exist in the absence of some significant degree of cognitive impairment, a good argument can be made that the ABA/APA formulations of cognitive insanity should obviate the need for any independent volitional test.[30]

Another recent development in the evolution of nonresponsibility jurisprudence is the advent of laws permitting the verdict of guilty but mentally ill (GBMI). Twelve states currently have such laws.[31] Although in at least two of these states, Georgia[32] and Indiana,[33] it is clear that persons with mental retardation may be found GBMI (guilty but mentally retarded [GBMR] in Georgia), in other states it is not so clear.[34] To the extent that these laws are intended to provide an alternative to the verdict of not guilty by reason of insanity, however, it is likely they would be interpreted to apply to anyone who might raise an insanity defense, including persons with mental retardation.

That GBMI laws apply to persons with mental retardation should not be cause for celebration, however. Indeed, the independent verdict of GBMI has been roundly criticized.[35] To begin with, critics point out, the verdict carries no real benefit for the defendant: he or she is convicted of the offense charged and the court imposes whatever sentence is prescribed by law; the only variation from ordinary sentencing is that the defendant is specifically considered a candidate for treatment or habilitation while serving his or her sentence. But of course, any prison inmate with a mental disability is a candidate for treatment or habilitation.[36] Indeed, as the Illinois Court of Appeals has ruled, the right to such services following a GBMI verdict is no stronger than the constitutional right to medical care accorded all prisoners.[37] There is emerging evidence, moreover, that very few defendants found GBMI ever receive treatment. Of the 45 defendants found GBMI in Illinois in the first 13 months after Illinois's GBMI law took effect, all were committed directly to the

Department of Corrections. None was hospitalized.[38] Thus, to view these laws as protreatment may be folly. What, then, is their purpose? As the governor of Illinois openly admitted when introducing that state's GBMI legislation, the real purpose of these laws is to "'protect the public from violence inflicted by persons with mental ailments who slipped through the cracks in the criminal justice system.'"[39] In other words, these laws exist to distract the trier of fact (the judge or jury) in an insanity trial from the moral question of criminal responsibility and, thus, permit the conviction of morally blameless persons on a misplaced trust that treatment will be provided. As Richard J. Bonnie has astutely observed, this is a "moral sleight-of-hand which simply will not do."[40]

MENS REA

Apart from concerns about legal insanity, the law traditionally has required for conviction of a crime proof that the defendant had some culpable state of mind—mens rea—at the time of the offensive act. "Cases of strict liability aside, all crimes include a mental element, a *mens rea,* that the prosecution must prove."[41]

In a general sense, mens rea may be viewed as intent. Many different kinds of mens rea are recognized in the law, however, and not all comport with standard notions of intent. Some mens rea (e.g., negligence) are objective in nature; others (e.g., premeditation) are subjective. Objective mens rea make reference to what the ordinary, reasonable person would have believed under the circumstances surrounding an act. To satisfy the requirements of objective mens rea, it is not necessary that the defendant, in fact, have held a particular belief or intended a particular consequence at the time he or she acted—only that the ordinary, "reasonable," person would have under the same circumstances. Accordingly, evidence concerning a defendant's subjective beliefs or intent at the time of an offense would be irrelevant and, therefore, inadmissible. For example, if the ordinary person would recognize that starting a barbecue with gasoline entails a substantial risk of explosion, then, in the prosecution of someone for another's death resulting from such an explosion, the accused's actual failure to be aware of this risk may provide no defense to a charge of manslaughter, an offense that typically carries the objectively defined mens rea of negligence.

To establish subjective mens rea, on the other hand, the prosecution must prove that the defendant in fact held a particular belief or intended a particular consequence at the time he or she acted. Logically, it would seem, any evidence relevant to the question whether, in fact, the defendant had the requisite belief or intent would be admissible. In many states, this "rule of logical relevance" permits the introduction of evidence concerning the defendant's mental state at the time of the offense as it bears on the question of subjective mens, rea. For example, if a defendant in such a state were charged with burglary—an offense requiring proof that the defendant broke into a dwelling house with the *specific intent* to commit a felony in the house— evidence that the defendant, because of mental retardation, entered the house impulsively, without any thought about what he or she would do upon entry, presumably would be admissible to negate the requisite mens rea. The defendant might be guilty of breaking and entering, an offense typically seen as having no specific subjective mens rea, but not burglary.

The ALI Model Penal Code would permit the introduction of any logically relevant evidence to address questions of subjective mens rea,[42] as would the ABA Criminal Justice Mental Health Standards.[43] Among the approximately 27 states in accord are Idaho, Montana, and Utah, the 3 states that have abolished the insanity defense. Sixteen states have specifically rejected the admissibility of evidence concerning a defendant's mental condition on questions of mens rea. Several states have not ruled on the issue.[44]

Although it seems clear that the courts should permit the introduction of evidence of the defendant's mental condition if that evidence is logically relevant to some subjective mental state that constitutes an element of the crime charged, the rule permitting the introduction of such evidence should not be allowed to substitute for the defense of insanity, as some have proposed[45] and as the legislatures of Idaho, Montana, and Utah have declared. Indeed, in many of the most morally compelling insanity cases, the presence of mens rea is undeniable (e.g., the defendant who kills under the delusion that he or she is acting in self-defense). Is it morally correct that a person with mental disability suffer conviction and punishment for a clearly intentional act committed under the misapprehension that the act was necessary and justified?[46]

INFANCY

One final legal doctrine that must be considered in any discussion of the relevance of mental retardation to criminal responsibility is the defense of infancy. At common law, before the advent of the juvenile court, children below the age of 7 were conclusively presumed not to be criminally responsible for their misdeeds, either because they were incapable of forming mens rea or because they had insufficient capacity to distinguish right from wrong. Children between the ages of 7 and 14 were presumed not to be responsible, but that presumption was rebuttable.[47]

Many of the early English insanity cases referred to the mental infancy of adult "idiots" as a basis for their nonresponsibility for crime. In 1778, Sir Matthew Hale declared that the "best measure" of responsibility was whether the accused had "as great understanding as ordinarily a child of fourteen hath."[48] Relying on Hale's declaration, a Connecticut court in 1873 instructed a jury in a criminal case as follows: "Inasmuch as children under fourteen years of age are prima facie incapable of crime, imbeciles ought not to be held responsible criminally unless of capacity equal to that of ordinary children of that age."[49] This instruction may be unique in American law, however. Indeed, as Ellis and Luckasson have observed, even with the development of intelligence tests designed to assess "mental age" with greater objectivity, the courts in the last century consistently have rejected defense claims that the laws protecting children should be extended to adult defendants with low mental ages.[50] "The presumption of the lack of power of thought and capacity in favor of a child is due more to the number of years he has lived than to the character of the development of his mind . . . . Deficiency of intellect is a species of insanity. . . . "[51]

Nonetheless, inasmuch as many persons with mental retardation, like children, may fail fully to appreciate the significance of their behavior, the notion of establishing for them a system of justice modeled on the juvenile court system—a system concerned with the best interests of subjects rather than their punishment—has appeal. In the final analysis, however, such a notion probably is not desirable, for three reasons: first, many persons with mild or moderate mental retardation *do* have sufficient capacity to form mens rea and to distinguish right from wrong and, thus, may be deserving of at least some degree of blame and punishment; second, there may be therapeutic value in requiring some persons with mental retardation to face the ordinary consequences of their behavior; and, finally, to relegate persons with mental retardation, as a class, to the status of children would significantly set back the movement to normalize this population.

MENTAL RETARDATION AND CRIMINAL RESPONSIBILITY IN THE LATE 20TH CENTURY

Many observers in recent years have objected to laws treating persons with mental retardation in the same manner as mentally ill persons for the purpose of determining criminal responsibility. To begin with, virtually every advocate for persons with mental retardation objects to the label "insanity"—an archaic mental disease construct—as applied to their constituents. The ABA Criminal Justice Mental Health Standards' rejection of this label in favor of the more generic label "mental non-responsibility" is to be applauded.

More substantive criticism of the application of traditional insanity defense formulae to people with mental retardation centers on the fundamentally different effects of mental illness and mental retardation on a person's thinking and behavior. Burgess conceded that "moron offenders of the lower level appear to be 'intellectually' cognizant that their acts were morally and legally wrong"[52] and, thus, will not likely qualify for a strict, M'Naghten defense; but, she argued, their "social inefficiency"—their impaired capacity to lead an unsupervised life—nevertheless raises significant questions about their moral accountability for acts beyond their "capacity for self-direction."[53]

> It is thus in social judgement rather than intellectual cognition that morons are fatally defective from the legal point of view. Morons are less capable of inhibition than normal persons, and generally follow their impulses without restraint of judgement. They are easily led, and often are brought into crime by the virtue of submitting without question to the directions of others on the promise of a small reward.[54]

Although Burgess recognized some utility in the ALI's "volitional," or control, formulation, ultimately she concluded that defendants with mental retardation rarely are sufficiently impaired to qualify for complete exculpation. Rather, she contended, they should be seen as "partially responsible" and dealt with accordingly.

To some extent, Burgess's concerns are addressed by laws permitting evidence of mental abnormality to negate mens rea. As discussed earlier, defendants found to have lacked requisite mens rea for the offense charged typically are convicted of a less serious offense—one whose mens rea is less specific[55]—and thus qualify for a lighter sentence. Unfortunately, however, because of the strictures of the mens rea rule, defenses based on lack of mens rea rarely are successfully.[56]

Burgess's proposal would be accommodated nicely by the English doctrine of "diminished responsibility," under which degrees of culpability may have significance for the offense of conviction without reference to particular mens rea. Under English law, for example, a defendant charged with first degree murder (an offense carrying the mens rea of "premeditation") may be convicted of the lesser offense of manslaughter on a finding of diminished mental responsibility, notwithstanding evidence that the defendant in fact premeditated the killing. Such an outcome, however, is not currently possible under the law in any jurisdiction in the United States.[57] Moreover, given the trend in recent years toward very strict judicial interpretation of mens rea requirements,[58] it is not likely this will change. Diminished responsibility in this country may be a consideration at the sentencing stage of a criminal trial—at least in states that permit discretion in the selection of sentence[59]—but, unless the defendant's mental disability negates requisite mens rea, guilt or innocence on a given charge is unaffected.

J. Tupin and H. Goolishian focus on the learning difficulty of people with mental retardation, arguing that this deficit may prevent a person from

> acquiring the information necessary to provide a sound basis upon which to make judgments about right and wrong. This is not to say that he cannot learn right and wrong as fact; rather, he finds it difficult to generalize or form abstract concepts and to apply the information to specific situations.[60]

Like Burgess, Tupin and Goolishian have argued that M'Naghten's restrictive cognitive formula—requiring a total lack of knowledge of wrongfulness—is too difficult for many deserving defendants with mental retardation to meet. Although the defendant may have an "intellectual appreciation of the act and its consequences," he or she may "lack . . . appreciation for the subtleties of social interaction and abstract concepts of right and wrong that impair his behavior."[61] Unlike Burgess, however, Tupin and Goolishian believe that the American Law Institute's formulation of cognitive insanity provides meaningful protection for defendants with mental retardation: "These changes provide for recognition of the individual and his life predicament, considering the question of mental illness as fact rather than as a function of procedural rule."[62] Certainly, they open the door wider to defense arguments of impaired judgment and understanding. Relieved of the burden to show total lack of knowledge of wrongfulness, the defendant with mental retardation stands a significantly improved chance of relief under the ALI rule.

At least one study has concluded that neither the traditional tests for mental nonresponsibility nor the doctrine of partial responsibility provides adequate protection for defendants with mental retardation. Finding unacceptable the punishment of anyone with mental retardation whose offensive behavior was caused by his or her disability, a 1963 Task Force on Law, of the President's Panel on Mental Retardation, issued a report essentially calling for the establishment of a product test of responsibility for defendants with mental retardation, patterned on the *Durham* rule that prevailed in the District of Columbia at that time:

> Once it has been determined that an offender is mentally retarded to a degree and in a manner making it reasonable to believe his affliction caused the conduct in question, then we think it axiomatic that he should be treated according to his condition. For such persons, imprisonment for the sake of punishment is never appropriate.[63]

The task force specifically rejected the doctrine of partial responsibility, as proposed by Burgess, "because, in practice, it entails punishment for the mentally retarded, as for 'normal' offenders, albeit somewhat less severe."[64] One might ask, of course, whether this rationale does not also apply to persons with mental illness. If such a person would not have committed some offensive act "but for" his or her disability, is he or she any more culpable than a person with mental retardation under the same circumstances? Perhaps the product test should be extended to *all* defendants with mental disability. The *Durham* experience in the District of Columbia courts, however, suggests that this would be a mistake. Indeed, as a number of commentators have observed, judges and juries require more precise guidance than the product test provides as to the proper boundaries of criminal responsibility.[65]

Most proposed reforms for dealing with defendants with mental retardation of course have had as their goal greater access to the insanity defense.

One recent proposal, however, takes a different tack. The Model Developmentally Disabled Offenders Act, a project of the American Bar Association's Commission on the Mentally Disabled, would altogether deny defendants with mental retardation access to the insanity defense, however formulated, leaving these defendants to argue claims of "diminished capacity," or lack of mens rea.[66] The Model Act justifies its position on five grounds:

> First, it [diminished capacity] focuses on the legal issues most likely to be affected by the impairments related to developmental disabilities; [s]econd, it avoids many of the procedural complexities which accompany the insanity defense" [e.g. bifurcation of the trial]; [t]hird, [because diminished capacity often can be established without the use of experts,] the confusion often wrought in applying psychiatric and psychological theory to legal axioms, is substantially reduced; [f]ourth, rather than the all or nothing imperative of the insanity defense, diminished capacity recognizes that the degree to which a developmental disability affects the ability to form the state of mind required to commit a criminal offense varies from individual to individual, and therefore, that the degree of culpability should vary; [and, fifth,] it is anticipated that providing separate defenses for developmental disabilities and mental illnesses will help to increase awareness of the distinctions between these conditions . . . ."[67]

As discussed previously, however, it is a fallacy to believe that concerns for mens rea cover the moral waterfront. Far too many morally blameless defendants can be said to have formed the mens rea specified for the offense charged.[68] Moreover, it should not be necessary to exclude persons with mental retardation from consideration for an insanity defense to clear the way for a mens rea claim. Even without abolition of other nonresponsibility defenses, the mens rea argument should be available. Finally, any notion that the mens rea approach will permit a subtler grading of culpability in a significant percentage of cases is unrealistic. Successful mens rea challenges are simply too infrequent.[69] It seems highly likely that the authors of this act are operating under a false set of assumptions about the effect of the "diminished capacity" defense on determinations of responsibility in American courts. Indeed, it would appear that they have confused diminished capacity with the English doctrine of "diminished responsibility," which, as discussed earlier, has no bearing on determinations of guilt under American law.

In a recent essay, Karl A. Menninger, II, has taken issue with those critics who would establish special rules for determining the criminal responsibility of defendants with mental retardation. Although he recognizes that persons with mental retardation as a class have distinct and special needs, out of deference to the principles of normalization he would recognize differing standards of criminal nonresponsibility only if necessary to guarantee these persons an "equal opportunity to be justly excused from criminal responsibility."[70] With this in mind, Menninger has reviewed the requirements of M'Naghten, the irresistible impulse defense, and the ALI test, observing that the objections made on behalf of persons with mental retardation to these various formulations apply with equal force to persons with mental illness. He noted, for example, that, just as there are defendants with mental retardation who would fail a strict "knowledge" of wrongfulness test but perhaps pass an "appreciation" of wrongfulness test, there are mentally ill defendants in the same situation. As measures of culpability keyed to functional considerations, these tests do not unfairly discriminate, Menninger concluded. Accordingly he saw no need for a special test for defendants with mental retardation. Finally, he reviewed several court decisions that have flatly rejected attempts to establish a separate test, demonstrating the futility of the idea.

CONCLUSION

Norvill Morris once remarked that "rivers of ink, mountains of printer's lead, and forests of paper have been expended on an issue [the insanity defense] that is surely marginal to the chaotic problems of effective, rational, and humane prevention in treatment of crime."[71] It is true that the attention the insanity defense has received in the professional literature is significantly out of proportion to its effect on the administration of justice. Very few defendants raise the insanity defense, and, of those who do, only a fraction in fact are acquitted by reason of insanity.[72] Moreover, it appears that of those few who are successful in their claims of insanity, only a handful bear a primary diagnosis of mental retardation.[73] Nonetheless, if only for that handful, it is important that we fashion meaningful and fair standards. Taking into account the peculiar difficulties encountered by persons with mental retardation—clouded social judgment, impulsivity, and susceptibility to being led by others, but rarely a complete lack of knowledge of the significance of their behavior—a good argument can be made that a strict M'Naghten formulation provides inadequate protection against the conviction and punishment of morally blameless persons with mental retardation. Either the APA/ABA formulation, allowing for consideration of the defendant's impaired *appreciation* of wrongfulness, or the ALI formulation, encompassing not only appreciation of wrongfulness but also capacity to control behavior, is preferable.

As for other criminal responsibility issues, advocates for people with mental retardation, as suggested earlier here, should fiercely resist: 1) laws that restrict the admissibility of relevant mental state evidence on the question of mens rea, 2) laws that recognize the independent verdict of guilty but mentally ill (or guilty but mentally retarded), and 3) determinant sentencing laws that eliminate mental retardation as a factor in mitigation at sentencing.

It is critical to the fair administration of justice that criminal defendants with mental retardation be provided a meaningful opportunity to have evidence of their disability taken into account at trial and at sentencing on the question of their responsibility. Advocates for people with mental retardation must be ever vigilant in their protection of these interests.

NOTES

1. W. Blackstone, (1775–1779), *Commentaries on the laws of England* 24 (London).
2. Penry v. Lynaugh, 492 U.S. 302 (1989). Note, however, that the American Association on Mental Deficiency has defined "idiot" as "an obsolete term used centuries ago to describe all retarded persons and during the 19th and early 20th century to describe persons who would today be called profoundly or severely retarded" ([1983], *Classification mental retardation* [Washington, DC: Author]).
3. Fitzherbert, (1524), *La nouvelle natura brevium* (London), quoted in N. Walker, (1968), *Crime and insanity in England* (Edinburg: Edinburg U.P. [pp. 1967–73]).).
4. M. Dalton, (1618), *The countrey justice* (London).
5. *M'Naghten's Case,* 10 Clark, F.200 8 Eng. Rep. 718 (H.L. 1843). Although the M'Naghten test spoke of "disease of the mind," the courts quickly recognized its application to "feebleminded" persons (persons with intellectual deficiency) as well (H. Weihofen, [1954], *Mental disorder as a criminal defense* [Buffalo, NY: Dennis] [p. 120].)
6. New Hampshire relies on a "product" test (see note 14) and Rhode Island uses a "justly responsible test" (see note 12). Three states have abolished the insanity defense: Idaho, Montana, and Utah (American Bar Association, [1989], *ABA Criminal Justice Mental Health Standards, 1989* (commentary to Std. 7-6.1) (Washington, DC: Author).
7. I. Ray, (1838), *A treatise on the medical jurisprudence of insanity* (Boston: C. Little and J. Brown).
8. Parsons v. State, 81 Ala. 577, 596 (1896).
9. Thompson v. Commonwealth, 193 Va. 704, 718 (1952).
10. A. Goldstein, (1967). *The insanity defense* (p. 80) (New Haven, CT: Yale University Press).
11. *Great Britain, Report of Royal Commission on Capital Punishment (1949–1955), Report: Presented to Parliament by Command of Her Majesty Sept. 1953* (p. 80), (1953). *Royal Commission on Capital Punishment 1949–1953* (1980) (Westport, CT: Greenwood Press).
12. More recently, the commission's recommendations were endorsed by the Rhode Island Supreme Court, which held that defendants should be excused from criminal liability if they were "so substantially impaired" at the time of the offense that they cannot "justly be held responsible" (State v. Johnson, 121 R.I. 267 [1979]).
13. Durham v. U.S., 214 F. 2d 862 (D.C. Cir. 1954).
14. New Hampshire, however, had recognized a similar test for years and continues to today (State v. Pike, 49 N.H. 399 [1869]).
15. "Sociopathic personality disturbance," known today as "antisocial personality disorder," is a condition defined in large part by a history of criminal or otherwise antisocial behavior. See American Psychiatric Association, (1987), *Diagnostic and statistical manual of mental disorders* (3rd ed., rev.) (Washington, DC: Author).
16. L. Becker, Jr., (1977), Obstacles to the presentation of psychiatric testimony remain, in R. Bonnie (Ed.), *Psychiatrists and the legal process: Diagnosis and debate* (p. 57) (New York: Guilford Press).

17. Id.
18. McDonald v. U.S., 312 F.2d 847, 850–51 (D.C. Cir. 1962).
19. G. Melton et al., (1987), *Psychological evaluations for the courts* (p. 117) (New York: Guilford Press).
20. *American Law Institute,* (1985), *Model Penal Code* (perm. ed. with rev. commentary), Section 4.01 (1) (Philadelphia: Author).
21. S. Morse, (1978), Crazy behavior, morals, and science: An analysis of mental health law, Southern California Law Review, 527, 640–645.
22. American Bar Association, *Criminal Justice Mental Health Standards* (commentary to Std. 7-6.1), n. 15.
23. American Bar Association, (1983), *Summary of action of the House of Delegates,* Mid-year Meeting (Washington, DC).
24. American Psychiatric Association, (1984), Statement on the Insanity Defense, in *Issues in Forensic Psychiatry* (Vol. 1) (Washington, DC: Author).
25. Credit goes to Richard J. Bonnie, Professor of Law, University of Virginia Law School, who worked closely with both organizations.
26. Interestingly, the American Psychiatric Association test retains the label, "insanity," whereas the American Bar Association test speaks in terms of "mental non-responsibility."
27. Id., pp. 339–340.
28. American Psychiatric Association, Statement on the Insanity Defense, p. 16. But see R. Rodgers, (1987), American Psychiatric Association's position on the insanity defense: Empiricism versus emotionalism, *American Psychologist, 42,* 840.
29. American Bar Association, *Criminal Justice Mental Health Standards,* (commentary to Std. 7-6.1).
30. R. Bonnie, (1983), The moral basis of the insanity defense, *American Bar Association Journal, 69,* 194.
31. Alabama, Delaware, Georgia, Illinois, Indiana, Kentucky, Michigan, New Mexico, Pennsylvania, South Carolina, South Dakota, and Utah. See C. Slobogin, (1985), The guilty but mentally ill verdict: An idea whose time should not have come, *George Washington Law Review, 53,* 494.
32. Ga. Code Ann. Sec. 17-7-131 (b) (1) (Michie Supp. 1989) 35-36-2-3 (Burns Ind. Stat. Ann. 1985) as added by Acts 1981, P.L. 298 Sec. 5, Art. 36 Ch. 1 Sec. 1.
33. Ind. Code Ann. Sec.
34. See J. Ellis and R. Luckasson, (1985), Mentally retarded criminal defendants, *George Washington Law Review, 53,* 414, 442–443.
35. Slobogin, Guilty but mentally ill verdict; Bonnie, Moral basis of insanity defense; American Bar Association, *Criminal Justice Mental Health Standards,* 7-6.10(b); American Psychiatric Association, *Statement on the Insanity Defense;* National Mental Health Association, (1983), *Myths and realities: A report of the National Commission on the Insanity Defense* (pp. 32–34) (Arlington, VA : Author).
36. Slobogin, Guilty but mentally ill verdict.
37. *People v. Marshall,* 114 Ill. App. 3d 217, 233 (1983).
38. Statement of Terry Brelje, (1982, October), Illinois representative at the Mental Health Directors Third Annual Conference, Chicago.
39. Thompson, (1981, April 23), *A message to the Eighty-second General Assembly,* state of Illinois. Technicalities in the criminal justice process: Closing the loopholes through which the guilty escape (quoting People v. Seefeld, 95 Mich. App. 197, 199 [1980]).
40. Bonnie, Moral Basis of insanity defense.

41. S. Morse, (1984), "Undiminished confusion in diminished capacity," *Journal of Criminal Law & Criminology, 75,* 1, 5.
42. *American Law Institute Model Penal Code,* Section 4.01 (1).
43. American Bar Association, *Criminal Justice Mental Health Standards* (Std. 7-6.2).
44. American Bar Association, *Criminal Justice Mental Health Standards* (Commentary to Std. 7-6.2), n. 2.
45. N. Morris, (1982), *Madness and the criminal law* (Chicago: University of Chicago Press).
46. See R. Bonnie and N. Morris, (1986–1987), "Should the insanity defense be abolished? An introduction to the debate," *Journal of Law & Health, 1,* 113.
47. L. Fitch, (1989), Competency to stand trial and criminal responsibility in the juvenile court" in E. Benedek & D. Cornell (Eds.), *Juvenile homicide* (p. 145) (Washington, DC: American Psychiatric Press).
48. M. Hale, (1847), *History of pleas of the Crown* (Vol. 1) (p. 3) (Philadelphia: R.H. Small).
49. State v. Richards, 39 Conn. 591 (1873), quoted in Ellis and Luckasson, Mentally retarded criminal defendants, p. 434.
50. Ellis and Luckasson, Mentally retarded criminal defendants.
51. State v. Schilling, 95 N.J.L. 145, 148 (1920); for a different view, see Pieski, (1962), Subnormal mentality as a defense in criminal law, *Vanderbilt Law Review, 15,* 769, 788–90.
52. H. Burgess, The mental defective and the law, 23 *Intramural Law Review, 23* 115, 123.
53. Id.
54. Id.
55. See notes 41–46 and accompanying text.
56. Morse, Undiminished confusion.
57. Id.
58. Id.
59. Many states in recent years, in an effort to eliminate disparity in sentencing have enacted determinate sentencing laws that have the effect of significantly restricting the court's authority to reduce a sentence based on a finding of "diminished [mental] responsibility." For example, the Federal Sentencing Guidelines disallow consideration of the defendant's mental condition as a mitigating factor at sentencing except where the offense is a nonviolent offense. See Laski chapter 7, this volume.
60. J. Tupin and H. Goolishian, (1969), "Mental retardation and legal responsibility," 18 *DePaul Law Review, 18* 673, 675.
61. Id., p. 677.
62. Id., p. 678.
63. President's Panel on Mental Retardation, (1963), *Report of the Task Force on Law* (p. 39), (Washington, DC: U.S. Department of Health, Education, and Welfare.). The chairman of the task force was Judge David L. Bazelon, the same figure who established the product test as the law of the District of Columbia in Durham v. U.S. (see note 13).
64. Id., pp. 38–39.
65. See American Bar Association, *Criminal Justice Mental Health Standards,* (commentary to Std. 7-6.1).
66. B. Sales, (1982), "Model Developmentally Disabled Offenders Act," in *Disabled persons and the law: State legislative issues* (p. 748) (New York: Plenum Press).

The act is designed to apply to persons with a range of disabilities, including epilepsy, autism, cerebral palsy, and mental illness, as well as mental retardation. Defendants with mental illness, however, are specifically exempted from the act's insanity defense provision. Thus, the act would provide no bar to assertion of an insanity defense by a defendant with mental illness.

67. Id.
68. Fitch, Competency to stand trial.
69. Morse, Undiminished confusion.
70. K. Menninger, II, (1986), Mental retardation and criminal responsibility: Some thoughts on the idiocy defense," *International Journal of Law and Psychiatry, 8,* 343, quotation at 347.
71. N. Morris and G. Hawkins, (1970), *The honest politician's guide to crime control* (Chicago: University of Chicago Press).
72. See Petrella, chapter 4, this volume.
73. Id. Of course, this may be partly owing to the underidentification of defendants with mental retardation by attorneys and others in the criminal justice process.

Chapter 7

SENTENCING THE OFFENDER WITH MENTAL RETARDATION
Honoring the Imperative for Intermediate Punishments and Probation

FRANK J. LASKI

A T A TIME when the President's Committee on Mental Retardation is pressing forward with attempts to address issues of defendants with mental retardation it must now confront a criminal justice system that is overloaded, overwhelmed, and nearly out of control. After two decades of unprecedented expansion, prisons and jail populations are past the breaking point. From 218,000 state and federal sentenced prisoners in 1974, the nation had increased its inmate population to 700,000 at the start of 1990, and is rapidly moving to the million mark (Bureau of Justice Statistics, 1986). Nearly all urban jails and prisons are operating in violation of court-ordered prison caps. In Philadelphia, for example, the September 1990 prison census of 5,370 is 41% above its capacity and is the highest in the city's history, putting the city on the brink of halting all new prison admissions (Goodman, 1990).

Those segments of the criminal justice system traditionally used as alternatives to prisons are similarly overloaded. In the mid-1980s alone (1984–1988), the probation alternative increased its population by 35%, and the parole increase was 53%. Limited resources severely curtail the availability of these punishment alternatives in most jurisdictions. The result is virtual paralysis to the point of decriminalizing nonviolent crime on the one hand, and on

I wish to acknowledge the research assistance of Barbara Ransom, J.D., Temple University School of Law, Philadelphia.

the other hand, of simply warehousing violent criminals—for example, using wall-to-wall mattresses in prison gymnasiums as beds.

There is no doubt that the in extremis condition of the criminal justice system today perpetuates and aggravates the previously documented problems of persons with mental retardation in that system. Even more, the near-term response to the criminal justice crisis—construction of more prisons and high-tech alternatives to incarceration, such as electronic monitoring—fails to consider the special needs of offenders with mental retardation.

This chapter focuses on the sentencing process, the one point in the system where there is an opportunity to respond to both the needs of offenders with mental retardation and the needs of the community for appropriate control, supervision, punishment, and treatment.

SENTENCING

Imposition of the sentence is one of the most critical points in the criminal justice system. It is the judgment that determines how, where, and under what conditions an offender should be dealt with. With each sentence, a judge must balance, by constitutional means, and within the limits of the sentencing statute, the not completely consistent goals of rehabilitation, protection of the public, confinement of those offenders considered dangerous, and public acceptance of the sentencing decisions.

> A just and efficient sentencing system should include a range of punishments and not merely a choice between imprisonment and probation. A variety of intermediate punishments, along with appropriate treatment conditions, should be part of a comprehensive, integrated system of sentencing and punishment. (Morris & Tonry, 1990, p. 38)

The critical importance of sentencing becomes obvious when one considers that the great majority of persons formally charged plead guilty (in some jurisdictions up to 90%). Further, there is some basis for suggesting that the defendant with mental retardation is more likely to plead guilty and to do so without benefit of a plea bargain than defendants without mental retardation (Brown & Courtless, 1967; Santamour & West, 1979). Characteristics associated with the disability of mental retardation frequently result in the defendants being viewed as poor risks for probation and other diversionary noninstitutional programs (Haskins & Friel, 1973; Santamour & West, 1979). In addition, research shows that the offender with mental retardation has a higher and more rapid recidivism rate than other former offenders (Coffey, Procopiow, & Miller, 1989). These high recidivism rates, combined with the increased probability of incarceration and a practical lack of access to any prison-based rehabilitation, add to the already enormous problems of prison overcrowding and probation overload.

The sentencing stage is furthermore crucial because it is the first decision point in the process where the individual with mental retardation is labeled a convict. As a lawbreaker, the criminal stereotype attaches without qualification, with no more presumption of innocence and no more bows to procedural safeguards. The person faces sentencing with the earned stigma of outlaw and the unearned stigma of mental retardation. Instead of laying claim to the sympathy and services that society rations for those with disabilities, the offender now is the one who deserves what he or she gets, even if it be in a correctional warehouse away from family and the rest of society.

Although jurists commonly acknowledge that sentencing is the most difficult function of a trial judge, demanding "the best that [she] has in wisdom, knowledge and insight" (Council of Judges of the National Council on Crime and Delinquency, 1974, p. 1), it is commonly a subjective judgment often made speedily, without real standards, without explanation or purported justification, and, in all but rare cases, without an evidentiary record or contest as to the record. Sentencing is an individualized decision, but it is not, in practice, an individual determination bounded by a process that a qualified mental retardation professional in an education or treatment setting would recognize.

SENTENCING REFORMS

Decisions of appropriate sentencing and disposition practices must take into account recent trends and impacts of sentencing reform. During the century before 1975, every state and the federal system had "indeterminate" sentencing systems, under which the legislature sets the maximum lawful sentences; the judge uses his or her discretion to set the minimum or maximum term; and with even more discretion, the parole board sets the release date.

> Under the indeterminate sentencing structure the legislature, the prosecutor, the judge, the prison staff, the governor, the parole board, and the probation and parole officer all exercise important and immediate decision-making powers which affect not only the duration of the criminal's sentence but also the quality and nature of the penalty imposed upon him or her. (Shane-DuBow, Brown, & Olsen, 1985, p. 7)

Indeterminate systems "were characterized by nearly unlimited judicial discretion to set minimum and maximum sentences and by comparable board parole discretion to set release dates" (Tonry, 1987, p. iii).

In the late 1960s and early 1970s, the indeterminate sentence structure was subjected to intense and wide-ranging criticism. The resulting reforms, beginning in 1975 when Maine abolished parole release, have produced a great diversity of sentencing systems (Tonry, 1987). The broad range of reform systems classified as "determinate" sentencing systems sought to standardize the length of the sentence, eliminate the judge's use of discretion, and, in some instances, eliminate parole releases. "Determinate sentencing laws do not affect the decisions whom to imprison, . . . and are at best a partial approach to comprehensive sentencing reform" (Tonry, 1987, p. 100). By 1987, 10 states—California, Colorado, Connecticut, Illinois, Indiana, Maine, Minnesota, New Mexico, North Carolina, and Washington—had abolished parole release. Most jurisdictions, however, maintain the parole board system within the broad framework of indeterminate sentencing.

By 1983, 49 jurisdictions had enacted mandatory sentencing laws (Tonry, 1987). Some, such as California and North Carolina, have adopted determinate sentencing laws. Other jurisdictions use presumptive (normal and expected) sentences or presumptive sentencing guidelines whereby the legislature is "responsible for weighing the importance of many variables which normally are present in different crime situations. For example, whether a loaded gun should be treated the same as an unloaded gun in the case of a robbery" (Shane-DuBow et al., 1985, p. 8). Similarly, parole guidelines control parole discretion in states such as Oregon, New York, and Maryland.

A complete discussion of the origins, rationale, and results of the recent sentencing reform efforts is beyond the scope of this chapter. However, three general points should be noted in relation to study and reform of sentencing for offenders with mental retardation. The first point is that, historically, both the ideological principle and political impetus for the indeterminate sentencing structure, that which allows for the most individualized focus on the offender's characteristics and needs, came from those most interested in the rehabilitation of the offender. Indeterminate sentencing assumed that the offender could be treated and rehabilitated and relied greatly on expert and professional treatment. In its purest form, this type of sentencing makes individualized rehabilitation the paramount goal in sentencing and setting parole. The salient political point is that reform of indeterminate sentencing procedures was conceived and brought to universal acceptance, not by the courts or the legal professions, but by correctional professionals and prison administrators.

The second point—a counterpoint—is recent history. The critique of indeterminate-individualized sentencing in the 1970s, although having both conservative and libertarian vectors, revolved around "the failure of rehabilitation" and the lack of empirical data that treatment works to rehabilitate the offender. A substantial body of evaluation literature that accumulated in the 1970s looked at the effects of "treatment programs" on recidivism and concluded that research did not demonstrate that correctional programs worked. Incarceration for rehabilitation, so it claimed, could not be justified (in Tonry, 1987).

Judge Marvin Frankel's 1973 devastating critique was typical:

> While we pour increasing numbers of people into prisons . . . the most basic of asserted justifications, the program of rehabilitation, is absent. In a host of cases, then, when somebody says a prisoner must stay locked up because he is not

"ready" for release, the ultimate Kafkaism is the lack of any definition of "ready." Facing the facts, we know that "treatment" is mostly an illusion in our prisons. There is powerful evidence that the majority of prisoners deteriorate—become poorer risks and lesser people—rather than improve in prison. . . . It is bracing doctrine, of course, . . . that our prisons must be improved to make rehabilitation a reality. Assuming that is feasible—assuming we can on any scale rehabilitate people while keeping them locked up—the point of transcending consequence at the moment is that we are not doing so. Because we are not, the main prop for indeterminate sentences is a hollow reed. (Frankel, 1973, p. 93)

Judge Frankel railed against the proposition that all prisoners can be rehabilitated. It must be emphasized, however, that many prisoners, including those with mental retardation, can be rehabilitated. Through special programming and assistance, persons with mental retardation caught in the correctional system can be taught to learn and cope (Coffey et al., 1989, p. 15).

Penal sanctions as they currently exist in criminal jurisprudence are commonly characterized as either punishment or treatment. In deciding on an appropriate penal sanction, the judge is constrained by social, political, and economic realities.

One of the reasons why American criminal justice systems have failed to develop a sufficient range of criminal sanctions to apply to convicted offenders is that the dialogue is often cast in the pattern of punishment or not, with prison being punishment and other sanctions being seen as treatment or, in the minds of most, "letting off." And, sadly, the popular view proves on closer inspection to be broadly accurate, with widespread nonenforcement of such custodial sentences. (Morris & Tonry, 1990, p. 5)

Unless the public at large and those responsible for various aspects of administering the system are convinced otherwise, existing ideas about penal sanctions will remain in place and be applied arbitrarily to offenders with mental retardation.

The assorted critiques of the effectiveness of rehabilitation efforts in correctional facilities have thus produced a consensus that offender rehabilitation or treatment is not a justification for confinement (as reflected in the American Bar Association [ABA] Standards for Criminal Justice: Sentencing Alternatives and Procedures, 1986b, 18-2.5; hereinafter cited as ABA Sentencing Standards).

The preceding two historical points lead to the third observation, that sentencing for offenders with mental retardation must address the effectiveness of sentence and disposition, independent of ideology and doctrine. Unfortunately, the belief that correctional rehabilitation is ineffective coupled with the growing emphasis on retribution, rather than rehabilitation, as the justification for punishment (Von Hirsh, 1976) serve to inhibit reform proposals that would make sentencing for offenders with mental retardation fairer and more effective.

All proposals and recommendations in regard to sentencing must be carefully studied and reviewed in the context of each jurisdiction's sentencing system. For example, in a state with determinate sentencing, to effectively implement standard 7-9.3 of the American Bar Association's Criminal Justice Mental Health Standards (1986a) that "retardation should be considered as a possible mitigating factor in sentencing a convicted offender" may depend on a legislative designation of mental retardation as a mitigating factor or the recommendation of a sentencing commission. In states that maintain an indeterminate sentencing structure, the same objective may be accomplished through training of judges and the defense bar in the characteristics of mental retardation and in how mental retardation may be shown to extenuate or reduce the degree of moral culpability for particular crimes.

The American system's approach to sanctions for criminal acts is limited: capital punishment, prison and jail, fines, house arrest, probation, community service orders, intermittent imprisonment, forfeiture, restitution and compensation, and electronic monitoring (Morris & Tonry, 1990). Breaking these factors into their common denominators, temporarily disregarding fines and capital punishment, the courts have available four types of sentences, ranging from relatively non restrictive supervision to total confinement. The ABA Sentencing Standards (1986b) set forth available sentences as follows: 1) probation, 2) partial confinement, 3) total confinement, and 4) the use of a special facility. The ABA Criminal Justice Mental Health Standards (1986a) conform to the ABA Sentencing Standards, making explicit the offender's right to habilitation under all sentences and assigning "seriously mentally retarded offenders to retardation facilities in lieu of incarceration" (Commentary to Standard 7-9.8).

PROBATION

Probation is generally acknowledged to be the preferred disposition when offenders are not a threat to the safety of others or themselves. The ABA Sentencing Standards (1986b) recommend that probation be available in every case, with the exception of capital crimes. The standards call for probation as the presumptive sentence to be used unless affirmative reasons for selecting another sentence are established.

As a corollary to the probation preferences, the standards relating to incarceration clearly state that total confinement is not to be selected as a sentence without affirmative reasons. The two stated reasons are:

> (i). Confinement is necessary in order to protect the public from further serious criminal activity by the defendant; or
> (ii). Confinement is necessary so as not to unduly depreciate the seriousness of the offense and thereby foster disrespect for the law. . . .
>
> Neither community hostility to the defendant nor the apparent need of the defendant for rehabilitation or treatment provides acceptable reasons for imposing a sentence of total confinement. (ABA Sentencing Standards, 1986b, 18-2.5)

The American Law Institute's Model Penal Code also supports the contention that offender habilitation is best achieved in the community. It states:

> The common sense of the matter, borne out in the main by available research, is that it is better to maintain the offender in the environment in which he must eventually learn to live rather than to place him in one that contains all of the artificial, and potentially harmful, factors of imprisonment. (1985, Standard 7.01, Commentary)

The ABA Mental Health Standards protect the presumptive probation option for offenders with mental retardation by stating: "An offender should not be denied probation solely because the offender requires . . . retardation treatment or habilitation" (1986a, 7-9.2). The standards notwithstanding, there are some reports that probation is a less frequent option for offenders with mental retardation (Haskins & Friel, 1973; Santamour & West, 1979).

The rationale for the preference of community-based disposition in the form of probation closely parallels the arguments in favor of community-based habilitation programs and will sound familiar to professionals in mental retardation. The ABA Criminal Justice Standards for Probation are based on the proposition that:

> Other things being equal, the odds are that a given defendant will learn how to live successfully in the general community if he is dealt with in that community rather than shipped off to the artificial and atypical environment of an institution of confinement. Banishment from society, in a word, is not the way to integrate someone into society. Yet imprisonment involves just such banishment. . . . (1970, p. 1)

Therefore, it follows that the goals of reintegration, as well as avoidance of future crime, are likely to be furthered much more readily by orienting the criminal sanction toward the community setting and working with offenders in the community rather than in prisons or other institutional settings.

Not only is institutional confinement purposely designed to be the antithesis of a normalized living environment where habilitation is possible, but what we know about how people with mental retardation fare in prison virtually eliminates prison as a habilitative or rehabilitative option. The hardship and vulnerability of inmates with mental retardation is summarized by Ellis and Luckasson:

> They are more likely to be victimized, exploited, and injured than other inmates. They are also more likely to be charged with disciplinary violations and . . . to serve longer sentences. Finally they are unlikely to receive any habilitation designed to address the problems caused by their mental retardation. (1985, pp. 479–480)

Today, prison overcrowding fueled by increasing populations make even the delivery of basic health and medical services problematic. It is highly doubtful that more sophisticated intensive habilitation services will be available anytime in the near or distant future. Moreover, to the extent that particular correctional institutions can claim to be exceptions to the rule of non-availability of rehabilitation resources, the "creaming" phenomenon common in all human services operates to exclude inmates with mental retardation.

All of the preceding considerations reinforce and confirm the proposition that the intermediate punishment of community-based probation is the most favored disposition and most effective vehicle for offenders with mental retardation.

It is of interest that the ABA Mental Health Standards view probation in the context of mental retardation as a mitigating factor in determining the appropriate sentence. The commentary states that "retardation should be considered as a mitigating factor, rendering a sentence of probation more appropriate than a sentence of incarceration" (ABA, 1986a, 7-9.3, Commentary).

Traditionally, probation standards reflect a different approach, emphasizing probation as an affirmative correctional tool. Explicitly rejected is the

> automatic response of many in the criminal justice system that imprisonment is the best sentence for crime unless particular reasons exist for 'mitigating' the sentence . . . [Instead] the automatic response in a sentencing situation ought to be probation, unless particular aggravating factors emerge in the case at hand. At least if such aggravating factors cannot be advanced as the basis for a more repressive sentence, probation offers more hope than a sentence to prison that the defendant will not become part of the depressing cycle which makes the gates of our prisons resemble a revolving door rather than a barrier to crime. (ABA Criminal Justice Standards, 1986b, p. 386)

The standards are not entirely grounded in the proposition that probation is effective or most therapeutic but, rather, that it is the most humane alternative or the least restrictive alternative.

> The judgment that the court should commence its thinking by according priority to a non-imprisonment sentence constitutes a rejection of the conclusion that probation is "an act of grace" or that the defendant, once having been convicted "owes" society the time represented by the maximum authorized sentence. This way of thinking about probation, ... is out of date and unrealistic. (American Law Institute, 1985, Standard 7.01, Commentary)

INTENSIVE PROBATION

Probation is perhaps the most flexible disposition the sentencing court can make. It can be individualized based on presentence investigation and in-depth study. It can consist of minimal supervision of intensive supervision with requirements for specific living arrangements and participation in educational, vocational, and/or specialized treatment programs.

The Model Penal Code characterizes probation as a pertinent disposition alternative in a "properly functioning sentencing system" (American Law Institute, 1985, Standard 7.01, Commentary). Probation is most effective when careful consideration is given to both the individual and the available resources. Such individualized disposition alternatives fall under the general heading of "intensive probation" and cover "the enforcement of a variety of restrictions on freedom in the community and a diversity of programs designed to reduce future criminality by the convicted offender" (Morris & Tonry, 1990, pp. 6–7). Their common feature is that the participating offender, not limited to the offender with mental retardation, is subjected to controlled supervision within the community with a requirement to demonstrate positive social behavior. Intensive probation programs frequently are touted for their cost-effectiveness; however, neither the offender with mental retardation nor society is likely to be served well if these programs are viewed primarily in terms of cost-effectiveness or leniency.

Intensive probation programs are functioning in several state systems and in the federal system. Judges praise the more than 115 such programs that operate in 27 states involving 15,000 offenders (The Sentencing Project, 1990). Georgia, for example, instituted its Intensive Probation Supervision (IPS) program in 1982 to restrain the growth of its prison population. "The evidence indicates that IPS diverted a substantial number of offenders from prison (84% between 1982 and 1985)" (Erwin & Bennett 1987, p. 3).

Massachusetts and New Jersey also have model intensive probation programs geared to lower the recidivism rates, reduce prison overcrowding, and improve the effectiveness of the habilitation process. Massachusetts matches the level of intensity of supervision to the assessment of risk associated with offenders of a similar type. An important feature of the New Jersey plan is

> the careful development of a life plan for each offender while on probation; his work, study, and community service obligations, the requirement that he be employed or in vocational training full-time; that he perform acts of community service; and the use of a community sponsor to assist each probationer and thus to extend the control and supportive reach of the probation officer. (Morris & Tonry, 1990, p. 182)

A number of specialized probation models for offenders with mental retardation have been reported to be successful in preventing recidivism, including the Nebraska Individual Justice Plans and the Lancaster County Mentally Retarded Offender Program, the latter serving as a prototype for 11 programs now operating throughout Pennsylvania (White & Wood, 1988).

LEAST RESTRICTIVE ENVIRONMENT

The strong presumption against incarceration is consistent with the principle of using the least restrictive environment (LRE) as a sentencing guide. The ABA Mental Health Standards (1986a) acknowledge an LRE principle similar in effect to statutory requirements for court-ordered civil commitments of persons with mental retardation. Court-ordered civil commitments are based on a need for treatment generally and are considered appropriate when there is "a determination of clear and present danger . . . , inability to care for himself, creating a danger of death or serious harm to himself" (Pennsylvania Statutes Annotate Title 50, §7304[a], 1978). In Pennsylvania, for example, "inpatient treatment shall be deemed appropriate only after full consideration has been given to least restrictive alternatives" (Pennsylvania Statutes Annotate, Title 50, §7304[f], 1978).

Although acknowledging that the principle of LRE means different things to different people, the Model Developmentally Disabled Offender Act adopts a least restrictive environment standard similar to that used for civil commitment. "[T]he court shall impose the least restrictive alternative consistent with the needs of the defendant and public safety" (Ellis & Luckasson, 1985, p. 472, n. 322).

The ABA Juvenile Justice Standards (Institute of Judicial Administration, 1980) are explicit on least restrictive environment. Dropping the public safety prong and incorporating mitigating factors, they make it clear that the burden of showing less-severe sentencing alternatives rests with the state. Standard 2.1 reads:

> In choosing among statutorily permissible dispositions, the court should employ the least restrictive category and duration of disposition that is appropriate to the *seriousness* of the offense, as modified by the degree of *culpability* indicated by the circumstances of the particular case, and by the age and *prior record* of the juvenile. The imposition of a particular disposition should be accompanied by a statement of the facts relied on in support of the disposition and the reasons for selecting the disposition and rejecting less restrictive alternatives. (Administration, 1980, emphasis added)

The ABA Mental Health Standards do not themselves adopt the least restrictive guide, and in fact where LRE principles are referenced—for example, in the case of postconviction commitment—the standards modify the principle with concern for, inter alia, "the offender's history, the offense, the sentence," and "institutional security requirements" (1986a, 7–9.10).

The lack of consistency in the application of LRE principles in the ABA Criminal Justice Standards and codes is not fatal, if the nonincarceration preference is honored. The LRE principle has been a touchstone in the habilitation process for retardation for decades, but has been rightfully criticized for its lack of clarity and assumption that some restriction is justified (e.g., in some cases, the institution is the least restrictive environment). Instead, Taylor, Racino, Knoll, and Lutfiyya (1987) proposed nonrestrictive environment principles to guide habilitation practices. Among those principles are:

1. All people with developmental disabilities belong in the community.
2. People with severe disabilities should be integrated into typical neighborhoods, work environments, and community settings.
3. People with severe disabilities should be placed in homes and natural community settings whenever possible.

4. Community living arrangements should be family-scale.
5. The development of social relationships between people with severe disabilities and other people should be encouraged.
6. Participation in community life and the development of community living skills should be fostered.

These straightforward principles can be applied easily in a probation or other intermediate punishment framework.

The ABA Mental Health Standards, although noteworthy and commendable for being the first comprehensive consideration of the problem of offenders with mental retardation, fall short in their address of the sentencing and disposition of offenders with mental retardation. Given what we know about the habilitation potential of offenders in community settings and the limits of programs based in institutional settings, offenders with mental retardation who participate in a community-based program have an increased potential for a successful return to community life.

Two important features of the ABA Mental Health Standards are the requirements that mental retardation be taken into account in sentencing "to ensure individualized sentencing" and that all offenders with mental retardation, no matter what the sentence, have a right to habilitation. However, the promise of individualization and habilitation standards is seriously undercut by the Mental Health Standards' classification of offenders with mental retardation as those who are "seriously mentally retarded" and those who are not (1986a). Ninety percent of all people with retardation fall into the classification of mild mental retardation. Qualifying their departure from the traditional definitions and classifications of the American Association on Mental Deficiency, the commentary to the ABA Mental Health Standards explains that all persons with moderate, severe, or profound mental retardation are "serious," but it does not say who among people with mild mental retardation are so defined, leaving it to the courts to "evaluate the totality of the circumstances" (1986a). The operational significance of the definition is that the classification determines, in effect, where the person will be confined and purportedly habilitated.

The ABA Mental Health Standards provide for habilitation of less-disabled convicts with mental retardation in correctional facilities and of those with more serious mental retardation in facilities supervised by a department of mental health or mental retardation. Under the scheme set forth in the standards, "some mildly retarded offenders will be sentenced to regular incarceration while others appropriately will be committed to mental retardation facilities" (1986a, 7-9.1, Commentary). The standards seem to go in a circle: a person who has serious retardation should not be confined to a correctional facility, but the determination of whether a person has serious retardation turns on whether services in a correctional facility are available to him or her.

As Ellis and Luckasson (1985) have pointed out, the standards fall into a quagmire by attempting to treat people with mental illness and mental retardation in a parallel manner. The result is that the standards imply that the universe of offenders with mental retardation will either be habilitated in correctional facilities or committed to facilities for people with mental retardation.

The first of these propositions is absurd, considering what we know about correctional facilities, and is out of line with the general sentencing standards' approach to treatment. The second proposition, that postconviction civil commitment will deliver offenders with mental retardation to noncorrectional treatment facilities, is equally misplaced. As a technical matter, a greater number of offenders, particularly those convicted of property crimes, will not be committable under a dangerousness-to-self-or-others standard. Plus, with deinstitutionalization priorities and tightening of admissions, state mental retardation officials will resist commitment of convicts to their facilities, particularly under the conditions set forth in the ABA Mental Health Standards (i.e., in-patient habilitation only).

The difficulties encountered by the approach suggested in the ABA Mental Health Standards are illustrated by Connecticut's experience and practice. Connecticut state law mandates that the court apply the least restrictive environment when finding defendants with mental retardation not competent to stand trial. The court will "dismiss the charges and either release the defendant or put him into the custody of the Department of Mental Retardation, the Department of Mental Health, or the Department of Children and Youth Services" (Hierta, 1989, p. A1). Connecticut Department of Mental Retardation (DRM) clients accused of a crime are often found not mentally competent to stand trial and then are sent back to the DMR, which has the mandate "to allow all clients to live in the least-restrictive setting possible." This usually means that the person will be placed back in his or her environment or in a group living arrangement with no practical rehabilitation relating to the criminal activity. Like the mental retardation agencies of most states, Connecticut's DMR, although well able to handle the characteristics relating to the client's mental retardation, is ill equipped to address the criminal behaviors that demand attention (Hierta, 1989). The inability of any state agency alone to deal with offenders with mental retardation caused such an impasse that the U.S. District Court overseeing the deinstitutionalization of Mansfield State School sought the involvement of Connecticut's Departments of Corrections, Mental Health and Adult Probation to develop a plan to effectively serve class members with retardation who are caught in the criminal justice system.

The ABA Mental Health Standards' division of offenders with mental retardation into two classes that will be served in separate systems fails to take into account that the offender with mental retardation tends not only to have a low priority in both corrections and retardation systems but also represents a class of clients that both systems argue they cannot and should not serve.

Both on the basis of the specialized programs that have been developed to date and professional knowledge about the conditions necessary for habilitation, it is possible to develop a system of services to meet the needs of offenders with mental retardation. Well-accepted habilitation procedures dictate that services must be based on an understanding of individual needs and incorporated into an individualized habilitation program. Outside of correctional settings, the elements of the individual program are prescribed in detail and are universally accepted, if not always followed, in determining appropriate programming.

Although there certainly are constraints in the criminal justice system to applying individualizing mechanisms such as the individualized education program (IEP) and the individualized written rehabilitation plan (IWRP) to offenders with mental retardation, it should be noted that individualized decision making and treatment are accepted as necessary for effective programming particularly in probation and parole settings and juvenile settings. Objections to individualized habilitation approaches within the criminal justice system can be overcome by adopting and implementing time-limited habilitation plans and effectively implementing those plans. Habilitation programs for offenders that emphasize education, vocational training, and employment are most suited to meet objectives that are common to the criminal justice system and to the agencies responsible for habilitation services.

CONCLUSIONS AND RECOMMENDATIONS

Sentencing of individuals with retardation must be both fair and just. "Fairness requires that general standards apply to all offenders; justice requires that decisions concerning each offender be made in light of general punitive purposes as they interact with each offender's individual circumstances" (Morris & Tonry, 1990, p. 40). These two requirements can be advanced significantly if the following six recommendations are adopted:

1. *In accord with the ABA Criminal Justice Standards, mental retardation must be given due consideration by the sentencing court. Based upon a complete presentence report, the court should consider mental retardation as a mitigating factor and should also consider the effect on the individual with mental retardation of alternative dispositions, including confinement.*

Failure to recognize mental retardation and to give it appropriate consideration will nearly always result in a disposition that is neither fair, just, nor effective. There is indisputable evidence that most people with mental retardation differ from those without mental retardation in their capacity to make the benefit-risk analyses involved in committing a crime with the degree of reason the criminal justice system assumes is present. To the extent that the postconviction phase of the criminal justice system continues to treat offenders with mental retardation who have different degrees of blameworthiness-competency and response to punishment as though they were equal to offenders without mental retardation, the system cannot be fair or effective.

In addition to moral culpability, the court must take into account, based upon advice of both mental retardation professionals and correctional experts, the capacity of persons with mental retardation to tolerate or survive conditions of confinement.

2. *State legislatures should enact and courts strictly apply a strong presumption that probation is the disposition to be used for offenders with mental retardation, and that offenders with mental retardation should not be sentenced to total confinement unless such confinement is necessary to protect the public from further serious criminal activity by the defendant.*

3. *Probation should be applied as an intermediate punishment. Conditions of probation should be individualized to meet the habilitative needs of the offender and incorporated into an individualized service plan. The service plan should include educational, vocational, and life-skills objectives necessary to assist the probationer to acquire the skills necessary to avoid further criminal activity and to assume a productive role in the community.*

4. *Specialized and intensive probation supervision and support, modeled upon the Lancaster County [Pa.] Special Offender Program, should be available to all offenders with mental retardation.*

5. *The state-federal vocational rehabilitation process and program, including its independent living and supported work components, should be made available to probationers with mental retardation.*

The related benefits of the probation-vocational rehabilitation collaboration would include:

- A written individualized habilitation plan with long-term goals supporting the federal mandates of employment, independence, productivity, and community integration for offenders with mental retardation.
- Improved diagnosis and record-keeping related to offenders with mental retardation.
- Closer monitoring of the condition, treatment, and habilitation of offenders with mental retardation.
- Access to data on the effectiveness of programs, activities, and resources used in habilitating offenders with mental retardation.

6. *When submitting their comprehensive plans under the Developmental Disabilities and Bill of Rights Act (42 U.S.C. §§6021–6024), states' developmental disabilities agencies should include specific activities for offenders with mental retardation.*

The history of federal-state developmental disabilities programs has demonstrated that federal priorities can generate state planning and program development activities that far exceed the influence of direct federal resources. The priorities established for community living and employment for persons with developmental disabilities, for example, have enabled states to launch and sustain important statewide initiatives. Federal priority for offenders with mental retardation—linked to formal state plan requirements through federal-state programs targeted to persons with developmental disabilities— would stimulate necessary state action on behalf of offenders with retardation.

Persons with mental retardation should not be cut off from community mental retardation services when they are labeled as offenders. To the contrary, they should receive priority attention. Neither the court system nor the community mental retardation service system acting alone or sequentially with the same "client-offender" can marshal the resources or expertise to deal with the offender with retardation. The success or failure of individualized sentencing and intermediate punishments associated with probation depends upon strong, ongoing linkages between the probation system and community retardation systems.

REFERENCES

American Bar Association. (1970). *Criminal justice standards for probation.* Washington, DC: Author.

American Bar Association. (1986a). *Criminal justice mental health standards.* Washington, DC: Author.

American Bar Association. (1986b). *Standards for criminal justice: Sentencing alternatives and procedures* (Vol. 3, 2nd ed.). Boston: Little, Brown.

American Law Institute. (1985). *Model Penal Code and commentaries, part I: General provisions.* Philadelphia: American Law Institute.

Brown, B.S., & Courtless, T.F. (1967). *The mentally retarded offender.* Washington, DC: President's Commission on Law Enforcement and Administration of Justice.

Bureau of Justice Statistics. (1986). *Correctional populations in the United States.* Washington, DC: U.S. Department of Justice.

Coffey, O.D., Procopiow, N., & Miller, N. (1989, January). *Programming for mentally retarded and learning disabled inmates: A guide for correctional administrators.* Washington, DC: U.S. Department of Justice, National Institute of Corrections.

Council of Judges of the National Council of Crime and Delinquency. (1974). *Guides for sentencing.* Hackensack, NJ: Author.

Developmental Disabilities Assistance and Bill of Rights Act, as amended: 42 U.S.C. §§6021–6024, P L 100–146, Title II, §201(b), Oct. 29, 1987.

Ellis, J. W., & Luckasson, R. A. (1985). Mentally retarded criminal defendants. *George Washington Law Review, 53* (3–4), 414–493.

Erwin, B. S., & Bennett, L. A. (1987, January). *New dimensions in probation: Georgia's experience with intensive probation supervision (IPS).* Washington, DC: U.S. Department of Justice, National Institute of Justice.

Frankel, M.E. (1973). *Criminal sentences: Law without order*. New York: Hall & Wang.

Goodman, H. (1990, September 5). Prison plan could free up to 261. *Philadelphia Inquirer*, pp. B1.

Haskins, J., & Friel, C. (1973). *Project CAMIO: The mentally retarded in an adult correctional institution* (Vol. 4). Huntsville, TX: Sam Houston State University.

Hierta, D. (1989, August 1). Rape cases reveal flaw in law on retarded. *New London Day*, p. A1.

Institute of Judicial Administration. (1980). *American Bar Association Juvenile Justice Standards: Standards relating to disposition*. Cambridge, MA: Ballinger.

Morris, N., & Tonry, M. (1990). *Between prison and probation: Intermediate punishments in a rational sentencing system*. New York: Oxford University Press.

Pennsylvania Statutes Annotate. Title 50 Mental Health, §7304, PL 1362, No. 324 §1, Nov. 26, 1978.

Santamour, M. B., & West, B. (1979). *Retardation and criminal justice: A training manual for criminal justice personnel*. Washington, DC: President's Committee on Mental Retardation.

Sentencing Project, The. (1990). *Factsheet: Alternative sentencing*. Washington, DC: The Sentencing Project.

Shane-DuBow, S., Brown, A. P., & Olsen, E. (1985). *Sentencing reform in the United States: History, content, and effect*. Washington, DC: U.S. Department of Justice, National Institute of Justice.

Taylor, S., Racino, J., Knoll, J., & Lutfiyya, Z. (1987). *The nonrestrictive environment: On community integration for people with the most severe disabilities*. Syracuse, NY: Human Policy Press.

Tonry, M. H. (1987, February). *Issues and practices: Sentencing reform impacts*. Washington, DC: U.S. Department of Justice, National Institute of Justice.

Von Hirsch, A. (1976). *Doing justice: The choice of punishments*. New York: Hill & Wang.

White, D. L., & Wood, H. (1988). The Lancaster County Mentally Retarded Offenders Program. In J. A. Stark, F. J. Menolascino, M. H. Albarelli, & V. C. Gray (Eds.), *Mental retardation and mental health: Classification, diagnosis, treatment, services* (pp. 402–408). Washington, DC: President's Committee on Mental Retardation.

Chapter 8

A MODEL FOR HABILITATION AND PREVENTION FOR OFFENDERS WITH MENTAL RETARDATION
The Lancaster County (PA)
Office of Special
Offenders Services

HUBERT R. WOOD AND DAVID L. WHITE

THE DIFFICULTIES AND inappropriate treatment encountered by citizens with mental retardation who break the law have been extensively documented by research during the past 30 years. Abuses occur at every phase of the criminal justice process from time of arrest, in prosecution and defense, during incarceration or detention, and while under supervision of probation or parole departments (Santamour, 1988). Little research has been conducted on how to habilitate offenders with mental retardation so that their involvement in the criminal justice system can become a benefit instead of a nonstop revolving door journey through the criminal justice system. In particular, there has been little research on specific programming for the habilitation of offenders with mental retardation who are now in the criminal justice system. Finally, missing in current research is an examination of the development, implementation, and effectiveness of prevention programs to assist citizens with mental retardation in avoiding contact with the criminal justice system.

The Lancaster County, Pennsylvania, Special Offenders Services program offers some answers and insights to these long-standing issues. It provides a model specifically designed to deal with the problems encountered by persons with mental retardation who become involved with the criminal justice system. It also encompasses methods of providing services to habilitate offenders with mental retardation, as well as to help prevent some citizens with mental retardation from breaking the law.

This chapter examines the design of the Lancaster model, as well as the programming and habilitation it provides for the offender. It also discusses the preventive techniques used to teach citizenship in schools, and techniques to prevent crime among active probationers and parolees with mental retardation.

THE LANCASTER MODEL

History

In 1980 the Pennsylvania Commission on Crime and Delinquency provided 2 years of funding to the county of Lancaster to develop a Special Offenders Services program to serve clients with mental retardation. Specific program goals were to: 1) identify the population, 2) increase the use of community services, 3) increase employment, 4) reduce recidivism, and 5) provide training for criminal justice personnel.

The first priority addressed was that of training criminal justice personnel in issues involving offenders with mental retardation. Without training, many of the systems' abuses would continue. It was important, in this connection, to take into account that the criminal justice system is a continuum of events in which each step affects further steps. For the criminal justice system to work appropriately for offenders with mental retardation, all the actors must cooperate effectively, which requires that everyone understand the nature of mental retardation. For example, police officers arresting a person with mental retardation must know that the district justice will support their prosecution and not dismiss it because of the offender's mental retardation. District justices need to be aware that the district attorney's office will follow through with prosecution. Judges can also be more comfortable sentencing citizens with mental retardation to probation because of special programs that are available to them. Defense attorneys should have an alternative to incarceration to offer the court. All parts of the system can then work as a team. If the criminal justice system does not operate as a team, the habilitation and restoration of offenders with mental retardation to full citizenship are not likely to succeed.

Philosophy

The Lancaster model is based upon the philosophy that most adults and juveniles with mental retardation who break the law have a "right" to be arrested. If not arrested, citizens with mental retardation may feel that they are above the law because of their disability. What needs to be taught is that citizens with mental retardation, like all others, are accountable and responsible for their actions. There are, of course, some individuals with mental retardation who, because of their incompetence, are unable to be prosecuted and tried (White & Wood, 1986). However, experience with this program indicates that the vast majority of offenders with mental retardation are high functioning (in terms of mental retardation) intellectually, extremely streetwise, and competent enough to be held accountable for their actions.

The overall goal of the Lancaster program is to enable offenders with mental retardation to successfully complete probation or parole. This is accomplished by providing teaching, training, services, and counseling in a habilitation plan specifically designed to meet the needs of each offender. The habits, routines, and mores learned in this setting by offenders with mental retardation apply to all areas of their lives, helping them to successfully participate in society, and not just to probation and parole.

The Office of Special Offenders Services believes that the granting of probation and parole are privileges bestowed upon the offender, whereupon he or she owes a debt to the community and the court. This debt is paid through obeying probation and parole rules and working on behaviors that contribute to becoming a member of the community. Although behavioral change is difficult in traditional criminal justice services, the experience of the Lancaster model demonstrates that it can be accomplished if appropriate and adequate supervision and services are offered to offenders with mental retardation.

Model Design

Historically, the community mental health/mental retardation (MH/MR) system has often been unaware of, uninterested in, or overwhelmed by the special needs of offenders with mental retardation. Once a citizen with mental retardation becomes an offender, the advocacy system tends to regard the criminal justice system as responsible for the client and for his or her actions. Conversely, the criminal justice system expects mental retardation "experts" to provide the needed services or intervention for the offender. Workers in both the criminal justice system and the community MH/MR system often do not know how to deal effectively with the reciprocal system, or lack the means or time to do so. This results in offenders with mental retardation falling through the cracks and receiving less than appropriate and adequate services from either system.

The Lancaster program is a joint systems model whereby the criminal justice and MH/MR systems have combined resources and professionals to habilitate offenders with mental retardation. A joint systems model is an effective way to provide programs for offenders with mental retardation to improve their skills, assist them to recognize and change problem behaviors, and help them obtain employment. In essence, these are life changes that were brought about by habilitation services and were initiated by arrest. Staff on the project include two probation officers and two case manager specialists who work with adult and juvenile offenders.

This program accepts only offenders with a diagnosis of mental retardation. Caseload sizes for the entire office have averaged about 50 adults and 35 juveniles yearly. Obviously, these numbers are considerably lower than traditional probation or case management caseloads for either system.

A client's right to treatment is an important MH/MR issue. However, Special Offenders Services' clients cannot refuse treatment without risk of going to prison since they have broken the law and been sentenced to probation or parole. Because of probation/parole rules and regulations, the expectations of the probation officer and case manager can be legally enforced. Clients who refuse to abide by the rules and regulations of probation or parole eventually are placed in the Lancaster County Prison as violators. These clients then have a hearing before their original sentencing judge, who hears the facts of the violation and decides whether or not to continue incarceration. Usually the first violation hearing and lecture from a judge is enough to effect positive behavior changes in the client. If behavioral changes do not occur, the client is again returned to prison. Obviously, cooperation on the part of the court is essential in establishing the authority of the Lancaster program.

Behavioral Approaches

Many probation officers and case managers measure their personal successes by the number of referrals they make for their clients. The Special Offenders Services program established a different philosophy. Instead of making an immediate referral, the program requires that the client indicate behaviorally that he or she is interested in the service, in personal growth, or in skill building. The client then earns the right to receive a service. For example, a client who is immediately referred to vocational evaluation is less likely to succeed than one who has learned the value of being on time, of dressing appropriately, and of having an awareness of, or appreciation of, the work ethic. Through counseling, the client is informed of the benefits of the vocational evaluation, and that there are consequences for not completing this evaluation. The Special Offenders Services' staff are knowledgeable about community services, leading to appropriate referrals and a high degree of success and positive experiences for clients.

Initially, upon being placed in Special Offenders Services, clients report every day. This develops a routine and allows the program team to learn about their new client, assess his or her needs, and evaluate client willingness to comply with probation/parole rules and regulations.

Accountability and responsibility for one's behavior is stressed with every client throughout the period of supervision. Clients learn that their behavior controls much of what happens to them while on probation and parole as well as in the community. All clients become aware of the consequences of their actions and are helped to evaluate consequences before acting, thus promoting a more positive reception in the community and the development of self-esteem.

Client Profile Information

Tables 1 and 2 include client profile data on adult and juvenile offenders with mental retardation in Lancaster County.

Recreation

One of the social skills most lacking among clients in Lancaster Special Offenders Services is that of knowing how to use their free time. It is difficult to become involved in community events or to visit historic sites or scenic locations when one neither reads nor drives. Without the benefit of recreational activities, most offenders are trapped into spending time with the people with whom, and in the places where, they got into trouble.

By developing social skills and self-confidence and learning specific recreational behaviors, many offenders find they enjoy activities in life that they were afraid to attempt previously.

MENTAL RETARDATION AND THE LAW

Why do citizens with mental retardation become lawbreakers? Based on the experience of Special Offenders Services, three factors seem to be prevalent: low self-esteem, the influence of more experienced peers, and lack of knowledge of consequences for one's actions.

Low self-esteem is a common trait among offenders with mental retardation. Often, breaking the law, being arrested, and going to jail are viewed as successful achievements by this population: for the first time in their lives, they can be accepted as belonging to a group. Low self-esteem develops from doing poorly in school, low expectations of family, lack of support and encouragement, and never feeling or experiencing self-worth or success at overcoming problems. Special Offenders Services is successful in developing positive self-esteem among its clients because no expectations are placed upon them that they cannot achieve. Small successes are built upon to develop stronger feelings of positive self-worth. This is accomplished through an intensive, firm, and sensitive approach.

The second factor leading to criminal justice system involvement of citizens with mental retardation is the influence of one's peers. Because success is such a rarely experienced feeling for persons with mental retardation, they are easily manipulated and often taken advantage of by other more intelligent and/or more experienced individuals. Most of the Lancaster program's clients have been arrested with another person. Persons with mental

Table 1. Juvenile special offenders profile: Lancaster County, PA

	Sept. 1986	Sept. 1987	Sept. 1988	Sept. 1989
Male	86%	83%	82%	84%
Race				
Caucasian	51%	57%	53%	58%
Black	24%	23%	24%	16%
Hispanic	25%	20%	23%	26%
Average age	16	16	16	16
Average IQ	67	66	67	68
Living with parents/family	76%	77%	65%	90%
Average grade level	8th	9th	10th	9th
Previous contact with base service unit	43%	31%	24%	10%
Dually diagnosed	14%	20%	53%	50%
First offenders	62%	69%	79%	84%
Informal probation	35%	40%	35%	40%
Formal probation	50%	46%	53%	40%
Parole	0%	4%	3%	2%
Clients in placement	15%	10%	9%	18%
Felony offenses	29%	29%	21%	50%
Misdemeanor offenses	72%	71%	79%	50%
Most common offense	Theft	Theft	Theft	Theft
Recidivism rate				
Short-term	5%	0%	3%	8%
Long-term	0%	3%	3%	12%
Court costs paid while in S.O.S.	38%	47%	53%	42%
Court appearances prior to S.O.S.	15	19	19	26
Court appearances after S.O.S.	1	1	2	8
Community services completed	90%	90%	77%	90%
Average length of community services	55 hrs.	55 hrs.	52 hrs.	50 hrs.

S.O.S., Special Offenders Services.

Adjudication Cycle

Criminal offense in Lancaster County ---- Arrest ---- Process 1, 2, or 3 (below)

1. Informal probation — Admits offense — Presiding officer or investigator referral to S.O.S. ---- S.O.S. staff interview & appraisal ---- Psychological evaluation ---- S.O.S. staffing ---- S.O.S. program or return to traditional supervision

2. Formal probation — Adjudication in juvenile court ---- Presiding officer or investigator referral to S.O.S. ---- S.O.S. staff interview & appraisal ---- Psychological evaluation ---- S.O.S. staffing ---- S.O.S. program or return to traditional supervision

3. Detention — Barnes Hall ---- Adjudication in juvenile court ---- Presiding officer or investigator referral to S.O.S. ---- Evaluation
   1. S.O.S. staff
   2. Psychological evaluation
   ---- S.O.S. program or return to traditional supervision ---- Court order placement or S.O.S. probation

Treatment Cycle

Probation commences ---------- Intake interview ---------- Unified treatment plan ---------- Treatment individual/group & other agencies ---------- Coordinated monitoring of client's progress

S.O.S. PROVIDES FOR CLIENTS:
—Specific referrals depending on client's needs
—Personal counseling
—Family counseling
—Budgeting assistance
—Housing assistance
—Vocational testing
—Job readiness
—Employment counseling
—Job placement
—Coordination of services

S.O.S. PROVIDES FOR COMMUNITY:
—Training for criminal justice and social service professionals
—Consultation for others requesting S.O.S. information
—Coordination of services to population with mental retardation
—Prevention programs in schools, residential programs
—Consultation with outside professionals concerning "potential" offenders
—Cost-effectiveness
—Cost savings for the criminal justice system

Table 2. Adult special offenders profile: Lancaster County, PA

	Sept. 1981	April 1983	Dec. 1985	Dec. 1987	Dec. 1989
Male	N.A.	N.A.	83%	87%	87%
Caucasian	N.A.	N.A.	91%	91%	90%
Single	N.A.	N.A.	73%	81%	82%
Average age	23	25	26	30	28
Average IQ	66	66	66	65	65
Average highest grade completed	10th	9th	10th	9th	9th
Prior MH/MR clients	3%	30%	37%	47%	48%
Prior state MR institution residents	15%	11%	12%	12%	9%
Dual diagnosis	22%	20%	47%	51%	56%
Living with parents	50%	60%	55%	53%	52%
Unemployed at arrest	70%	95%	71%	76%	69%
First offenders	60%	60%	71%	75%	72%
Prior probation/parole clients	40%	40%	29%	25%	28%
Most common offenses	Arson & theft	Theft & burglary	Theft & criminal conspiracy	Theft & criminal conspiracy	Theft & ind. assault
Presentence investigation ordered	N.A.	N.A.	17%	17%	20%
Average probation sentence	31 mos.	30 mos.	26 mos.	23 mos.	27 mos.
Average parole sentence	6–23 mos.	6–22 mos.	6–23 mos.	6–21 mos.	6–22 mos.
Felony offenses	68%	67%	45%	64%	82%
Misdemeanor offenses	32%	33%	55%	36%	64%
Court appearances prior to S.O.S.	41	77	164	226	266
Court appearances after S.O.S.	6	15	34	53	69
Pre-/post-court incarceration	50%	60%	56%	59%	58%
Recidivism	3%	5%	0%	5%	2%

N.A., data not available

S.O.S., Special Offenders Services.

Eligibility and Review Cycle

Criminal offense in Lancaster County --- Arrest --- Sentencing in criminal court --- Presiding officer or investigator referral --- S.O.S. staff interview & appraisal --- Psychological evaluation --- S.O.S. staffing --- S.O.S. program or return to traditional supervision

Adjudication cycle

1. Incarceration --------- Pa. State Penitentiary --------- No S.O.S. services

2. Incarceration ---- Lancaster county prison ---- Evaluation --- Pre-planning for release --- Probation/parole ---- S.O.S. program
   1. S.O.S. staff
   2. Psychological

3. Placed on Lancaster County Probation --------- Evaluation --------- S.O.S. Program --------
   1. S.O.S. staff
   2. Psychological

Treatment Cycle

Probation commences --------- Intake interview --------- Unified treatment plan --------- Treatment individual/group & other agencies --------- Coordinated monitoring of client's progress

S.O.S. Provides for Client:

—Specific referrals depending on client's needs
—Personal counseling
—Family counseling
—Budgeting assistance
—Housing assistance
—Vocational testing
—Job readiness
—Employment counseling
—Job placement
—Coordination of services

S.O.S. Provides for Community:

—Training for criminal justice and social service professionals
—Consultation for others requesting S.O.S. information
—Coordination of services to population with mental retardation
—Prevention programs in schools, residential programs
—Consultation with outside professionals concerning "potential" offenders
—Cost-effectiveness
—Cost savings for the criminal justice system

retardation are more often followers and not leaders in breaking the law. Often, to be accepted by others, citizens with mental retardation become the lookout for a burglary, carry a forged check into a bank, attempt to sell stolen merchandise, or drive a vehicle for a "friend." In becoming an accomplice in these offenses, the person with mental retardation is often interested only in being accepted and does not consider the consequences of his or her behavior.

The third factor in criminal justice system involvement of citizens with mental retardation is lack of knowledge regarding consequences for one's actions. Many Lancaster program clients are shocked to learn the potential jail sentences they face for their offenses. Because society's expectations for people with mental retardation are minimal, it is assumed they will not become involved in the criminal justice system or, if they do, that minimal punishment will be imposed. School curricula have not been developed to teach community law and the legal consequences for criminal behavior. Offenders with mental retardation are held accountable for laws and rules they have never been taught or only vaguely understand. Without special programming such as that offered by Special Offenders Services in the criminal justice system, the first-time offender with mental retardation is often destined to become a lifelong member of the system. A potential solution for this dilemma is offered in the next section of this chapter.

CRITICAL FACTORS IN RECIDIVISM PREVENTION

During the past 9 years, Special Offenders Services has maintained a recidivism rate of 5%, compared to the often-cited national rate of 60% (Santamour, 1986). What factors make this program so successful?

First, this model has recognized that it is critical when working with offenders with mental retardation to establish a joint systems approach. The criminal justice system cannot be successful without the assistance of the MH/MR system. The easiest solution to resolving systems problems for clients with mental retardation is to create one department to oversee probation/parole and MH/MR services. This team approach helps the offender to receive the best services of both systems.

Second, programs often try to do too much for too many clients at any one time. Special Offenders Services is successful because it works within its program limits, providing services only to offenders with mental retardation in Lancaster County. Services are not offered to persons with learning disabilities, or who are mentally ill, or who abuse drugs and/or alcohol. However, offenders with a dual diagnosis are accepted as appropriate for services, if mental retardation is the primary diagnosis.

Third, Special Offenders Services offers intensive supervision to probation/parole or MH/MR clients. No other program in Lancaster County offers the consistency and intensity provided by the Office of Special Offenders

Services. Initially, clients are seen on a daily basis. All crisis situations are dealt with immediately. Clients are placed in situations where they can be successful, and these successes are built upon. As much as possible, services are provided directly to the client by Special Offenders Services' staff. Areas such as mobility training, job search, budgeting and banking skills, and comparison shopping are all dealt with by the program team.

Finally, Special Offenders Services focuses consistently on the need for clients to be responsible and accountable for all of their own behaviors. This applies to violating probation rules, getting along at home, dealing with problems at work, and maintaining appropriate relationships in the community. Clients are consistently rewarded for positive changes and counseled regarding difficulties they are experiencing. Ultimately, if necessary, the court provides reinforcement or punishment for positive or negative behaviors.

Training and Prevention

If we assume that there will always be citizens with mental retardation involved in the criminal justice system, what can we as a community do? Special Offenders Services believes that it is important to protect the rights of citizens with mental retardation as they move through the criminal justice system. In Lancaster County, the authors provide training to all members of the criminal justice community as an essential step toward achieving this protection. This training focuses on the roles and responsibilities of each individual in the criminal justice system, whether dealing with an offender or a victim with mental retardation. Even though the roles of personnel are adjusted to meet the needs of offenders with mental retardation, the one consistent factor that all members of the system in Lancaster County agree on is that citizens with mental retardation who break the law should be prosecuted. Because of training and sensitivity on the part of all members of the criminal justice community in this county, offenders with mental retardation are assisted to understand the consequences of their actions.

Training is made available to all criminal justice personnel on an ongoing basis, and consultation with Special Offenders Services' staff is available on request. These consultations could include the case manager being present for the questioning of a suspect with mental retardation, or the case manager participating in the decision-making process regarding whether or not to arrest a suspect with mental retardation.

Prevention

From the time each of us was very young, we were taught rules to abide by in our homes. As we grew older and socialized outside the family in clubs, schools, and churches, other rules had to be learned and obeyed. Finally, upon becoming a young adult and a member of our community at large, we were expected to abide by more rules, the laws of the community. As we moved from family into the community, the consequences for breaking rules become more and more severe. It is the belief of the staff of Special Offenders Services that many citizens with mental retardation break the law because they have never been taught society's consequences for misbehavior.

Increased community acceptance, mainstreaming, and normalization have contributed to greater levels of independent living for citizens with mental retardation, resulting in a growing number of adolescents and young adults with mental retardation now living in the community. At the same time, social service and criminal justice professionals are seeing many youths with mental retardation becoming involved in the criminal justice system. Although most citizens with mental retardation know the difference between right and wrong, they do not fully understand the significance of their actions and the consequences that follow from them. It appears that many younger citizens with mental retardation do not recognize their responsibility to know and understand the law because they are so used to being protected by family and friends. This protected life has led many offenders with mental retardation to believe that there is no accountability for their criminal behavior, and even upon arrest, they cling to the notion that someone will rescue them.

Although educational programs for students with mental retardation emphasize academic skills such as mathematics and reading, professionals must become more involved in preparing adolescents to obey community standards. Social mores and community laws are often very confusing for people with mental retardation, because these mores and laws are not very concrete or are not taught repetitively, as are academic subjects. The result is an inadequately prepared individual who is recognized by the community as "different," but is still expected to be a fully responsible member of the community.

In response to the growing problem of the presence of citizens with mental retardation in the justice system, the Office of Special Offenders Services in Lancaster has developed a school prevention program to educate special education students about the laws of their community and the consequences of breaking the law. Training by Special Offenders Services staff includes education about kinds of, and reasons for, laws, arrest procedures, the detention center, placement facilities, the responsibility of citizens to obey the law, and the consequences of breaking the law. Probation rules and responsibilities are also reviewed. Students are presented with ways their freedom of movement could be restricted or lost. Because young people with mental retardation are used by peers and others to commit crimes, the students are provided with information to assist them in decision making and problem solving to avoid being exploited by others.

Educators and social service professionals consistently support the school prevention program and have expressed their appreciation. As a follow-up to the program, many teachers have developed lesson plans on community responsibility and the legal consequences of breaking the law. The students demonstrate a high level of interest and participate eagerly in the discussions. After the presentation, many students express their commitment to be responsible members of their communities and to be law-abiding citizens.

Prevention programs need to be initiated at a young age. Adolescents with mental retardation must be taught that with independence and citizenship come responsibility. This may prevent adults with mental retardation from committing crimes and going to county jails and state prisons or perhaps, ultimately, to their execution.

Schools have been extremely willing, supportive, and interested in receiving these presentations. Students attending these programs will be followed for 3 years to determine if they become involved in the criminal justice system. This will allow the authors to measure the effectiveness of the Lancaster County program.

CONCLUSION

The Lancaster County Office of Special Offenders Services has shown that with special intervention, citizens with mental retardation can be better prepared for community life as law-abiding citizens. This has been demonstrated by a 10-year recidivism rate in the county of 5%, an extremely low rate in any offenders program. Parents and professionals must recognize the need to educate citizens with mental retardation to the legal consequences of their behavior before they become part of the criminal justice system, and must actively reinforce the individual's responsibility to his or her community as a law-abiding citizen. Advocates for citizens with mental retardation must recognize that it is normal to expect citizens with mental retardation to obey laws, or else face arrest and potential detention.

The Lancaster model offers solutions to many problems discussed throughout the literature. It offers: prevention of crime in the community, training for criminal justice system staff, protection of individual rights with prosecution of the guilty, individual treatment of clients, training for clients, a way to reduce jail crowding, a way to reduce recidivism, and cost-effectiveness.

REFERENCES

Santamour, M.B. (1986, Spring-Summer). The offender with mental retardation. *Prison Journal, 66*(7), pp. 3–18.

Santamour, M.B. (1988). *The mentally retarded offender and corrections.* Laurel, MD: American Correctional Association.

Stark, J.A., Menolascino, F. J., Albarelli, M. H., & Grey, V. C. (Eds.). (1988). *Mental retardation and mental health: Classification, diagnosis, treatment services.* New York: Springer/Verlag.

White, D.L., & Wood, H.R. (1986). The Lancaster County, Pennsylvania, Mentally Retarded Offenders Program. *Prison Journal, 65*(1), 77–84.

Chapter 9

CORRECTIONAL SERVICES FOR INMATES WITH MENTAL RETARDATION
Challenge or Catastrophe?

JANE NELSON HALL

ALTHOUGH SERVICES IN correctional facilities for inmates with mental retardation remain inadequate, changes in social policy have stimulated intervention programs for this population. The situation provides both mental retardation and correctional professionals with a compelling challenge—that of uniting to develop and implement a comprehensive and integrated intervention program for people with mental retardation in an environment where most of the variables are controlled. This approach would enable staff to effect significant changes in persons who have reached developmental stages that facilitate learning, yet who have had the negative experience of the loss of freedom. Such a restriction may create a concomitant motivation: an intrinsic need to learn and to change behavior.

However, fragmented recognition of the situation could exacerbate difficulties for both correctional staff and mental retardation service providers, leading to catastrophe. Inmates with mental retardation who were not provided adequate services could prove to be exceedingly difficult to manage.

I wish to extend appreciation to several people who supported this chapter in a variety of ways. Without their consistent encouragement and critical thought, it would not have been a possibility. Special thanks to John Moore, National Institute of Corrections; Herbert Goldstein, Professor Emeritus, New York University; Jerry Thomas, Georgia State Prison; Albert Duncan, Georgia Department of Corrections; and Shirley Paris, Princeton, New Jersey Regional School System. As always, I thank Heather.

They could interrupt the flow of institutional activities, cause damage to property, or injure other inmates, staff, or themselves.

Persons with mental retardation are still overrepresented in correctional facilities and underrepresented in program participation (Brown, 1989). In 1980, DeSilva found so few services for this population in correctional facilities that he referred to it as a "problem without a program." Less than a decade later, the National Institute of Corrections (NIC) responded to steadily increasing demands for technical assistance in this area by designating certain grant funds to improve programs for offenders with mental retardation. Coffey, Procopiow, and Miller (1989) were able to locate sufficient resources to generate a guide for correctional administrators. However, despite significant progress, programs and services remain inadequate. Less than 10% of all inmates with mental retardation receive any specialized services (Wolford, 1987).

This chapter has two major purposes. The first is to discuss the effect of certain aspects of the correctional culture on inmates with mental retardation. The second is to analyze common or universal problems in service delivery and compare different methods and/or models for responding to them. To these ends, emphasis is directed toward legal issues, theoretical perspectives, and structural features of comprehensive programs, keeping in mind the unique character of mental retardation service delivery systems within correctional environments. Discussion is limited to adult facilities; the legal distinctions and administrative differences of juvenile offenders are beyond the scope of this chapter.

FACTORS INFLUENCING GROWTH OF MENTAL RETARDATION SERVICES IN CORRECTIONS

Deinstitutionalization

A number of factors have been proposed as contributing to the increase in programs for inmates with mental retardation. To begin with, the number of persons with mental retardation has probably increased, although existing data are too weak to confirm this hypothesis. Statistics support a dramatic rise in the number of individuals under correctional supervision in general. The rate of incarceration in the United States is the highest in the world (Rutherford, Nelson, & Wolford, 1985); in the last 15 years, the adult prison population in this country has doubled (Wolford, 1987). One can reasonably assume that persons with mental retardation represent a part of this increase.

The deinstitutionalization movement of the 1960s may also be a possible contributor (Cohen, 1985; Steelman, 1987). Although there are no empirical data to support the theory of a direct relationship between the *decrease* in populations in state-operated mental hospitals and schools for persons with mental retardation and the *increase* in prison inhabitants, it is widely believed that problems associated with persons with handicapping conditions in prisons have increased in number and complexity (Hardy, 1984; National Institute of Corrections, 1982). Indeed, Steelman (1987) stated:

> It is clearly the perception of those who work in the criminal justice system, and particularly those who work in the prison system, that the problems being presented by mentally impaired offenders are more difficult now and different from what they once were. (p. 3)

One can reasonably infer that some people who would have been in institutions end up in prisons instead.

An increase in number of inmates demands at least a proportional enlargement in number of staff; this is particularly so as the inmate populations become more heterogeneous and include a greater proportion of inmates with developmental disabilities. Regarding inmates with mental retardation, Santamour and West (1977) have observed: "Institutions report that this group requires greater attention and therefore larger staffing. This takes away from services provided to the nonretarded in prison" (p. 9). Rowan (1976) and Smith, Schmid, Clark, Crews, and Nunnery (1988) agree, stating: "When special attempts were made to address the needs of mentally retarded prisoners, manpower was necessarily diverted from the rest of the inmate population" (p. 9). Failure to adequately increase funding, then, has meant that correctional administrators have continued to face the dilemma of how to allocate available scarce resources among different prison populations (Brown, Courtless, & Silber, 1970).

Changing Social Attitudes

A major part of the impetus to deinstitutionalize was the concept of normalization. Nirje (1969) defined normalization as "making available to the mentally retarded patterns and conditions of everyday life which are as close as possible to the norms and patterns of the mainstream of society" (p. 369). Logically, it would follow that people with mental retardation would thus be responsible for complying with normal expectations; violation would result in punishment. This is particularly the case when one considers the shift in social attitudes away from the concept of rehabilitation toward a punitive reaction to crime (Rutherford et al., 1985; Wolford, 1987).

Mental retardation professionals have not, however, been united in their interpretation of normalization as it relates to corrections. Haywood (1976), for example, contended that incarceration is one means by which society deals with deviant or inappropriate behavior; by sentencing a person with mental retardation who has been found guilty of a crime, society is punishing the behavior, rather than the condition of mental retardation. In another view, McDaniel (1987) stated:

> Normalization may be defined as the use of certain important social norms to help mentally retarded people function better in normal or natural settings. Using this definition for mentally retarded offenders means using a particular set of positive rules or behavior principles that are modeled in the prison and in wider society. (p. 184)

Santamour (1989), however, stated: "*Normal* opportunities in prison do not exist for anyone. Therefore, it is not feasible to apply this principle in the prison setting" (p. 10).

This fundamental disagreement over what normalization means in a correctional setting also complicates perceptions regarding the services that should be provided to offenders with mental retardation. Combined with increasing rates of crime and incarceration, overcrowded facilities, and "staggering levels of illiteracy" among offenders (Wolford, 1987) this complication furthermore establishes corrections as a system in crisis. Although there is no factual evidence that either deinstitutionalization or increasing emphasis on normalization has deepened the problems of operating correctional facilities, it seems to correctional administrators, line staff, funding agents, and other advisory personnel that one or the other movements must have negatively affected them.

Court Involvement

Another variable influencing the growth of mental retardation services in corrections has been the increased willingness of the federal courts to involve themselves in the operation of correctional institutions (Snarr & Wolford, 1985). Beginning with granting prisoners the right of access to the courts in *Coleman v. Peyton* in 1966 and extending to the actual removal of correctional systems from state control in cases such as *Newman v. Alabama* in 1976, the federal judiciary influenced the nature, range, and quality of services. Although courts have, for the most part, held that the individual with mental retardation has no clear constitutional right to treatment under the medical model that protects the person with mental illness, they have also indicated that the person with mental retardation does indeed "possess a constitutionally protected liberty interest in personal safety and freedom from undue restraint" (Cohen, 1985, p. 34).

In several situations, judges have directly addressed the responsibility of departments of corrections to inmates with mental retardation. For instance, in a case in Georgia, Judge Alaimo ordered corrections officials to provide for the care and treatment of inmates with mental retardation (*Guthrie v. Evans,* 1981). And in Texas, Judge Justice ruled, based upon his interpretation of the Eighth Amendment to the U.S. Constitution:

> The evidence shows that Texas Department of Corrections (TDC) has failed to meet its constitutional obligation to provide minimally adequate conditions of incarceration for mentally retarded inmates. Their special habilitation needs are

practically unrecognized by TDC officials, and they are subjected to a living environment which they cannot understand and in which they cannot succeed. Moreover, prison officials have done little to protect these mentally handicapped inmates from the type of abuse and physical harm which they suffer at the hands of other prisoners. Their conduct is judged by the same standards applicable to prisoners of average mental ability, and they are frequently punished for actions the import of which they do not comprehend. (*Ruiz v. Estelle,* 1980, p. 1346)

In other states, such as South Carolina, services for inmates with mental retardation have been initiated as a result of departments of corrections' recognition of the special needs of offenders with handicaps and the problems such inmates present to facility operation (Coffey et al., 1989).

In summary, correctional involvement with services to inmates with mental retardation has increased in the last decade. Catalytic factors seem to be radical alterations in social attitudes, including the deinstitutionalization and normalization movements, rapid growth in prison populations, public disillusionment with the concept of rehabilitation, and increasing advocation of punishment. In addition, more persons with mental retardation have been placed in community settings, where they are offered fewer alternatives to incarceration when they violate laws. Although there has been an increased willingness of the federal judiciary to involve itself in the operation of correctional institutions, no clear policy or procedure has been developed at the federal or state levels to deal with the problems of offenders with mental retardation.

GENERAL PROBLEMS OF SERVICE DELIVERY

Conflicting Missions

The foremost responsibility of a department of corrections is the secure containment of those individuals remanded to its custody (Snarr & Wolford, 1985). A secondary objective is to maintain order, protecting first staff and then inmates. The emphasis in prisons, then, is on security and control. Although few correctional administrators would disagree that meaningful training and habilitation programs offer tools to assist in maintaining order, it is unreasonable to conceptualize prisons as care and treatment facilities. If advocates for offenders with mental retardation adopt such a posture, the results, as suggested earlier, could be disastrous. Correctional administrators would then have more reason to disown the problems associated with offenders with mental retardation (DeSilva, 1980; Rockowitz, 1986).

The presence of inmates with mental retardation creates conflict at multiple layers of correctional operations. Security staff perceive their own function as that of administering legally imposed sanctions of control. Effective performance of this activity does not require extensive concern with the etiology of the inmate's behavior. An officer, consequently, is more concerned with the fact that the inmate has broken the rules than with why the inmate has done so.

Counselors, clinicians, teachers, and social workers, on the other hand, see their task, particularly with inmates with disabilities, as that of enabling or enhancing their abilities. Clinical staff are thus concerned with underlying environmental causes and with the stimuli that accompany the behavior. To the officer, the inmate may be simply a "bad actor"; to the counselor, he may be a developmentally delayed individual who is using the best behavioral responses in his repertoire.

The more time the inmate has served, the more complicated the situation may become. An inmate with mental retardation whose circumstances have placed him or her among brighter peers without support may well learn to survive through aggression. Such an individual's immediate reaction to *any* perception of danger is to strike out physically. Experience suggests that this behavior is initially rewarded (e.g., the inmate is not bothered as often by peers). If incarcerated long enough, however, the inmate will probably become the object of force from groups of other inmates or staff.

In the natural course of prison operation, the inmate may be placed in disciplinary isolation. The stress of such a placement increases frustration; the inmate with mental retardation may resort to the only behavior that "worked" in the past, which was to strike out verbally and/or physically. Continuous attempts by the inmate, for example, to assault staff, project urine and feces, and self-mutilate by cutting or head-banging result in such a complicated diagnostic and behavioral picture that neither security nor clinical staff can efficiently manage the inmate alone. Intervention with these individuals strains both facets of correctional operations and threatens the most positive of working relationships.

Although maintaining order and increasing the functioning ability of inmates are not intrinsically incongruent, achieving success in both areas depends, in large part, upon strong leadership, in-service training, open discourse, and mutual respect. Each objective might be considered an aim unto itself; none can be assumed to exist in any bureaucratic structure, particularly one so burdened as corrections. Cohen (1985) has stated:

> Even the most casual observations will reveal the tension between security and treatment staff in virtually any prison setting where they coexist. Clinical personnel will complain about having disciplinary problems foisted on them and security staff will be angry and bewildered at how quickly some inmates believed to be "out of it" are returned from a treatment unit. (p. 36)

There are other problems. Most authorities (e.g., Coffey et al., 1989; Nelson, Rutherford, Jr., & Wolford, 1987; Rockowitz, 1986; Santamour, 1989) agree that meaningful intervention depends, at least in part, on interagency agreements between departments of human resources, corrections, and education. Many offenders with mental retardation also have emotional or personality disorders that lead to behavior problems. Santamour (1989) stated:

> Owing to a lag in development, retarded persons often fail to master both social and cognitive skills. As a result, (1) they misunderstand how to use institutions in society to attain desired goals in legally sanctioned fashion, (2) they strike out against society in frustration stemming from their own limitations and feelings of rejection, and (3) they are naively unable to foresee or appreciate the consequences of their own behavior. (p. 13)

A repercussion is that no agency wants the problem of managing offenders with mental retardation. The inappropriate behavior of some clients may threaten public support of community-based mental retardation services; in addition, the low tolerance of these clients for frustration, their poor judgment, and their aggressiveness may be perceived to endanger more seriously impaired persons in residential mental retardation facilities (Giagiari, 1981; Santamour & West, 1977). Meanwhile, in prison, these clients may be abused or victimized (Santamour, 1989). Their personal property may be stolen, they may be forced to participate in homosexual acts, or they may be used by more intelligent inmates to violate institutional rules. Even if agencies were genuinely motivated to serve this population, the "endless bureaucracy in all systems" (Rockowitz, 1986, p. 21) would complicate the matter.

Definition, Classification, and Identification

Classification is an integral part of correctional operations and exemplifies the unique nature of mental retardation services in corrections. For operational purposes, "inmates are classified on the basis of age, sex, conviction offense, educational level and security classification or risk" (Smith et al., 1988, p. 9). Although intellectual functioning may be evaluated, this is done for purposes of assignment rather than treatment. Whereas the importance of the effect of mental retardation on the individual's behavior and on the development of treatment plans may be recognized, this recognition is a secondary concern. The addition of treatment as an objective of classification requires a more intensive assessment of individuals and introduces new problems and issues.

According to the definition of mental retardation established by the American Association on Mental Retardation (AAMR) (Grossman, 1983), an individual must meet three criteria to be designated as having mental retardation:

1. Significantly subaverage general intellectual functioning as measured by an individually administered and standardized test of intelligence
2. Deficits in adaptive behavior as appropriate for age and cultural group
3. Onset during the developmental period (prior to chronological age of 18)

To measure these criteria satisfactorily in any setting may be difficult. Filler et al. (1975) and Wechsler (1974) are among those who have addressed at length the strengths and limitations of standardized measures of intellectual functioning. The literature is also replete with discussions of the problems involved in measuring adaptive behavior (Brooks & Baumeister, 1977; Greenspan, 1979; Mahoney & Ward, 1979; Mercer, 1965, 1970, 1974, 1979). Since inmates in general are more likely than average citizens to be poor, undereducated, and members of minority groups (Giagiari, 1981; MacEachron, 1979), they are, given the current state of the art, at highest risk for error in assessment of both intellectual functioning and adaptive behavior.

Because the nature and characteristics of the correctional setting exacerbate the individual's problems (Browning, 1976), it is especially important to clarify at each *stage* the purpose of evaluation. Initial efforts at identification should be directed at classification with no assumption that the individual identified as having mental retardation will receive treatment.

Whereas the identification process has generated negative concern in the public arena or "free world" because of the purported effects of labeling and the possibility of stigmatizing individuals, the opposite effects are true in the correctional setting. Within a prison, failure to identify inmates with mental retardation may result in serious problems not only for individual inmates but also for the entire facility (Rutherford et al., 1985).

Assessment of Intelligence   In any population and/or situation, the validity of an IQ score is partially dependent upon the extent to which procedures for administration are followed. On a fundamental level, one must deal with the environmental conditions of testing. Correctional institutions are established to maintain a secure environment, and locating areas that conform to standardized test conditions is difficult. This is particularly so as prison overcrowding becomes a larger concern.

On a more abstract level, one must consider the attitudes of the participants. Ideally, evaluation would be conducted by a forensic psychologist who is familiar with the realities of the correctional culture. The test administrator should be sensitive to the array of factors that might invalidate the evaluation, such as the inmate's history as it affects his or her current physical and/or psychological state, attitude toward the test, and hidden motivations. Some examples are the culture shock experienced by an inmate who has been sent to prison for the first time, the effects of detoxification, and/or the deliberate attempt to score poorly to obtain some secondary gain such as protective housing. In addition, it is possible that the test administrator might be frightened of the inmate, who, in turn, may be suspicious of the reasons for testing and behave in a hostile or aggressive manner. The presence of security measures (e.g., a correctional officer, one-way mirror, or video camera) could increase the anxiety of both participants.

If correctional evaluators are not available, contract personnel may have to be recruited from local school systems or nearby colleges and universities. Such test administrators often have to arrange testing at night, on weekends, or holidays. This situation could affect test validity, particularly if inmates are forced to sacrifice a favored activity for testing. Prior to acceptance of the validity of an IQ score, institutional mental retardation staff should review both the psychological interpretation of the testing and the raw test data to rule out irregularities. The focus of review should be the spread of the subtest scores on the protocol; the test administrator's comments regarding the inmate's effort, attitude, and/or unusual behavior during testing; and any anecdotal information that might discredit the test's validity (Hall, 1985).

Assessment of Adaptive Behavior. The measurement of adaptive behavior is extremely difficult. To begin with, no instrument or standard for assessing adaptive behavior meets the levels of reliability and validity of standardized intelligence tests. In addition, adaptive behavior is situation specific; behavior that is acceptable in one situation may not be appropriate in another. Since prison life is very different from that of the free world, skills necessary for adaptation in a penal setting may be dissimilar and, in some cases, directly opposite from those required in society-at-large. An example might be the displaying of ingenuity. Society-at-large often rewards the innovative individual. In the prison setting, however, compliant behavior and following of orders is valued. The person who fails to understand this and thinks of other ways to perform a task is likely to be punished rather than praised.

It can be argued that anyone who is incarcerated has exhibited maladaptive behavior. There is, however, no instrument available for objectifying the nature of the inappropriateness of the behavior. The existing standardized scales, such as the Vineland Adaptive Behavior Scales (Sparrow, Balla, & Cicchetti, 1985) and the Adaptive Behavior Scales (Nihara, Foster, Shellhaas, & Leland, 1974), are not appropriate (Denkowski, Denkowski, & Mabli, 1983) for adults with mild impairment. Thus, the literature offers little direction for a clinical determination of impaired adaptive behavior. Improved strategies for meeting this criterion are particularly important in the correctional setting because of the prevalence of limited educational backgrounds and the proportionate overrepresentation of minority groups among inmates.

Howell (1987) has suggested that "for social behavior problems, the best survey procedures are often observations of and interviews with the client and/or his/her acquaintances" (p. 183). A structured interview with the inmate and line staff combined with a review of preincarceration social history and institutional adjustment would provide a measure of adaptive behavior. Such a procedure is time consuming and requires that the evaluator be skilled in interview techniques and social observation and familiar with the customs, mores, and intricacies of prison culture. This evaluation would be treatment oriented or program oriented and would be only so good as the person who conducted it.

Age of Onset Since mental retardation is a developmental disorder, onset must occur before chronological age 18. Although this criterion may seem insignificant in determining eligibility for treatment programs, it may well have programming implications. This is particularly so for persons whose functioning has been affected by a head injury or substance abuse. In addition, age of onset may be important for legal reasons.

If interagency agreements between departments of correction, human resources, and education are functional, this criterion might be easily documented in areas where the population is relatively stable. With younger inmates, the process should become easier as special education becomes more widespread and computer networks more available. There are, however, conditions that impede opportunities for meeting the criterion. One such condition is the exceedingly short sentence served by many young offenders, resulting from a combination of judicial leniency afforded many youthful or first offenders and overcrowded conditions that force agencies to release those deemed "least dangerous." Experience indicates that by the time the inmate has been permanently assigned and documentation of history established, release is imminent; hence, valuable time can be lost in waiting for documentation of age of onset. Another factor is the itinerant life-style of some people in the United States. The best interagency agreement cannot be expected to reach across the entire country to facilitate expedient information exchange between states that are geographically remote.

In other cases, the inmate may be the only source of information available to staff. If the inmate is indeed a person with mental retardation, he or she will have a difficult time recalling and relating developmental indicators, or may attempt to deny the presence of childhood disability or special classes. For any number of reasons, the family may also have difficulty supplying this information. Finally, the prevalence of persons who appear to have functional mental retardation as a consequence of substance abuse seems to be high in the correctional setting. Although the determination of time of onset for these and other inmates may be a vital factor in meeting legal criteria and in some cases in determining programmatic funding patterns, it may be unjustifiably time consuming. Careful thought should be directed, therefore, toward whether benefits of proper identification outweigh the costs of treatment for persons whose difficulties in functioning occurred after age 18.

Conclusions and Implications

Identification of offenders with mental retardation will continue to be complicated by the nature of the correctional environment. The potential gains of early identification of inmates with mental retardation seem to outweigh any negative effects of the handicapped label and recommend a more liberal inclusion policy than one might encounter in the free world. However, it may be unreasonable and counterproductive to expect correctional systems to provide comprehensive treatment to special-needs inmates when, because of overcrowding and limited budgets, they are financially unable to supply decent housing, clothing, and food.

In summary, careful strategies for identifying inmates with mental retardation are critical for several reasons. First, the realities of the prison culture place the person with mental retardation at risk. Although there is no legal precedent regarding liability for failure to identify *and* protect the inmate with mental retardation, growing interest in the issue by advocacy groups in New York (Steelman, 1987), Delaware (H. Risley, personal communication with author, May 19, 1989), and other areas raises the possibility of such a lawsuit. Intervention assumes accurate identification. Error in either direction—failing to identify a person with mental retardation or labeling as mentally retarded a person who malingers—may obstruct the efficacy of treatment programs and invalidate evaluative studies.

INTERVENTION

Because mental retardation services for persons in correctional facilities operate within the existing bureaucratic structure, many factors influence the nature of the program. Perhaps the most obvious is the mission of the facility. Under the umbrella of supervision and control, specific activities will vary as a function of the makeup of the inmate population. At the same time, institutions within the same system may have very different missions. An effective intervention matches its goals to the institution's function and the characteristics of the inmate population. Goals suitable to facilities serving young adults with short sentences who require low security would be inappropriate in maximum security prisons housing violent inmates with extensive sentences.

Although certain program elements would be consistent across settings, each program should be expected to have goals and objectives that are specifically matched both to the facility in which the program operates and to the needs of the inmates it serves. Simply stated, there is no best way to intervene.

In planning services, then, a meaningful intervention for inmates with mental retardation should be developed proactively and sequentially as an element of comprehensive operations (Hall, 1987). Specifically, the program should be planned *before* it is put into place in a manner that facilitates step-by-step operationalization. Mental retardation services must be a collaborative effort (i.e., they belong to *all* facility staff and not just to mental retardation professionals). The need for consistent responses from all persons with whom inmates with mental retardation come into contact is critical to instruction of this population.

Cognitive (Piaget, 1970) and moral (Kohlberg, 1969) developmental theory suggest that young adults with mental retardation may have reached key stages of developmental intervention. Consistent reinforcement of behavior through verbal intervention and modeling (Bandura, 1977) may yield genuine learning that will not only transfer but possibly generalize. For example, the inmate may learn to control physical aggression first with staff, then by transfer to situations involving peers. In time, the inmate may realize that nonaggressive behavior makes life easier and may generalize the skill from physical to verbal aggression. He or she will only cease fighting and hitting but also cursing and name-calling. Indeed, in this respect, correctional institutions have a unique opportunity because they typically house persons with mild disabilities and potentially control most variables in a person's daily life.

For several reasons, line correctional staff are the most important element of programming. First, they spend more routine time with the inmate than care and treatment staff. This allows them to observe the inmate's behavior away from the treatment setting and to supply program personnel with qualitative data regarding changes in individuals and their relationships with others. Second, they are in a position to provide the inmate with symbolic extrinsic control mechanisms. The inmate with mental retardation is able to *see* a uniformed correctional officer who is able to stop any inappropriate behavior the inmate may exhibit. The officer can apply immediate consequences for both appropriate and inappropriate behaviors. With mediated repetition of the meaning of the officer's presence (i.e., if the inmate is taught that the officer is present to help the inmate control his or her own actions, the inmate may be able to develop intrinsic control strategies). If taught effectively, the inmate may be able to conduct himself or herself more appropriately.

Finally, as the representative of security staff, the correctional officer is able to alert program staff to security issues providing or reinforcing critical cross-training. The officer can explain *why* an idea will not work or is dangerous.

The recent development of mental retardation services within the correctional setting necessitates that extensive in-service training be planned and implemented as an initial component of program development. Certain program factors are critical:

1. The desired outcome/result of in-service training should be specified.
2. The anticipated benefits of this training *both* for the inmate and for the operation of the facility should be identified and presented succinctly to administrative staff. In a proactive model, administrators must be able to see that short- and long-term benefits outweigh costs.
3. Selection of content, language, and style is crucial. Prisons are pragmatic places, and there is little need for theory except to explain why certain actions are preferable to others. To illustrate the problem within a correctional context, a new inmate with mental retardation might not know what "failure to follow instructions" and "insubordination" mean. The inmate might not know how to ask about this. His or her confusion might lead to anger, causing the inmate to do something he or she would not ordinarily do. A good correctional officer would recognize the confusion

and clarify it for the inmate, thereby preventing trouble for the institution, the inmate, and himself or herself.

Theoretical Foundation

Historically, intervention with individuals with mental retardation has rested upon two models: medical and social systems (Mercer, 1974). The medical model defines mental retardation as an illness that should be treated. The social systems perspective regards retardation as a delay in development causing behavior that deviates from social norms and/or expectations. Intervention is based upon determining the individual's level of functioning and teaching more appropriate behaviors. Ideally, programming is both multifaceted and integrated so that the same skills are being presented in various aspects of the individual's daily life.

Selection of a theoretical base affects the nature of intervention. The correctional mental retardation literature (Nelson et al., 1987; Rutherford et al., 1985; Santamour, 1989) advocates a social systems approach directed at habilitation. Since judicial action has been a major force in the development and implementation of services, understanding of the legal position of persons with mental retardation is important.

Legal Basis for Services

The theoretical position adopted for legal interpretation is clear. According to this position, mental retardation is a developmental condition and not a disease. Therefore, it can neither be cured in prison nor caused by being placed there. Because the deinstitutionalization movement included *both* persons with mental illness and persons with mental retardation, and because these groups tend to be placed organizationally under the same bureaucratic umbrella (e.g., Division of Mental Health/Mental Retardation), there is an unfortunate proclivity to equate requirements of care. Cohen (1985), however, provided a specific differentiation between the legal bases for intervention. With respect to the inmate with mental illness, he stated:

> The most fundamental obligation of a prison system . . . is to maintain the life and health of those in its charge. This obligation of basic care now clearly includes the physical and psychological dimensions of the person and has moved from the exclusive domain of private (or tort) law to include the public domain of constitutional law.
>
> The Eighth Amendment's proscription of cruel and unusual punishment has been interpreted to require that state and federal prison officials must avoid deliberate indifference to the serious medical needs of inmates. (p. 36)

In the area of services to inmates with mental retardation, Cohen (1985) stated:

> Although a state is not constitutionally bound to provide services for the mentally retarded, once a service *is* provided, a set of rights and reciprocal obligations

arises. In *Youngberg v. Romeo* (1981) . . . , the Court's first decision involving the substantive rights of involuntarily committed, mentally retarded persons, it was determined that such persons—along with convicted prisoners—possess a constitutionally protected liberty interest in personal safety and freedom from undue restraint.

Liberty interests are individual rights traceable to the word 'liberty' contained in the Due Process Clause of the Fourteenth Amendment to the United States Constitution. (p. 34)

Although the *Romeo* case arose in the civil commitment area and did not deal with criminal protection, it is important to this discussion for several reasons. First, it addresses *minimum* rights guaranteed persons with mental retardation who are civilly committed. Second, it compares these rights to those afforded "convicted prisoners." It seems safe to assume that this ruling may affect the definition of protection and freedom from restraint for offenders with mental retardation.

In conclusion, courts have not been willing to equate treatment with habilitation (Cohen, 1985). *Guthrie v. Evans* (1981) and *Ruiz v. Estelle* (1980) are the exceptions rather than the rules of judicial response to intervention with offenders with mental retardation. This is not to imply that correctional agencies have been judicially relieved of responsibility for developing and implementing programs for inmates with mental retardation. In the future, federal courts might be willing to examine in more detail specific application of the nature of protection and freedom from undue restraints, especially in cases where violations were evident. In addition, the programs created in response to court intervention in Georgia and in Texas have demonstrated their worth not only for the individual inmates involved but also for the correctional facilities. Although data remain scarce, there is evidence that serving inmates with developmental disabilities reduces the number and severity of disciplinary infractions this population incurs. It is important, however, that those seeking to promote intervention understand the constitutional base upon which intervention for inmates with mental retardation may rest and the subsequent need to ensure that programs are developed to complement and support the mission of the overburdened correctional system.

Structural Features

A primary mode of mediation in a social system habilitation model is that of special education. Rutherford et al. (1985) identified six components that are essential to a meaningful correctional special education program. They are as follows:

1. Procedures for functional assessment of strengths and weaknesses of individual offenders.
2. Curriculum which directs instruction in functional academic and daily living skills.
3. Provision for vocational training.

4. Policies and procedures for transitional services between the correctional program and the community.
5. Comprehensive system for providing institutional and community services to handicapped inmates.
6. Provisions for in-service and pre-service training for staff. (p. 66)

Immediate difficulties can be identified in operationalizing these components in correctional settings. Wolford (1987) has stated:

Most adult correctional institutions are faced with burgeoning populations and are forced to make institutional assignments based almost exclusively on security and space determinations. Typically, the correctional classification process neither considers educational needs nor effectively screens new arrivals for educational needs. Institutional educational programs are typically voluntary and have no effective process for identifying handicapped offenders; the potential special education student slips into a correctional crack, avoiding the school program in which he or she has already failed on the streets. (p. 79)

When faced with making a decision that appears to be that of providing either security or education, the correctional administrator has no choice. His or her mission *is* security. The burden rests, then, upon clinical staff to work with security so that education or treatment becomes a viable means of helping to maintain order and control.

Common goals must be established through cross-training (i.e., care and treatment staff must understand the responsibilities of security and see themselves as important elements in fulfilling this mission). Likewise, security personnel, from administrators to line correctional staff, must be familiar with the objectives of the educational program and the way these objectives fit with their mission. Although there may be initial resistance from both sides, this is a common-sense position: namely, educators cannot teach in a chaotic and uncontrolled environment, and the inmate who comprehends expectations is more predictable and less likely to exhibit unanticipated violence.

COMPARISON OF PROGRAMS

South Carolina Department of Corrections Habilitation Unit

To illustrate the importance of these factors, three programs are discussed and compared here. The first is the Habilitation Unit at the Stevenson Correctional Institution in Columbia, S.C. This unit was established in 1975 as a proactive measure of the South Carolina Department of Corrections.

The Habilitation Unit provides housing and services for 32 male inmates and day services for 18 females. Each of these inmates has been identified as having developmental disabilities (this program is not limited to inmates with retardation but also includes inmates with physical and/or sensory impairments) and is accepted into the program upon the advice of a multidisciplinary review team. The team has the right to refuse to accept an inmate or to require that he or she complete certain prescribed activities prior to consideration. The security level of the facility is minimum, indicating that the inmates do not pose a serious threat to each other or to the community as a whole. Ninety-six percent of the inmates are first offenders; the average sentence is 9 years.

Comprehensive services include special education, life-skills and vocational training, recreation, counseling, and prerelease services. These services are provided by a team of clinical psychologists, special education teachers, and vocational rehabilitation specialists. The goal of the unit is increased socialization skills. Work programs include training in behaviors that promote job acquisition and retention as well as actual work in washing cars, horticulture, or contracted piecework in a sheltered workshop. Because the facility is a specialized unit, staff are able to contract with the private industries for work. Recreation emphasizes building interpersonal skills through team sports and learning constructive use of leisure time by table games and arts and crafts. Counseling focuses on values clarification and resolution of emotional conflict.

Since the unit is minimum security, inmates are able to participate in a variety of activities that would be inappropriate for inmates considered more dangerous. Examples include the use of kitchen areas and the granting of furloughs for shopping. (Maximum security inmates, in most cases, would not be allowed access to various normal housekeeping activities because such areas contain items that might be fashioned into weapons.)

Inmate aides are selected from the "normal" inmate population to serve as paraprofessional staff. In this capacity they not only assist residents in structured activities but also serve as role models for more appropriate behavior. There is extensive pre-service and in-service training. Long-standing interagency agreements exist between the state Departments of Corrections and Education and the South Carolina Protection and Advocacy Agency.

Although there has been no formal evaluation of the various aspects of the program at the Habilitation Unit, staff take pride in a number of accomplishments. The unit has continued to focus on the more positive notion of habilitation at a time when social attitudes have advocated stricter punishment. In so doing, it has been able to maintain its position as an integral component of correctional services. In addition, there has been a significant decrease in the recidivism rate for inmates discharged or paroled from this program.

Mental Retardation
Program, Georgia State Prison

The Mental Health/Mental Retardation (MH/MR) Program at Georgia State Prison (GSP) operates in a maximum security facility. Although intellectual functioning and social history are evaluated for each inmate entering the Georgia system, this factor is not of primary significance in determining assignment to GSP. The operational criterion is level of security/custody or degree of dangerousness. It is particularly important in this situation that the goals of the mental retardation program be compatible with both the mission of the institution and the characteristics of the inmate population.

Administrative and medical files for each inmate assigned to GSP are reviewed by the MH/MR staff. Inmates who score below an IQ of 80 on a group screening test are considered candidates for reevaluation in areas of intellectual functioning and adaptive behavior. Although inmates have no choice in their assignment to GSP, they can refuse evaluation or program participation. A continuum of services is available to inmates with mental retardation, ranging from housing in a separate unit with intensive programmatic intervention to residence in the general prison population with supportive counseling and special education.

Decisions regarding the nature and intensity of services are made by multidisciplinary teams composed of a mental retardation specialist, special education teacher, mental retardation counselors, consulting clinical psychologist, and security staff. Inmates may refuse segregated, sheltered housing unless they are determined to be a danger to themselves or others or to be grossly unable to care for themselves in areas ranging from personal hygiene to inability to protect themselves from exploitation by other inmates. When either situation applies, the inmate is granted due process rights to protest confinement.

Like the Habilitation Unit in South Carolina, services at GSP include special education focusing upon socialization and life-skill development; structured recreation; and vocational instruction ranging from on-the-job training in custodial maintenance, groundskeeping, and furniture assembly to training in attitudes and behaviors compatible with job success. There are, however, notable differences. GSP inmates are uniformly repeat offenders; most have been convicted of violent crimes, and more than half have at least one life sentence. Of the approximately 60 men who qualify for the program, half are in lock-down status (confined to individual cells except for shower and exercise) for the bulk of the 24-hour day because they have committed rule infractions so serious as to pose a threat to safety of staff and other inmates. These men are served in their individual cells or in secured counseling offices within the dormitory.

There is a graduated behavioral modification program throughout the entire institution so that inmates may earn their way from lock-down status to less-restrictive living units. Those who work in the furniture assembly shop have demonstrated that they can be responsible in work habits and the use of tools. Great emphasis is placed, however, on tool control to prevent introduction of weapons into the living areas.

Since most of the inmates will be confined for longer than 10 years, the nature of instructional goals and material is very different from that of the South Carolina Habilitation Unit and of most minimum security facilities.

Emphasis is placed on institutional adaptation (understanding not only rules but also rights, privileges, and procedures for everything from making telephone calls and receiving packages to moving through the institution and meeting with staff in various departments) and social skills that are applicable not only in the prison itself but also beyond in society at large. In recreation, the focus varies according to the inmate's status. For inmates in lock-down, there is emphasis upon in-cell exercise programs and independent activities such as puzzles and needlework.

Much time has been spent in developing innovative motivational and reward strategies that pose no security risk and in working reciprocally to train correctional staff to recognize behaviors associated with retardation and to intervene in a consistent manner.

The Mental Health/Mental Retardation Program operates two supportive living units (SLU); one unit has an objective of long-term care and support. The other serves as a transitional center, or "halfway house," between the staff intensive unit and the general prison population. Inmates who need intensive intervention are assigned to an SLU on the basis of their daily functioning rather than their diagnoses. Inmates whose IQs would place them in the moderate range of mental retardation (below 50) might live in the transitional unit for 6 months to a year and then be integrated into the general population. Likewise, some inmates whose testing indicates that they should function on a higher level might be unable to adjust to incarceration and remain in the long-term SLU for several years.

Inmates with mental retardation who violate institutional rules or assault staff or other inmates are placed in disciplinary lock-down, as are their "normal" peers. Before an inmate with mental retardation can be sanctioned (placed in lock-down, restricted from commissary or entertainment privileges), he or she must be evaluated by MH/MR staff. If placed in a lock-down status, the inmate is assigned to a specific area within the disciplinary or special management unit, where he or she receives counseling and special education.

Although an inmate's sentence does not change, his or her security can be increased or reduced. If an inmate exhibits good behavior, he or she will, in time, earn a reduction in security status and a transfer to a less-restrictive facility. Approximately 5 percent of the inmate population qualifies for mental retardation services. A recent survey (Duncan, 1987) of the 19,000 inmates throughout the Georgia Department of Corrections (GDC) indicated that this percentage is representative. Supportive living units for persons with mental retardation are available in 10 correctional institutions operated by the Georgia Department of Corrections.

Interagency agreements have been negotiated between the GDC and the Georgia Department of Human Resources (DHR). Postrelease services for inmates who complete their sentences or who are paroled are negotiated through DHR agencies. Contacts are made with community-based service centers and vocational rehabilitation counselors in the areas to which the inmates will return. If possible, conference calls are made among the inmate, his or her family, and the rehabilitation counselor who will serve essentially as a case manager. With the inmate's permission, information regarding his or her programming in the GDC is released to DHR agencies, thus helping to promote continuity of care.

Texas Department of Corrections Mentally Retarded Offender Program

The Texas Department of Corrections (TDC) Mentally Retarded Offender Program (MROP) was developed in response to a class-action lawsuit, and varies from the South Carolina and Georgia programs in several ways. Rather than selecting the inmates most likely to benefit from treatment or receiving inmates as a function of security/custody designations, the TDC screens *all* inmates and assigns those with mental retardation to a separate and special facility. This results in a much larger and more heterogeneous population than either the South Carolina Habilitation Unit or the MH/MR program at Georgia State Prison.

The goal of the Texas program is to provide inmates with the chance "to learn academic, vocational, and social skills which will enable them to function independently in the community upon release from the prison setting" (Pugh, 1986, p. 45). The MROP has four areas of emphasis: habilitation, social support, security, and continuity of care (Pugh, 1986). Habilitation includes functional special education services, life-skills, and vocational training, and is a mixture of classroom and applied activities. Because the facility houses inmates of varying security levels, the nature of an individual inmate's participation is a function of his or her security designation. Theoretically, an inmate may be motivated to reduce his or her security risk-level in order to enjoy more privileges and participate in hands-on activities.

Social support is based on the case management model. Each of the 900 inmates in the MROP is assigned to a professional who coordinates services and operates as the inmate's advocate. The advocate endeavors to provide the individual with the consistency he or she might have missed during the developmental stages, which, in turn, may increase the inmate's chances for success in institutional adjustment. At the same time, this social support may contribute to the inmate's chances for maximal program participation, parole, and adjustment to society at large.

In terms of security, the MROP emphasizes the importance of uniting security with care and treatment by designating its correctional officers as rehabilitation aides. Persons who work in this capacity receive 2 weeks preservice training in areas relevant to mental retardation. They serve as vital members of the treatment teams and, to ensure consistency, they work on the same posts with the same inmates.

The final aspect of the MROP involves continuity of care. Interagency agreements are used not only with institutions in the department of human resources but also with the Board of Pardons and Parole. Ideally, an inmate who has received maximum benefit from the MROP would be granted parole under the auspices of a specialized parole officer (Pugh, 1986). These persons would work as case managers in the larger social sphere.

SUMMARY AND RECOMMENDATIONS

Although persons with mental retardation are still overrepresented in correctional facilities and underrepresented in habilitative programming, there has been a significant increase in the development and implementation of services in recent years. Many factors are thought to have contributed to both aspects of growth. Among them are the deinstitutionalization and normalization movements, changing social attitudes toward crime and rehabilitation, and a willingness of the federal judiciary to involve itself in the operation of correctional facilities. Any analysis of correctional mental retardation services must acknowledge the uniqueness of such services from both positive and negative perspectives. From a negative standpoint, there must be a realization that the need for such services reflects the failure of other institutions to effect maximal adaptation. On the positive side, correctional mental retardation services possess unparalleled opportunities. Not only are correctional mental retardation staff able to control most variables, but they also have the chance to work with adults with mild impairment.

Correctional and mental retardation professionals are faced with an important choice—that of uniting to regard the situation as a challenge or of splintering off in diverse directions, with serious repercussions both to individual inmates and to the correctional system. If a positive approach is adopted, staff must be willing to integrate the elements of two very different missions: the protection of society and the enhanced social adjustment of inmates with mental retardation. Although these objectives are not mutually exclusive, their incorporation requires energetic leadership, mutual respect, open communication, and cross-training at various levels. These requirements strain both systems; this is particularly so, given the tremendous needs and demands of the population to be served.

To maximize the chances for success, staff must develop proactive and comprehensive interventions. Programs should be congruent with the overall mission of corrections and the particular function of individual facilities. They should also address in an integrated and consistent manner the needs of inmates with mental retardation. There must be acceptance and mutual respect for the role of each staff member, as well as effective communication among staff members. Finally, there must be procedures for evaluating programs.

Although there is no "one best way" to develop and implement programs, certain common approaches have proven to be effective. For instance, the three programs selected for discussion here share a multidisciplinary approach directed toward socialization. Each focuses on life-skills training through special education, vocational activities, recreation, and case management, and each relies heavily on line correctional officers. The three programs differ primarily as a function of varying security levels of the inmates they serve. Other distinctions arise, however, from departmental policies concerning eligibility criteria, scope of services, and the types of facilities in which they are provided.

The following recommendations are offered to improve correctional services for inmates with mental retardation:

1. There is a need for a public information effort to inform policymakers of the growing numbers of offenders with mental retardation, their special needs, and the stress they place upon a burdened correctional system.
2. Research and development in prison mental retardation services is needed. Particular emphasis should be directed toward:
   a. Standardizing identification procedures.
   b. Implementing programs that meet the needs of inmates in different correctional categories (e.g., minimum security inmates with short sentences, maximum security inmates with life sentences, inmates in protective custody).
   c. Using quasi-experimental research designs to evaluate innovative programs for inmates with mental retardation.
   d. Supporting the continued development and implementation of in-service training programs focusing upon inmates with mental retardation.
3. There is a need to develop meaningful interagency agreements (e.g., between mental retardation and developmental disabilities agencies and departments of corrections) that facilitate development of a continuum of services extending from alternatives to incarceration to community-based facilities for persons released from prison.
4. Correctional mental retardation coursework at the undergraduate and graduate levels for students in both criminal justice and special education should be initiated.

REFERENCES

Bandura, A. (1977). *Social learning theory*. Englewood Cliffs, NJ: Prentice-Hall.
Brooks, P., & Baumeister, A.A. (1977). A plea for consideration of ecological validity in the experimental psychology of the mentally retarded. *American Journal of Mental Deficiency, 81*, 407–416.
Brown, B., Courtless, T., & Silber, D.E. (1970). Fantasy and force: A study of the

dynamics of the mentally retarded offender. *Journal of Criminal Law, Criminology and Police Science, 61,* 71–77.

Brown, R. (1989). Introduction. In *Programming for mentally retarded and learning disabled inmates: A guide for correctional administrators* (p. IX). Washington, DC: U.S. Department of Justice, National Institute of Corrections.

Browning, P.L. (Ed.).(1976). *Rehabilitation and the retarded offender.* Springfield, IL: Charles C Thomas.

Coffey, O.D., Procopiow, N., & Miller, N. (1989, January). *Programming for mentally retarded and learning disabled inmates: A guide for correctional administrators.* Washington, DC: U.S. Department of Justice, National Institute of Corrections.

Cohen, F. (1985). Legal issues and the mentally disordered inmate. In *Sourcebook of the mentally disordered prisoner.* Washington, DC: U.S. Department of Justice, National Institute of Corrections.

Coleman v. Peyton, 302 F2d 905 (4th Cir. Ct. App., 1966).

Denkowski, G.C., Denkowski, K.M., & Mabli, J. (1983). A fifty state survey of the current status of residential treatment programs for mentally retarded offenders. *Mental Retardation, 21,* 197–203.

DeSilva, B. (1980). The mentally retarded offender: A problem without a program. *Corrections Magazine, 6,* 24–33.

Duncan, A.S. (1987). *An empirical survey of retarded inmates in the Georgia Department of Corrections.* Atlanta: Georgia Department of Corrections.

Education for All Handicapped Children Act of 1975, 20 U.S.C. §1400–1461.

Filler, J.W., Jr., Robinson, C.C., Smith, R.A., Vincent-Smith, L.J., Bricker, D.D., & Bricker, W.A. (1975). Mental retardation. In N. Hobbs (Ed.), *Issues in the classification of children* (Vol. 1, pp. 194–238). San Francisco: Jossey-Bass.

Giagiari, S. (1981). The mentally retarded offender. *Crime and Delinquency Literature,* 559–577.

Greenspan, S. (1979). Social intelligence in the retarded. In N.R. Ellis (Ed.), *Handbook of mental deficiency* (pp. 483–520). Hillsdale, NJ: Lawrence Erlbaum Associates.

Grossman, H.J. (Ed.). (1983). *Classification in mental retardation* Special Pub. 9. Washington, DC: American Association on Mental Retardation.

Guthrie v. Evans, 93 F.D.R. 390 (S.D. GA, 1981).

Hall, J.N. (1985). Identifying and serving mentally retarded inmates. *Journal of Prison and Jail Health, 5,* 29–38.

Hall, J.N. (1987, November). *Model program for mentally retarded and severely learning disabled inmates.* Paper presented at American Correctional Association Seminars on Program Development for Mentally Retarded and Severely Learning Disabled Inmates, St. Louis.

Hardy, S.L. (1984). Dealing with the mentally retarded and emotionally disturbed. *Corrections Today, 46,* 16–18.

Haywood, H.C. (1976). Reaction comments. In M. Kindred, J. Cohen, D. Penrod, & T. Shaffer (Eds.), *The mentally retarded citizen and the law* (pp. 677–680). New York: Free Press.

Howell, K.W. (1987). Functional assessment in correctional settings. In C.M. Nelson, R.B. Rutherford, Jr., & B.I. Wolford (Eds.), *Special education in the criminal justice system.* Columbus, OH: Charles E. Merrill.

Kohlberg, L. (1969). Stage and sequence: The cognitive-developmental approach to socialization. In D. Goslin (Ed.), *Handbook of socialization theory and research.* (pp. 212–260). Chicago: Rand-McNally.

MacEachron, A.E. (1979). Mentally retarded offender: Prevalence and characteristics. *American Journal on Mental Deficiency, 84,* 168–176.

Mahoney, M.P., & Ward, M.P. (1979). *Mental retardation in modern society.* New York, Oxford University Press.

McDaniel, C.O. (1983). Is normalization the answer for mentally retarded offenders? *Corrections Today, 49,* 184–189.

Mercer, J. (1965). Social systems perspective and clinical perspective: Frames of reference for understanding career patterns of persons labeled mentally retarded. *Social Problems, 13,* 17–34.

Mercer, J. (1970). Sociological perspectives on mild mental retardation. In H.C. Haywood (Ed.), *Socio-cultural aspects of mental retardation* (pp. 378–391). New York: Appleton-Century-Crofts.

Mercer, J. (1973). *Labeling the mentally retarded.* Berkeley: University of California Press.

Mercer, J. (1979). *Technical manual: System of multicultural pluralistic assessment.* New York: Psychological Corp.

National Institute of Corrections. (1982, July). *NIC annual program plan for fiscal year 1983.* Pub. No. 15. Washington, DC: Department of Justice.

Nelson, C.M., Rutherford, R.B., Jr., & Wolford, B.I. (Eds.). (1987). *Special education in the criminal justice system.* Columbus, OH: Charles E. Merrill.

Newman v. Alabama, 406 F. Supp. 318 (M.D. Ala. 1976).

Nihara, K., Foster, R., Shellhaas, M., & Leland, H. (1975). *American Association on Mental Deficiency Adaptive Behavior Scale.* Washington, DC: American Association on Mental Deficiency.

Nirje, B. (1969). The normalization principal and its human management implications. In R.B. Kigel & W. Wolfensberger (Eds.), *Changing patterns in residential services for the mentally retarded* (pp. 112–124). Washington, DC: President's Committee on Mental Retardation.

Piaget, J. (1970). Piaget's theory. In P.H. Mussen (Ed.), *Carmichael's manual of child psychology,* (Vol. 1, 3rd ed., pp. 231–276). New York: John Wiley & Sons.

Pugh, M. (1986). The mentally retarded offenders program of the Texas Department of Corrections. *Prison Journal, 66,* 39–51.

Rockowitz, R.J. (1986). Developmentally disabled offenders: Issues in developing and maintaining services. *Prison Journal, 65,* 59–71.

Rowan, B. (1976). Mentally retarded citizens in correctional institutions. In M. Kindred (Ed.), *The mentally retarded citizen and the law* (pp. 63–71). New York: Free Press.

Ruiz v. Estelle, 503 F. Supp. (S.D. Tex. 1980.).

Rutherford, R.B., Nelson, C.M., & Wolford, B.I. (1985). Special education in the most restrictive environment: Correctional special education. *Journal of Special Education, 19*(1), 59–71.

Santamour, M.B. (1989). *The mentally retarded offender and corrections.* Washington, DC: American Correctional Association.

Santamour, M.B., & West, B. (1977). *The mentally retarded offender and corrections.* Washington, DC: Law Enforcement Assistance Administration.

Smith, C., Schmid, R.E., Clark, L.R., Crews, W.B., & Nunnery, N. (1988). The mentally retarded inmates: Prison adjustment and implications for treatment. *Journal of Offender Counseling, 9,* 8–17.

Snarr, R.W., & Wolford, B.I. (1985). *Introduction to corrections.* Dubuque, IA: William C. Brown.

Sparrow, S.S., Balla, D.A., & Cicchetti, D.V. (1985). *Vineland Adaptive Behavior Scales.* Circle Pines, MN: American Guidance Service.

Steelman, D. (1987). *The mentally impaired in New York's prisons: Problems and solutions.* New York: Correctional Association of New York.

Wechsler, D. (1974). *Selected papers of David Wechsler.* New York: Academic Press.

Wolford, B.I. (1987). Correctional education: Training and education opportunities for delinquent and criminal offenders. In C.M. Nelson, R.B. Rutherford, Jr., & B.I. Wolford (Eds.), *Special education in the criminal justice system* (pp. 53–82). Columbus, OH: Charles E. Merrill.

Youngberg v. Romeo, 102 S. Ct. 2452 (1982).

Chapter 10

ADVOCACY SERVICE SYSTEMS FOR DEFENDANTS WITH MENTAL RETARDATION

CHRISTINE DeMOLL

T HIS CHAPTER REVIEWS the types of advocacy service systems that may be available to defendants with mental retardation. Overall, very few advocacy programs have been established in this country for defendants with mental retardation. Nevertheless, failure to cite any particular program here should not diminish the importance of all of the available programs and services.

A variety of individual and systematic responses has emerged to assist defendants with mental retardation as they confront the criminal justice system. Protection and Advocacy Systems, Planning Councils on Developmental Disabilities, University Affiliated Programs, Client Assistance Programs, and Vocational Rehabilitation Programs are federally mandated to assist persons with developmental disabilities, including defendants with mental retardation. Advocacy organizations for persons with mental retardation, such as the Association for Retarded Citizens of the United States and the American Association

Special thanks to the following individuals for providing information on their services: Michele Alexander, Department of Public Advocate, New Jersey; Kathy Burton, Advocacy Center for Persons with Disabilities, Florida; Kim Chumley, Arizona Center for Law in the Public Interest; Comstock-Galagan, Advocacy Center for the Elderly and Disabled, Louisiana; Peter Cubra, New Mexico Protection & Advocacy System; Curt Decker, National Association of Protection & Advocacy Systems, Washington, D.C.; Eric Evans, Nebraska Advocacy Services; Steve Gaulke, Washington State Protection & Advocacy Agency; Dee Kifowit, Project Chance— Texas Council of Offenders With Mental Impairments; Joseph Lavey, Michigan Protection & Advocacy Service; Walter McNeil, Developmentally Disabled Offenders Project, ARC-New Jersey; Steve Onken, Advocacy, Inc.; Louise Ravenel, Protection & Advocacy System for the Handicapped, South Carolina; Gwenson Yuen, Protection & Advocacy for Hawaii.

on Mental Retardation, have pursued important policy reform of the criminal justice system at the national level.

The following discussion highlights some of the existing available resources.

ASSOCIATION FOR RETARDED CITIZENS

The **Association for Retarded Citizens of the United States** (ARC-US) is a national organization of parents of children with mental retardation that advocates for the human and legal rights and the physical and social well-being of persons with mental retardation and their families.

The ARC-US has taken a leadership role for defendants with mental retardation, beginning indirectly through the association's instrumental work in the passage of PL 94-142, the Education for All Handicapped Children Act of 1975. This law mandated states to provide public education to all children with disabilities.

In effect, the education agencies may have been the first system to address the needs of defendants with mental retardation by providing opportunities for training, special education, and daily supervision. However, inattention to the importance of teaching functional skills produced a phenomenon of special education "dropouts," many of whom had mental retardation, were unprepared vocationally, and were unable to care for themselves independently.

The ARC local and state affiliates provide a range of services and supports, such as: vocational opportunities, family support, education and training, legislative activities, residential services, citizen advocacy, and case management services. For many communities, the ARC was the first to organize efforts to address the needs of defendants with mental retardation, and to function as a mediator between the social service and criminal justice systems. Assuming a primary role as advocates for defendants with mental retardation, however, has caused unfortunate conflicts within this organization. The ARC has spent over 40 years advocating for equal access and integration in all areas of community life for people with mental retardation. There are fears that public awareness of defendants with mental retardation will cause society to revert to believing in the historical myths about the dangerousness of people with mental retardation (Ellis & Luckasson, 1985).

The ARC has placed issues surrounding defendants with mental retardation on state and national conference agendas. They have been active in legislative reform of laws that discriminate against defendants with mental retardation. They have advocated changes in mental health and criminal codes to distinguish between the disabilities of mental illness and mental retardation. They have rallied against zoning and deed restrictions that would exclude group homes with defendants from certain neighborhoods. They have joined forces with other associations in promoting Medicaid reform and funding to develop community services. The ARC-US signed the amicus curiae brief (see Appendix A) in *Penry v. Lynaugh* (1988), which supports the abolition of the death penalty for persons with mental retardation, and the association has passed a national resolution calling for an end to executions of offenders with mental retardation.

Families, service providers, and criminal justice personnel often turn first to the local ARC instead of state institutions for assistance with the problems of the defendant with mental retardation. A number of ARCs throughout the country have implemented community services for offenders with mental retardation. Seven of these programs are described in this section.

1. The ARC-New Jersey houses the **Developmentally Disabled Offenders Project.** Since 1976, the project has served as the only project in the state that monitors the development of services and programs for offenders with developmental disabilities. The project advocates for the availability of diversionary options and correctional programs, and a coordinated system of service delivery. It also provides consultation services to the Division of Developmental Disabilities, the Department of Corrections, the Bureau of Parole, Probation Services, and any agency involved in providing services to offenders with developmental disabilities. The project provides independent case management services and assists in the formulation of an individual justice plan. Education and training are key components of the project, which seeks both to educate students of human services and criminal justice fields about the needs of people and offenders with mental retardation and to train local municipal law enforcers, the judiciary, and probation, correctional, and parole officers.

In 1988, the ARC-New Jersey created a national network for providers of services to offenders with mental retardation and developmental disabilities. Through a newsletter, the network publishes a list of service providers available throughout the country and provides subscribers with general information about legal cases and development of programs in the field.

2. The ARC of Raritan Valley in New Brunswick, New Jersey, operates the **Job Training Center Program,** which is designed to provide individualized and specialized services for offenders with mental retardation on probation. The program addresses the needs of clients by identifying appropriate community-based programs, coordinating services, identifying and evaluating persons suspected of having mental retardation who have been adjudicated, increasing employment and independent functioning, reducing recidivism, and educating the criminal justice community to the needs of offenders with mental retardation.

3. The ARC-Michigan **Special Needs Offenders Work Group** provides training on mental retardation and issues surrounding offenders with mental retardation to all service systems and professionals.

4. The ARC-Duluth, Minnesota, **Criminal Offenders Project** provides

independent case management based on coordination of services through an individual justice plan. This project provides direct advocacy to offenders with developmental disabilities, educating them about their rights, due process and the criminal justice system, the legal process, and available treatment programs. The case manager helps to protect the offender from neglect and abuse by investigating conditions during incarceration. The case manager works with the offender's attorney, family, employer, and corrections personnel, and provides support and follow-up during arrest, incarceration, release, pretrial, trial, sentencing, and probation/parole. The project promotes effective options for treatment and provision of community services by helping offenders secure specialized services such as treatment for substance abuse and sexual perpetration. The project provides consultation, information, and training to individuals and agencies regarding the needs of offenders with developmental disabilities.

5.   The **Mentally Retarded Offender Team Project** of Cuyahoga County, Ohio, aims to increase the effectiveness of the Mentally Retarded Offender Jail Unit by contracting with the Association for Retarded Citizens for independent case management services. The project team comprises a representative from the County Probation Department, staff from the ARC of Cuyahoga County, the project director of the Court Psychiatric Clinic, and representatives from appropriate community agencies. The team develops an individual justice plan for each offender with mental retardation and reviews the plans monthly for implementation, effectiveness, and need for revision.

6.   The **ARC-South Carolina** has been active in advocating the abolition of the death penalty for people with mental retardation and has provided expert testimony in death penalty cases. It also has urged the state mental retardation boards to develop community-based services for offenders with mental retardation.

7.   The ARC-Austin, Texas, operates **Project CHANCE,** which has been providing independent case management services to adult and juvenile offenders with developmental disabilities since 1984. Project CHANCE offers training to criminal justice personnel, human services professionals, correctional officers, law enforcement personnel, and the judiciary on client identification and provision of services. The project provides technical assistance to attorneys and conducts intellectual and educational evaluations as well as adult literacy and vocational readiness clinics. Substance abuse counselors who specialize in treating persons with mental retardation and can authorize inpatient residential treatment for substance abuse are also affiliated with the project. ARC-Austin has also been instrumental in promoting legislation to assist offenders with mental retardation, including the abolishment of the death penalty for persons with mental retardation.

Across the country, defendants with mental retardation have become a service priority for many, but not all, state and local chapters of the ARC.

AMERICAN ASSOCIATION ON MENTAL RETARDATION

The **American Association on Mental Retardation** (AAMR) is the nation's oldest and largest interdisciplinary organization of mental retardation professionals. This organization has taken a national leadership role in educating professionals in the mental retardation field to the problems and needs of defendants with mental retardation. The AAMR has promoted education at national and state levels and has encouraged criminal justice and human services personnel to learn and work concurrently. The association supports legislative Medicaid reform that would allow states federally matched dollars for providing services to people with mental retardation in community-based settings. (Currently, Medicaid allotments are primarily to institutions, such as state schools for mentally retarded persons and large nursing homes.) The AAMR is the leading advocate of change in laws to address the specific needs of individuals with mental retardation and to ensure their ability to exercise their legal rights. The AAMR supported the development of the amicus curiae brief, which favored abolishment of the death penalty in *Penry v. Lynaugh,* and passed a national resolution calling for an end to execution of people with mental retardation.

The association has also assumed key roles with respect to the training of professionals, advocating legislative reform, amending current laws and standards that adversely affect defendants, and coordinating with other national disability advocate organizations.

NATIONAL ASSOCIATION OF PROTECTION AND ADVOCACY SYSTEMS

The Developmental Disabilities Assistance and Bill of Rights Act of 1978 (D.D. Act), PL 95-602, as amended, established the Protection and Advocacy Program. As a condition for the receipt of federal funds under this program, Congress mandated the establishment of a **Protection and Advocacy System** in each state and territory to protect and advocate for the legal and human rights of persons with developmental disabilities (D.D. Act, Subchap. I, Sec. 6001).

Protection and Advocacy Systems are authorized to pursue legal, administrative, and other appropriate approaches to ensure the protection of persons with developmental disabilities who are, or may be, eligible for treatment, habilitation, or services. The goal is to enable them to achieve their maximum potential with increased independence, productivity, and integration into the community. These approaches include coordination, monitoring, planning, and evaluation of services. The federal mandate includes the authority to provide information on, and referral to, programs and services addressing the needs of persons with developmental disabilities. The Protection and Advocacy System has the authority to investigate incidents of abuse and neglect.

Some Protection and Advocacy Systems provide services for defendants with mental retardation—for example, obtaining appropriate education and rehabilitation services in the community or during incarceration. The Protection and Advocacy Systems have mandates to identify the legal right to habilitation and treatment services directed toward independent living, and to pursue the development of either new habilitation and treatment services or the opening up of existing programs to assist defendants in need of community alternatives. Some state Protection and Advocacy Systems have organized and/or participated with other service systems in interagency task forces to develop service options for defendants with developmental disabilities. Protection and Advocacy Systems encourage service systems to use individualized justice plans for offenders with developmental disabilities, in addition to providing information and training on the use of this plan and the development of specialized services. (The individualized justice plans are used to hold service providers accountable for meeting the needs of the defendant, to hold the defendant accountable for completion of the conditions of the plan, and to facilitate communication and partnerships between service systems and the criminal justice systems.)

Protection and Advocacy Systems assist defendants with developmental disabilities in obtaining equal access to their legal rights. The assistance includes, but is not limited to, assistance with due process protections under the law, investigation and correction of incidents of abuse within prisons and jails, and monitoring of treatment programs and community services to ensure coordinated, comprehensive delivery of services to defendants with developmental disabilities in a nondiscriminatory manner.

Protection and Advocacy systems also provide outreach to defendants not yet identified as having a developmental disability or mental retardation, but who are incarcerated or unable to access traditional correctional services (Yuen, 1989), by assisting jails and prisons to establish routine procedures to diagnose and identify persons with developmental disabilities. Once identified, however, many defendants with developmental disabilities and/or mental retardation are unwilling to access services offered, due to their fear of being stigmatized as a "special needs offender" and not wanting to have their lives controlled by social workers and service providers.

Defendants with developmental disabilities have historically been subject to discrimination by the criminal justice system (Ellis & Luckasson, 1985). The Protection and Advocacy Systems work to hold service systems accountable for the protection of persons with developmental disabilities from abuse, neglect, and due process violations. To increase the criminal justice system's responsiveness to the protection of these rights, the Protection and Advocacy Systems have worked with public defenders, court-appointed attorneys, and the private bar in providing technical assistance, training in defense strategies, differentiation of the disabilities of mental illness and mental retardation, information on traditional services available to clients as alternatives to incarceration, and awareness of the issues regarding competency, communication, characteristics of developmental disabilities, sentencing alternatives, and community resources.

The National Association of Protection and Advocacy Systems (NAPAS) has supported language changes in the federal mandate to specifically incorporate the need for Protection and Advocacy Systems to be responsive to offenders with developmental disabilities who are incarcerated in jails and prisons. The NAPAS has sponsored training sessions at its annual conferences that have afforded Protection and Advocacy Systems the opportunity for education on current legal cases and the development of services to defendants with developmental disabilities. The NAPAS has taken a position against application of the death penalty to offenders with mental retardation by signing the amicus curiae brief in *Penry v. Lynaugh*.

Some state Protection and Advocacy Systems have shied away from significant involvement in the area of defendants with developmental disabilities, for fear that the demand for services could drain their resources. Although the state protection and Advocacy Systems are under the auspices of the federal mandate, they also must be guided by each state's laws, public policies, and service systems. The remainder of this section outlines specific efforts by Protection and Advocacy Systems in a number of states. (Note that despite varying titles, each state program described is a Protection and Advocacy System.)

The Washington State Protection and Advocacy Agency provides technical assistance to attorneys who represent people with mental retardation charged with criminal offenses. The system has a volunteer with an office in the state prison to investigate abuse and to help develop a parole plan. The Washington State Protection and Advocacy System monitors the Department of Mental Health, the Department of Developmental Disabilities, and the Department of Corrections' implementation of service delivery to defendants with mental retardation.

The Washington State Protection and Advocacy System has organized a statewide task force to create legislation to address the needs of offenders with mental retardation. The task force is composed of representatives from the Protection and Advocacy System, the Planning Council on Developmental Disabilities, the Department of Social and Health Services, legislators, and consumer advocates. Its primary focus is on offenders with mental retardation who committed felonies, with specific attention to sexual offenses. The task force recommended a program to address reform of the criminal codes affecting offenders with mental retardation and also recommended that assistance from a professional with expertise in mental retardation be available.

Nebraska Advocacy Services provides individual legal assistance for clients with mental retardation who are charged with crimes and have concerns about the quality of legal representation available to them. The system also provides technical assistance to attorneys who need to be better informed about people with mental retardation. Nebraska Advocacy Services works with the public defender to achieve alternative sentencing and facilitation of community-based services. Nebraska Advocacy Services monitors legislative activity and provides testimony and other forms of information relevant to legislation that affects the lives of defendants with mental retardation (Evans, 1989).

The Arizona Center for Law in the Public Interest provides training on defendants with developmental disabilities to police and to corrections, criminal justice, and social services personnel. The training includes information necessary to assist in identifying people with developmental disabilities. Information is also provided on how to communicate effectively with such individuals, how to locate community resources, and on understanding fundamental basic rights. Developments of the Arizona Center's *Guide for Law Enforcement Officers* was funded by the Arizona Council on Developmental Disabilities.

The New Jersey Department of Public Advocate has formed a task force on defendants with developmental disabilities. Composed of both attorneys and advocates, the task force is analyzing data from the state corrections department and the court systems to determine the needs of the defendants in the criminal justice system. Prior to the task force's study, there had been no systematic identification or count of people with developmental disabilities or mental retardation in the criminal justice system. The task force provides training throughout the state on defendants with developmental disabilities, including information on identifying persons with developmental disabilities, available services, and developing effective working relationships with defendants with developmental disabilities. The Task Force is working to identify deficits in service delivery systems to juvenile offenders. The Department of Public Advocacy aims to address the inequity of having one moderate security unit for male offenders with mental retardation located on the grounds of a state school, but *no* facilities for women.

The issue of defendants with developmental disabilities is a priority area for the state criminal justice system in New Jersey, but the State Department of Human Services places a low priority on this issue. Thus, the public advocate's goal is to raise the priority status of the defendant with developmental disabilities within the Department of Human Services.

An attorney with the New Mexico Protection and Advocacy System has been monitoring the state's prison system, which is under federal court supervision, to ensure correction of unconstitutional conditions, including the appropriate provision of mental health services. The correctional system has created a 12-person Mental Retardation Offender Unit for men. The New

Mexico Protection and Advocacy System has provided training to the prison staff on delivery of service to offenders with developmental disabilities, and has given legal rights training to inmates with either mental illness or developmental disabilities. The New Mexico system's staff advocates and attorneys provide some case management services to certain inmates with developmental disabilities and/or mental illness. They assist the inmates with: obtaining appropriate vocational rehabilitation programs; informal and formal administrative appeals procedures within the prison setting; prerelease procedures (i.e., obtaining Social Security Supplemental Income); and locating a place to live. The New Mexico system advocates for inmates to receive special educational services within the prison setting (the state prison has inmates as young as age 15). The system also provides technical assistance to attorneys and law students in the form of training on how to effectively represent clients with developmental disabilities in the areas of civil and criminal law. In addition, the system is in the process of training all of the public defenders in New Mexico.

The Michigan Protection and Advocacy Service has created a task force on offenders with mental illness and/or developmental disabilities. The task force is surveying the criminal justice and social service systems throughout the state on the local, county, and state levels to determine what services are in existence and which ones are in need of development. The task force is also publishing a manual for criminal justice personnel working with offenders with developmental disabilities. The Michigan Protection and Advocacy Service is developing an individual justice plan and an Identification of Legal Rights Protection project for offenders with mental impairments through the Michigan State Bar Association.

The Michigan Department of Corrections has a "Social Skills" unit that uses Adaptive Behavior case criteria to work with inmates who have mental illness and/or developmental disabilities. The prison systematically identifies inmates with developmental disabilities upon entry into the prison. The state Department of Corrections has attempted to enlist the state Department of Mental Health in addressing the needs of offenders with developmental disabilities, but has so far been unsuccessful.

The Ohio Legal Rights Services has assisted in the development and production of a training manual, *And Justice For All: Building Understanding of Citizens With Developmental Disabilities*. The manual is a training program to assist law enforcement officers to identify, communicate, and work with people with developmental disabilities.

The Protection and Advocacy System for Hawaii organized the Developmentally Disabled and Handicapped Prisoners Steering Committee for the State of Hawaii and developed a plan of action that addressed the needs of prisoners with developmental disabilities. The committee focuses primarily on identification of inmates within the prison and jails, identification of services available to the inmates, and implementation of a specialized case management system to ensure service delivery.

The Hawaii system provides individual advocacy on behalf of offenders in prison by investigating incidents of abuse and due process violations. The system provides technical assistance to attorneys representing defendants with developmental disabilities, as well as information and training to the public (Yuen, 1989).

The South Carolina Protection and Advocacy System for the Handicapped has made offenders with developmental disabilities a priority area. The system has provided staff advocates at the state prison to investigate abuse and rights violations, and has worked with the state Juvenile Justice Services. The system advocates appropriate, coordinated delivery of community services for offenders. It has provided technical assistance to attorneys, and its staff are called as expert witnesses in trials of defendants with mental retardation charged with capital offenses. The system has advocated for the abolishment of the death penalty for persons with mental retardation at the state and national levels.

The North Dakota Protection and Advocacy Project has worked closely with the state Planning Council on Developmental Disabilities to organize annual conferences focused on the needs of offenders with developmental disabilities. The Protection and Advocacy Project has designated offenders with mental retardation as a priority area and has assigned an advocate whose primary expertise is the offender.

The Louisiana Advocacy Center for the Elderly and Disabled began its outreach to defendants with mental retardation in 1986 with a grant from the State Planning Council for Developmental Disabilities for legal advocacy to minority youths. The Advocacy Center has represented adolescent juvenile defendants with developmental disabilities and mental retardation in juvenile court, and has trained all juvenile judges and all indigent defenders on issues surrounding developmental disabilities. *Disabled Youth and the Juvenile Court System,* a guide for attorneys and judges to use with juveniles with developmental disabilities, was written by the Advocacy Center. The center also serves as a resource for technical assistance to attorneys representing adults with developmental disabilities.

The Protection and Advocacy System for Texas—Advocacy, Inc.—assisted in the organization and development of the legislative mandate of the Texas Council on Offenders with Mental Impairments. This council has an unprecedented legislative charge to collaborate with criminal and juvenile justice systems, social service and education agencies, and advocacy organizations and policy councils to develop community-based sentencing alternatives for offenders with mental retardation, developmental disabilities, and/or mental illness. The council is responsible for the ongoing determination of the status of offenders with mental impairments, the identification and creation of necessary services, and for overseeing the reform of criminal codes that discriminate against offenders with mental impairments. The council is also charged with the development and implementation of independent case management services programs throughout the state.

Currently, two pilot projects are operational, one for offenders with mental retardation and developmental disabilities and one for offenders with mental illness. Expansion of these projects into five major metropolitan areas in the state is expected. The council has also conducted research studies on management of the "violent" offender, as well as an analysis of sex offenses committed by offenders with mental impairments. The council has submitted a resolution to the legislature on mental retardation as a mitigating factor in sentencing in capital cases, and has also recommended requiring both mandatory presentence investigation on all convicted felons suspected of having a disability and pretrial service reports on all offenders incarcerated in county jails who are identified as potentially having mental impairment. These reports would be used by the prosecutor's office in determining pretrial diversion from the criminal justice system. The council has requested funding for the state Education Agency, Rehabilitation Commission, Mental Health and Mental Retardation Department, and Commission on Alcohol and Drug Abuse to provide treatment and (re)habilitation services to offenders with mental impairments. Expansion of Medicaid has also been sought, to include (re)habilitation and service options for offenders with mental retardation. In addition, the council recommended that the Texas Adult Probation Commission and Board of Pardons and Parole provide specialized caseload supervision to offenders with mental impairments.

The council is composed of governor appointees and the directors of numerous state departments and commissions, as well as advocacy organizations. Representatives from Advocacy, Inc., sit on the Legislative and Developmental Disabilities subcommittees, and staff from Advocacy, Inc., chair the advisory committee to the independent case management project for offenders with mental retardation and developmental disabilities.

Advocacy, Inc., provides case management and legal services to offenders who experience problems with the criminal justice and/or legal systems. Provision of technical assistance to attorneys appointed to represent offenders with developmental disabilities is also a priority service. Case management services are available to offenders with mental retardation on death row and to the inmates of the Texas Department of Correction's Mentally Retarded Offender's Unit. Advocacy, Inc., provides training to criminal justice and social service personnel and to advocacy organizations regarding all issues affecting offenders with mental retardation and developmental disabilities. Information and referral are also provided to families, attorneys, advocates, and service systems regarding available resources for offenders with developmental disabilities.

Protection and Advocacy Systems in states that have committed resources to provision of services appear to have had a significant positive impact on the legal system, service delivery systems, and individual defendants with developmental disabilities. The National Association for Protection and Advocacy Systems should continue its efforts to make defendants a service priority in every state.

VOCATIONAL REHABILITATION

The Rehabilitation Act of 1973, amended by PL 99-506, requires that states establish client assistance programs (CAPs) to help inform all clients and client applicants of all available benefits under the Rehabilitation Act. The assistance can include pursuing legal, administrative, or other appropriate remedies to ensure the protection of individual rights under the Rehabilitation Act (Sec. 112 [A]).

Some Vocational Rehabilitation Commissions have specific regulations requiring that attention be given to prisoners at the time of their parole. For states lacking such specific policies, CAPs can often prove to be a valuable resource to offenders with mental retardation. CAPs can supervise referrals to the Vocational Rehabilitation Commissions, mediate services, and ensure that Vocational Rehabilitation counselors are sensitive to the needs of offenders. For example, many offenders with mental retardation are in need of treatment for drug abuse. Vocational Rehabilitation Commissions have been a traditional resource for substance abuse programs (Project Chance, 1989). CAPs also have the ability to advocate for changes within the Vocational Rehabilitation service delivery system, such as training of counselors on the needs of offenders with mental retardation.

By assisting with the referral process and advocating for appropriate services, CAPs can furthermore help offenders obtain services through the Independent Living Centers, a community resource to help defendants adapt to community living. CAPs are used also as a resource for defense attorneys, providing information regarding vocational rehabilitation services that may be alternatives to incarceration, as well as regarding the vocational potential of their clients.

The CAPs are an underutilized resource to defendants with mental retardation. In the past, persons with mental retardation were often categorized as having disabilities that were too severe for Vocational Rehabilitation services. With the advocacy efforts of the CAPs, some offenders have been able to gain access to these services.

PLANNING COUNCILS
ON DEVELOPMENTAL DISABILITIES

The state planning councils on developmental disabilities were established by the Developmental Disabilities Assistance and Bill of Rights Act of 1978 (D.D. Act). The councils are charged to act as advocates for persons with developmental disabilities; to develop state plans jointly with the administering agency; to monitor, review, and promote coordination of services; and to promote coordination of services. The councils are furthermore charged with demonstrating new ways to enhance the independence and productivity of persons with developmental disabilities as well as their integration into the community.

The individual justice plan and the independent case management models that many service systems have adopted help to fulfill the State Planning Council's mandate to promote productivity, integration, and coordination of services. In some states, special projects for offenders with developmental disabilities funded by State Planning Councils have demonstrated "new ways to enhance" community diversion alternatives and increased independence of offenders with developmental disabilities. Some Planning Councils have generated interest in the development of specialized treatment for offenders with substance abuse treatment needs and sexual offense counseling needs. Some councils have also encouraged the use of "cognitive interpreters" to assist professionals who work with defendants with mental retardation. The councils have provided grants for development and promotion of education and training guides regarding defendants with mental retardation and/or developmental disabilities for all personnel in the service and criminal justice systems. The councils have, in addition, proven to be an effective resource for instrumental coordination and development of interagency task forces that can be established to review and address the needs of defendants with mental retardation.

In 1981, the Nebraska Developmental Disabilities Planning Council funded a project entitled Crime and Community Program. This program developed the individual justice plan as a tool to coordinate community services, to address the habilitation needs of offenders with mental retardation, and to hold all agencies and involved parties accountable for the successful completion of the offender's parole or probation. The program focused on development of community-based alternatives to incarceration in four communities. Unfortunately, when the 3-year grant ended, so did the services. Nevertheless, the concept of the individual justice plan for offenders with mental retardation has spread throughout the country and has been utilized as an important tool for advocates, criminal justice personnel, and service providers nationwide.

The New York State Planning Council on Developmental Disabilities established a Criminal Justice Task Force whose purpose was to develop a screening model that included a diagnostic assessment component for professionals working with offenders with developmental disabilities. The assessment has been utilized to help develop service options for such offenders through the existing service delivery system. The New York Department of Health and Human Services Administration and the Developmental Disabilities Planning Council funded the preparation of a brochure listing applicable state statutes, describing characteristics of mental retardation, and providing information on how to identify a person with mental retardation.

In 1979, the Mentally Retarded Offender Project was funded jointly by the Ohio Department of Mental Retardation and Developmental Disabilities, the Law Enforcement Assistance Act, the Federation of Community Planning, and the Common Pleas Court. These entities cooperated to write *Mentally Retarded Offenders: A Handbook for Criminal Justice Personnel.* Partly as a result of this project, the Cuyahoga County Court of Common Pleas' Probation Department established the Mentally Retarded Offender Unit in 1980 to provide a probation officer who specializes in working with offenders with mental retardation. The Ohio Department of Mental Retardation provides psychological testing, evaluation, and treatment plans to the Mentally Retarded Offender Unit.

The unit identifies all offenders with mental retardation at the time of initial entry into the criminal justice system and provides segregated confinement if deemed appropriate. A supervised release program provides supervision for indigent defendants unable to pay bail pending their cases and monitors attorneys assigned to represent defendants with mental retardation. These case managers ensure that the defendants appear for hearings, and they assist attorneys with preparing cases and with understanding their clients' potentials and needs.

The North Dakota Governor's Task Force on Developmental Disabilities has organized annual statewide conferences on defendants with mental retardation through a grant from the North Dakota Developmental Disabilities Planning Council. A comprehensive manual for professionals working with defendants with developmental disabilities was developed, and a format of the individual justice plan was designed specifically to provide case management services for offenders with developmental disabilities. The intent of the conference was to promote a cooperative effort between the criminal justice, judiciary, legal community, and human services systems to meet the needs of defendants with mental retardation.

The Arizona Planning Council funded the development and publication of *A Guide for Law Enforcement Officers,* used for training professionals in the criminal justice system.

The State Planning Council in Florida funded an attorney with expertise in developmental disabilities and mental retardation to provide technical assistance to public defenders representing defendants with developmental disabilities and mental retardation in criminal matters. The attorney also furnished education and training for other components of the criminal justice system and assisted in the coordination of services through the State Human Resource Services.

The Colorado Planning Council on Developmental Disabilities has organized a task force to develop policy directions on alternative sentencing for offenders with mental retardation.

The Louisiana Planning Council on Developmental Disabilities has funded a state protection and advocacy system to provide legal representation to juvenile offenders with developmental disabilities.

The Texas Planning Council on Developmental Disabilities is a member of the Texas Council on Offenders with Mental Impairments. The Planning Council has also provided grant monies for independent case management program services.

The State Planning Council of South Carolina funded an advocate from the Protection and Advocacy System to be housed at the State Correctional Facility to investigate incidences of abuse and rights violations for inmates with developmental disabilities and to represent the inmates in fair hearings (L. Ravenel, personal communication, 1989).

UNIVERSITY AFFILIATED PROGRAMS

The Developmental Disabilities Assistance Act provides for university affiliated programs (UAPs). These programs are public or nonprofit agencies associated with a college or university. The University Affiliated Programs' activities include interdisciplinary training for personnel concerned with developmental disabilities, demonstration of integrated community services, technical assistance, and the dissemination of information (D.D. Act, Subchap. I, Sec. 18).

University affiliated programs have not yet been established in every state, but this can be expected to occur within a few years. Although a UAP specializing in offenders with mental retardation has not yet been formed, the UAPs can contribute to this area by conducting applied research, assisting in the design and development of specialized evaluative instruments, and analyzing pilot projects designed to provide services for offenders with mental retardation. They can provide research and demonstration funds to evaluate the feasibility of merging education, community mental retardation services, and criminal justice service systems. The UAPs can also test locus of responsibility questions to determine which authorities or agencies are most effective in working with offenders.

CONCLUSION

The mental retardation service system and the criminal justice system have had limited success in addressing the needs of defendants and offenders with mental retardation in the United States. This country has often relied on the criminal justice system as an interim measure between the past practice of institutionalizing all persons with mental retardation and creating new community-based alternatives. As a result, by incarcerating potentially productive citizens with mental retardation in an expensive criminal justice system, we have paid a higher price than the cost of developing viable community programs.

States originally wrote mental health laws (few specified the disability of mental retardation) to reflect the view that state institutions would control, care for, and treat offenders with mental impairments. The advocacy systems must work to bring about a reorientation of the law, legislatures, and criminal justice and service systems to reflect community-based options and equality under the law. Advocacy service systems must ensure that funding schemes are equitable in the allocation of money for community services and for targeted specialized services for offenders with mental retardation (Talbott, 1985).

REFERENCES

Alperin, H., Jones, W., Moschella, A., & Teahan, W. (1971, June–August). Representation of a mentally retarded criminal defendant. *Massachusetts Law Review, 103*–166.

Blackhurst, A.E. (1968). Mental retardation and delinquency. *Journal of Special Education, 2,* 379–391.

Brown, B.S., & Courtless, T.S. (1971). *The mentally retarded offender.* Rockville, MD: National Institute of Mental Health, Center for Studies of Crime and Delinquency.

Developmental Disabilities Assistance and Bill of Rights Act of 1978, PL 95-602, as amended.

DeWeaver, K. (1983, November–December). Deinstitutionalization of the developmentally disabled. *Social Work, 28*(6), 435–439.

Dickerson, M. (1981). *Social work practice with the mentally retarded.* New York: Free Press.

Dorwart, R.A. (1988). A ten-year follow-up study of the effects of deinstitutionalization. *Hospital and Community Psychiatry, 39,* 287–291.

Dudley, J. (1987, January–February). Speaking for themselves: People who are labeled as mentally retarded. *Social Work, 32*(1), 80–85.

Education of All Handicapped Children Act of 1975, PL 94–142.

Ellis, J., & Luckasson, R. (1985). Mentally retarded criminal defendants. *George Washington Law Review, 53*(3–4), 414–493.

Findholt, N.E., & Emmett, C.G. (1990). Impact of interdisciplinary team review on psychotropic drug use with persons who have mental retardation. *Mental Retardation, 28*, 41–46.

Greacen, J., & Morris, N. (1977). *Improving the responsiveness of the police to the mental health problems of citizens.* Working paper for President's Commission on Mental Health. Washington, DC: Police Foundation.

McAfee, J., & Gural, M. (1988). Individuals with mental retardation and the criminal justice system: The view from states' attorney general. *Mental Retardation, 26*(1), 5–14.

Morell, B. (1979). Deinstitutionalization: Those left behind. *National Association of Social Workers, 24*(6), 528–532.

Report of the Task Panel on Community Support Systems (Vol. 2, pp. 139–236). (1978, February 15). Submitted to the President's Committee on Mental Retardation. Washington, DC: President's Committee on Mental Retardation.

Ruiz v. Estelle, 503 F. Supp. 1265 (S.D. Tex. 1980). Aff'd in part and vacated in part, 679 F. 2d 1115 (5th Cir.), amended in part, 688 F. 2nd 266 (5th Cir. 1982), cert. denied, 460 U.S. 1042, 103 5th Cir., 1483, 765 L. Ed 2nd 795 (1983), now styled Ruiz v. McCotter, pursuant to Fed. R.C.V.P. 25 (d) (1).

Sprague, R.L., & Baxley, G.B. (1978). Drugs for behavior management. In Inwords (Ed.), *Mental retardation and developmental disabilities* (Vol. 10, pp. 92–129). New York: Brunner/Mazel.

Talbott, J. (1985, January). The fate of the public psychiatry system. *Hospital and Community Psychiatry, 36*(1), 46–50.

Texas Council on Mentally Impaired Offenders. (1989, February). *Project Chance evaluation.* Austin, TX: Austin Association for Retarded Citizens.

Wolfensberger, W. (1974). Will there always be an institution? The impact of new service models. *Mental Retardation, 9*, 31–37.

Yuen, G. (1989). *Punishment or treatment in prisons for persons with developmental disabilities. . . . Fair or right? An issue for protection and advocacy.* Working paper for National Association of Protection and Advocacy Systems, National Conference. Washington, DC: National Association of Protection and Advocacy Systems.

Chapter 11

PEOPLE WITH MENTAL RETARDATION AS VICTIMS OF CRIME

RUTH LUCKASSON

N O ONE IS immune to criminal victimization, but it appears that people with mental retardation are at higher risk than others. Not only are they subject to all the typical crimes, but they may be victims of additional crimes based on their disability. Evidence also suggests that people with mental retardation are less likely to receive just treatment from the American judicial system.

This chapter addresses the incidence of criminal victimization of people with mental retardation, the types of crimes in which they are victimized, the fear of crime and its consequences, and possible strategies the justice system can employ to address the needs of victims with disabilities. The issues faced by these individuals in the judicial system have unique components and thus require careful analysis, policy evaluation, and, occasionally, innovation and special accommodation. Rather than attempt to offer answers to the many questions that arise as the judicial system seeks to administer justice for victims with mental retardation, this chapter provides information that, it is hoped, will explore some of the more troubling aspects of the issues.

PREVALENCE OF VICTIMIZATION

Americans are more likely to be victims of crime than citizens of any other industrialized democracy ("Study Says Americans Lead as Crime Victims," 1990). According to a report by the U.S. Department of Justice's Bureau of Justice Statistics, in 1987 approximately 34.7 million crimes were committed against individuals or households in the United States (1989, Table 1). The report, often referred to as the National Crime Survey (NCS), summarizes data that are collected continuously across the United States and are categorized and analyzed on the basis of factors such as type of crime, age, region, gender, and identity of victimizer. Conducted by the U.S. Bureau of the Census, the National Crime Survey is the largest and most complete survey of rates of victimization. It is federally funded and is considered authoritative by policymakers.

The National Crime Survey does not, however, shed light on the victimization of people with mental retardation. People with mental retardation are not specifically identified in the data, so there is no way to know their number, or any information about the types of crimes in which they are victims, their rate of victimization, or any other information. The Bureau of Justice Statistics is not alone in this omission. Little research has been done on the victimization of people with disabilities by researchers in any sector (Balkin, 1981).

What research is available on victimization rates focuses almost exclusively on abuse and neglect. However, some small studies suggest the gravity of the overall problem of victimization. The Seattle Rape Relief Project, for example, found that 75% of the people it studied with developmental disabilities had survived at least one sexual assault, and that 99% of these assaults had been committed by someone known to the victims (Beyette, 1987). In addition, the Los Angeles Commission on Assaults Against Women estimated that an even higher percentage of people with developmental disabilities were victimized by sexual assault (Beyette, 1987).

LIMITATIONS OF DATA ON VICTIMIZATION

Based on the limitations described in this section, it is fair to assume that the actual rates of victimization of people with mental retardation are much higher than those reported in current crime surveys. For example, information on the abuse and neglect of people with disabilities is not collected in the Bureau of Justice Statistics data. Yet, since at least anecdotally it appears that much of the victimization of individuals with mental retardation may be classified as abuse and neglect, the omission of this category probably results in severe underreporting of victimization.

It is unclear why the victimization of people with disabilities is so frequently classified as abuse and neglect. The specific acts that occur—for example, torturing and perhaps killing an individual, violating an individual's body, hitting, yelling, withholding food, subjecting someone to dangerously unsanitary living conditions, depriving an individual of necessary medical care—are similar, if not identical to, the acts that occur in more serious crimes such as rape.

How and when does this classification occur? Is the classification dependent on the setting in which the act occurs? Who selects the classification of abuse and neglect? Does this classification assist prosecutors? Does it allow social service agencies to perform certain functions? Is it advantageous to victims to have their victimization classified as abuse and neglect rather than as crimes?

Perhaps use of the terms *abuse and neglect* reflects society's attitudes toward people with disabilities. It has been suggested that euphemisms are used to label the victimization of people with disabilities (cf. Lamb, 1991). For example, attacks on group homes for people with disabilities are frequently called "discrimination," rather than the bias-related hate crimes they really are; similarly, homicides of these victims are sometimes referred to as "mercy killings." Moreover, the National Crime Survey (NCS) (U.S. Department of Justice, 1989) depends in its data collection on first-person reports and descriptions provided by individuals who are capable and willing to report what happened to them: "Victimization surveys like the NCS have proved most successful in measuring crimes with specific victims who understand what happened to them and how it happened and are willing to report what they know" (p. 1). Unfortunately, many victims with disabilities do not have the skills or opportunity to respond to surveyors.

Several other problems exacerbate the shortcomings of victimization data. Any reports from people with disabilities that do make it into the national data probably come from proxies. The methodology for the NCS indicates, "In the case of . . . persons who are physically or mentally incapable of granting interviews, interviewers may accept other household members as proxy respondents, and in certain situations nonhousehold members may provide information for incapacitated persons" (U.S. Department of Justice, 1989, p. 119). Some, or perhaps many, victims with mental disabilities have been victimized by fellow household members. It is highly unlikely that proxy reporters who have victimized a person with mental retardation will provide data on that victimization to an interviewer. Moreover, although some "group quarters" such as dormitories, rooming houses, and religious group dwellings were included in the NCS data collection, the environment in which many victims with disabilities live—institutions—was excluded (p. 119). Add to these limitations the fact that, in 1987, among all populations, only 37% of all crimes were reported to the police (p. 10). Several factors make it likely that the overall rate of reporting by all victims with disabilities is lower than the average. First, some of these victims are in dependent relationships with people who provide care to them, and may fear graver personal harm if they make a report. Second, many of these individuals are devalued, and thus their reports may not be taken seriously by unsympathetic officers or lawyers. Third, many victims with mental retardation do not have the social supports or financial or emotional resources to sustain them through a difficult prosecution.

Collection of accurate national and local data is necessary for several reasons. First, this information is needed to help evaluate and document the need for additional services such as transportation to court and assistants to help individuals understand the judicial process; the justice system cannot be expected to respond to challenges to improve treatment of victims with mental retardation unless the need is proven. Second, and more important, all individuals have a basic need for personal safety and to protect their money and possessions. People with mental retardation and their families should be provided a realistic picture of the risks of victimization, so that they can learn to protect themselves, to organize their lives so as to avoid unnecessary risks, and to evaluate the need for extra precautions (e.g., using a fanny-pack rather than carrying a purse and installing home security devices such as door peepholes and burglar alarms).

CRIME PATTERNS

The increased vulnerability of people with disabilities to criminal victimization is based on many factors, such as:

- Their impaired judgment and intellectual abilities
- Their deficits in adaptive behavior
- Their accompanying physical disabilities
- The high-risk environments in which they often must live and work
- Their frequent contact with unscrupulous "benefactors"
- Their lack of basic knowledge of how to protect themselves
- The misinterpretations of their limitations and behaviors by courts and law enforcement officers

People with disabilities are plagued by certain crimes at a higher rate than the rest of the population. For example, the firebombing of newly opened group homes for individuals with mental retardation can be placed within the category of hate crimes. Such prejudice-driven crime is particularly pernicious because of its terrifying and tragic effect on its victims and its escalating effect on neighborhood tensions. Even though these crimes are analogous in every essential way to traditionally defined hate crimes, they may be excluded from statutory protections in many jurisdictions because of a lack of knowledge and understanding about the lives of people with mental retardation. Although Congress recently authorized the Justice Department to compile national statistics on hate crimes (Hate Crimes Statistics Act, 1990), such offenses against people with disabilities were not specifically included.

The deaths of individuals with disabilities, especially when at the hands of family members, are often reported as "mercy killings," limiting justice for the victims. For example, one prosecutor categorized a husband's "aided suicide" of his mentally disabled and elderly wife as similar to the "mercy killing" of a 38-year-old man with mental retardation by his father who did not want his son to outlive him (Lopez, 1990). Similarly, a woman gave her granddaughter with mental retardation and cerebral palsy an overdose of sleeping pills "to put the girl out of her misery"; and a 20-year-old man beat his stepson to death because the child had mental retardation and epilepsy and the stepfather was "tired of dealing with him" (Vegetable Speak-out, 1989).

Certain economic crimes are also likely to occur more often to people with mental retardation. For example, many individuals with mental retardation rely on state and federal benefits payments to support themselves. Frequently, these payments are forwarded through third parties such as Social Security representative payees. The November 1988 case of the Sacramento landlady in whose backyard the police found the bodies of eight Social Security beneficiaries brought this issue to national attention in a graphic way. Victimization is widespread, and some appointees have been accused of murder, larceny, and "slave trading," in which beneficiaries are sold from payee to payee (Tolchin, 1989). The Social Security Administration's most recent study of representative payees in 1983 found problems in 20% of the cases (Tolchin, 1989). Other types of financial victimization include consumer schemes and other buncos such as those involving encyclopedia sales, the "bank examiner" (swindlers claim to be bank officials trying to apprehend a dishonest teller), the pigeon drop (victim is offered a share of a large amount of money if victim contributes some "earnest money"), the charity switch (swindlers claim to be collecting money for a charity), and home improvements and repairs. The follow-up to financial victimization may extend beyond the loss of property: victims may suffer loss of self-esteem, a blow to hard-earned independence, personal guilt and self-blame for a crime in which they were actually an innocent victim, and fear that restrictions such as a guardianship or institutionalization might be forced on them.

Victimization of a vulnerable individual by a third-party payee may involve the loss of more than money. Slavery of another sort than the "slave trade" involving Social Security recipients was alleged in the case of *United States v. Kozminski* (1988). The victims in that case had mental retardation, had worked on the Kozminskis' farm for years, 7 days a week, 17 hours per day, living in a squalid, unheated trailer, receiving little or no pay, but unable to escape due to psychological duress. (They were told they would be institutionalized if they tried to leave the farm.) Although the U.S. Supreme Court ruled that the Kozminskis could not be prosecuted under the 13th Amendment's prohibition of slavery, the case did illustrate in vivid detail another way in which people with mental retardation are victimized. It also demonstrates how courts may fail to understand fully the nature of coercion when the victim is especially vulnerable due to mental retardation.

Experience informs us that some people with disabilities are also at risk of being victimized by their caregivers. The special relationship between vulnerable people and the individuals hired to provide their care can create unique opportunities for victimization, including physical and psychological harm, and financial loss. Even when caregivers are not directly responsible for the victimization, they may neglect to report and seek prosecution of suspected victimizers. Motivation for failure to report crimes will vary, but may include a desire to protect the reputation of the care facility or that of a colleague or another resident.

Clearly, any analysis of criminal victimization of people with disabilities must include both the typical range of offenses as well as other less frequently considered crimes to which these persons are especially vulnerable.

FEAR OF CRIME
AND ITS CONSEQUENCES

Criminal victimization is a national problem, a threat to the well-being of all citizens. But for people with mental retardation, it is a compellingly immediate and omnipresent threat. For example, in a 1986 Louis Harris survey (ICD Survey, 1986), nearly 60% of all people with disabilities whose activities were limited said they feared that their disabilities exposed them to high risks of being victimized by crime.

The fear of criminal victimization in itself can have profoundly negative effects on people's mental health and normal life functioning, causing them to deprive themselves of opportunities for activities they love—interactions with friends, shopping, and recreation (Berg & Johnson, 1979).

Case Examples

The following composite episodes, drawn from real cases, illustrate some of the issues related to the victimization of people with mental retardation.

1.   Bob, a man with mental retardation, lives in a boarding home run by Sam. For the 18 years since Bob was deinstitutionalized into his care, Sam has claimed to be Bob's guardian. However, no legal documents have ever been produced to substantiate this claim. Bob has held a well-paying job in a local business all these years. Bob's only time away from the boarding home is at his job. The remaining time he spends on the floor of his small window-less room, putting puzzles together on the mattress that serves as his bed. Sam has regularly threatened that, if Bob is dissatisfied, he can go back to the institution "with the other vegetables." Bob no longer suggests activities or changes he would like in his life.

Bob and Sam jointly hold the bank account into which Bob deposits money. Each payday, Sam accompanies Bob to the bank where Bob's check is cashed. Bob retains $20 spending money, while Sam retains an unknown but large amount for his "expenses." The remaining $25 – $50 is deposited in the bank account. Bob's co-workers worry that he is becoming increasingly depressed and withdrawn at work. They have noticed that he is limping and losing weight. Several bruises have appeared on his face. One payday after the close of business, a co-worker who happened to stay late saw Sam arrive to pick Bob up. Sam screamed at Bob that he hadn't waited at a particular spot and then chased him around the parking lot, Bob running as fast as he could and Sam pursuing him in his pickup truck. The co-worker telephoned the district attorney's office to report this assault, but the district attorney refused to prosecute the case because "the retarded are like children and children can't testify in court," and because "even if Bob could testify, no one would ever believe a retarded witness."

2.   Ruby is a young woman with mental retardation who recently moved from her family home to a group home. Her parents consider this move an essential step toward independence, and they trust that the agency supplying support services will provide the necessary assistance to their daughter. Ruby looks forward to getting married and having a family as soon as possible. She rides the bus to and from work each day. During her waits at the bus stop, she has met many men who tell her that they want to "marry" her. During the physical contacts that have occurred with these men, several of the men have, according to Ruby, "gone too far" after she asked them not to. At least one of the men has claimed to have a weapon, and several have threatened to tell the bus driver not to let her ride the bus any more if she reports her rapists to the driver.

Following a recent incident, a friend drove Ruby to the hospital. The hospital personnel did not collect the evidence necessary to prosecute a rape case, but instead sent Ruby to the emergency mental health center so that she could be evaluated for civil commitment and receive drugs to "calm her down." After the next incident, Ruby went instead directly to the police station. She was not able to describe the incident in a complete manner, and the police did not take a report or pursue the rapist. They did, however, give her a ride back to the group home. The police officers told the group home operators that the "kids" from the group home were causing too much trouble, and if they expected to stay in a "normal" neighborhood they better "act normal" and stop "expecting the police to handle all their little problems."

The victim assistance counseling program in Ruby's city refuses her requests for help because they "don't feel prepared to deal with mental retardation." The psychologist who provides contract services to the group home is unfamiliar with criminal justice issues.

3.   Annie has profound mental retardation and accompanying physical disabilities that cause her to be nonambulatory. She has lived in a large congregate institution her entire life. She recently became pregnant. A witness has reported suspicious circumstances involving an employee of the

institution. Although it appears likely that either a staff member or another resident raped Annie, she is unable to report the crime. Fearful of the reaction of the employees' union and the possibility of adverse publicity, the institution's administration declines to report the crime to the district attorney and, instead, conducts an "internal investigation." Subsequently, the only other action taken by the facility is to create a new rule forbidding private visits to residents unless a staff member is present the entire time.

    4.   John, who had mental retardation, was murdered by a neighbor in his apartment building. The defendant was prosecuted and found guilty under a special statute making the victimization of a person with a physical disability a felony. The state court of appeals overturned the conviction because it had been obtained under an improperly applied statute—mental retardation is not a physical disability and thus does not come within the protections of the statute. The statute had been passed by a well-meaning state legislature in an attempt to recognize the special vulnerability of victims whose disabilities made them easy targets.

    After his original conviction was overturned, the murderer could not be tried again. Prosecution under the ordinary homicide statute would now violate the principle of double jeopardy. This tragic result might have been foreseen had the legislature received guidance on proper consideration of the disabilities of victims of crimes, and on the risks and benefits of creating separate crimes or providing enhancements to sentences when the victim is especially vulnerable due to a disability.

    John was the first from his group home to move into an independent apartment. Since his death, his friends from the group home are refusing to move from the group home into independent living arrangements because they fear victimization and believe their victimizers will not be punished. The families of these young people have also lost enthusiasm for independent living. Several newspaper editorials have urged that all people with mental retardation need the protection of supervised group living arrangements. The service providers had never anticipated these criminal justice system issues. They need assistance in dealing with John's victimization, the fears of his friends and their families, and the community backlash against independent living.

    5.   Sara and Al are both 35 years old. Sara has mental retardation, and Al sustained brain damage in a car accident when he was 19. They are best friends, have dated for 15 years, and have long had plans to marry and move into their own apartment once one of them gets a steady job. Meanwhile, they spend all their free time together, as they have since they met. One night 6 months ago, Sara and Al made love while her parents were out of the house. Her parents returned unexpectedly, discovered the couple, called the police, and charged Al with raping their daughter. Al protested that Sara had "consented," but under the law in his state, people with mental retardation cannot,

by definition, "consent" to sex. Thus any sexual partner of an individual with mental retardation is guilty of statutory rape.

Sara wanted to testify in Al's defense, but the judge was confused by the legal doctrines and ruled that "if a mentally retarded person is incompetent to engage in sex, she must be incompetent to be a witness and incompetent for everything else." Al was found guilty of rape. When the time came for his sentencing, the judge would not let Al exercise his right to allocution (to speak formally to the court) because he was "retarded."

As these case examples suggest, many concerns particular to people with disabilities require considerations beyond the typical victim issues.

POSSIBLE STRATEGIES FOR THE JUSTICE SYSTEM

How might the justice system improve its response to the issues of victimization of people with mental retardation? Some possible strategies include:

1. Civil damage actions seeking large financial awards could be used for "routine" abuse such as verbal abuse, leaving the person in excrement, or failure to provide physical therapy (Lewin, 1990).

2. Sentence enhancements could be implemented for the victimizers of people with disabilities. (This writer is conducting research on the existence of these statutory enhancements, to be published in 1991.) Should an individual convicted of committing a crime against a victim with mental retardation be automatically subject to an enhanced punishment? What would be the justification for enhancements in these crimes? Would enhancements increase a tendency to stereotype these victims? If enhancements are determined to be a good idea, should they be discretionary or mandatory? Might an enhancement statute be counterproductive? Might it make a judge *less* likely to sentence the convicted individual? What factors should judges consider when using sentence enhancements?

3. Specialized victim assistance services could be provided, including: counseling, transportation to court, escorts to court, accommodations such as hearing aids in court, follow-along services to enable victims to understand court scheduling and proceedings, help with arranging medical treatment following victimization, or alternative dispute resolution services.

4. Disability advocates could be recruited to assist police and the judicial system with some aspects of these cases. Perhaps assistants could facilitate the investigation of certain aspects of these cases, provide psychological support to the victims during the judicial process, or help analyze the puzzling "fabric" of a case in which the victim's personal character and life are best understood in terms of the disability. Disability advocates might be helpful in reporting back to the court on the particular effects of victimization (Jaycox, 1981).

5. Alternative dispute resolution, such as noncourt mediation, could be used in some cases in which people with disabilities are the victims of crime. Hoffman and Wood (1987) have sensitively described the possible benefits of this strategy with elderly people. However, they pointed out that some experts oppose the strategy in situations where individual resolution might jeopardize the pursuit of class claims, where due process rights are likely to be unprotected, or where the balance of power is so overwhelmingly weighted against one party that justice is unlikely.

6. Further research on victimization issues is needed. There is an almost total lack of useful and accurate data on people with disabilities as victims of crime, and of their interactions with the judicial system.

7. Inappropriate reliance on the "abuse and neglect" classifications should be reduced. It appears that much of the victimization of people with disabilities gets termed "abuse and neglect." The actual actions in individual cases could often be identified as more serious offenses such as rape, homicide, and battery.

8. Policymakers should explore the possibility of special criminal statutes when victims have mental retardation.

9. Some assert that the impact of victimization is especially severe for people with disabilities. For example, the effects of an injury on an individual who is already frail owing to a physical handicap may be more damaging in terms of how much his or her body "can take." The victimization is likely to be more psychologically damaging, since the victim may become more fearful of another attack in light of the increased vulnerability of his or her body. Should courts conduct specialized inquiries into the unique trauma sustained by victims who have disabilities before sentencing the defendant? Should the court appoint professionals who specialize in the problems of people with disabilities to report back on the effects of the victimization? Should a group of assistants (Jaycox, 1981) who are disability advocates perform such a service for the courts?

GENERAL STRATEGIES FOR VICTIM ASSISTANCE

Certainly, people with mental retardation require victim assistance as much as, or perhaps more than, other crime victims. However, some victim support and counseling groups may not accept these individuals, believing that their needs are too specialized. Such groups might also express an attitude of devaluation toward the needs of victims with mental retardation.

Some victims with disabilities may need particular types of assistance—for example, materials written at a lower reading level (see, e.g., Baladerian, 1986). Some may also require counselors who are skilled in communicating with individuals who have disabilities. In other cases, the assistance program might be willing to accept the individual, but the individual may lack access to transportation or other resources necessary to participation in the program.

There are several specialized victims' assistance services that the justice system should consider developing to address the unique needs of victims with disabilities. These include:

- Counseling
- Transportation to court
- Escorts to court
- Accommodations such as hearing enhancement devices in court
- Follow-along services to enable victims to understand court scheduling and proceedings
- Help with arranging medical treatment following victimization
- Alternative dispute resolution services
- Access to individuals in environments such as nursing homes to monitor possible victimization

CONCLUSION

The problem of crime victims who have disabilities are complex. When proposing solutions, however, in addition to all the other considerations that must be kept in mind, it is critical to remember the basic value of all individuals, including those who have disabilities, and the principles of normalization, dignity of risk, and the right to treatment and habilitation.

REFERENCES

Baladerian, N., with Dankowski, K., & Jackson, T. (1986). *Survivor: Special edition for people with developmental disabilities, who have been sexually assaulted. Booklet I: For those who read best with few words.* Los Angeles: Los Angeles Commission on Assaults Against Women.

Balkin, S. (1981). Toward victimization research on the mentally retarded. *Victimology: An International Journal, 6*(1–4), 331–337.

Berg, W.E., & Johnson, R. (1979). Assessing the impact of victimization: Acquisition of the victim role among elderly and female victims. In W.H. Parsonage (Ed.), *Perspectives on victimology* (pp. 58–71). Beverly Hills: Sage Publications.

Beyette, B. (1987, March 5). Pages of good advice about "bad touches": New self-help guide for disabled persons. *Los Angeles Times,* p. 1.

Louis Harris and Associates, Inc. (1986, March). *The ICD survey of disabled Americans: Bringing disabled Americans into the mainstream.* (Conducted for ICD–International Center for the Disabled, in cooperation with National Council on the Handicapped). New York: ICD–International Center for the Disabled.

Hate Crimes Statistics Act, PL 101-275. (1990). 28 USC Sec. 534.

Hoffman, R., & Wood, E.F. (1987, Summer). Mediation and the elderly: A time for exploration. *BIFOCAL, American Bar Association Commission on the Legal Problems of the Elderly, 8.*

Jaycox, V. (1981). *Creating a senior victim/witness volunteer corps: An introductory brochure.* Washington, DC: National Council of Senior Citizens.

Lamb, S. (1991). Acts without agents: An analysis of linguistic avoidance in journal articles on men who batter women. *American Journal of Orthopsychiatry, 61,* 250–257.

Lewin, T. (1990, July 12). Neglect at nursing home: In a first, suits are won. *New York Times,* p. A1.

Lopez, S. (1990, January 19). Schwartz to handle "aided suicide" case. *Albuquerque Journal,* p. A1.

Study says Americans lead as crime victims. (1990, April 1). *New York Times,* p. 14.

Tolchin, M. (1989, March 22). U.S. trying to halt abuses of incompetent pensioners. *New York Times,* p. A9.

United States v. Kozminski, 108 S.Ct. 2751 (1988).

U.S. Department of Justice. (1989). *Criminal victimization in the United States, 1987.* Washington, DC: Bureau of Justice Statistics, U.S. Department of Justice.

Vegetable speak-out. (1989, September/October). *Disability Rag, 10,* 33.

Chapter 12

Training Programs and Defendants with Mental Retardation
History and Future Directions

Ruth Messinger
and Philip W. Davidson

MEETING THE NEEDS of offenders with developmental disabilities is complicated by the vast systematic differences between the developmental disabilities network and the criminal justice systems. In addition, there is a lack of qualified personnel to address the comprehensive needs of clients in all of the systems, and a paucity of intersystem technology transfer to improve communication and knowledge.

This gap in the workforce in these two systems has been addressed in previous reviews (Rockowitz, 1986; Santamour, 1975). The reasons for the gap include a limited number of pre-service university-based training opportunities for students to learn about developmental disabilities and about the criminal and justice systems, as well as a host of barriers for providing effective in-service training opportunities to personnel in all segments of the systems.

Limitations on educational resources are not a principal cause for the gap; rather, the available resources have not consistently and effectively ad-

The authors acknowledge the assistance of two people in particular in conducting the University Affiliated Program survey: William E. Jones, Executive Director of the American Association of University Affiliated Programs for Persons with Developmental Disabilities (AAUAP), and Roland Loudenborg, of the AAUAP Central Office staff. We also wish to recognize Virginia Potter's invaluable leadership in conducting the program evaluation project for the New York State Developmental Disabilities Planning Council summarized here.

221

dressed the need. This chapter reviews those resources, describing successful program models and highlighting directions for the future.

REVIEW OF EXTANT MODELS

A small but not insubstantial number of training efforts concerning offenders with developmental disabilities have been undertaken over the past 20 years. The first substantive activity was a Conference on the Naive Offender, organized by Santamour (1971) and held in Newport, Rhode Island. Sponsored by the President's Committee on Mental Retardation (PCMR), the conference assembled professionals from law enforcement and mental retardation to educate people in both bureaucracies about each other and about defendants with mental retardation. Santamour's effort predated a survey by Wood (1976) citing the lack of training about mental retardation for judges, prosecutors, public defenders, and private attorneys in the state of Missouri. Wood's survey also found that most correctional staff had no training regarding mental retardation.

Norley (1976) published the first manual for police training concerning defendants with mental retardation. This manual dealt with the recognition and handling of citizens with mental retardation and was notable for three reasons: 1) it urged mandatory training for police officers in every state, 2) it suggested that local parents should be used as local educators about mental retardation, and 3) it advocated that persons with mental retardation attend police training sessions so there could be intervention with them during the course of the training.

About the same time, a symposium was held in South Carolina to define problems and needs of offenders with mental retardation. Following this symposium, a manual was published discussing mental retardation, describing methods for law enforcement staff to assist offenders with mental retardation, and suggesting alternate strategies (Hoffman, 1978). The manual was subsequently adopted by the South Carolina law enforcement system for staff training.

In the late 1970s, some training programs were developed by University Affiliated Programs (UAPs) addressing youthful offenders with mental retardation. At Georgetown University's Child Development Center, juvenile justice system judges, probation officers, and vocational rehabilitation counselors were trained side by side with State Developmental Disabilities Planning Council members, parents, and local service agencies. Regional workshops and in-service training sessions were held in Virginia, West Virginia, and the District of Columbia. In Florida, the Youth Alternatives Project at the Mailman Center of the University of Miami developed a screening test called the Florida Developmental Screening Quicktest (McGrath & Owen,

1979). This test, the first such instrument for use in the criminal justice system, is still used by juvenile officers or other personnel untrained in administering psychological tests to screen for mental retardation among adolescents in detention. The test was accompanied by a training manual.

What can be said regarding the impact of these programs? Reichard, Spencer, and Spooner (1980) found that by the late 1970s only 11% of all states had training programs for judges and lawyers regarding defendants with mental retardation. About a decade later, McAfee and Gural (1988) surveyed all the states' attorneys general concerning identification and treatment of persons with mental retardation. Their findings suggested that such identification still was "neither systematic nor probable" and that "progress that has been made has been small, mostly informal and isolated in a few states" (p. 11).

NEW YORK STATE AS A MODEL

New York State has for some time emphasized the implementation of specialized high-quality community-based services for its citizens with developmental disabilities. However, Shilit in 1979 found that 90% of police officers, lawyers, and judges in the state had no training regarding mental retardation. Since then, the state has developed several training programs that can serve as models for other states.

In 1981, the University Affiliated Program for Developmental Disabilities, University of Rochester, was awarded a grant from the federal Office of Human Developmental Services to develop a comprehensive model for coordinating services to adult offenders with developmental disabilities in a local jail setting. As part of this project, a training program was developed that consisted of identifying logical target audiences for training, including sheriff's deputies, jailers, local police, district attorneys, judges, public defenders, probations officers, and a wide variety of private voluntary and state agencies serving persons with developmental disabilities. Special training materials were developed, including a 25-minute slide/tape show and an accompanying lecture. These materials were then "infused" into existing periodic training forums for in-service criminal justice and developmental disabilities (DD) professionals, as well as being integrated into the curriculum of the police academy. Posttraining follow-up studies revealed that the materials had an impact upon both the knowledge and attitudes of trainees.

In 1984, the New York State Developmental Disabilities Planning Council (NYS DDPC) adopted the issue of defendants with developmental disabilities as a major initiative, which led to several important statewide efforts. For one thing, the NYS DDPC formed a task force with membership from state and voluntary developmental disabilities and corrections and law enforcement agencies. The task force stimulated discussion at state, regional, and local levels and recommended the funding of 21 projects by the state DDPC.

In 1988, the NYC DDPC commissioned the University Affiliated Program for Developmental Disabilities, University of Rochester, to analyze activities in the criminal justice system resulting from the 21 projects (Rockowitz, Potter, & Davidson, 1989). The analysis revealed that approximately $200,000 of the state DDPC's funds were allocated to 4 projects emphasizing training, although most of the other 17 grantees performed some staff training as part of their effort.

Different training approaches and products were developed and utilized by the 21 grantees. One grantee trained criminal justice staff and inmates about epilepsy. Another grantee supported the creation at New York University of a curriculum and training guide in developmental disabilities (Heller, 1986). Separate modules in this curriculum described each particular disability and how it affected a person's status as a victim, a witness, or a perpetrator. Each module could be used independently or in combination with others, and included group training exercises.

A grant to one campus of the State University of New York (SUNY) supported a Clearinghouse on the Offender with Developmental Disabilities, with information about state grants, as well as resource materials, a speakers' registry, and publication of a quarterly newsletter. The university also developed a Certified Master's Level Program in Corrections Education within the SUNY system to help the state perform continuing education functions and create an opportunity for coordination of training efforts.

Training activities were neither measured for service system impact nor for changes in the way individual offenders were identified and managed. However, grantees reported that in some locales training did make a difference, and in several locations, it was continued and integrated into ongoing activities after the NYS DDPC grants ended.

The combined impact of the efforts sponsored by the NYS DDPC task force exceeded the results and products of the individual training grant sites. The task force both allowed cross-system "turf" issues and knowledge deficits to be resolved, and it served as a catalyst for cooperation between state agencies. Among the significant contributions of the task force were: 1) increased awareness of the issues involving defendants with developmental disabilities, 2) education of state legislators, and 3) greater networking across programs. Several recent efforts in New York State may be at least partially or indirectly the result of awareness raising by the state DDPC. These include:

1. The Commission of Corrections designated a staffperson for issues involving offenders with developmental disabilities.
2. Within the state administering agency for mental retardation and develop-

mental services, money has been appropriated to create a Bureau of Forensic Services to provide training that, among other things, keeps persons with developmental disabilities from becoming deeply enmeshed in the corrections system.

3. The New York State Department of Mental Health has established mobile units that offer training to local probation departments.

SURVEY OF TRAINING ACTIVITIES IN UNIVERSITY AFFILIATED PROGRAMS

University Affiliated Programs (UAPs) are federally funded centers with primary missions of interdisciplinary training, exemplary service, technical assistance, and information dissemination to improve services to persons with developmental disabilities. There are 54 UAPs, linked in a national network by membership in a national association and by frequent and extensive information exchange.

UAPs have long undertaken various educational and research projects germane to defendants with developmental disabilities, and many of the training projects reviewed here have involved UAPs in some way. To address issues of national resources in personnel preparation and in-service training concerning defendants with developmental disabilities, the authors decided to survey the UAPs. The project was conducted in collaboration with the staff of the American Association of University Affiliated Programs for Persons with Developmental Disabilities (AAUAP).

In the spring of 1989, a short survey was developed and sent to each of the UAPs. Questions included what training they had done in the last 3 years, the training focus, the intended target audience, how the efforts were financed, who the trainers were, available training materials, future plans, barriers encountered, and other agencies doing training. Out of 54 questionnaires sent, 40, or 74%, were returned. Table 1 lists the 13 UAPs indicating they had been involved in some training efforts concerning offenders with disabilities during the 1987–1990 period.

Table 2 shows that eight UAPs reported conducting pre-service training. Programming occurred in a variety of disciplines, from art educators in Georgia, to special educators at Temple University (Philadelphia) and the University of Kentucky (Lexington). Pre-service training was financed by core grants, fellowship training, and contract funds. Most of the training occurred at regular university training sites.

Table 3 lists the nine UAPs that reported providing in-service training. These projects focused on audiences primarily from justice, law enforcement, or corrections agencies. No consistent pattern appeared in the amount, format, or timing of the training. In-service training was funded mainly by UAP core and administrative grants or by state DDPCs. Although other sources of

Table 1. University Affiliated Program (UAP) training projects addressing defendants with developmental disabilities: 1987–1990

UAP	Location
Neuropsychiatric Institute, University of California, Los Angeles	Los Angeles
University Affiliated Program on Developmental Disabilities, University of Connecticut	East Hartford, CT
University Affiliated Program of Georgia, University of Georgia	Athens, GA
Human Development Institute, University of Kentucky	Lexington, KY
Developmental Evaluation Clinic, Children's Hospital, Boston	Boston
Rose F. Kennedy Center, Albert Einstein College of Medicine	Bronx, NY
University Affiliated Program for Developmental Disabilities, University of Rochester, School of Medicine and Dentistry	Rochester, NY
University Affiliated Cincinnati Center for Developmental Disabilities, University of Cincinnati	Cincinnati
Nisonger Center, Ohio State University	Columbus, OH
Crippled Children's Division, Child Development and Rehabilitation Center, University of Oregon Health Services Center	Portland, OR
Developmental Disabilities Center, Temple University	Philadelphia
South Dakota University Affiliated Program, Center for Developmental Disabilities, University of South Dakota	Vermillion, SD
Developmental Center for Handicapped Persons, Utah State University	Logan, UT

financial support were mentioned, only Georgia indicated that some of its efforts were paid for by the state's prison system.

Table 4 summarizes products and materials developed by the five UAPs reporting materials development activities. In most instances, the materials were developed to meet the needs of the particular UAP training effort. However, some of the materials, such as the testing material being validated by the Rose F. Kennedy Center, might be suitable for much wider use.

Most of the training at the UAPs resulted from modification or supplementation of existing training materials or development of new materials. A wide variety of products were mentioned. However, three UAPs stated that they had nothing already available. Few UAPs acknowledged awareness of, or

UAP	Level of training				Discipline trained	Location and support source of training
	Undergraduate	Graduate	Postgraduate	Other		
Neuropsychiatric Institute, University of California, Los Angeles			X		Child/adolescent Psychiatry Fellows	Child psychiatry follow-up
University Affiliated Program of Georgia, University of Georgia, Athens	X	X			Art education/ therapists	UAP trainee stipend
Human Development Institute, University of Kentucky, Lexington	X				Rehabilitation counseling Social work Special education	UAP core course
Developmental Evaluation Clinic, Children's Hospital, Boston			X		Psychiatry	UAP core course
University Affiliated Program for Developmental Disabilities, University of Rochester, School of Medicine and Dentistry			X	X	Psychology Social work Special education, pediatrics	UAP advanced seminar
Crippled Children's Division, Child Development and Rehabilitation Center, University of Oregon, Portland	X	X			Law enforcement Law students	UAP core grant
Developmental Disabilities Center, Temple University, Philadelphia	X				Special education Social administration	UAP core grant
Developmental Center for Handicapped Persons, Utah State University, Logan				X	Foster parents	State Department of Social Services

Table 3. University Affiliated Program (UAP) continuing, in-service education: 1987–1990

UAP	Recipient of training	Extent of training	Funding source
University Affiliated Program on Developmental Disabilities, University of Connecticut, East Hartford	Law enforcement officers	Twelve 2-hr. sessions	DDPC
University Affiliated Program of Georgia, University of Georgia, Athens	Judges Recreational staff at state prison	Workshops	UAP and prison
Developmental Evaluation Clinic, Children's Hospital, Boston	Court staff	Clinical work	
University Affiliated Program for Developmental Disabilities, University of Rochester (NY), School of Medicine and Dentistry	DD agency staff Interfaith Jail Ministry Volunteers	2-hr. lecture 2-hr. lecture for new volunteers three times/year	UAP core grant
University Affiliated Cincinnati Center for Developmental Disabilities, University of Cincinnati	Police department staff Judges, probation officers, public defenders, bail/bond staff, court administrators DD service providers 20 teams from DD/law enforcement	Five 3-hr. sessions 4-hr. session 2-hr. session 7-hr. train-the-trainer	CoMH DDPC
Nisonger Center, Ohio State University, Columbus	National Juvenile Forensic Center		State
Crippled Children's Division, Child Development and Rehabilitation Center, University of Oregon Health Services Center, Portland	Law enforcement, judicial personnel		UAP core grant

Developmental Disabilities Center, Temple University, Philadelphia	Law enforcement DD service agencies	Annual conference, other	UAP core grant Philadelphia Office of Mental Retardation
South Dakota University Affiliated Program, Center for Developmental Disabilities, University of South Dakota, Vermillion	State DD Offender Task Force		State Department of Social Services

DDPC, Developmental Disabilities Planning Council.
DD, Developmental Disabilities.
CoMH, Community Mental Health.

Table 4. University Affiliated Program (UAP) training products and materials: 1987–1990

UAP	Description of materials
University Affiliated Program on Developmental Disabilities, University of Connecticut	For training law enforcement officers
University Affiliated Program of Georgia, University of Georgia	Manual to do artwork with prisoners Copied video, "Justice, Accountability, and the DD Offender"
Rose F. Kennedy Center, Albert Einstein College of Medicine, Bronx, NY	Testing materials to identify and divert offenders with learning disabilities
Developmental Disabilities Center, Temple University, Philadelphia	For annual conference for personnel in criminal justice and mental retardation For continuing education
Developmental Center for Handicapped Persons, Utah State University, Logan	For biological or foster parents of youths with handicaps who are in custody

local availability of, many of the materials shown in Table 4. In addition, few respondents indicated the extent and nature of activities in this area by agencies other than UAPs. Almost all respondents indicated that there were training resources available through other state-level agencies. In general, scant information was offered about local training efforts and less about training being done in criminal justice or corrections systems.

Respondents were asked to identify barriers to their conduct of effective training concerning identification and treatment of defendants with developmental disabilities, as a function of whether the UAP engaged in training for that population. Table 5 shows the distribution of positive responses expressed as a percentage of all respondents ($N = 40$). For those UAPs not currently conducting any training, the subject of defendants with developmental disabilities was either not a priority or could not be addressed by knowledgeable staff. Insufficient linkage with the criminal justice system was identified as a barrier for all respondents, but the most frequently mentioned barrier was lack of funding.

Even given the barriers mentioned, the majority of the 13 UAPs reporting current training efforts indicated an intent to continue these programs; 3 other UAPs plan to begin new programs. None plan to conduct a rigorous evaluation of training methods. Those UAPs most involved with defendants with developmental disabilities over the past 10 years gave no indication of plans to do future training, citing a lack of funding as the principal reason.

Table 5. Barriers to training identified by responding University Affiliated Programs (UAPs): 1987–1990

Barriers	Percentage of all UAPs responding yes		
	Training (n = 13)	Not training (n = 27)	Total (N = 40)
No barriers	5	2.5	7.5
Not a priority of UAP	2.5	32.5	35
Inadequate training materials	10	5	15
Inadequate awareness of training need	10	12.5	22.5
Funding constraints	22.5	25	47.5
Lack of staff knowledge or commitment about offender	10	20	30
Insufficient collaborative links with criminal justice system	12.5	17.5	30
Not a priority within criminal justice system	2.5	0	2.5
Other organizations already doing it	0	5	5

Note: Columns and rows do not total 100% because some respondents answered yes to more than one barrier.

Overall, our data indicate that UAPs are not taking a leadership position in training concerning defendants with developmental disabilities. Although training efforts address audiences in particular geographical areas, there is little communication, coordination, or collaboration among UAPs active in this area.

INTERPRETATION OF UNIVERSITY AFFILIATED PROGRAM SURVEY FINDINGS

As indicated earlier, of the 54 University Affiliated Programs, 40 responded to our survey. Assuming that the 14 nonrespondents to the survey are not active in this area, then the 13 UAPs that are active represent about 25% of all UAPs. UAPs have a large range of missions, and there is substantial diversity of programs across the UAP network. A commitment to a particular problem by one-fourth of the programs may be viewed as substantial, especially recognizing the complexity of this particular issue.

In the area of model services and outreach training, UAPs are charged with developing cutting-edge programs and inculcating them in alternative community sites once they have been perfected. To this end, UAPs finance their functions through extramural support. They persist in their initiatives so long as: 1) the need continues; 2) the funding continues; and 3) there is a network to which the initiatives can be related, either academic or provider (Davidson & Fifield, 1989).

Although the needs continue concerning offenders with developmental disabilities (and they may even have increased as more and more persons with developmental disabilities become integrated in community settings), the funding for training is inconsistent and sporadic. Also, the networks are not in place. As stated, there is little communication among UAPs, less intersystem communication, and even less academic focus across the nation on this domain. Therefore, it is not surprising to see a waning of interest among UAPs that have been involved in this area.

THE REMAINING NEEDS

What are the remaining and ongoing training needs concerning defendants with developmental disabilities? First, if we are to accomplish the systematic modification required in the criminal and justice systems to accommodate the needs of this population, there is a continuing need for training in developmental disabilities for individuals working in the criminal and justice systems at all levels (judges, prosecutors, lawyers, police, parole and probation workers, prison personnel, public defenders, corrections specialists, etc.). Second, although some model training programs and some curricular materials have been developed, they have not been widely disseminated. Resource sharing to avoid duplication of effort should be a continuing priority. Third, products have been developed, but they have not been thoroughly evaluated for effectiveness and impact upon trainees or upon the clients they serve. Such rigorous evaluation is essential to improve the products. Fourth, there is a continuing need for a critical mass of experts with a hybrid specialization to address both sides of the issue. Such a nucleus of specialized personnel will increase the probability of cross-system knowledge and technology transfer.

What role might UAPs play in addressing these needs? The UAPs may be a unique national resource. They have both a networking capability through the American Association of University Affiliated Programs and, within their own ranks, there is already a concentration of documented expertise in this area. The UAPs have also demonstrated a capacity to link systems and program resources through interagency collaboration at the national level. As part of the 1987 reauthorization of the Developmental Disabilities Assistance and Bill of Rights Act (PL 100-146), the U.S. Congress authorized the funding of special training initiatives in UAPs. The focus of these initiatives was restricted to early intervention, enhancing skills involved in the direct care of persons with developmental disabilities, and aging and developmental disabilities. Each UAP was given an opportunity to submit a request for support to address one of these areas.

In 1988, the Administration on Developmental Disabilities (ADD) awarded training initiative funds to 33 UAPs. Each successful applicant was required to develop its project in collaboration with appropriate components of the service delivery system that employed persons in the target areas for training. All projects had to address both pre-service and in-service training. The projects were also mandated to network among participating UAPs, creating a resource-sharing and collaborative potential. The funded programs were then assisted by the ADD to establish national networks including themselves and a number of other UAPs interested in the targeted training areas, but which did not receive training initiative awards. These groups meet periodically and correspond regularly.

Project outcomes for two years included training materials, curricula, resource directories and newly developed training opportunities for thousands of staff in the service system. In one training area—aging and developmental disabilities—the network of UAPs was successful in influencing interagency collaboration within the federal government, leading to the development of a Memorandum of Understanding concerning joint training efforts on aging and developmental disabilities by the ADD and the Administration on Aging of the U.S. Department of Health and Human Services.

Public policy should be developed to ensure that funding, priority setting, and longevity become integral components of any future attempt to address training issues concerning defendants with developmental disabilities. This may require an increase in federal interagency collaboration, such as the UAP special training initiative just described, and should involve the ADD and the U.S. Department of Justice. This approach may allow the developmental disabilities network to take advantage of federal interests and priorities at the state level through the state DDPCs, Protection and Advocacy Agencies, and the UAPs.

REFERENCES

Coffey, O.D., Procopiow, N., & Miller, N. (1989, January). *Programming for mentally retarded and learning disabled inmates: A guide for correctional administrators,* Washington, DC: U.S. Department of Justice, National Institute of Corrections.

Davidson, P., & Fifield, M. (1989). *Developing and maintaining quality in university affiliated programs.* Silver Spring, MD: American Association of University Affiliated Programs for Persons with Developmental Disabilities.

Heller, D. (1986). *Recognizing and interacting with developmentally disabled citizens: A training guide for law enforcement personnel.* New York: New York Universities Department of Human Services and Education, Developmental Disabilities Project.

Hoffman, K.S. (1978). *The South Carolina law enforcement officer's guide to the recognition and handling of the developmentally disabled offender.* Columbia: University of South Carolina, University Affiliated Facilities.

McAfee, J.K., & Gural, M. (1988). Individuals with mental retardation and the criminal justice system: The view from states' attorney general. *Mental Retardation, 26*(1), 5–14.

McDonald, J.A., & Beresford, G. (1984). *Mentally retarded adult offenders in the criminal justice system.* Austin: Texas Council on Crime and Delinquency.

McGrath, F., & Owen, R.G. (1979). *The Youth Alternatives Program: A demonstration project serving the retarded juvenile offender.* Miami: University of Miami, Mailman Center for Child Development.

Norley, D. (1976). *Police training in the recognition and handling of retarded citizens. Guidelines and materials.* Arlington, TX: National Association for Retarded Citizens.

Reichard, C.L., Spencer, J., & Spooner, F. (1980). The mentally retarded dependent offender. *Journal of Special Education, 14,* 113–119.

Rockowitz, R.J. (1986). Developmentally disabled offenders: Issues in developing and maintaining services. *Prison Journal, 66*(20).

Rockowitz, R.M., Potter, V.S., & Davidson, P.W. (1989). *Offenders with developmental disabilities in New York State: A study of activities sponsored by the Developmental Disabilities Planning Council and their impact on barriers to comprehensive services.* Rochester, NY: University Affiliated Program for Developmental Disabilities.

Santamour, M.B. (Ed.). (1971). *Format and essays: Naive offender—New England seminar on retarded youth and the law enforcement process.* Newport, RI: Salve Regina College.

Santamour, M.B. (Ed.). (1975). *Mentally retarded citizens and the criminal justice system—Problems and programs.* Washington, DC: President's Committee on Mental Retardation.

Santamour, M.B., & West, B. (1979). *Retardation and criminal justice: A training manual for criminal justice personnel.* New Brunswick: New Jersey Association for Retarded Citizens.

Schilit, J. (1979). The mentally retarded offender and criminal justice personnel. *Exceptional Children, 46,* 16–22.

South Carolina Department of Corrections. (1974). *Mentally retarded offenders in the South Carolina criminal justice system—A proposed program.* Columbia: Author.

Wood, H.V. (1976). *Retarded persons in the criminal justice system: (1976). Proceedings of the 106th Annual Congress of Corrections.* College Park, MD: American Correctional Association.

Chapter 13

WHERE WE NEED TO GO
Perspectives on the Judicial,
Mental Retardation Services,
Law Enforcement, and Corrections Systems

JAMES G. EXUM, JR.,
H. RUTHERFORD TURNBULL III,
ROBERT MARTIN, AND JOHN W. FINN

A T THE CONCLUSION of the Presidential Forum that provided the impetus
for the present volume, the four participants who had initially summarized the issues concerning mental retardation and criminal justice from the
perspectives of law enforcement, the judiciary, corrections, and mental retardation services (see Chapter 1) were asked to discuss what they believed
should be the next steps toward improving the procedures for dealing with
these issues. The remarks of these four speakers subsequently were expanded
for presentation in this concluding chapter.—*The Editors*

A PERSPECTIVE ON THE JUDICIARY

James G. Exum, Jr.,
Chief Justice, North Carolina Supreme Court
Despite some evidence to the contrary, lawyers are teachable. Judges are also,
if to a somewhat lesser extent, teachable. In the future I am going to operate
on that belief and try to get people interested in sensitizing judges to the
problems discussed in the preceding chapters. We can then try to educate
lawyers about the existence of people and organizations concerned with the
rights and needs of people with mental retardation in the context of the
criminal justice system, so that attorneys will be informed about sources of
help and what to look for.

This is what I see ahead of me in North Carolina. First, however, I need to find out more about what is already being done in this area. I know of a number of resources already in place, such as the Institute of Government in Chapel Hill, the faculty at the University of North Carolina, the North Carolina State Bar, and the North Carolina Bar Association. We have programs of mandatory continuing legal education for lawyers sponsored by the North Carolina State Bar and judges sponsored by the North Carolina Supreme Court. I propose that the problems of people with mental retardation as they interact with the criminal justice system, both as victims and defendants, be incorporated into these mandatory continuing legal education programs for both judges and lawyers.

A PERSPECTIVE ON MENTAL RETARDATION SERVICES

H. Rutherford Turnbull III, Professor
of Special Education, The University of Kansas

It is my hope that the issues discussed in this book will raise the levels of knowledge and consciousness of many people regarding the involvement of people with mental retardation in the criminal justice system, and that reforms will be forthcoming. We should also be aware that we are enmeshed in a very political process, namely, considering and recommending action at the local, state, and federal levels.

What strikes me as unfortunate, however, is that we have gone about our business without the participation of any of the major professional or family organizations in the field of mental retardation except one—the American Association on Mental Retardation (AAMR). By and large, the "field" has not been greatly involved. I am sure that a major explanation for this is that the interaction between people with mental retardation and the criminal justice system represents a problematic issue.

The issue is problematic for several reasons. First, the number of people with mental retardation who come into contact with the criminal justice system is, fortunately, small. Second, the criminal justice system itself is unfamiliar to many people in the mental retardation field, most of whom are not lawyers, police officials, corrections officials, or judges. Third, the dominant focus of the field has been on the development of services for people with mental retardation and their families. Criminal justice systems are not regarded as services comparable to special education, vocational rehabilitation, social services, medical services, income-maintenance programs, family support services, and so on. Fourth, there is probably some reluctance on the part of the field to confront the fact that the stigma of mental retardation is exacerbated when the label "criminal" is added to it; the problems of appropriately serving people with mental retardation are confounded by these people's involvement with other "deviant" populations, making it all the more difficult for those who advocate for *other* services for the great majority of people with mental retardation (who are not involved with the criminal justice system) to address the problem or give it priority for even a short while.

Creating Awareness and Initiatives

Yet it is precisely because of the complexity of the issues surrounding mental retardation and the criminal justice system that they deserve special attention. For one thing, we need one or more highly placed officials in the federal government who will give the matter visibility and attention. Attorney General Richard Thornburgh's remarks (see Foreword) encourage all of us, and we look to him for that leadership. Second, we need an interdepartmental initiative, at both the federal and state levels, to focus attention and money on preventing criminal behavior by people with mental retardation. Cooperative efforts by the U.S. Departments of Justice, Education, and Health and Human Services might take the form of special funding opportunities for research, model development, and training/technical assistance efforts. Third, we need to have the professional and family associations (such as the AAMR, the Association for Persons with Severe Handicaps, the Association for Retarded Citizens-USA, and the National Down Syndrome Congress) sponsor symposia in their conferences, and give priority in their policy agendas to issues relating to mental retardation and the criminal justice system. Fourth, we need to have the police and corrections officials address the topic through their associations, such as the International Association of Chiefs of Police and the Fraternal Order of Police. Fifth, we need to have the issues brought to the states by way of thoughtful and deliberate technical assistance from the National Conference of State Legislatures, National Conference of Governors, and National Conference of State Court Judges. Finally, we need to help professors of law develop the ability to teach about these issues with concern for the human dimensions of mental retardation. In short, we need to mainstream the issues into the usual and ordinary spheres of activity of all people and organizations that address the issues of mental retardation and criminal justice, separately or holistically.

Training

Clearly, however, specific steps must be taken to ensure that people with mental retardation are, first, not involved in the criminal justice system and, second, when involved, dealt with appropriately. These efforts should result in the creation of a national capacity, not—again—of islands of excellence.

We must start with efforts to train people with mental retardation and those who work with them. In special education and other direct-training systems, we should concentrate on assisting people with mental retardation to develop the skills they need to be law-abiding citizens, to know the difference between lawful and unlawful behavior, and to model their own behavior accordingly. Currently, there is precious little effort to teach decision-making and self-advocacy techniques to people with mental retardation. Yet, those skills and techniques may be most helpful in forestalling behavior that snares people in the criminal justice system.

We should concentrate, too, on training law students, lawyers, and judges in issues related to mental retardation and the criminal justice system. Likewise, we should train those who enforce the law by other means—police and corrections officials, including probation and parole officers and officials.

In addition, we need to do a better job of training forensic professionals concerning mental retardation and its special relevance to criminal justice issues. Psychiatry and psychology, in particular, are ripe for developing better capacities for engaging the subject of mental retardation in forensic aspects of their disciplines.

Models and Their Replication

We have heard that there is a great need to change the systems that affect people with mental retardation in direct and often life-affecting ways. In particular, we have heard that the forensic system (the evaluation of people with mental retardation and the assessment of their behavior for criminal justice purposes) is in need of repair. We have been told the same is true with respect to the corrections and postdischarge (parole and probation) systems. Yet, we know there are models of effective systems. We need, therefore, to do a better job of studying, replicating, evaluating, and modifying the models and the existing nonmodel systems. We know there are islands of excellence, but we need to create peninsulas and then continents of state-of-the-art.

Quality Assurance and Attorney Decision Making

We have heard that too often counsel for people with mental retardation are unaware of the fact of mental retardation or of how to make clear its significance on behalf of their clients. We need to develop capacities to assist these counsel, and not simply through preservice and inservice (continuing legal) education. We need units of special forensic experts that would be available to defense counsel alone; special teams in the public defender system; national and state leadership by judges to help ensure that the federal and state courts are better able to try people with mental retardation fairly; and, perhaps, carefully controlled systems for third-party consent on behalf of people with mental retardation who themselves are incapable of giving or withholding consent for important pretrial, trial, and posttrial decisions.

Assurance of Equal Opportunities

Attorney General Thornburgh makes a particularly compelling point when he says that laws and policy should not "free" people with mental retardation from a system of specialized services just to incarcerate them in other systems (see Foreword). His caution against creating nothing more than purely equal treatment, rights, and opportunities is germane to the policies and opportunities that people with mental retardation have in the criminal justice system. We have heard about the New York State statute that results in automatic involuntary commitment upon a plea of not guilty by reason of mental disability or a verdict of not guilty by reason of mental disability. But we have not received assurances that such an approach is necessarily or even usually the most appropriate for the purposes of deterrence, prevention, and punishment of crime and habilation of the offender.

Capital Punishment

A consensus exists that capital punishment of people with mental retardation should be prohibited by federal and state laws. It already is prohibited under the current federal laws and the laws of some states. But because it is not unconstitutional under the Eighth Amendment (which prohibits "cruel and unusual punishment"), the U.S. Congress and the states have the option to impose it.

We cannot permit capital punishment of any person who meets the characteristics of mental retardation, no matter how mild the degree of retardation. To have mental retardation means that there is a ceiling of intellectual and behavioral capacity that the person simply cannot exceed. To put to death those who by definition have mental retardation is simply unacceptable.

To prevent capital punishment from being carried out, we need to have special funding for groups to represent capital defendants with mental retardation. A national capacity, augmented by state and local capacity, must be created. Simultaneously, the present vigorous effort to exempt people with mental retardation from federal and state laws regarding capital punishment must continue, and on an enlarged scale.

Corrections

Just as it is always impermissible to execute anyone with mental retardation, so must there be other presumptions in favor of such individuals in the corrections system. Another irrefutable presumption must be that mental retardation will always be taken into account by any sentencing authority as well as by parole and probation authorities. In addition, there should be a presumption in favor of probation in lieu of incarceration. This may be a rebuttable presumption.

I recommend that the vocational rehabilitation system be modified so that it is encouraged, if not required, to serve people with mental retardation who have been convicted and have completed their sentences. Without a job to anticipate, discharge from prison is a dead end.

Inservice education for corrections officers clearly is needed and is even likely to be welcomed by those officers. Similarly, interagency agreements between corrections and community-based service providers (e.g., vocational rehabilitation, mental retardation/developmental disabilities) would provide corrections officers the opportunity to work with those agencies' officials so that corrections becomes a device not only to control but to enable people with mental retardation to be more effective citizens. Such agreements also would make it possible for the person leaving prison to be more appropriately integrated into the receiving community.

A further point is that federal funding would aid in developing and standardizing instruments used by forensic specialists to determine if a person has mental retardation and, if so, the degree of disability. A far more precise and reliable measure of retardation, for forensic purposes, would be very useful to everyone involved in the criminal justice process.

There are several model state and local corrections programs. It is important to know how they work and what improvements are necessary, and to replicate them nationally.

Sentencing

It is clear that the American Bar Association (ABA) Criminal Justice Mental Health Standards do not take sufficient account of the fact of mental retardation in persons charged or convicted of crime. Likewise, the Federal Sentencing Guidelines do not permit sufficient flexibility to judges in sentencing people with mental retardation who have been convicted of crime. The ABA and U.S. Sentencing Commission should return to their tasks, giving special emphasis to the implications for their previous work of the fact of mental retardation.

Victimization

We know that people with mental retardation are victims of crime. What we do not know, however, is the degree to which they are victims or the crimes that victimize them most often. Moreover, we know that people with mental retardation are subject to various forms of "hate crimes," and that the law does not prohibit perpetrators from making people with mental retardation the objects of their behavior. We need much better systems for collecting data on the victimization of people with mental retardation. And we need especially to acknowledge that, in addition to hate crimes, people with mental retardation are victims of crimes against their property and against their body by people who purport to be their caregivers. Sexual, physical, and emotional abuse, and other forms of abuse and neglect, are too frequent in institutions and community settings, and protection against the criminal behavior of caregivers is too scant.

One response to victimization—other than better reporting, enacting more laws to protect people with mental retardation against victimization, and enforcing those laws more vigorously—would be a national system for screening applicants who seek jobs working with people with mental retardation. Such a system would help identify those who have been dismissed from previous work with this dependent population because of having committed crimes or otherwise harming people with mental retardation. Another response would be to augment the protection and advocacy systems, or to create other legal defense capacities to facilitate the reporting and prevention of crimes against people with mental retardation. Likewise, making rape-victim services more readily available to people with mental retardation would be a means to ensure decent follow-up after rape and to help detect and punish perpetrators of sexual crimes. Finally, a whistle-blower statute—enacted federally and by each state—that protects the person who reports the perpetrators of crimes may be useful in preventing and punishing crime.

Conclusion

The authors contributing to this book have made their own recommendations. I have but highlighted those that seem to have special merit. I would also reiterate the plea that special consideration be given to the problems discussed in this book. Clearly, specific and narrow reforms are overdue.

It is especially necessary—indeed, indispensable, if there are to be other reforms—for the issue of mental retardation and criminal justice to be elevated to a national priority, not by those people and groups who clamor for law and order at any price, but by those who are the guardians of law and order under the restraint of the Constitution and with knowledge of and sensitivity to the effects of mental retardation upon victims and perpetrators. These are the groups that represent professionals, people with mental retardation and their families, police and corrections officials, judges, and lawyers. Until the issue becomes politically important, I fear it will not attract the widespread attention, and capacity for reform, that it needs.

In closing, my recommendations are, first, that those of us who care about the issue elevate it on the policy agendas, and, second, that we be forever vigilant to ensure that, in the name of reform, we avoid doing more damage than good.

A PERSPECTIVE ON LAW ENFORCEMENT

Robert Martin, Commanding Officer, Detective Headquarters Division, Los Angeles Police Department

How many people concerned with mental retardation and the criminal justice system know their local police agency's stance on this issue? Very few! It is important to go find out. How many know how their community service agencies react when contacted by the police about a suspected offender with mental retardation?

When police officers pick up an individual with apparent mental retardation on the street, they may contact a professional person at a social service, mental health, or mental retardation facility to acquire information or assistance on the disposition of the individual before taking him or her to the police station or jail. Unfortunately, most professionals in the service system don't want to assume any responsibility for assisting the suspected offender or admitting him or her to their facility. The police officer is then left with one course of action—taking the individual to the police station and, perhaps, placing him or her under custody (i.e., in jail). Then, the judge is the next person who will be responsible for the disposition of the individual. There is a need for the service system to be more responsive to the police. Otherwise, the police become progressively more inclined simply to release the individual on the street or to take the individual directly to the police station and subsequently to jail without checking with a service provider.

It is important for advocates in the mental retardation field to discuss these issues with their local police officials, and, similarly, to find out what is happening in their local communities. Find out what motivates police officers and other components of the criminal justice system. I guarantee that what police officers respond to is what every other employed person responds to—the bases on which they are evaluated.

One may prefer that police officers were evaluated on the basis of all those warm cuddly things they ought to do. But the bottom line is that the police department wants to know things like: How many arrests did they make? How many tickets did they write? How many people did they throw in jail? We do not ask the number of people with mental retardation that were assisted.

The next level of review is at the prosecution agency. Essentially, they are evaluated on the conviction rate based on cases filed. To a degree, this favors people with mental retardation, because one of the things that prosecutors always look for is the diminished capacity defense. If there is any possibility of that, or if the case is weak, they will disregard the case against the person with mental retardation. Unfortunately, that is a two-edged sword, because now the person with mental retardation is put back on the streets rather than in an appropriate treatment program.

Another area requiring serious attention is that of statistics. Research is needed into improved methods of collecting data on offenders with mental retardation. In Los Angeles, a number of recommendations have been made for improving the data on mental disabilities. Usually, recommendations amount to passing the buck: we make the recommendations and we expect someone else to implement them. But what happens? The usual responses from government bureaucrats are that they don't have enough money or enough equipment; or, they may not respond at all.

My most urgent recommendation to practitioners and other advocates involves the need to identify the people who should be involved in improving services to offenders with mental retardation, and to find ways to get the message to them, particularly through trade magazines (i.e., those of the legal profession), newsletters, conferences, and so on. In the law enforcement area, the International Association of Chiefs of Police is a powerful organization with a magazine to which mental retardation professionals should consider submitting articles. Journals of the state police officers' associations should also be queried. Advocates also need to find out where the police unions are. For example, the Fraternal Order of Police on the East Coast is very influential. Sheriffs' organizations too, should not be overlooked. I suggest that by whatever means, advocates should talk directly to the people they are trying to influence. There is an untapped audience out there that can do wonderful things.

A PERSPECTIVE ON CORRECTIONS

John W. Finn, Director, Forensic Services,
New York Office of Mental Retardation
and Developmental Disabilities

I offer two cautions to those responsible for dealing with the issues highlighted in this book. First, I believe we must all resist the tendency to make public policies based upon the extremes of issues. Most of the problems discussed here have some areas of agreement as well as substantial areas of controversy. Too often we pass over the areas of agreement and focus on the extremes of controversy when deciding questions of public policy. Although, clearly, we must continue to articulate our differences, it is even more important to cultivate areas of common interest and agreement. Most of the work that needs to be done on behalf of persons with mental retardation and developmental disabilities who are involved in the criminal justice system will not be of national significance, nor will it receive national attention. Most of the work will occur in the mainstream of the human services and criminal justice systems, not on the peripheries where the controversies are most intense. Most of what we do to help our clients is rather mundane, sometimes tedious, and often frustrating. We must remember that although it is important to win the wars, it is also important to fight valiantly in the little battles that erupt every day.

Another caution is that we not confuse bad practice with bad policy or bad law. We must not compromise our standards of practice because we have not achieved our goals in policy or laws. Our clients need us to continue to work within the existing structures on their behalf, while we advocate for the more broadly based changes that are also clearly needed.

The challenges in helping persons with mental retardation and developmental disabilities who are involved in the criminal justice system are undeniable, as are the adversities and risks. But the opposite side of adversity is opportunity. Our challenge is to seize the opportunity presented by the adversity and use it to make a difference in our clients' lives.

Appendix A

Brief of American Association on Mental Retardation et al. as Amici Curiae in Support of Petitioner in re Johnny Paul Penry, Petitioner, v. James A. Lynaugh, Director, Texas Department of Corrections, Respondent

James W. Ellis and Ruth Luckasson
(with an introductory essay by Richard Burr)

SOMETIMES WE ARE less civilized and less humane than our ancient ancestors. In the Middle Ages, the death penalty was used far more frequently, and for a much broader array of crimes, than it is today. Nevertheless, people in the Middle Ages were unequivocal about one thing: death should not, indeed must not, be a sentence for a person with mental retardation who committed a capital crime. In *Penry v. Lynaugh* (492 U.S. 302 [1989]), the United States Supreme Court rejected this ancient rule of humanity, holding that the imposition of a death sentence in the case of a mentally retarded offender is not prohibited as a cruel and unusual punishment.

The argument against the death penalty for offenders with mental retardation was eloquently presented in *Penry* through an amicus curiae brief by the American Association on Mental Retardation, the American Psychological Association, the Association for Retarded Citizens of the United States, and eight other professional and voluntary associations interested in and knowledgeable about people with mental retardation. Despite the power of the

245

amicus argument and the wise humanity of our heritage, the Supreme Court was not moved to spare persons with mental retardation from condemnation. The indignity of the Supreme Court's decision should be an affront to all of us, proponents and opponents of capital punishment alike.

How great an indignity *Penry* is can best be understood by reading the amicus brief reproduced on the pages following this essay. It is helpful first to have an overview of the legal argument presented to the Court, the Court's response, and the need to move beyond *Penry.*

A sentence of death is a cruel and unusual punishment under the Eighth Amendment if it is imposed on a person who lacks sufficient moral culpability for the murder that has been committed. Moral culpability is measured by the mental state of the person at the time of the murder. To bear sufficient moral culpability, the person must have killed *purposefully*—with the intent that the victim die—and *immorally*—with at least reckless disregard for the rights and well-being of the victim. Under these criteria, the amicus curiae brief in *Penry* argued that a person with mental retardation lacks the degree of moral culpability necessary for the imposition of the death penalty.

The great majority of people in this country concur with the Eighth Amendment's mandate: They do not believe that the death penalty should be imposed on people with mental retardation. In two recent national polls conducted by respected public opinion analysts for *Time* and Cable Network News (CNN) and for the NAACP Legal Defense and Educational Fund, Inc. (1989) nearly two-thirds of all respondents were opposed to the death penalty for people with mental retardation, even though three-fourths of the respondents were in favor of the death penalty for persons convicted of murder. Similar results were obtained in recent public opinion surveys in Georgia, Florida, Texas, and South Carolina. Significantly, no public opinion survey conducted within the past 5 years—the period within which most modern-era executions have occurred—has reported contrary results.

Notwithstanding the clear command of the Eighth Amendment and the public's disavowal of the death penalty for people with mental retardation who are convicted of murder, the Supreme Court decided, by a 5–4 vote on June 26, 1989, in *Penry,* that the death penalty for this population is not a cruel and unusual punishment. The majority rested its decision on two grounds. Disregarding and distorting the amicus curiae presentation, the Court was unconvinced "that all mentally retarded people of Penry's ability [mild-moderate retardation]—by virtue of their mental retardation alone, and apart from any individualized consideration of their personal responsibility—inevitably lack the cognitive, volitional, and moral culpability associated with the death penalty." (106 L.Ed.2d at 290–91). To reach this conclusion, the Court relied only on the notion that the abilities of people with mental retardation vary widely; it ignored the teaching of the mental retardation professionals that despite these variations in ability, the universal disabilities of mental retardation preclude the offender with mental retardation from acting with sufficient moral culpability to be sentenced to death. The second ground for the Court's decision was that only one state (now five states) and the federal government (in federal criminal prosecutions) prohibit capital sentencing for offenders with mental retardation. The Court did not discount the public opinion surveys as reliably reporting public sentiment. However, it held that until this sentiment "find[s] expression in legislation, . . . there is insufficient evidence of a national consensus against executing mentally retarded people convicted of capital offenses for us to conclude that it is categorically prohibited by the Eighth Amendment" (106 L.Ed.2d at 289).

The Supreme Court's decision thus failed to act upon the clear and unequivocal evidence that the disabilities of mental retardation do categorically lessen the moral culpability of offenders with mental retardation, and that capital punishment for this population is unacceptable to the people of this country.

The alternative provided by the Court—the consideration of mental retardation simply as a mitigating circumstance in a death penalty trial—is inadequate protection for offenders with mental retardation, for three reasons. First, people with mental retardation are more likely than nonretarded people to be convicted and sentenced to death for capital murders they did not commit or in which they were only passive accomplices, because they are vulnerable—owing to their disabilities—to assuming the blame for and confessing to far more than they could accurately be held accountable for. Accordingly, there is frequently less assurance that the capital prosecution process has functioned reliably when the offender has mental retardation. Second, even though a mentally retarded person's disabilities should always preclude the death sentence, if those disabilities are only considered as a mitigating factor, in some cases the disabilities will so pale in comparison to the apparent brutality or senselessness of the murder that they will carry no weight in the sentencing calculus. Third, in some cases the offender's mental abilities will be viewed as establishing a risk of future violent behavior, which weighs heavily in favor of a sentence of death.

Accordingly, remedial legislation is sorely needed. Legislation prohibiting capital punishment for people with mental retardation who are convicted of murders that are otherwise death-penalty-eligible must be recommended to the states. Further, since the U.S. Congress has jurisdiction to effectuate the Due Process Clause of the Fourteenth Amendment—through which the Eighth Amendment applies to the states—Congress has the authority to enact legislation prohibiting capital punishment for offenders with mental retardation.

Finally, no such remedial legislation can be effective without a concurrent change in the frequency and quality of pretrial mental health evaluations for persons accused of capital murder. At present, no accurate estimate can be

made of the number of persons on death row who have mental retardation. The reason for this is that pretrial mental health evaluations frequently are inadequate for the detection and assessment of mental retardation. They are inadequate because virtually every person charged with capital murder is poor and is thus dependent on the state to provide resources for a mental health evaluation. Almost inevitably, however, the resources provided are professionally inadequate. Thus, the mental health evaluators funded by the state often fail to obtain the accused's school records, they fail to obtain an accurate social, medical, psychiatric, and family history, they fail to conduct intellectual testing, or they fail to utilize intellectual tests that are known to be reliable—or sadly, they fail in several of these respects. Accordingly, no remedial program designed to protect the offender with mental retardation from capital punishment can be meaningful unless, at the same time, the professional quality of the pretrial mental health evaluations provided to poor people accused of capital murder is significantly improved to meet or exceed the diagnostic-evaluative procedures necessary for reliable assessment.
—*Richard Burr*

REFERENCES

NAACP Legal Defense and Educational Fund, Inc. (1989, January 11). *NAACP Legal Defense and Educational Fund, Inc., survey reveals "solid base of support for positive action on race relations."* New York: Author.

No. 87-6177

In The
Supreme Court of the United States
OCTOBER TERM, 1988

———

JOHNNY PAUL PENRY,
Petitioner,
v.

JAMES A. LYNAUGH, DIRECTOR, TEXAS DEPARTMENT
OF CORRECTIONS,
Respondent.

———

On Writ of Certiorari to the United States
Court of Appeals for the Fifth Circuit

———

BRIEF OF AMERICAN ASSOCIATION ON MENTAL
RETARDATION, AMERICAN PSYCHOLOGICAL
ASSOCIATION, ASSOCIATION FOR RETARDED
CITIZENS OF THE UNITED STATES, THE
ASSOCIATION FOR PERSONS WITH SEVERE
HANDICAPS, AMERICAN ASSOCIATION OF
UNIVERSITY AFFILIATED PROGRAMS FOR THE
DEVELOPMENTALLY DISABLED, AMERICAN
ORTHOPSYCHIATRIC ASSOCIATION, NEW YORK
STATE ASSOCIATION FOR RETARDED CHILDREN,
INC., NATIONAL ASSOCIATION OF PRIVATE
RESIDENTIAL RESOURCES, NATIONAL ASSOCIATION
OF SUPERINTENDENTS OF PUBLIC RESIDENTIAL
FACILITIES FOR THE MENTALLY RETARDED,
MENTAL HEALTH LAW PROJECT, AND NATIONAL
ASSOCIATION OF PROTECTION AND ADVOCACY
SYSTEMS AS *AMICI CURIAE* IN SUPPORT
OF PETITIONER

———

Of Counsel:

BARBARA BERGMAN
DONALD N. BERSOFF

JAMES W. ELLIS
Counsel of Record
RUTH LUCKASSON
1117 Stanford, NE
Albuquerque, New Mexico 87131
(505) 277-2146
Counsel for Amici Curiae

WILSON - EPES PRINTING CO., INC. - 789-0096 - WASHINGTON, D.C. 20001

TABLE OF AUTHORITIES
CASES

Booth v. Maryland, 107 S. Ct. 2529 (1987)

California v. Brown, 107 S. Ct. 837 (1987)

City of Cleburne v. Cleburne Living Center, 473 U.S. 432 (1985)

Coker v. Georgia, 433 U.S. 584 (1977)

Coleman v. United States, 357 F.2d 563 (D.C. Cir. 1965)

Commonwealth v. Green, 396 Pa. 137, 151 A.2d 241 (1959)

Commonwealth v. Irelan, 341 Pa. 43, 17 A.2d 897 (1941)

Enmund v. Florida, 458 U.S. 782 (1982)

Ford v. Wainwright, 477 U.S. 399 (1986)

Franklin v. Lynaugh, 108 S. Ct. 2320 (1988)

Furman v. Georgia, 408 U.S. 238 (1972)

Giles v. State, 261 Ark. 413, 549 S.W.2d 479 (1977)

Hitchcock v. Dugger, 107 S. Ct. 1821 (1987)

Lockett v. Ohio, 438 U.S. 586 (1978)

Miller v. State, 373 So. 2d 882 (Fla. 1979)

Pickett v. State, 37 Ala. App. 410, 71 So. 2d 102 (1953)

Regina v. Higginson, 174 Eng. Rep. 743 (1843)

Spaziano v. Florida, 468 U.S. 447 (1984)

State v. Behler, 65 Idaho 464, 146 P.2d 338 (1944)

State v. Hall, 176 Neb. 295, 125 N.W.2d 918 (1964)

Sumner v. Shuman, 107 S. Ct. 2716 (1987)

Thomas v. State, 97 Tex. Crim. 432, 262 S.W. 84 (1924)

Thompson v. Oklahoma, 108 S. Ct. 2687 (1988)

Tison v. Arizona, 107 S. Ct. 1676 (1987)

Woodson v. North Carolina, 428 U.S. 280 (1976)

STATUTES

Ga. Code Ann. § 17-7-131(j) (1988 Supp.)

18 U.S.C. § 17(a) (Supp. IV 1986)

TABLE OF AUTHORITIES—Continued

TABLE OF AUTHORITIES—Continued

Kohlberg, *Moral Stages and Moralization: The Cognitive-Developmental Approach,* in *Moral Development and Behavior: Theory, Research and Social Issues* 31 (T. Lickona ed. 1976)

K. Lewin, *A Dynamic Theory of Personality* (1936)

Lind & Smith, *Moral Reasoning and Social Functioning Among Educable Mentally Handicapped Children,* 10 Austl. & N. Zealand J. Developmental Disabilities 209 (1984)

Litrownik, Freitas, & Franzini, *Self-Regulation in Mentally Retarded Children: Assessment and Training of Self-Monitoring Skills,* 82 Am. J. Ment. Defic. 499 (1978)

Lives in Process: Mildly Retarded Adults in a Large City (R. Edgerton ed. 1984)

Mahoney & Mahoney, *Self Control Techniques with the Mentally Retarded,* 42 Exceptional Children 338 (1976)

C. Mercer & M. Snell, *Learning Theory Research in Mental Retardation* (1977)

J. Piaget, *The Moral Judgment of the Child* (Free Press ed. 1965)

Polloway & Smith, *Changes in Mild Mental Retardation: Population, Programs, and Perspectives,* 50 Exceptional Children 149 (1983)

Rueda & Zucker, *Persuasive Communication Among Moderately Retarded and Nonretarded Children,* 19 Educ. & Training Ment. Retarded 125 (1984)

S. Sarason, *Psychological Problems in Mental Deficiency* (3d ed. 1959)

Spitz & Borys, *Performance of Retarded Adolescents and Nonretarded Children on One- and Two-Bit Logical Problems,* 23 J. Exper. Child Psychol. 415 (1977)

TABLE OF AUTHORITIES—Continued

No. 87-6177

JOHNNY PAUL PENRY,
Petitioner,

v.

JAMES A. LYNAUGH, DIRECTOR, TEXAS DEPARTMENT
OF CORRECTIONS,
Respondent.

On Writ of Certiorari to the United States
Court of Appeals for the Fifth Circuit

BRIEF OF *AMICI CURIAE* AMERICAN ASSOCIATION
ON MENTAL RETARDATION, *ET AL.*
IN SUPPORT OF PETITIONER

INTEREST OF *AMICI CURIAE*

Amici curiae are professional and voluntary associations interested in people with mental retardation. They represent a broad spectrum of viewpoints within the field of mental retardation.[1]

THE AMERICAN ASSOCIATION ON MENTAL RETARDATION (AAMR), previously named the Amer-

---

[1] The Petitioner and Respondent in this case have consented to the filing of this brief.

ican Association on Mental Deficiency, is the nation's oldest and largest interdisciplinary organization of professionals in the field of mental retardation. Founded in 1876, AAMR has long been interested in legal issues involving people with mental retardation and has appeared before this Court as *amicus curiae* in cases such as *City of Cleburne v. Cleburne Living Center*, 473 U.S. 432 (1985) and *Bowen v. American Hospital Association*, 476 U.S. 610 (1986).

THE AMERICAN PSYCHOLOGICAL ASSOCIATION (APA) is a nonprofit, scientific and professional organization. With over 70,000 members, it is the major association of psychologists in the United States. This case is of special interest to the APA Division on Mental Retardation, as well as thousands of other APA members who are engaged in scholarly research and the development of people with mental retardation.

THE ASSOCIATION FOR RETARDED CITIZENS OF THE UNITED STATES (ARC) is a national voluntary association of parents, families and friends of people with mental retardation, along with members who have mental retardation. ARC, which has a national membership of over 160,000 people organized in some 1,300 local and state-wide chapters, is directed and led by active volunteer parents.

THE ASSOCIATION FOR PERSONS WITH SEVERE HANDICAPS (TASH) is an organization of over 8,000 teachers, researchers, administrators, parents, medical personnel, and other professionals dedicated to making appropriate education and services available to persons who experience severe disabilities.

THE AMERICAN ASSOCIATION OF UNIVERSITY AFFILIATED PROGRAMS FOR THE DEVELOPMENTALLY DISABLED (AAUAP) is a national organization of university-based research, training, and model demonstration programs in the field of mental retardation.

THE AMERICAN ORTHOPSYCHIATRIC ASSOCIA-
TION is an interdisciplinary professional organization of
more than 10,000 mental health professionals, including
psychiatrists, psychologists, social workers, educators and
allied professionals concerned with the problems, causes,
and treatment of mental disabilities, including mental
retardation.

THE NEW YORK STATE ASSOCIATION FOR RE-
TARDED CHILDREN, INC. (NYSARC) is a state-wide
organization of 65 chapters and 53,000 members, including parents and others concerned with the needs of people
who have mental retardation. NYSARC provides services
to 25,000 clients on a daily basis and is also an advocacy
organization. (NYSARC is not affiliated with the Association for Retarded Citizens of the United States.)

THE NATIONAL ASSOCIATION OF PRIVATE
RESIDENTIAL RESOURCES represents approximately
650 agencies in 49 states and the District of Columbia
that together provide residential services to more than
40,000 people with mental retardation and other developmental disabilities. Members offer a full range of residential services in a variety of settings designed to enhance the development and independence of those served.

THE NATIONAL ASSOCIATION OF SUPERIN-
TENDENTS OF PUBLIC RESIDENTIAL FACILI-
TIES FOR THE MENTALLY RETARDED is composed
of approximately 200 directors of public facilities which
serve people with mental retardation.

THE MENTAL HEALTH LAW PROJECT is a
Washington, D.C.-based public interest organization
founded in 1972 to advocate the rights of children and
adults with mental disabilities. It has brought major
cases decided by this Court establishing the rights of
people with mental disabilities, including *Addington v.
Texas, O'Connor v. Donaldson,* and *Bowen v. City of New
York.* It has participated as *amicus curiae* in this Court
in more than a dozen additional cases.

THE NATIONAL ASSOCIATION OF PROTECTION AND ADVOCACY SYSTEMS represents Protection and Advocacy systems in 50 states and six territories, created pursuant to Section 113 of the Developmental Disabilities Assistance and Bill of Rights Act, 42 U.S.C. § 6042 (Supp. II 1982). These agencies have the statutory mandate to advocate for the rights of persons with developmental disabilities, including mental retardation.

Amici agree with Petitioner that he is entitled to a reversal on the first question on which certiorari was granted, because the Texas system does not allow jurors to give adequate consideration to mental retardation as a mitigating factor, but *amici* will limit this brief to an analysis of whether the execution of a person with mental retardation is invariably a violation of the Eighth Amendment, as applied to the states by the Fourteenth Amendment.

SUMMARY OF ARGUMENT

The Eighth Amendment limits the imposition of the death penalty to those defendants whose blameworthiness is proportional to society's most extreme and irrevocable sanction. This Court has held death to be a disproportionate punishment where the characteristics of the offense or of the offender did not match the high level of culpability required by the Constitution.

Capital defendants who have mental retardation lack this constitutionally required level of blameworthiness. The effects of their disability in the areas of cognitive impairment, moral reasoning, control of impulsivity, and the ability to understand basic relationships between cause and effect make it impossible for them to possess that level of culpability essential in capital cases.

The execution of a person with mental retardation, such as Johnny Paul Penry, cannot serve any valid penological purpose, and as a result it is "nothing more than the purposeless and needless imposition of pain and suf-

fering." *Coker v. Georgia,* 433 U.S. 584, 592 (1977).
Such an execution offends modern standards of decency.

ARGUMENT

I. THE DISABILITIES THAT ACCOMPANY MENTAL RETARDATION ARE DIRECTLY RELEVANT TO THE ISSUE OF CRIMINAL RESPONSIBILITY AND TO THE CHOICE OF PUNISHMENT FOR THOSE CONVICTED OF CRIMES.

A. Mental Retardation Is A Substantial Disability Which Impairs An Individual's Capacity To Understand And Control His Actions.

Every individual who has mental retardation experiences a substantial disability in cognitive ability and adaptive behavior. The universally accepted definition requires that any person who is classified as mentally retarded must have "significantly subaverage general intellectual functioning existing concurrently with deficits in adaptive behavior" and requires that the disability must have been "manifested during the developmental period." American Association on Mental Deficiency [now Retardation], *Classification in Mental Retardation* 1 (H. Grossman ed. 1983) (hereafter cited as "AAMR, *Classification*"). This means that a mentally retarded individual's measured intelligence is at least two standard deviations below the average person's.[2]

---

[2] General intellectual functioning is measured by IQ tests, and to be classified as having mental retardation, a person generally must score below 70 (depending on which test is employed). The average IQ for the overall population is 100; more than 97 percent of all persons score above 70.

Persons with IQ scores between 70 and 85 are sometimes erroneously described as having "borderline retardation," but this classification has long since been abandoned by professionals in the field. AAMR, *Classification* at 6. Individuals with IQ scores in the 70s and 80s, while not mentally retarded, do have reduced cognitive ability, although the reduction is not as severe as for those who have

People with mental retardation are capable of learning, working, and living in their communities. *See generally* J. Conroy & V. Bradley, *Pennhurst Longitudinal Study: A Report of Five Years of Research and Analysis* (1985); *Systematic Instruction of Persons with Severe Handicaps* (M. Snell 3d ed. 1987). Special educators and other professionals have made substantial advances in developing techniques to assist people with mental retardation, and legislatures have acted to attempt to assist such individuals. *City of Cleburne v. Cleburne Living Center*, 473 U.S. 432, 444 (1985). But advances in our capacity to help people with this disability do not change the reality that mental retardation is a substantial disability and that people who have mental retardation "have a reduced ability to cope with and function in the everyday world." *Cleburne*, 473 U.S. at 442.

This reduced ability is found in every dimension of the individual's functioning, including his language, communication, memory, attention, ability to control impulsivity, moral development, self-concept, self-perception, suggestibility, knowledge of basic information, and general motivation. Among the many substantial intellectual impairments resulting from mental retardation, the most serious occur in logical reasoning, strategic thinking, and foresight. Spitz, *Intellectual Extremes, Mental Age, and the Nature of Human Intelligence*, 28 Merrill-Palmer Q. 167, 178 (1982). The ability to anticipate consequences is a skill requiring intellectual and developmental ability. White, *Critical Influences in the Origins of Competence*, 21 Merrill-Palmer Q. 243, 246 (1975). A defendant in a

---

mental retardation. Mental disability that falls short of mental retardation should be considered as a mitigating circumstance at the penalty phase of capital trials, just as the youth of a person who is 19 or 20 should be considered. *See, e.g., Hitchcock v. Dugger*, 107 S. Ct. 1821, 1824 (1987); *see also Commonwealth v. Green*, 396 Pa. 137, 151 A.2d 241 (1959) (chronological age of 15 not enough to preclude death penalty, but an IQ of 80 tips the balance to require life imprisonment).

capital case whose understanding of causation and ability to predict consequences are substantially limited by mental retardation lacks an essential ingredient of culpability.

The problems caused by a mentally retarded defendant's substantial intellectual deficits are aggravated by intellectual rigidity, which is often demonstrated by an impaired ability to learn from mistakes and a pattern of persisting in behaviors even after they have proven counterproductive or unsuccessful. *See generally* K. Lewin, *A Dynamic Theory of Personality* (1936); S. Sarason, *Psychological Problems in Mental Deficiency* (3d ed. 1959); Rueda & Zucker, *Persuasive Communication Among Moderately Retarded and Nonretarded Children*, 19 Educ. & Training Ment. Retarded 125 (1984). One feature of this rigidity is that a person who has mental retardation often cannot independently generate in his mind a sufficient range of behaviors from which to select an action appropriate to the situation he faces (particularly a stressful situation).

A related consequence of mental retardation is impairment in the ability to control impulsivity. *See* S. Kirk & J. Gallagher, *Educating Exceptional Children* 144 (1983); Litrownik, Freitas, & Franzini, *Self-Regulation in Mentally Retarded Children: Assessment and Training of Self-Monitoring Skills*, 82 Am. J. Ment. Defic. 499 (1978); Mahoney & Mahoney, *Self Control Techniques with the Mentally Retarded*, 42 Exceptional Children 338 (1976). This appears to be related to problems that people with mental retardation encounter in attention span, attention focus, and selectivity in the attention process. *See generally* C. Mercer & M. Snell, *Learning Theory Research in Mental Retardation* 94-141 (1977). Such an impairment in the area of impulsivity is, of course, directly relevant to the level of an individual's ability to conform his conduct to the law's requirements and therefore to the degree of a defendant's culpability.

Moral development is also affected by mental retardation. It is widely accepted by researchers that moral reasoning ability develops in stages, incrementally over time, and is dependent on an individual's intellectual ability and developmental level. J. Piaget, *The Moral Judgment of the Child* (Free Press ed. 1965); Kohlberg, *Moral Stages and Moralization: The Cognitive Developmental Approach,* in *Moral Development and Behavior: Theory, Research and Social Issues* 31 (T. Lickona ed. 1976). Thus, mental retardation limits the ability of individuals to reach full moral reasoning ability. *See* Israely, *The Moral Development of Mentally Retarded Children: Review of the Literature,* 14 J. Moral Educ. 33 (1985); Lind & Smith, *Moral Reasoning and Social Functioning Among Educable Mentally Handicapped Children,* 10 Austl. & N. Zealand J. Developmental Disabilities 209 (1984). This does not mean, of course, that people with mental retardation are immoral or that they should escape responsibility for their actions. But it does mean that where mental retardation has placed an upper limit on a defendant's attainment of full moral reasoning ability, he cannot be held to have that level of culpability that would justify punishment by death.

Nor do *amici* contend that people with mental retardation are unusually likely to commit crimes.[3] Most people with mental retardation are law abiding. A complex mix of environmental influences and individual differences unrelated to intelligence determines whether individuals engage in criminal acts. But those individuals with mental retardation who do commit crimes do so with a limited

---

[3] The false belief, widely held in the early years of this century, that mental retardation was a cause of much of society's criminality is now understood to be a result of the eugenics hysteria of that era. Biklen & Mlinarcik, *Criminal Justice, Mental Retardation and Criminality: A Causal Link?,* 10 Mental Retardation and Developmental Disabilities 172 (J. Wortis ed. 1978); Ellis & Luckasson, *Mentally Retarded Criminal Defendants,* 53 Geo. Wash. L. Rev. 414, 425-26 (1985).

understanding of causes and effects and a reduced ability to govern their own behavior.

A minimal level of cognitive ability and moral reasoning development are necessary for the level of culpability that will satisfy the requirements of the Eighth Amendment in capital cases. Defendants with mental retardation have serious impairments in intellectual and moral reasoning, strategic thinking, and the ability to foresee consequences. The combination of these substantial limitations is directly relevant to the degree of the disabled defendant's moral culpability for his criminal actions.

B. Mental Retardation Has Long Been Recognized As Relevant To The Choice Of Appropriate Punishment For Crime.

For centuries, Anglo-American law has accepted the principle that the degree of criminal culpability of people with mental retardation is reduced by the effect of their disability. The common law exempted "idiots" from criminal responsibility. 4 W. Blackstone, *Commentaries* *24; M. Dalton, *The Countrey Justice* 223 (1619 & photo. reprint 1973). When English law adopted the *M'Naghten* test for insanity, courts almost immediately extended its applicability to mentally retarded defendants. *Regina v. Higginson*, 174 Eng. Rep. 743 (1843). The modern American formulations of the insanity defense almost invariably speak in terms of "mental disease or defect," the latter referring to defendants with mental retardation. *See, e.g.,* 18 U.S.C. § 17(a) (Supp. IV 1986). Similarly, the weight of authority holds that even when it does not constitute a complete defense, a defendant's mental retardation should be taken into account as a mitigating factor in determining an appropriate sentence. *See, e.g., Coleman v. United States*, 357 F.2d 563, 569 (D.C. Cir. 1965); *Thomas v. State*, 97 Tex. Crim. 432, 262 S.W. 84 (1924) (evidence of "a low order of mentality"); *A.B.A. Standards for Criminal Justice* 7-9.3 (1984). *See gen-*

erally Lockett v. Ohio, 438 U.S. 586 (1978) ("mental deficiency" was one of the mitigating factors that had been prescribed by the Ohio statute). Even before this Court held that the Constitution required consideration of mitigating evidence, state appellate courts reduced sentences of death to life imprisonment on the basis of the mitigating effect of a defendant's mental retardation. *E.g. State v. Behler*, 65 Idaho 464, 146 P.2d 338 (1944); *State v. Hall*, 176 Neb. 295, 125 N.W.2d 918 (1964). *Cf. Giles v. State*, 261 Ark. 413, 549 S.W.2d 479 (1977) (post-*Gregg*).

The reason that mental retardation has been so widely accepted as relevant to the degree of punishment, whether through a finding of nonresponsibility or mitigation, is that courts and legislatures have recognized the disability's relationship to the degree of a defendant's blameworthiness. For example, the Supreme Court of Pennsylvania vacated a death sentence because expert testimony showed that the defendant's subnormal intelligence produced "a smaller range of selectivity as to action than would be had by the average human being" (quoting expert testimony) and meant that the defendant lacked "the ability to think things through to a logical conclusion." *Commonwealth v. Irelan*, 341 Pa. 43, 46, 17 A.2d 897, 898 (1941) (involving a defendant whose mental disability apparently was less severe than actual mental retardation).

American law has never held, nor do *amici* contend, that people with mental retardation cannot be held responsible or punished for criminal acts they commit. Some defendants who have mental retardation are entitled to acquittal because the effect of their disability matches the jurisdiction's test for insanity or because they lack the requisite *mens rea*. Other mentally retarded defendants properly can be convicted and subject to appropriate punishment. But mental retardation always involves a substantial impairment that reduces a defendant's level of blameworthiness and moral culpability for a capital offense.

II. THE DEGREE OF REDUCTION IN MORAL BLAMEWORTHINESS CAUSED BY A DEFENDANT'S MENTAL RETARDATION RENDERS IMPOSITION OF THE DEATH PENALTY UNCONSTITUTIONAL.

A. Punishment By Death Is Reserved For Those Selected On The Basis Of Their Blameworthiness And Moral Guilt.

Unique considerations attend issues that determine which defendants may be put to death. As this Court has observed, "the penalty of death is qualitatively different from a sentence of imprisonment, however long. Death, in its finality, differs more from life imprisonment than a 100-year prison term differs from one of only a year or two." *Woodson v. North Carolina*, 428 U.S. 280, 305 (1976) (plurality opinion). Therefore, the flexibility that states have in devising appropriate sentences for noncapital cases is more strictly circumscribed in cases which may result in a death sentence.

Under modern capital punishment statutes, only a small minority of those individuals who commit willful criminal homicide are actually sentenced to death. *See Thompson v. Oklahoma*, 108 S. Ct. 2687, 2697 (1988) (plurality opinion). This Court has made clear that States cannot select candidates for the death penalty in an arbitrary or unprincipled fashion or solely on the basis of the offense committed. *Furman v. Georgia*, 408 U.S. 238 (1972); *Sumner v. Shuman*, 107 S. Ct. 2716 (1987). "There must be a valid penological reason for choosing from among the many criminal defendants the few who are sentenced to death." *Spaziano v. Florida*, 468 U.S. 447, 460 n.7 (1984).

This Court's Eighth Amendment opinions make clear that the decision to impose the death penalty must be "directly related to the personal culpability of the criminal defendant." *California v. Brown*, 107 S. Ct. 837, 841 (1987) (O'Connor, J., concurring). The Court has reversed death sentences that were based on factors unrelated to the defendant's blameworthiness. *Booth v. Maryland*, 107 S. Ct. 2529 (1987). The degree of a defendant's blameworthiness and moral culpability are thus the key criteria for determining who may be put to death and who may not. *Enmund v. Florida*, 458 U.S. 782 (1982).[4]

A principal component of any defendant's culpability is his mental ability and state of mind at the time of the offense. This Court has observed that:

> A critical facet of the individualized determination of culpability required in capital cases is the mental state with which the defendant commits the crime. Deeply ingrained in our legal tradition is the idea that the more purposeful is the criminal conduct, the more serious is the offense, and, therefore, the more severely it ought to be punished.

Tison v. Arizona, 107 S. Ct. 1676, 1687 (1987).

The obverse is equally true; a substantial reduction in the purposefulness of a defendant's criminal acts or impairment in his comprehension of them and their consequences must surely indicate that a less severe penalty is warranted. *Cf. Thompson v. Oklahoma*, 108 S. Ct. 2687, 2698-99 (1988) (plurality opinion). As Justice O'Connor has observed, our society long ago agreed "that defendants who commit criminal acts that are attributable to . . . mental problems[] may be less culpable than defendants who have no such excuse. This emphasis on culpability in sentencing decisions has long been reflected

---

[4] *Tison v. Arizona*, 107 S. Ct. 1676 (1987), which distinguished *Enmund*, does not weaken its central holding that a defendant's moral culpability is the key criterion for imposing the death penalty. In *Tison*, the Court found that the defendants' conduct was "sufficient to satisfy the *Enmund* culpability requirement." 107 S. Ct. at 1688.

in Anglo-American jurisprudence." *California v. Brown,* 107 S. Ct. 837, 841 (1987) (O'Connor, J., concurring). Mental retardation significantly affects the degree of purposefulness and impairs the comprehension of every defendant who has the disability and commits a capital offense.

B. The Death Penalty Is Disproportionate To The Degree Of Culpability Of Any Defendant With Mental Retardation.

No defendant who has mental retardation is "capable of acting with the degree of culpability that can justify the ultimate penalty." *Thompson v. Oklahoma,* 108 S. Ct. 2687, 2692 (1988) (plurality opinion).

Amici acknowledge that there is substantial variation among people with mental retardation regarding the degree of their disability and its effect on their reasoning capacity and adaptive behavior. Individuals with IQs in the 50s or 60s differ substantially from persons with IQs in the range of "profound" mental retardation.[5] But this variation would be relevant to the Eighth Amendment issue only if some individuals in the "mild" mental retardation category had such minimal disabilities that they were capable of the level of culpability and moral blameworthiness required for the death penalty. This

---

[5] The AAMR classification system divides people with mental retardation into four categories: mild, moderate, severe and profound. "Mild" mental retardation includes individuals with IQ scores between approximately 50 or 55 and 70. "Moderate" mental retardation includes those whose IQ scores are between approximately 35 or 40 and 50 or 55. (The precise boundaries depend on the particular intelligence test that is employed.) AAMR, *Classification* at 13. "[C]riminal justice personnel unfamiliar with this classification scheme may find the labels of 'mild' and 'moderate' to be euphemistic descriptions of individuals at those levels of disability." Ellis & Luckasson, *Mentally Retarded Criminal Defendants,* 53 Geo. Wash. L. Rev. 414, 423 (1985). Approximately 89 percent of people who have mental retardation fall within the "mild" mental retardation category.

is not true. The highest functioning individuals in the "mild" mental retardation category have substantial cognitive and behavioral disabilities. *See* Polloway & Smith, *Changes in Mild Mental Retardation: Population, Programs, and Perspectives,* 50 Exceptional Children 149 (1983); *Lives in Process: Mildly Retarded Adults in a Large City* (R. Edgerton ed. 1984).

Comparison with nonretarded teenagers may illuminate this issue.[6] Most teenagers are of average intelligence,

---

[6] The question upon which this Court granted certiorari is framed in terms of "an individual with the reasoning capacity of a seven year old." This is similar to the concept of mental age, a tool used in the field of mental retardation to describe the severity of an individual's disability. Mental age is calculated as the chronological age of nonretarded children whose average IQ test performance is equivalent to that of the individual with mental retardation. *See* D. Wechsler, *The Measurement and Appraisal of Adult Intelligence* 24 (4th ed. 1958). The equivalence between nonretarded children and retarded adults is, of course, imprecise. An individual's mental age can simultaneously underestimate and overestimate attributes of the adult to whom it is applied. An adult will have the physical development and some of the interests and experiences of his non-disabled age peers; mental age suggests underestimation in these areas. But mental age substantially overestimates important problem-solving abilities. Mental age markedly overstates the ability of adults with mental retardation to use logic and foresight in solving problems. *See, e.g.,* Spitz & Borys, *Performance of Retarded Adolescents and Nonretarded Children on One- and Two-Bit Logical Problems,* 23 J. Exper. Child Psychol. 415, 428 (1977); Haywood & Switzky, *Intrinsic Motivation and Behavior Effectiveness in Retarded Persons,* 14 Int'l Rev. Research Mental Retard'n 1 (N. Ellis & N. Bray eds. 1986). *See generally* Spitz, *Intellectual Extremes, Mental Age, and the Nature of Human Intelligence,* 28 Merrill-Palmer Q. 167, 178 (1982).

Courts appear to have grasped intuitively the strengths and weaknesses of mental age as an estimation of disability. They have rejected claims that an adult with a mental age below 12 automatically lacks criminal responsibility because children of a similar chronological age are deemed incapable of criminal intent. But courts have frequently used mental age as a shorthand description of an individual's level of reasoning ability when discussing issues and a minority (as with any age group) have superior intelligence. The common trait of teenagers is relative immaturity (although a few are unusually mature or sophisticated). *Thompson v. Oklahoma*, 108 S. Ct. 2687, 2709 (1988) (O'Connor, J., concurring in the judgment). But their lives have been lived with varying degrees of mental ability, and those varying abilities produce differences in their life experiences. By contrast, people with mental retardation *never* have average, let alone superior, intelligence. The result of this impairment is that their abilities to comprehend concepts such as causation will vary but will never rise above a certain ceiling. The substantial variation among people with mental retardation always occurs below that ceiling. Thus, all persons with mental retardation lack that level of ability that would allow them to be capable of the level of culpability required for the death penalty.

The essence of *amici's* argument is not that jurors, or this Court, should feel sorry for capital defendants with mental retardation and as a result exempt them from the death penalty. Some jurors may reach that conclusion after hearing evidence about a defendant's disability in argument for mitigation. Rather, *amici's* Eighth Amendment argument is wholly different. The nature of mental retardation is sufficiently severe that any person who has that disability and commits a capital offense lacks, by definition, that level of culpability that would allow the state to take his life. Therefore, the case involving people with mental retardation bears no resemblance to hypothetical arguments that "blind people . . . or white-haired grandmothers . . . or mothers of two-year-olds" or "other appealing groups" should be spared from execution. *Thompson v. Oklahoma*, 108 S. Ct. 2687, 2721 (1988) (Scalia, J., dissenting). None of these

---

such as voluntariness of confessions, competence to stand trial, mitigation, and the insanity defense. *See, e.g., Pickett v. State*, 37 Ala. App. 410, 71 So. 2d 102 (1953).

groups uniformly lacks the ability necessary to achieve the Eighth Amendment's required level of culpability. *Amici's* argument arises not from the "appeal" or sympathetic character of people with mental retardation, but rather from the real and practical effects of their disability.

III. A RULING THAT THE EIGHTH AMENDMENT BARS THE EXECUTION OF PEOPLE WITH MENTAL RETARDATION IS APPROPRIATE AND NECESSARY.

This Court has held that the death penalty violates the Eighth Amendment if it is disproportionate to the circumstances of the case for which it is prescribed. Most frequently, this is because of characteristics of the offense. *Coker v. Georgia,* 433 U.S. 584 (1977); *Enmund v. Florida,* 458 U.S. 782 (1982). The death penalty may also be excessive and therefore unconstitutional because of characteristics of the defendant for whom it is proposed. *Thompson v. Oklahoma,* 108 S.Ct. 2687 (1988).

Although the Court has repeatedly emphasized the importance of individualized determinations of culpability through the system of weighing aggravating and mitigating circumstances, each of these holdings is categorical in nature. It is significant that in each instance, the claim of disproportionality was available in individual cases as an argument for mitigation. The cases reached this Court, and merited its attention, only because the system of considering mitigating circumstances did not invariably preclude the death penalty under the circumstances at issue. Even if most jurors (or most voters or legislators) would conclude, if asked, that the death penalty was inappropriate for non-murdering rapists, peripheral participants in crimes that led to homicides, or children under the age of 16, some trials may still result in a sentence of death under those circumstances. This Court's rulings teach that a function of the Constitution's ban on cruel and unusual punishment is to reflect society's "evolving standards of decency" and to impose them where the system of considering mitigating circumstances in individual cases has failed to reflect those standards by prescribing punishment that is clearly disproportionate to the defendant's culpability.[7]

The possibility that a person with mental retardation could be executed in America has only recently become apparent. The first modern case to receive any substantial publicity was Georgia's execution of Jerome Bowden in 1986, and in that case, the existence and degree of his disability (IQ 65) were not recognized widely in Georgia until after his death. In response to the outrage that many expressed at the spectacle of a person so disabled being executed, Georgia passed a statute banning the execution of people with mental disability. Ga. Code Ann. § 17-7-131(j) (1988 Supp.); *Georgia To Bar Executions of Mentally Retarded Killers*, N.Y. Times, April 12, 1988, at A26, col. 4. Legislatures in other states have not "rendered a considered judgment approving the imposition of capital punishment" on people with mental retardation because the reality of this possibility has not been apparent. *Thompson v. Oklahoma*, 108 S. Ct. 2687, 2708 (1988) (O'Connor, J., concurring in the judgment). Polling data strongly indicate that when supporters of the death penalty are asked whether they approve of the execution of people with mental retardation, they oppose

---

[7] In each of these cases, the Court has banned the use of the death penalty under the circumstances in question. In his dissenting opinion in *Thompson v. Oklahoma*, 108 S. Ct. 2687, 2712 (1988), Justice Scalia raises the possibility of a rebuttable presumption regarding a defendant's culpability that could be grounded in the Eighth Amendment. *Amici* strongly believe that the Eighth Amendment should be held to preclude any execution of a person with mental retardation, and we are unclear about how such a rebuttable presumption would be structured and implemented. The possibility of such a presumption has not been argued in this case, nor has it been considered by the courts below.

such sentences. Blume & Bruck, *Sentencing the Mentally Retarded to Death: An Eighth Amendment Analysis*, 41 Ark. L. Rev. 725, 759-60 (1988) (reporting results of scientific surveys).[8]

Despite the consensus that is now becoming apparent, people with mental retardation may still be sentenced to death. Just as the mitigation system was inadequate to prevent unconstitutionally disproportionate punishment of defendants in *Coker*, *Enmund*, and *Thompson*, Johnny Paul Penry's presence on Death Row demonstrates that the system of considering factors in mitigation cannot be relied upon exclusively to assure that defendants with mental retardation will not be executed.[9] Jurors in an individual case may be confused about the relevance of mental retardation to culpability and may even believe perversely that it should be considered as an aggravating circumstance. *Cf. Miller v. State*, 373 So. 2d 882 (Fla. 1979). Similarly, reviewing appellate courts may misperceive the impact of mental retardation on culpability.

---

[8] The identifiable objective indicia of societal opinions on this question, while consistent, are less numerous than those available, for example, on the issue of executing minors. However, this Court has indicated that it looks to objective indicators as part of its own process of deciding whether a punishment is excessive, but that "it is for us ultimately to judge whether the Eighth Amendment permits imposition of the death penalty" in particular circumstances. *Enmund v. Florida*, 458 U.S. 782, 797 (1982). In the case at bar, the objective indicia are not numerous because the possibility of a person with mental retardation being executed has only recently become clear. Once the prospect becomes clear, the indicia suggest that Americans consistently reject the execution of persons with mental retardation.

[9] *Amici* acknowledge that the instant case may not be an ideal vehicle for resolving the Eighth Amendment issue, since the Texas system of jury instructions may give jurors inadequate opportunity to evaluate the relevance of mental retardation as a mitigating circumstance. *See Franklin v. Lynaugh*, 108 S. Ct. 2320, 2333 (1988) (O'Connor, J., concurring in the judgment).

IV. EXECUTION OF A PERSON WITH MENTAL RE- TARDATION SERVES NO VALID PENOLOGICAL PURPOSE.

The principal reason that *amici* have concluded that execution of a person with mental retardation violates the Eighth Amendment is that it is "grossly out of pro- portion" to such a defendant's culpability. *Coker v. Georgia*, 433 U.S. 584, 592 (1977) (plurality opinion). But *Coker* also made clear that a punishment is unconsti- tutionally excessive if it "makes no measurable contribu- tion to acceptable goals of punishment and hence is noth- ing more than the purposeless and needless imposition of pain and suffering." *Id.* The death penalty for people with mental retardation also violates this principle.

This Court has held that retribution is a valid peno- logical purpose, and that in proper cases it can support imposition of the death penalty. But this Court has also concluded that valid exercise of the state's interest in retribution must be related to the degree of the defend- ant's blameworthiness. *Enmund v. Florida*, 458 U.S. 782, 800 (1982). "The heart of the retribution rationale is that a criminal sentence must be directly related to the personal culpability of the criminal offender." *Tison v. Arizona*, 107 S. Ct. 1676, 1683 (1987).

Deterrence has also been recognized as an acceptable purpose for punishment. But the likelihood that an in- dividual with mental retardation would be deterred from committing a capital offense by the prospect of the death penalty is even smaller than was true for teenagers, since some teenagers have above average intelligence. *Cf. Thompson v. Oklahoma*, 108 S. Ct. 2687, 2700 (1988) (plurality opinion). Similarly, removing the small num- ber of capital offenders with mental retardation from the prospect of execution "will not diminish the deterrent value of capital punishment for the vast majority of [nonretarded] potential offenders." *Id. See generally Ford v. Wainwright*, 477 U.S. 399, 407 (1986) (citing

Sir Edward Coke for the proposition that execution of an insane person is "a miserable spectacle, both against Law, and of extream inhumanity and cruelty, and can be no example to others"); *A.B.A. Standards For Criminal Justice* 7-5.6 (1987) (opposing execution of inmates whose incompetence results from either mental illness or mental retardation).

Amici believe that execution of a person with mental retardation is invariably disproportionate to the level of that individual's culpability and is "nothing more than the purposeless and needless imposition of pain and suffering." *Coker*, 433 U.S. at 592. Therefore, we believe that this Court should hold that such executions violate the Eighth Amendment's ban on cruel and unusual punishments.

CONCLUSION

For the reasons set forth above, *amici* urge this Court to reverse the judgment of the Fifth Circuit.

Respectfully submitted,

JAMES W. ELLIS
   Counsel of Record
RUTH LUCKASSON
1117 Stanford, NE
Albuquerque, New Mexico 87131
(505) 277-2146
Counsel for Amici Curiae

Of Counsel:

   BARBARA BERGMAN
   DONALD N. BERSOFF

September, 1988

APPENDIX

AMERICAN ASSOCIATION ON MENTAL RETARDATION RESOLUTION ON MENTAL RETARDATION AND THE DEATH PENALTY JANUARY, 1988

WHEREAS, the AMERICAN ASSOCIATION ON MENTAL RETARDATION, the nation's oldest and largest interdisciplinary organization of mental retardation professionals, has long been active in advocating the full protection of the legal rights of persons with mental retardation.

WHEREAS, the AMERICAN ASSOCIATION ON MENTAL RETARDATION recognizes that, archaic stereotypes and prejudices to the contrary notwithstanding, the vast majority of people with mental retardation are not prone to criminal or violent behavior.

WHEREAS, the AMERICAN ASSOCIATION ON MENTAL RETARDATION recognizes that some people with mental retardation become involved with the criminal justice system and are often treated unfairly by that system. This mistreatment often results from the unusual vulnerability of individuals with mental retardation and from the failure of many criminal justice professionals to recognize and understand the nature of mental retardation.

WHEREAS, the United States Supreme Court has made clear that in *all* capital cases the judge or jury must consider any mitigating circumstances which would indicate that the death penalty is inappropriate or unjust. Among these mitigating circumstances are any which would tend to reduce the individual offender's personal culpability and moral blameworthiness for the act he or she committed.

WHEREAS, mental retardation is a substantially disabling condition which may affect an individual's ability to appreciate and understand fully the consequences of actions, and which may impair the individual's ability to conform his or her conduct to the requirements of the law. Thus mental retardation should always be considered to be a mitigating circumstance in selecting an appropriate punishment for a serious offense.

WHEREAS, the current system of permitting judges and juries to determine the relevance of mental retardation as a mitigating circumstance on a case-by-case basis has failed to prevent the unjust sentencing of several mentally retarded persons to death.

AND WHEREAS, the competence of individuals with mental retardation to stand trial or enter a guilty plea, and to face execution are always subject to question, raising serious doubts as to the legality of an execution in any particular case.

THEREFORE the AMERICAN ASSOCIATION ON MENTAL RETARDATION resolves that *no person who is mentally retarded should be sentenced to death or executed.*

Appendix B

OBSERVATIONS FROM THE FIELD

COLLECTED BY RONALD W. CONLEY

M ANY OF THE chapters in this book derive their inspiration from the discussion and debate at the Presidential Forum on Offenders with Mental Retardation and the Criminal Justice System, held in September 1989 by the President's Committee on Mental Retardation. Some of the observations made by panelists and other conference participants have been excerpted and are presented below. We believe that the viewpoints expressed here will help readers grasp the diversity of opinion among advocates and disability professionals concerning the criminal justice system and people with mental retardation, as well as introduce additional perspectives on many of the issues raised in this book.—*The Editors*

Commentators whose remarks appear in this appendix are listed below. (Full affiliations are listed only for those commentators whose affiliations do not appear in the contributors list on pp. ix to xi of this book.)

George S. Baroff, Ph.D.
Professor of Psychology
Director
Developmental Disabilities Training
  Institute
CB 3370, Hill Commercial Building
University of North Carolina at
  Chapel Hill
Chapel Hill, North Carolina
  27599-3370

Richard J. Bonnie, LL.B.

Richard H. Burr, J.D.

Philip W. Davidson, Ph.D.

Christine DeMoll, M.S.S.W.

James W. Ellis, J.D.

James G. Exum, Jr., LL.B.

John W. Finn, Ph.D.

Robert Martin, Cpt.

Ruth J. Messinger, M.S.W.

Dolores Norley, J.D.
Attorney & Counselor at Law
529 N. Sans Souci Avenue
DeLand, Florida 32720

Russell C. Petrella, Ph.D.

Louise R. Ravenel
Executive Director
South Carolina Protection &
  Advocacy System for the
  Handicapped, Inc.
3710 Landmark Drive, Suite 208
Columbia, South Carolina 29204

Maurice H. Richardson
First Justice
District Court Department
Dedham Division
631 High Street
Dedham, Massachusetts 02026

Clarence J. Sundram
Chairman
Commission on Quality of Care for
  the Mentally Disabled
99 Washington Avenue
Suite 1002
Albany, New York 12210

**H. Rutherford Turnbull, III,
LL.B., LL.M.**

David L. White

DEFENDANTS WITH MENTAL RETARDATION

MESSINGER: I was watching a videotape in which a man with mental retardation was giving a very, very damaging confession to four police
officers. It was clear that each of those officers knew that the man was a
person with mental retardation. It was also clear that they had an understanding of how that mental retardation was directly leading to this confession, and
that they were, in fact, manipulating him on the basis of his mental retardation
into giving a very damaging confession.

RAVENEL: Limmie was 26 years old in June 1987. He had been
convicted of killing his neighbor and had been sentenced to death. Limmie sat
on death row for 2 years before anybody realized he was mentally retarded.

One thing I realized was that the judge and the solicitor had absolutely no
understanding of what mental retardation was. The judge thought Limmie was
a poor farmer. The solicitor felt that the reason Limmie hadn't learned how to
read was that he didn't try hard enough in school. Limmie was smiling shyly
and was totally unaware that he had been resentenced to death.

THE SERVICE SYSTEM FOR
DEFENDANTS WITH MENTAL RETARDATION

SUNDRAM: With the exception of a small percentage of offenders
who have committed truly serious crimes, and for whom the correctional
system is probably the only appropriate place, many of the other offenders
with mental retardation who come into the criminal justice system do so

because the other social supports have broken down and there aren't any alternatives available other than jail.

PETRELLA: They aren't going to recover in a maximum security mental health forensic facility. They aren't going to get appropriate training. They languish in these facilities for lengthy periods of time because their condition doesn't change.

BONNIE: In Virginia, once people are in the forensic services system, apparently methods are not readily available to get them into the civil side, in part because there aren't secure placements within the mental retardation services system.

THE POLICE

MARTIN: If a violent crime is committed, that's not the time when the police are going to sit down and administer tests to find out if this person is mentally retarded. In fact, a uniformed field officer is more likely to be talking to victims and witnesses.

DAVIDSON: I don't think it's unfair to say that police on the beat do case management to a certain degree, and make on-the-spot decisions about how to resolve a situation that may exclude bringing a person downtown and booking him. The investigating officer becomes the broker for prying loose whatever services there are.

THE *MIRANDA* WARNING

BAROFF: In the cases I've been involved with, I've been struck by how extraordinarily distorted understanding of their *Miranda* warning has been for people who have confessed to crimes, some of whom have been charged with first-degree murder and some of whom are on death row.

EXUM: I think the courts are very concerned with whether people who waive their *Miranda* rights do so knowingly and understandingly.

BURR: In death penalty cases and in many serious felony prosecutions, confessions have several consequences. If they are complete confessions and are found to be credible by the police, they cut short further police investigation. They will cut off consideration of other suspects. They will cause the police to shape the evidence to fit the person who has confessed. In death cases, if there is a confession, it's the centerpiece of the state's case.

People with mental retardation usually don't have the ability to argue with the police on their understanding of their *Miranda* rights. It seems that issues concerning the knowing and understanding of *Miranda* warnings are major and have not been addressed to any great extent by the courts.

ELLIS: I think there is independent value, and the courts have held that there is independent value, in the right to counsel and the right to be free from coerced, self-incriminatory statements that are independent of guilt or innocence. People with disabilities are the ones least likely to be able to exercise these rights. I come across cases in which factual innocence after conviction, in both capital and noncapital cases, is a real question. Invariably, these cases involve confessions or guilty pleas. I know of one case where a person thought "rights" were the opposite of "lefts" and that "waiving" was a gesture. That person had pled guilty. He also thought that guilt meant that you felt badly because something had happened.

EVALUATION

PETRELLA: No one likes to say that the emperor has no clothes, but in reality, many psychiatrists and clinical psychologists don't know a lot about mental retardation, don't consider it very carefully in forensic evaluations, and don't do a very good job of documenting it.

RICHARDSON: In Massachusetts, we're looking at the issue of how to deal with defendants with mental retardation. What I envision happening is that we're not going to be able to afford to have a truly expert forensic evaluation for persons with mental retardation. What we're going to be able to do, I think, is train the mental health forensic team to be alert to and recognize those indicia that would lead them to think they may be dealing with persons with mental retardation. In these cases, they would involve local people in carrying out a further evaluation. If a defendant doesn't want to be tested, you appoint an attorney. The attorney, under our reading of the law, can sit in on the evaluation by the clinician. He can advise his client not to answer or participate.

NORLEY: The courts seem to be as intimidated as the rest of us are by doctors and think that they'll have the answers—that's not always true.

EXUM: The competency issue, particularly with respect to the guilty plea, is troublesome. I recall when I was on the trial bench that a young defendant wanted to plead guilty. He was represented by counsel. I was going through all the questions that trial judges ask to ensure that the defendant understands the plea. The trial judge must make sure that the defendant understands what he is doing when he enters his guilty plea, that he understands that he is waiving certain rights, particularly the right to trial by jury. I asked this defendant if he was willing to waive his right to a jury trial. He said, "Yes, your honor," *and waved his hands*. Nobody suggested, nor did it occur to me, that he might be mentally retarded.

As a matter of tradition, not law, our trial judges may hear the evidence against the defendant before accepting a guilty plea. If the evidence seems weak, the judge will set aside the plea.

LEGAL COUNSEL

BURR: I have three observations to make about the issue of counsel, and the lack of knowledge and the need for training. One is that the client population we are concerned with consists of poor people who must rely on public defenders or court-appointed counsel. Almost invariably, my colleagues in that part of our profession don't expect much of their clients. We don't expect them to be very verbal or to give a lot of information. And that will continue. It makes very little sense to teach lawyers to get an intuitive feeling for who may be mentally retarded, because we will continue to expect very little from our uneducated, poor, predominantly black clients. That is how class and race works in our society.

My second observation is that if lawyers do what they are supposed to, which is investigate their cases, they will inevitably learn something about their clients which is highly relevant to the issue of mental retardation. Their client's school history is an extraordinarily reliable indicator. This information requires very little work and almost no lawyers do it.

My third observation is that defense counsel must have assistance form experts not publicly known by the state or the court to whom they can turn and talk to, and who will conduct an evaluation.

There is a case from the Supreme Court, *Ake v. Oklahoma* [105 S. Ct. 1087 (1985)], in which the Court said that as a matter of due process, in a death penalty case where mental health is an issue, an indigent defendant is entitled to have state-paid assistance that is not public and that is not available to the court or to the prosecutor.

RICHARDSON: As far as a situation where you have one judge and the same attorney representing the same type of cases day in and day out, you're going to get a situation where the attorney has to compromise certain cases, and bargain for a median level of representation. A committee of the Massachusetts Supreme Court felt that this made the attorney's representation less effective. To combat this, we have in each county a list of qualified attorneys who represent patients, which we utilize on a rotating basis.

NORLEY: One trouble with public defenders is that they don't stay on the job very long.

DEMOLL: We have court-appointed public defenders who get paid $50 a case. They have almost no resources with which to develop a case. We haven't had much success in getting training programs on agendas at state bar conferences.

POLICY CONSIDERATIONS

PETRELLA: My experience has been that there isn't a lot of interest or attention for defendants with mental retardation and that most policy makers would prefer that this issue go away. They typically make funding decisions for this group based on two factors—legal liability and public safety. They react to a consent decree, or to someone who is able to convince them that they are in great legal peril if they don't institute the program. Or, they are worried that if someone goes out on parole or probation and doesn't do well, it will get a lot of media coverage. Few people institute these programs because they think it's the right thing to do.

WHITE: I think there's great hope for diversionary programs because of prison overcrowding. In addition, it's cost-effective. It costs $15,000 a year to keep someone in a county prison while it costs only $1,000 a year to be in our program.

RAVENEL: For the past 3 years, we have written numerous separate grant proposals seeking extra support to beef up our advocacy for people with mental retardation. It's not a priority with any funding program at all.

SENTENCING

ELLIS: The sentencing guidelines for federal judges have a provision for departures downward from the fixed levels that would otherwise apply for what is called diminished capacity as a result of a mental condition that might help explain the offense. But unlike other departures in the guidelines, that provision is not available to people with mental retardation or mental illness who have committed a violent offense.

FINN: Last year we intervened in over 35 cases where a person was well on the way to being deemed incompetent to stand trial and committed to an institution. We asked the courts to entertain a more informal disposition or a probationary outcome with the client agreeing to participate in a plan of services. In more than half the cases we succeeded in arranging such dispositions which provided client services in more appropriate settings, ones which were much more therapeutic for the individuals. An essential element of this approach is that it makes clients responsible for choosing to participate in the services that are appropriate to their developmental needs. Sometimes they choose to participate in this type of disposition and sometimes they choose to take their chances and do their time.

BURR: I'm confident that in every death penalty state where a poll was conducted, you'd get two-thirds to three-fourths of the people agreeing that they did not want the death penalty for people with mental retardation.

RICHARDSON: In the house of correction in Dedham [Massachusetts], there is a federal cap on the number of people who can be incarcerated. The facility is overcrowded and archaic. Every time I order somebody committed to it, the master lets somebody out the back door. That is ridiculous. Therefore, I look for a disposition other than incarceration. When somebody has a particularly unique situation, a disability of some type—mental illness, mental retardation—and if this has been brought to the attention of the judge, many of us will follow what the federal courts do automatically—defer sentencing to another day, ask our probation officer to investigate the matter, and come back with a presentence report. If you can educate a judge to the nature of the problem and the alternatives, I think that of the problem and the alternatives, I think that judge, no matter now stony-hearted he or she may be, is going to opt for the alternative.

EXUM: We are living—more so than at any time in my judicial experience—in a law-and-order age. Judges, particularly in states that elect judges, are sensitive to the fact that people regard crime as serious and want judges to throw the book at criminals. Often, the only way to do that is to put people in prison. If a judge opts for an alternative for someone who has committed a serious offense, he gets excoriated in the local paper.

ELLIS: Fewer than 2 percent of the people who are convicted of capital murder are sentenced to death. Far fewer are executed. We have to continue our efforts with Congress to ensure that federal law doesn't put people with mental retardation on death row. We need to consider whether we want to ask Congress to mandate that the states not do so, a politically more difficult task. We need to continue our efforts in state legislatures. Finally, we need to begin looking at state courts. Each state's constitution has a provision roughly parallel to the Eighth Amendment's prohibition of cruel and unusual punishment.

VICTIMS

TURNBULL: I recall a state court which, in the few cases of criminal prosecution brought against the caregivers at the local institution, had great difficulty finding that they had committed any crimes, even when it was perfectly clear that they had committed very serious crimes against people who were institutionalized. Referring to victims, he once said: "Well, you know, they are retarded. They can't really feel pain."

ELLIS: In both capital and noncapital cases, there is the question of aggravating and mitigating circumstances. One instance that might usefully be thought of as an aggravating circumstance is when the perpetrator has selected his or her victim because of the vulnerability of that victim due to disability. In particular, where the perpetrator has fiduciary or custodial responsibility for that victim, it seems that that's the sort of circumstance that legitimately draws outrage which ought to be considered as an enhancement in punishment.

TURNBULL: It will be a major challenge to differentiate between sexual victimization on the one hand and autonomy and sexual expression in people with limited cognitive ability on the other. We must make sure that there are not statutes around the country in which it is defined as statutory rape to engage in sexual relations with someone who has a mental disability solely on the basis of the person's disability. When victims are unable to consent to these sexual relations, the perpetrator should be prosecuted.

DEMOLL: The protection and advocacy systems have a clear mandate to investigate incidents of abuse. If a person happens to reside in an institution or a community program, we can gain access to records with the consent of the individual or a parent or guardian. This is an area where protection and advocacy systems traditionally and unfortunately have thought of investigation of victims of physical abuse only within institutional settings, instead of victims of civil and legal rights abuses within the criminal justice system.

ELLIS: Most communities now have, in both their law enforcement and health provision systems, a rape intervention and crisis team that assists law enforcement and helps victims cope with the traumatic consequences of those crimes. There is no reason to think that the people running those operations have learned enough about people with mental retardation to be able to adopt their services to these people's needs.

One thing that we have not done sufficiently in our special education curriculum is adapt and develop elements of the curriculum that would help people with mental retardation to avoid becoming victims of crime.

INDEX